FIGURES
IN A
LANDSCAPE

FIGURES IN A LANDSCAPE

A History of
THE NATIONAL TRUST

JOHN GAZE

BARRIE & JENKINS
IN ASSOCIATION WITH
THE NATIONAL TRUST

British Library Cataloguing in Publication Data

Gaze, John
    Figures in landscape: a history of the
    National Trust.
    1. England. Landscape conservation.
    Organisations. National Trust to 1987
    I. Title
    719′.06′042

ISBN 0–7126–2065–6

Typeset by DP Photosetting, Aylesbury, Bucks
Printed and bound by Butler & Tanner,
Frome, Somerset

Contents

PUBLISHING NOTE

John Gaze very sadly died before he could complete this book, and an appreciation of his life and work has been provided by his great friend, Robert Latham, the Solicitor of the National Trust. A last chapter has also been written by Len Clark, a long-serving member of National Trust committees, former Chairman of the Southern Region, and a shrewd observer of the Trust at work over the past twenty-five years.

The Trust's work continues, and events have perforce moved on since John Gaze last worked on his manuscript. To try to keep the text updated as much as possible, the publications division of the Trust, in particular Lawrence Rich and Alison Rendle, have worked long and hard, with the help of many members of the National Trust staff.

Margaret Willes
Publisher to the National Trust
March 1988

JOHN GAZE: AN APPRECIATION

John Owen Gaze, who died in 1987, was a land agent on the staff of the National Trust from 1948 until his retirement in 1982. For the last six of those years he was the Trust's Chief Agent.

Born in Devon in 1920, John Gaze was at the Royal Agricultural College, Cirencester, after school at Wellington; but on the closure of Cirencester at the outbreak of war he joined up and served from 1939 in India, the Middle East, North Africa and Germany.

Between periods of active service, in 1944, he married his wife Susan in Iraq. He also met Ivan Hills, later to be his predecessor as Chief Agent of the National Trust, when they were chosen to instruct at an infantry school in the Middle East. Here he developed his gift of transmitting ideas and enthusiasm and also his practical teaching abilities – qualities which were to come into prominence in his work for the Trust when he, in turn, became its Chief Agent.

After being demobilised in 1946, Gaze returned to Cirencester and completed his training. Although offered a job on the staff there, and another with the War Agricultural Executive Committee, he accepted instead one with the National Trust. After eighteen months in its London head office he joined Ivan Hills who was then responsible for Trust properties in south-east England from an office at Polesden Lacey, Surrey. Before long Hills sent him to manage the Trust's Slindon Estate, West Sussex. Here he was largely responsible for replanting the woodlands devastated by wartime felling. John Gaze's passion for trees and forestry, however, was matched by his warmth of character and his concern for the Trust's tenants and others whose life was on the land. It was this understanding which has enabled him to set the history of the Trust into the context of the people involved in it.

Gaze's next move was to Devon as an agent for that county, Dorset and the Isle of Wight. His respect for geography however had him exchanging the Island for West Somerset before long. In 1965, while Gaze was in the West Country, the Trust launched Enterprise Neptune – its campaign to save the coast. Without question the finest of all coastal estates it has subsequently created is the composite Golden Cap Estate in Dorset. This was inspired by John Gaze and made a reality largely through his enthusiasm, persuasion and hard work.

Appointed land agent in the East Midlands in 1970, Gaze was next to consolidate the Trust's emerging High Peak Estate in Derbyshire. These years also saw him concentrating his talents to reconcile the needs of forestry with those of landscape and nature conservation. On the retirement of Ivan Hills in 1975, therefore, Gaze was the obvious choice to become Chief Agent. His experience of estate management was unequalled. Meanwhile the practical skills with which he was endowed were backed by enviable powers of persuasion and irresistable good humour. It was the latter which enabled him to promote the Trust's estates philosophy so successfully to conservation bodies and Government departments. John Gaze, in short, like all good land agents, was knowledgeable and experienced in land management, but unlike some he also knew how best to communicate that knowledge.

Robert Latham
Solicitor of the National Trust

The
Patron Saint

Although the formal establishment of the National Trust occurred just under a century ago, it is necessary to look further back if its origins and aims are to be understood. During the last two hundred years the world, and in particular Europe, has undergone immense changes. For the National Trust, these changes have especial significance because a large element in the philosophy of its founders consisted of a deliberate desire to arrest or avoid their effects, or to mitigate the adverse influences on people's lives.

Any starting point must be arbitrary, but we will take 1770, the year that William Wordsworth was born, for in him there is a valid symbol of the processes and pressures from which the movement grew. Wordsworth's lifetime, 1770 to 1850, spans the critical period in which England changed from an agrarian to an industrial nation, a period when the population doubled – from 7 to 14 million. Great numbers of people moved from the country to the towns to seek work, but usually found only hardship, poverty, disease and degradation. This was also the period when the ideas of the Age of Reason spread through the world, sparking off the French Revolution and threatening to turn the social order upside down.

Wordsworth was born in Cockermouth on the edge of the Lake District, and spent his childhood there. His father was agent to the Lowther Estate and this provided a respectable background solidly based in the rural economy, yet not so grand as to divorce him from his surroundings. He went to the Grammar School at Hawkshead, where he lodged in the village. It was said of him that at the school 'he imbibed the local sentiments of the rustic society of statesmen and peasants.'

The strength of these ties survived the next phases of his life. At seventeen, he went up to St John's, Cambridge, a breeding ground for radical opinion. Wordsworth had already begun to see more of England, visiting, among other places, the already well-established 'beauty spot' of Dovedale. Then in 1792 he was off to France where he tasted the heady wine of revolution and became, as did many other idealistic young men, an ardent – if temporary – republican.

A return to the English Lakes in 1799 was the first step in the formation of the small group known as the Lake Poets. Wordsworth was to remain in the Lakes for the rest of his life. Although he moved from house to house as his fortunes and domestic circumstances dictated – Dove Cottage, Allan Bank, the Grasmere Parsonage, Rydal Mount – he never again lived outside the district and his presence

9

and prestige formed a focus towards which his own especial friends, and a continuous stream of the curious and the great gravitated.

Quite unconsciously Wordsworth embodied two of the qualities that were fundamental to the creation of the National Trust: the literary concept of the romance of natural beauty and the identification of that romance with the English Lakes. The taste of the educated English for the beauty of 'natural' landscape had been evolving since the middle of the eighteenth century, and indeed earlier and it was to be a major part of the philosophy of the Trust's founders. In earlier centuries there had been an urge to tame and to civilise. Nature had been seen as a force to be controlled and used for agriculture or converted into parklands and pleasure grounds. The shires of England were enclosed for modern farming, their open fields divided and hedged, their scrublands formed into tiny woodlands for fox coverts and game birds, and for the production of larch and pine timbers for the new demands of the improved estates.

The very society which promoted this process also had its aesthetic appreciation formed by exposure to the influence of European art, often in the course of making the Grand Tour. The classical landscapes of the great painters of the previous century became the standard for natural beauty. However, such landscapes were scarcely to be found in the habitable parts of Britain and in the wilder parts they were sparse and scattered. Only where the counties of Cumberland, Westmorland and Lancashire joined could they be discovered in full measure.

The contrast that tourists found between the ordered, regulated prosperous lowlands and the dales and fells of the Lake District, then still largely unchanged from Tudor times, is conveyed by the poet, Thomas Gray. Making a visit to the district in 1769 he wrote 'not a single red tile, not a gentleman's flaring house or garden wall, break in upon this unsuspected paradise; but all is peace, rusticity and happy poverty, in its neatest most becoming attire.'

Gray's visit exemplifies the growing recognition of the special charms of the Lakes. Artists had begun to record those aspects of the scenery which were appropriate to the mood: 'Beauty, horror and immensity united' in the words of Dr Brown of Oxford, or alternatively, and perhaps more generally, 'The Beautiful, the Picturesque and the Sublime'. Prints were published in the 1750s and later; Gainsborough, Turner and Constable toured and painted. In 1778, Thomas West published a guide in which the tourist was directed to viewpoints or 'stations' from which the scenery might be observed composed in the most suitable way.

So, when William Wordsworth and his sister returned at the very end of 1799 to settle at Dove Cottage he was not creating a Lake District mystique and fashion. It was already there. In 1810 Wordsworth wrote *A Guide to the Lakes*, published anonymously as an adjunct to a book of prints. The first full and separate version under his own name came out in 1822 and the fifth and final edition in 1835. The work ranges from entirely basic advice to the tourist, through the evolution of the land use of the district, to a discussion of the concept of good and bad landscape. The crispest and most enjoyable of the writing is lifted directly from Dorothy's journal. Much of it, with little alteration, could have been the product of the conservation lobby of today. One passage in particular records, perhaps for the first time, the newly forming attitude of 'persons of taste throughout the whole island who ...

testify that they deem the district a sort of national property in which every man has a right and interest, who has an eye to perceive and a heart to enjoy.'

When Wordsworth died, on 23 April 1850, the eldest of the four founders of the National Trust was already twenty-five years old, two were twelve and five respectively and one was to be born the following year. They were close enough to his time not only to feel a degree of continuity but, perhaps more importantly, to come under the influence of those whose experience of 'Romantic England' was more direct than theirs.

CHAPTER I

The
Founding Quartet

There are three people who are usually acknowledged as the founders of the National Trust: Octavia Hill, Robert Hunter, and Hardwicke Rawnsley. Robin Fedden, author of *The Continuing Purpose*, an important account of the Trust written in 1968, gave them a chapter entitled 'The Trinity'. But in fact there was a fourth, Hugh Lupus Grosvenor, later Duke of Westminster whose place with the others was fully recognised by them. They were all four in their different ways of equal importance, not only because of what they did when the Trust was created, but for what they brought to it from their earlier experiences. The one distinction that may fairly be made is chronological, and so they are best discussed in order of their date of birth.

Hugh Lupus Grosvenor was born in 1825, named after his earliest forebear (in this country) who was nephew to William the Conqueror and became Earl of Chester. An early accretion of property, the Eaton Estate in Cheshire, came to the family by marriage in the reign of Henry VI, but most importantly in 1677 the third Grosvenor baronet married a girl called Mary Davies who brought with her the Manor of Ebury, running roughly from the Thames to Oxford Street. Today it is possible to walk from Oxford Street south down Davies Street and pass every variant on the Grosvenor family and territorial names until you reach Lupus Street by the Thames. On this development of the choicest land in the City of Westminster was the immense wealth of the Grosvenors founded. But although Hugh Lupus was very rich, it was his nature, his status, his interests and his friends which were significant for the history of the National Trust. By the time he came on the family scene, the Grosvenors had been ennobled and his father was Earl Grosvenor and Viscount Belgrave, which latter title he took by courtesy as son and heir. Country interests came early and were perhaps fostered by a visit to cousins in Sutherland when he was twelve. The north of Scotland, even now in places almost 'wilderness', was then still very remote and wild and took a strong grip on his imagination; in later years he was to acquire extensive interests there.

Predictably Grosvenor went to Eton and then to Balliol, an Oxford College that appears frequently in the story of the Trust. He was fortunate that Jowett, later a famous Master, was appointed tutor in 1842, the year before he went up, and coincidentally Matthew Arnold, poet and son of the great headmaster of Rugby, was in his third year. Palgrave, best remembered now for his *Golden Treasury*, was a freshman. The Rugby connection also featured in that Grosvenor's closest friend, Francis Lawley, had been at the school and may have been instrumental in bringing him together with Thomas Hughes, author of *Tom Brown's Schooldays* who became a distinguished lawyer and judge and who represents a link with other members of the Quartet.

Probably the most consistent thread in Grosvenor's life is politics: he entered Parliament as Member for Chester in 1846 when he was only twenty-one and continued to represent it for twenty-three years. Supporting Palmerston and Lord John Russell, he attracted national political notice in 1866 when he was wholly unwilling to support Gladstone's Franchise Bill. With him it was a matter of principle to try to remedy what he deemed unfair and opportunist and on the Second Reading he moved an amendment to broaden the basis for the representation of the people. In 1869 on the death of his father he went as Marquess of Westminster to the Lords. It does not seem that his earlier intervention against Gladstone marred the close friendship between the two men and their families, a fact that must be seen as a measure of the recognition of his genuine and disinterested principles.

Turning back to the other sides of his life, we see a man fully engaged in the pursuits of his station. He was an outstanding game shot, hunted the fox and kept his own hounds for some years. He went to the heart of the sporting masses, however, as a breeder of racehorses and, as breeder and owner of the Derby winner, Ben d'Or, he was as well known and popular as any man in the kingdom.

His marriage to Constance, daughter of the Duke of Sutherland, has an especial significance because the lovely girl was a great favourite with Queen Victoria and marriage led to a close association with the royal family which lasted his lifetime. It began with the marriage ceremony being held, by the Queen's wish, in the Chapel Royal in St James's Palace, which belonged to his mother-in-law, and prospered partly because Cliveden House in Buckinghamshire was so close to Windsor Castle. To this friendship as well as to that with Gladstone must be attributed Grosvenor's elevation as Duke of Westminster in the Dissolution Honours of 1874.

The warmth, accessibility and caring nature of the man is hinted at by the conduct of his business life and his choice of charitable works. He took a close and personal interest in the management of all his properties in Scotland, Cheshire and in London. Among his London benefactions were the provision of sites at peppercorn rents for new churches, rectories and schools and a public library in Buckingham Palace Road, while hospitals and nursing were among his particular interests. Florence Nightingale was one of his tenants (on what she described as 'munificent terms'). He played a large part in founding the Jubilee Institute for Nurses, which later became – as the Queen's Institute of District Nurses – one of the most effective and loved of all nursing charities. He was also involved with the RSPCA, the Metropolitan Drinking Fountains Association and the Cabmen's Shelter Fund.

Just one act illuminates his practical kindness and good sense. The park at Eaton was open to the public free on every day of the year. A well meant attempt by his agent to keep out noisy visitors by closing on Sundays was revoked by Grosvenor because it was the only day on which city workers were free to reach it on cycling expeditions. Indeed his last years in the Upper House were devoted to the welfare of that then down-trodden race, the shop assistants. His Bill to give statutory force to at least minimal rights for them was a small but highly constructive part of the social welfare measures which had begun to emerge from Parliament. It is especially worth notice that he conducted a programme of slum demolition in Chester and replaced the slums with modern houses and flats. He founded the Chester Cottage Improvement Society in 1892.

From this catalogue of worthy effort a picture emerges of a man of liberal mind, of high-standing, influential friends, and above all a full measure of human kindness. For all these things and more he was to be greatly valued by the other founders of the Trust.

Thirteen years younger and as emphatically middle-class in origin and circumstances as Hugh Lupus was aristocratic, Octavia Hill was born in Wisbech, Cambridgeshire, to a father who was a reforming radical and a free trader. He was a banker in what were to prove the last days of private banking, and suffered accordingly. His business failed in the difficult time of the Reform Act of 1832. He manfully re-started, paid his debts in full when, in 1840, disaster struck again, and his health gave out completely. The family broke up, the father going to a relative in Kent where he died thirty-two years later.

So, with her mother and sisters, Octavia, at the age of three, went to live at Finchley, just north of London. Her name needs an explanation; Mr Hill had three daughters by a previous marriage and five more in his second marriage, so his youngest was by that reckoning quite properly number eight – Ockie to her family. Her maternal grandfather was a man of some distinction, Dr Southwood Smith, who had taken a leading role in promoting the public health legislation which began to flow through Parliament in the second half of the century. It was largely through him that his daughter, Caroline, was able to keep her family going. He adopted the eldest girl, Gertrude, and helped support the others. Nevertheless, they led a very simple country life in straitened circumstances.

It is difficult to imagine Finchley as country, but one hundred and forty years ago it was. The children led a happy life, healthy and much out of doors. It was a life that Octavia loved and her efforts to enable others to enjoy it too appear again and again throughout the following years. There is a charming description of her as, 'a very ardent child with a quick sense of the ludicrous, partially hidden under a precise and determined manner'. One suspects that she changed little down the years!

When Octavia was in her early teens, Mrs Hill was offered the position of manager of the Ladies Co-operative Guild, a charity intended to help distressed gentlewomen to support themselves. It was associated with an enterprise known as Consolidated Glass, which taught and practised the technique of designing and producing decorative objects of painted glass. Miranda, who was sixteen and Octavia, then thirteen, were to be given training. This meant a move into central London, to Marylebone and the end of what she herself described as a 'happy country life'.

It did, however, bring her into an intensely Christian and radical milieu, for these enterprises had come under the aegis of the Society of Christian Socialists. She wrote to an enquirer some ten years later that 'the Society was composed of people of all religions and differing in politics – Chartists, Conservatives, Whigs, Radicals', and that 'the meeting point for all sorts of Socialists was the belief that fellow-work was stronger than isolation, union than division and generosity than selfishness.' She was much impressed with the Reverend F.D. Maurice, one of the Society's leading men, going to hear him preach at Lincoln's Inn Chapel and 'went twice to Mile End to hear Maurice and [Charles] Kingsley preach. I never leave London when Mr Maurice is here.' Maurice is worthy of notice because he represents the conscious endeavour of the radical element of the mid-nineteenth-century middle class to work by example and organisation for the betterment of their fellow men. If for no other reason, he should now be remembered for his part while at Cambridge in founding the Apostles Club. As a founder and first principal of the Working Men's College he provided a vehicle for good works for others for those who followed him.

Octavia's exposure to Christian Socialism was paralleled by her own experiences of London's poverty. Under the auspices of the Ladies Guild, she had taken over the supervision of the toy-making enterprise in which poor children of about her own age were employed. Still only a child herself, she had to organise and discipline her workers, market their products and keep her accounts. The London of that time was a curious mixture where considerable wealth and comfort lived within a stone's throw of the most appalling poverty. One of her toy-makers, nicknamed Robin 'for her bright eyes' came to her door one morning, turned out by her father, her mother having been 'dead and gone these eighteen months'. She was warmed, washed, fed and then placed with a woman who would look after her, but she later slipped off and disappeared. Octavia determined to trace her and in a letter to a friend she describes what she found.

'A low archway led through a way, now half-obstructed by a heap of dirt, to a wide paved court swarming from end to end with numberless children ... a crowd of blighted lives ... Down into a dark coal-cellar we looked; a ladder led to it, leaning against which, on the coals below, sat a girl with two very young children ... I can never forget the look of hopeless terror on her face.' So Robin was rescued and became a mainstay among the toy-makers, but Octavia never did forget.

On the day before her fifteenth birthday, another important thread of Octavia's make-up became woven into her life. She met John Ruskin. The meeting – at the Ladies Guild, where Ruskin was probably brought by Maurice, since the former was then teaching at the Working Men's College – was brief but important. Octavia's sister, Emily (later Maurice's daugher-in-law) introducing a selection of letters between Octavia and Ruskin, says that by the age of twelve she 'had read much of the first volume of *Modern Painters* and knew long passages by heart'. There developed what her sister describes as 'the beautiful and unique friendship ... which ... ripened gradually, as she matured with a deeper communion of thought'.

The relationship of Octavia and Ruskin developed within a 'business' framework. Ruskin employed Octavia to make copies of pictures in public galleries which he later used for reference when compiling his critical works. She was very proud when in the publication of the fifth volume of *Modern Painters* there was 'a word or two in the preface about me' and 'four of my own scraps'. That was in 1859, the same year in which he thanked her for 'the Claude, it is excellent and will do admirably' and soon after gave her grace to finish the next; 'Any time will do for the Salvator.' For ten full years she worked in her 'spare' time as a camera for his reference library.

The regular delivery of her work brought them much in contact and her letters to her Quaker friend, Mary Harris, are full of what Ruskin said and thought and wholly unrestrained in her admiration for him. His occasional moods of depression, which were to deepen in later years, soon came to her notice and she worried over them. Nevertheless she concluded that although 'there is occasionally a deep sad sense of want ... he has so much more joy than others ... so deep a trust in that which is beyond all the rest, that I feel that he is happy'.

Had the two never met and Octavia's aesthetic development been formed in other ways, John Ruskin would still have featured in this story as the embodiment of the artistic and social movements of that mid-century which constituted the climate of opinion in which the National Trust was formed. From painting he turned to architecture with the publication of his *Seven Lamps of Architecture* and later again to political and economic theory in which his polemic *Unto this Last* had a material influence on the philosophy of socialists such as William Morris, Walter Crane and George Bernard Shaw.

There was, however, one most particular result of his friendship with Octavia which specifically determined the course of her career and her contribution to the shape of the National Trust. After the Ladies Guild folded, through petty jealousies, she worked for £25 a year as secretary to the newly opened classes for working women, another development by Maurice at the Working Men's College. Later, with her sister Miranda and in her new home in Nottingham Place off the Marylebone Road, she also opened a school for young ladies. Three jobs, over-conscientiously carried out, led to recurrent bouts of ill health, surprising in one whose physique and mental strength seem in other ways to have been very robust.

The principal task of her life, and that on which her reputation properly rests, was engendered by her experience of the squalid housing conditions of the poor. This was reinforced when one of a group being given free tuition in the school's kitchen fainted and had to be helped home. Octavia was dismayed by the squalor: she wrote to her friend, 'How can the poor live?' Coincidentally Ruskin, having come into his father's sherry-importing fortune, was casting about for proper ways to use it for the general good, and consulted Octavia. Within a short space of time she had evolved plans for the acquisition of slum property, its repair and its improvement.

It is fascinating to follow the way in which Octavia developed her theory and practice. First we see compassion and courage, and hand-in-hand with that, discipline and business acumen. She must have seen the irony of the name of the first slum she tackled: Paradise Place. This was followed in 1866 by Freshwater Place and later Barretts Court, off Wimpole Street, an atrocious sink. Her system was simple; to be a good and strict landlord. She herself collected the rents – often in places were no policeman ventured alone – tolerated no arrears, but steadily, within the income so derived, cleaned the properties, repaired them and, little by little, got rid of the few incorrigible tenants.

One of the pupils at the Nottingham Place school, who went regularly to Barretts Court to teach a class of rough girls has left a description of the sort of conditions that existed there:

> There was a little crowd at the entrance to the court. I heard a man swearing and a woman screaming; he was holding her by the hair and striking her. I appealed to the men who looked on to interfere, but one of them said. 'We dursn't; he fights for money and a kick from him would lame you for life.'

16

I thought the poor woman would be killed. I sprang into the ring, seized the savage's nearest arm and said with tears, 'Please stop.' He was startled, he turned and hit, not me as I expected, but one of the men for not telling him that the 'little lady' was coming. The crowd dispersed, the man slunk away, the woman was taken home and the mother of one of the girls said, 'Miss October 'Ill and 'er young ladies wasn't afraid of nothing nor nobody.' The grown ups often stood outside to listen to the singing.

It was at Freshwater Place that Octavia made her first essay in providing an outdoor area for her tenants. She was particularly concerned with the state of the children confined either to overcrowded rooms and the squalor of the foetid courts or the hazards of the streets. 'And the children!' she wrote to Mary Harris. 'Their eyes all inflamed with continual dirt, their bare feet, their wild cries, disordered hair, and clothes looking as if dogs had torn them all around.' Again: 'No one can imagine the awfulness of the dirt and the disgustingness of the children.'

It was for these that she set about making a playground out of the patch of waste land adjoining the court. It was uphill work, bricks were stolen in the night from the wall being built round it, and then one day 'there lay the wall one tumbled mass of ruin'. Gradually, with continual supervision, organisation and the recruitment of devoted helpers, her first playground was established and prospered. Ruskin helped from a distance, with gifts of trees and creepers and the services of his gardener to see to the planting.

This concept of the need for people to have at least some space in the open air, first formed so early in Octavia's career, we shall later see developing into an altogether wider idea. Ironically, however, it was the breakdown of her own health through overwork which renewed and broadened her appreciation of the countryside. In 1867, just approaching her thirtieth birthday, she spent many months with Mary Harris, first at her home in the English Lakes, and later in Florence. Her first visit to Wales followed in 1871 when Sydney Cockerell, later her devoted slave, met her in the Hydro at Ben Rhydding and recorded this impression: '... an unobtrusive plainly dressed little lady whose face attracts you at first and charms you as you become acquainted with the power of mind and sweetness of character to which it gives expression, a lady of great force and energy with a wide open, well stored, brain but withal as gentle and womanly as a woman can well be, and possessed of a wonderful tact, which makes her the most attractive and pleasantest companion in the whole establishment.'

Besides leaving that eulogy for posterity, Cockerell deeply affected Octavia's life by introducing a young ex-Balliol barrister to help with the Barrett's Court Club. Edward Bond became her helper in other fields as well and in 1877 they became engaged to be married. The marriage did not take place and Octavia discouraged speculation as to why not, but it is assumed that Edward's tiresome and demanding mother continually caused him to postpone it, so that Octavia eventually saw that it would not work and broke it off herself.

Understandably Octavia was upset. In her forties the girl, who at seventeen had been surprised by friends with torn and muddied petticoats sliding down a bank on Hampstead Heath where she had taken her child toy-makers, became staid and aloof. More sadness was to follow. In 1877 Cockerell died, aged only thirty-five.

Worse still, perhaps, came a breach with Ruskin. The occasion was a harmless comment by Octavia – on the occasion of the resignation of two of his old friends from the Trusteeship of St George's Guild – that Ruskin was 'a visionary whose teaching could not always be taken literally'. Ruskin was enraged and probably mortified by the truth of it. He vilified Octavia in extreme terms in an issue of his *Fors Clavigera* pamphlet and though ten years later he 'forgave' her, his attack was never withdrawn.

The culmination of all these crises was a complete breakdown and provided the occasion for Harriot Yorke to attach herself to Octavia as friend and companion, a role which she performed up to, and in a sense after, Octavia's death.

Throughout the years Octavia's reputation in housing and social reform had grown and with it her opportunities for expanding her work. She was able to tell a Royal Commission in 1884 that, 'since 1864 I have never had to wait a day for money for houses', a long list of charitable investors being ready to supply it. Direct social work in the form of charitable relief was initiated by the Vicar of St Mary's, Marylebone, with Octavia in charge, succeeded and was enlarged to cover the whole parish. Later one of the vicar's former curates, Canon Barnett, persuaded her to take an interest in the problems of Whitechapel. It was he who founded the first University Settlement, Toynbee Hall, in Whitechapel.

Octavia began writing on her several subjects and was in demand as a speaker: she was, it was said, 'a convincing speaker who easily got through to her audience'. By 1875 – before her breakdown – she had become a member of the Central Council of the Charities Organisation Society and was at once in touch with all manner of people engaged in different fields, including the pre-eminent Earl of Shaftesbury, leader of the factory reform movement and chairman of the Ragged Schools Union. In 1884 her sister Miranda wrote to Mary Harris:

> It *has* come to a point! – when two peers and a Cabinet Minister call and consult her in one week. She had Fawcett [Postmaster General] here yesterday, Lord Wemyss [promoter of the volunteer movement] the day before to ask what he should say in the House of Lords, and the Duke of Westminster on Wednesday to ask what the Prince of Wales could do in the matter.

On that high note her career continued right up to her death in 1912.

The 1840s were anxious and unsettled times into which, in 1844, the third of the Trust's founders, Robert Hunter, was born. His parents were Ayrshire Scots by descent, but his Lachlan grandfather had founded a ship-broking business in London which prospered for four generations. His father was a sea-farer, whaling in the Antarctic in early days and then becoming a modestly successful ship-owner.

When Robert Hunter was born his family lived in the south London suburb of Camberwell. From there, when he was seven, they moved to Denmark Hill. At that time the place was still countrified: the garden and waste land beyond it was his first taste of living outside the suburbs. He must soon have begun to shake off the sickliness which had dogged his early years, because attendance at Denmark Hill Grammar School followed and he appears to have lived the life of any ordinary schoolboy, playing games – cricket in particular. A strong formative influence was provided by Leonard Seeley, who was engaged to give him private tuition before matriculation. Seeley's brother John was soon to write the controversial book *Ecce Homo*, the Christian moralism of which stirred the young of the time and the brothers constituted the first direct contact that Robert had with radical religious opinion.

This almost certainly led to the choice of University College, London, for the next stage of Robert's education. Its wide curriculum and acceptance of free thought in religious matters were in contrast to the restrictive attitudes lingering in the older Universities. He studied law here and joined the lively University Debating Society. He was at this time drawn by chance into the same orbit of socio-religious philosophy as Octavia Hill. Another student, Augustus Wilkins, lived not far away and they became not only daily travelling companions, but close friends. With Augustus and his two attractive sisters, Robert began to attend Claylands Chapel in the Clapham Road. There, captivated by the preaching of the Congregationalist minister, Baldwin Brown, he discovered the Christian Socialist movement and in extension of his admiration for Seeley's work began a serious study of Maurice and Kingsley.

Robert Hunter at twenty-two, with a degree in law, became articled to a firm of solicitors, Eyre and Lawson, in Bedford Row. He resorted to further study at the same time, getting his MA two years later and developing his private pleasure in reading history and the classics which he was to pursue throughout his life.

Robert Hunter was the only member of the Quartet to be plunged at the very start of his career into work which was to remain central to the creation of the National Trust. One evening in 1866 an uncle showed him a newspaper announcement of an essay-competition on the subject of 'Commons and the means of preserving them for the public'. Robert entered and won, and this proved to be his entrée into specialist work with eminent lawyers which made his reputation. At that time the extensive commons around London were very much at risk. Commoners had generally given up the exercise of their rights and there was no general public right to use them. They were suddenly becoming valuable for housing development, provided easy routes for railways and the lords of the manors were beginning to see them as new sources of wealth.

The following year Robert became engaged to Emily Browning, an old family friend. Obviously he desired an established position and a suitable income on which to support marriage. He began to negotiate with the eminent London lawyer, and supporter of the Commons preservation movement, Mr Lawrence, for a partnership. His first approach was met with an offer of a place in the office, an unspecified salary and no promise in the way of partnership. However, he decided on a trial run for six months. 'I think a little more work with a good firm will do me good, even if it should lead to nothing immediately it would give me a better chance of a partnership.'

So the right decision was taken. After a pause for reflection, the irascible Mr Lawrence quickly sized up Robert's capacity and willingness, putting him at once onto the very important case of Hampstead Heath and working him hard. Emily saw little of him and in his letters there are constant references to long hours: 'Monday night in Town till past nine, last night until past ten, tonight till past seven

... Mr Lawrence unfortunately does not subscribe to the Saturday Half Holiday movement.'

It all came right in the end because, two years later, Mr Lawrence gave up his practice on being appointed Solicitor to the Office of Works, and, with Fawcett and C.P. Horne, Robert bought the firm.

Robert Hunter at the age of twenty-four was then appointed solicitor to the Commons Preservation Society. He thus became responsible for the series of decisive law suits in process at the time which formed a key element in the earliest stages of what is now the conservation movement. In these long, involved and incredibly expensive battles he became acquainted with all the other principal protagonists in the field and emerged as the acknowledged expert.

While engaged in his day to day practice and even after 1882 when he was appointed solicitor to the Post Office, Robert found time to help, in and out of Parliament, with the promotion of legislation for the better preservation and management of open spaces. His daughter, Dorothy, affirms, probably correctly, 'It would be true to say that every measure passed between 1870 and 1913 ... was drafted either by or in consultation with ... (my father).'

Perhaps it would be wise at this point, when this description of Robert is tending towards the priggish, to conclude with Dorothy's description of her father: 'He was very sociable, loved music, danced, rowed on the river – (as a member of the University Boat Club) – drilled with a Volunteer Corps, and spent many holidays taking long country rambles and walking tours.'

September in the year of the Great Exhibition, 1851, saw the birth of the youngest member of the Quartet, Hardwicke Drummond Rawnsley, usually known as Hardie. His origins were unassailably middle-class, although his brother Willingham produced a family tree which has its roots in the Yorkshire Pennines in 1370, with one William de Ravenslawe, of Ravenslawe Cliff, near Halifax. There is a temptation to see in the rugged origins of the family the pattern of Hardwicke's equally rugged nature.

Hardwicke's father was at Rugby under the great Doctor Arnold. On taking Holy Orders he received the living of Shiplake near Henley-on-Thames. It was there that in 1850 he officiated at the wedding of Alfred Tennyson to Emily Sellwood, his mother's cousin. This apparently irrelevant incident was to have a most important influence on Hardwicke. Alfred Tennyson's father was rector of Somersby, almost next door to Partney at the southern end of the Lincolnshire Wolds. Here Hardwicke's father followed in 1861, and the families were close friends.

Tennyson became Poet Laureate and the literary symbol of the age and it is small wonder that a romantically inclined schoolboy should come to revere him in later life. Rawnsley was to write in a prefatory note to his book, *Memories of the Tennysons* published eight years after the death of the poet, in 1892:

> Each year my father paid a visit to the Poet at Farringford, and one heard
> talk of Tennyson when he returned. Each time a volume of poems was given
> to the world, a presentation copy came to my father's hands and we, as
> children, gathered in the eventide to hear the poems read in our ears with

such deep feeling that we were impressed by them even when we could not realise their beauty of thought and diction.

After a quiet and thoroughly country boyhood, first in the Thames valley and then where the tail of the Wolds slips into the fens of the Wash, Rawnsley was sent off to Uppingham, then in its heyday under the most liberal and progressive of headmasters, Edward Thring, his godfather. Then on to Balliol, where Jowett was in his last years as Master. It is at this stage that Rawnsley's immense energy and eclectic interests become clearly apparent. He was assiduous in academic work, reading Natural Sciences, but found time also to worry about social and economic problems and to attend the lectures of Ruskin, then Slade Professor of Fine Art. Indeed it was in attendance at Ruskin's lectures that one aspect of Rawnsley's mature character took form and it was the root of a devoted discipleship which endured until Ruskin died.

In common with so many public school and 'Varsity men of the time Rawnsley did a stint of social work in London. Going as lay-chaplain to the Newport Market Refuge in Crown Street, Soho, must have been a sufficiently harsh experience to have given him that permanent sympathy for the poor and distressed that marked his later work. He may also have met Octavia Hill, since a letter from Ruskin commended her to him as 'the best lady abbess you can find for London work'. That was followed by a spell with the Clifton College Mission from Bristol. Uppingham had been the first to found a public school mission and the Bristol school followed suit.

Between the two periods of voluntary social work there had been a period of recuperation from the effect of London on Rawnsley's health. It was spent with cousins at Wray, on the western side of Windermere. There he met the Fletcher family of Ambleside, and this visit was to bring first his ordination into the priesthood and his cousin's gift of the living of Wray. This was just before Christmas 1877. Five weeks later came marriage to Edith Fletcher. They undertook one of the most remarkable honeymoon journeys on record, to Egypt and thence across Sinäi to Petra, to Palestine and Syria and home via Turkey and Europe. Travel by sea or river was relatively civilised, but the rest of the journey was by horse, mule or camel, or on foot. Rawnsley's physique was especially robust but it says much for Edith that she seems to have taken it all in her stride. It is also remarkable that a young man, just appointed to his first job, should disappear from it forthwith for a six-month holiday!

However, Wray was important for it placed Rawnsley in the diocese of Carlisle, in which the whole of his ministry was to be spent, and for him that came primarily to mean the district of the English Lakes. In 1883 he moved to the more important parish of Crosthwaite near Keswick and was there until he retired in 1917. In 1909 he became a canon of Carlisle and in 1912 Chaplain to King George V. He might indeed have become a bishop in 1898 but the see on offer was that of Madagascar and he was prevailed upon by his friends to refuse, Octavia Hill writing most persuasively to dissuade him.

In the long course of his church career Rawnsley attracted attention in many other ways. Probably the most important, in that it illustrates one of the characteristic aspects of the Christian Socialist movement, was the founding of the Keswick

School of Industrial Art. The idea was that training should be given to occupy the leisure of those without jobs, or indeed those with, and to give them useful skills which would improve their earning capacity while at the same time keeping them out of mischief. In this Edith, who was a competent water colourist, took a major part and while the promotion of the school may be attributed to Rawnsley and inspired, indeed, by Ruskin, its continuing development and success were largely due to Edith.

Rawnsley turned out an immense amount of written work, some good, all of it pleasant. In verse his predeliction for the sonnet form never reached the level of poetry, and indeed called forth general hilarity, even getting noticed by *Punch* which alleged that he had just written his 30,000th! Such books, however, as *Literary Associations of the English Lakes*, published in 1894, and the later Lakeland books are still of interest and charm.

It was, of course, to Wordsworth that Rawnsley particularly attached himself and that poet came to equal Tennyson in his estimation. There were many still living who remembered Wordsworth and his sister, and Rawnsley assiduously collected their recollections and anecdotes until one feels that he enjoyed as close an acquaintance with the former Laureate as he did with the living one. A memorial to Wordsworth in the form of a fountain was erected in Cockermouth and unveiled by Matthew Arnold.

Edith died in 1916 and Hardwicke himself was very ill. He resigned from Crosthwaite in 1917 and went to Allan Bank, the great ugly house in which Wordsworth had spent some three years and which, with a multitude of late-eighteenth and nineteenth-century villas has turned the centre of the district into a strange sort of Lakeside suburbia. He married again, Eleanor Simpson, a family friend who had shared innumerable outings and holidays with Rawnsley and Edith. From then it was only a short three years to the end of his life.

Front man, ideas man, publicist, catalyst, Hardwicke Rawnsley provided the element of ebullience that the other three founders of the National Trust lacked, and which their infant organisation so badly needed.

CHAPTER II

The
Battle
for the
Commons

William Wordsworth, the Patron Saint, having enshrined his philosophy on landscape in his *Guide to the Lakes* entered the lists on behalf of preservation when the heart of his beloved Lake District was threatened by the approach of a railway from Kendal to Windermere. Originally designed to reach Low Wood at the northern head of the Lake, a revision placed the proposed terminus a mile from Bowness, where it now ends. In two very long letters to the *Morning Post* in late 1844 Wordsworth opposed the idea as strongly as he could, fearing that if the railway line were permitted there would be a further extension beyond Ambleside.

The railways were a catalyst in stimulating an active preservationist lobby throughout the country. In the first place, their very construction provoked alarm at the prospect of damage to the landscape. Increasingly, however, experience showed that subsequent social changes were likely to make an even greater impact. The open common lands were obvious temptations for railway engineers seeking routes into central London through the already congested environs. Wandsworth Common perhaps suffered most, two lines approaching Clapham Junction splitting it into three and providing excuses for further enclosure.

It would be unfair to blame the railways for the boom in housing development which characterised the second half of the nineteenth century. Boom there was, however, and until 1870 there was also a boom in agriculture. These two sources of potential wealth both called for new land and lords of the manor thought they had at their disposal the common lands of their manors over which, in and near large towns, commoners had almost ceased to exercise their rights.

One of the first cases in which Robert Hunter was involved concerned Wimbledon Common. This prompted Parliament to appoint, in 1865, a Committee to enquire into the best means of preserving commons in and around London, with the Member for Lambeth, Mr Doulton, in the chair and with Mr Shaw-Lefevre as a member. The latter, with Hunter's chief, Mr Lawrence at his elbow, managed the Committee adroitly and with wisdom and they adopted a report, which Hunter had drafted, with two main elements: first, the repeal of the antique Statute of Merton which purported to give lords of manors the right to enclose, and second a declaration that schemes of regulation should be made for the proper public use and control of commons.

Predictably, lords of the manor rushed to realise the value of their common lands before legislation could prevent them and so the battle was joined. George Shaw-Lefevre anticipated this and formed, in July 1865, the first and certainly the most influential of preservation organisations, the Commons Preservation Society. Among his supporters are names which crop up again and again in preservation history. One was John Stuart Mill, the philosopher and economist, who had originally advocated enclosure to achieve maximum productivity, but whose ideas had been reversed because of his experience, ten years earlier, of the injustices imposed upon labouring people by the arbitrary conduct of the lord of the manor in respect of the common of Burnham Beeches in Buckinghamshire. Other names include the Buxtons, and Professor Henry Fawcett, later Postmaster General, Sir Charles Dilke, W.H. Smith, the Duke of Westminster and Octavia Hill.

The legal cases that were fought read like battle honours each with some gallant leader:

> Berkhamsted and Augustus Smith
> Plumstead and Sir Julian Goldsmid
> Hampstead and Gurney Hoare
> Wimbledon and Sir Henry Peck
> Coulsdon and Batts
> Tooting Graveney and Thompson
> Dartford Heath and Minet
> Epping Forest and the Corporation of the City of London

Behind them all were Shaw-Lefevre, Lawrence, Hunter and then the solicitor, Birkett.

The legal points were abstruse and complicated. The cases were often bitterly fought, for there was much money at stake. Had Parliament acted on its Committee's report and repealed the Statute of Merton, all would have been easier, but it did at least pass the Metropolitan Commons Act in 1866 which provided for the schemes of regulation. But for an intervention by Lord Redesdale (of the first creation) the Act could have applied to all suburban commons in England and Wales. Still, the preservation of the metropolitan commons was an important start.

The most dramatic encounter was at Berkhamsted where on behalf of Lord Brownlow and to enlarge the park of Ashridge House, his agent, tired of the slow and diplomatic moves towards enclosure, erected iron fences. They were five feet in height with seven horizontal rails, and stretched in two lines across the 1,150 acre common, enclosing 434 acres of it and, being without gates or openings, severed all rights of way. Shaw-Lefevre 'meeting Mr Augustus Smith in the Commons' (hardly by chance one suspects) persuaded him to take up the case and 'to resort to the old practice of abating the enclosure by the forcible removal of all the fences ...' So a contractor was employed to send down a force of 120 navvies who duly arrived, though without anyone in charge, the contractor having got drunk at Euston *en route*. However, Mr Lawrence had sent a clerk to keep watch and he took charge, so that by 6 a.m. two miles of fence were down and stacked for removal. There were, of course, actions and cross-actions as a result, but Lord Brownlow's against Smith was failing when the plaintiff died and Smith's cross-suit was wholly upheld by the

Master of the Rolls. The land is now part of the Ashridge Estate of the National Trust.

Very soon another and greater battle was to be fought for the forests of Essex, Waltham, Hainault and Epping, a battle which was to make Robert Hunter's reputation. As the East End of London grew, the old Crown forests of Essex became the people's only playground and every Sunday and holiday they came in their thousands from Shoreditch, Stepney, Limehouse and Mile End, by train, by cart, or on foot. Yet at the same time the forests diminished, especially on the edge nearest the city. The position of the Crown in relation to the forests was peculiar, in that its rights over much of the land were limited to the preservation and pursuit of game – principally deer – and to matters connected with that. Ownership was vested largely in numerous manors, except at Hainault where, on the dissolution of the Abbey of Barking, the manors had reverted to the Crown. With tastes changing, the deer disappearing, and agricultural productivity booming, the Crown lost interest in forestal rights, which gave it much trouble and little revenue. From 1805 to 1848 sales and enclosures reduced the extent of the forests from 9,000 to 7,000 acres and then, at the instance of a Parliamentary Committee, Hainault was disafforested by an Act of 1851, half the 2,000 acres vesting in the Crown and the balance distributed among the commoners. The exceptionally fine King's Wood was grubbed out and the area laid out as farms. The timber value may be imagined from the fact that the cost of the work, £42,000, was met from timber sales. Within twelve years the revenue from the Crown's allotment was £4,000 per annum against £500 from the whole of the forest. This excellent business venture stimulated private owners of manors elsewhere to similar enterprise, assisted by the Crown's offer of its forestal rights for sale, which was taken up over half the forest for as little as £5 per acre. Enclosures proceeded apace, faintly challenged in Parliament, but otherwise unchecked until, twenty years later, half had been enclosed.

The first check came when the Rev. Maitland, the rector of the parish of Loughton and lord of its manor, enclosed at one blow the whole of his 1,300 acres. Here there had been a right of lopping, maintained actively up to that time, and on St Martin's Eve, in accordance with custom, one Willingale, a labouring man, and his two sons went out as usual upon midnight, broke through the lord's fences and lopped the trees. They were convicted of malicious trespass and, refusing to pay fines, went to prison on the very day the Berkhamsted fences came down. Old Willingale found a champion in Sir Thomas Fowell Buxton, a forest landowner and member of the Commons Society and a suit was entered against the rector, who not only resisted it at law but sought first to bribe the plaintiff and, failing in that, tried to drive him from the parish and so deprive him of his rights. Willingale was evicted from his cottage, refused employment and his character maligned. The case took years to come to court and before it did the old man died, but the action had maintained the *status quo ante bello*, and this particular enclosure was not revived.

The row stirred up public opinion on both sides and matters came to a head in 1870 with the promotion in the Commons of a Bill which ostensibly sought to protect rights of access but which in fact would have confirmed the legality of all previous enclosures, given a further tranche to lords of manors and have left but 600 acres in all as open land. Hunter wrote: 'The Bill, in fact, is an Enclosure Bill and not one for the preservation of the Forest. It is in direct opposition to the repeatedly expressed opinion of Parliament ....'

The Commons Society was far from unanimous as to the best course to take: there were those, very strongly supported by Hunter, who felt that the Bill must be opposed in the House as being directly against the principles of the society. Others were for compromise and settlement. It was John Stuart Mill who moved that the society 'do resist it to the utmost', but an amendment moved by the Member for the County of Essex only failed by one vote. On so slight a margin was this vital decision made. Fawcett took up the case in the Commons where the open space lobby in the House had become stronger in recent years, regularly fortified by Government ineptitude. The Bill was withdrawn on technical grounds, never to reappear.

At this juncture an ill-judged move by the Trustees of Lord Cowley, prominent among the despoilers of the forest, opened the way for preservationist victory. They enclosed some of the Wanstead Flats, including a fine avenue known as Queen Elizabeth's Walk and in doing so not only upset the populace of the East End, to whom it was the closest part of the forest, but more importantly the Corporation of the City of London who, as copy holders, had rights of common there. Hunter had been researching the history and laws of the forest and its commons and had concluded that rights of grazing were not limited by manorial boundaries, but extended throughout the whole forest.

In the train on his way to work Robert had his flash of inspiration: let the Corporation, which had the means to sustain the costs, make suit against the lords of nineteen manors on behalf of all occupiers of land within the forest, for rights of common of pasture over not only that which remained unenclosed but also all that had been enclosed within the previous twenty years! It says much for the city fathers that they readily embraced this wild idea, even engaging Hunter, young though he was, to act for them in conjunction with their own solicitor.

The Government continued its ham-fisted efforts to frustrate the preservers, using the device of a Royal Commission on the problem to postpone action and then, unbelievably, introducing a clause which would have stopped litigation and referred the dispute to a Government Commission. Even sending the Bill first to the Lords did not work: Lord Salisbury, not the most liberal of statesmen, roundly condemned it as 'violent and unconstitutional'.

In the two years that followed Hunter worked unceasingly in the preparation of the case, at the same time bringing numerous holding actions to prevent ploughing, building, felling and quarrying. At last on 25 June 1874 the case opened before Sir George Jessel, Master of the Rolls. Hunter's researches had been so detailed and extensive that the documents, ranging from the twelfth to the nineteenth century had to be barrowed into court in large tin boxes. He had found between seventy and eighty witnesses, all of whom he had examined personally, sometimes two or three times to ensure accuracy. The defence outdid him numerically but their one hundred and seventeen witnesses were so badly prepared that much of their evidence reinforced Hunter's case. The Master found for the Corporation and granted its claim over all the forest, an injunction to restrain any new enclosures and to throw open again all enclosed since 1851 (save only land already actually developed). Costs were given to the plaintiffs, the judge remarking of the defendants that 'they have taken other persons property for their own use, they will retain lands enclosed more than twenty years ago ... they have endeavoured to support their title by a vast bulk of false evidence.'

The importance of the Epping Forest case to the story of the Trust is two-fold. First, the furore caused and the populist nature of the victory provided an immense advertisement and boost for the open space lobby. Second, it illustrates the qualities of energy and integrity which were to characterise Hunter's life's work.

Octavia Hill meanwhile had been developing her own ideas about open spaces. Her initiative in providing a playground for her tenants at Freshwater Place coincided approximately with the formation of the Commons Preservation Society, although she did not join it until 1875. Meanwhile she developed her ideas in an essay entitled 'Open Spaces'. In this she pressed for the provision of small open areas for people 'which might be used by them in common as sitting rooms in summer. Even in England there are a good many days when at some hours sitting out of doors is refreshing, and when very hot days do come it seems almost a necessity.'

To understand the significance of what today may seem an unimportant and obvious statement, it is necessary to read on:

> I fancy you do not know what a narrow court near Drury Lane or Clerkenwell is on a sultry August evening. The stifling heat, the dust lying everywhere, the smell of everything in the dirty rooms, the baking dry glare of the sun ... making it seem intolerable – like an oven. The father of the family ... is round the corner at the public house, trying to quench his thirst with liquor which only increases it. The mother is either lolling out of the window, screaming to the fighting women below or sitting dirty and dishevelled ... side by side with a drunken woman who comments with foul oaths on all who pass. The children, how they swarm! ... from the neglected youngest crawling over the hot stones, clawing among the shavings and the potato peelings, on cabbage leaves strewn about, to the big boy and girl 'larking' in the vulgarest play by the corner ... the dustbins reek, the drains smell, the dirty bedding smells, the people's clothes smell.

It was for the relief of such conditions that Octavia sought the grace of small patches of open space within the cities. She was at the same time well aware that it would meet only one specific need, and that it was of supreme importance that wider areas of real countryside should be accessible to people in the city. When in 1875 the fields which then stretched from Swiss Cottage to the edge of the village of Hampstead came on the market as building land she was appalled. Those fields were within an easy walk of Marylebone, where her pioneering work was done. With Edward Bond at her side and with the backing of Grosvenor, newly created Duke of Westminster, she launched an appeal for funds with which to buy the land. She was within an ace of succeeding when the vendors, for no obvious reason, declined to sell and so today, as you pass along Fitzjohn's Avenue, instead of grass and trees and sky and space there is the dreary monotony of uninterrupted bricks and mortar.

The ill wind of that reverse brought two positive gains. Octavia joined the Commons Society, where she met Robert Hunter and became an active member of the Executive Committee. It also forged a working partnership with the Duke of Westminster (Three members of the 'Quartet' were now working together.).

Moreover, most subscribers to the appeal chose to leave the money in her hands and so she was obliged to work out both for herself and publicly by what principles she would be guided in spending it. 'I do not pledge myself to any one spot until I have prepared a general map to see where space is most needed. My impression is that I shall care most (now that the Swiss Cottage fields are gone) for small central spaces; but this may not prove to be the case.'

The Hills were a close and mutually supportive family and her elder sister Miranda collaborated closely with Octavia, first with the school and then with housing. It was to her school that Miranda read a paper suggesting a society 'For the Diffusion of Beauty'. It was taken up by Octavia who printed and circulated it and who, when the society was formed, became its first Treasurer. Named 'The Kyrle', after Pope's 'Man of Ross' who devoted himself to beautifying his town, the society's object was to provide entertainment for the poor and to secure for them the use of small open spaces in the city, close to their homes. Octavia celebrated the foundation of the society with a tribute to her mentor by decorating the Freshwater Place houses with de Morgan tiles, since this would 'please Ruskin who taught me to care for permanent decoration which should endear houses to men, for external decoration should be a common joy'.

Finding sites for open spaces, then winkling them out of the possession of their owners and persuading the vestries of parishes to help was a frustrating business and one in which she laboured at first alone. As late as 1878 she said to her sister Gertrude (about a proposed holiday), 'I am confident that my work in the houses will not really suffer in my absence but my open spaces will miss me, for nobody knows there are any.' Burial grounds were her prize target for most of those in London had been closed for some time since the ghastly over-use resulting in shallow burials, stench and disease (Dickens in *Bleak House* provides a vivid description) had eventually obliged the authorities to act. Nevertheless, to prevail upon the church authorities to part with them was a very different matter. Although she persisted and eventually won her battle for 'small central spaces', the frustration of slow progress may well have prompted her to embark upon consideration of wider issues.

Her housing work had developed to the point where, by 1874, she had fifteen blocks of housing under her management with between two and three thousand tenants. Her prestige and authority were recognised and she had begun publishing important papers of which 'Homes for the London Poor' appearing in *Macmillan's Magazine* in June that year got glowing reviews in the *Medical Times*, the *Builder* and the *Globe*. Two years later she published a paper entitled 'Our Common Land' and in 1877 a further one on 'The Future of our Common Land'. These were clearly prompted by her new association with the Commons Society and were designed in the first case to raise public support for improving the Home Secretary's Commons Bill and in the second, when it had become the Commons Act of 1877, to alert opinion to the dangers to commons still existing.

Shaw-Lefevre, Fawcett and others had worked hard in Parliament to get the Bill improved, but had succeeded only partially and the risk of enclosure remained. It is, however, for illustrations of the way in which her ideas were developing that the papers are directly relevant to this story.

Octavia complained that the Bill only dealt with suburban commons within six miles of the edge of a town. 'Now, I hardly know how far ... excursionists go, but I know they go every year farther and farther. I am sure a common twelve, nay twenty, miles off ... is accessible by cheap trains ...'. She identified the need to feel the freedom of unenclosed land quoting Hugh Miller:

> 'A thoroughly cultivated country is ... much less beloved by its people than a wild and open one. Rights of proprietorship may exist equally in both; but there is one important sense in which the open country belongs to the proprietors and the people too. All that the heart and intellect can derive from it are alike free to peasant and aristocrat; whereas the cultivated and strictly fenced country belongs usually, in every sense, only to the proprietor.'

Faced with the passage of a far from perfect Act she confronted the critical question '... whether, consistently with all private rights, there is any land in England which can be preserved for the common good; ... are we as a nation to have any flower gardens at all? Can we afford it? Do we care to set aside ground for it, or will we have beetroot and cabbages only?'

She also identified a change in attitude by country owners and occupiers caused by the growth of urban populations and the consequent pressures against rural interests which, beginning in the middle of the nineteenth century, is still in progress today. 'In self defence the landowners erect barriers and warn off the public' and where fields are laid up for hay 'the farmer is obliged to lock up his gate, put up his notices or, if a right of way exist, erect a fence which should leave the narrowest permissible pathway ....' Octavia saw this as an added and cogent reason for the preservation of all unenclosed land. 'The more these – (fields, meadows, streams and woods) – are and must be closed the more intensely precious does the common or forest, safe for ever from inclosure, become.'

The Commons Society and the open space lobby in Parliament were continually active, and the Kyrle Society formed a special Open Space Sub-Committee, but it was not until 1884 that a crisis arose which brought three of the Quartet into action together. The preservation of Hampstead Heath had given the Society trouble from the start, the lord of the manor, Sir Thomas Wilson, promoting a private Bill to overcome an entail to grant building leases not only on his demesne but on the Heath itself. This was defeated and it so rankled that in 1865 he told a Commons Committee '... it never entered my head to destroy the Heath until I found I was thwarted with my Bill in Parliament!' However, after Sir Thomas's death a few years later his successor sold out to the Metropolitan Board of Works, so all was well.

However, the Heath depended for much of its charm upon lands lying to the east and north, Parliament Hill and Kenwood, (belonging to the Earl of Mansfield, who had led the opposition to Wilson's Bill) and a small property owned by Wilson's successor. The latter had been put on market for building in 1884 and it had already become 'an offensive and unsightly brick field'. Lord Mansfield was very elderly and his heir made no secret of his intention to sell as soon as he inherited. A special Committee was set up to enlarge the Heath by buying these properties. The Duke of Westminster presided, with Shaw-Lefevre as his Executive Committee Chairman, and with Octavia Hill and Robert Hunter among the members. At Grosvenor House on Park Lane a public meeting was held at which Octavia presented a paper. It took five years to raise the money and complete the deal, but in the process an enlarged and permanent Hampstead Heath Preservation Society was formed with the Duke as President and as a generous subscriber. The result was a further enlargement so that by 1910 the original 240 acres of open space had grown to 614.

Away in the Lake District where he had been established for only seven years, Hardwicke Rawnsley had already begun the activities which were to earn him the sobriquet 'Guardian of the Lakes'. In 1882 he took up the fight, begun nearly forty years before, against railway encroachment. This time the proposal was to lay a line from the slate quarries above Newlands down to Braithwaite. He took a more direct approach than Wordsworth had done: 'Let the slate train once roar along the western side of Derwentwater, let it once cross the lovely vale of Newlands, and Keswick, as the resort of weary men in search of rest, will cease to be.' With the energy which he brought to his whole life, he bombarded every possible ally with demands for support, raised money for opposition through a countrywide appeal for a Borrowdale and Derwentwater Defence Fund, and in one way and another raised the issue to the level of a national *cause célèbre* and finally had the satisfaction of seeing the promotion grind to a halt in the House of Lords.

His next move was an interesting one, in that he conceived the idea of a permanent watch-dog organisation with ample funds for fighting undesirable developments. He put this to the Annual General Meeting of the Wordsworth Society in 1883, with the support of Matthew Arnold, its chairman, and as a result the Lake District Defence Society was born, which lives on, somewhat transmogrified, as the Friends of the Lake District. Wordsworth's fear that the Kendal to Windermere railway might lead to proposals to extend it proved only too real. However, forty years on, the vested interests of the ever increasing number of residents provoked an alliance which, with the major landowners and the pressure group of Hardwicke's Society, defeated that project and another, even more potentially damaging one, in Ennerdale.

How well, if at all, Rawnsley was at that time personally acquainted with the others of the Quartet it is not possible to say. Certainly with John Ruskin established in retreat at Brantwood, by Coniston Water, there was a possible link with Octavia Hill. In any event the two organisations – the Commons Society and the Lake District Defence Society – must have enjoyed mutual recognition. In 1885 a new row in the Lakes brought them all together. Landowners, alarmed by the ever-increasing pressure from tourists, and possibly also hoping to improve the development value of their land, stopped up the much used and popular footpath to Latrigg. Hardie Rawnsley pounced upon this undoubtedly illegal action and, reviving the Keswick and District Footpaths Association, which had almost died of inanition, mounted a crusade which recalls that of Augustus Smith at Berkhamsted. At the head of some 400 avengers he marched to Fawe Park and uprooted the barriers. Characteristically he had brought along Samuel Plimsoll, best known now for his loading line on shipping, but at that time regarded as a popular reforming politician. There seems no record of what Mr Plimsoll said when he addressed the gathering, but to Hardie his value lay in his nationally-known name.

Of course there was a riposte by the owners in the form of writs for trespass and, at Hardwicke Rawnsley's instance, both the Commons and Kyrle Societies appealed for national support against the closures, over the signatures of Robert Hunter and

Octavia Hill. There was an out of court settlement which recognised the right of access and so another conflict ended in victory.

The history of the late nineteenth century is peppered with incidents arising out of the new needs of the rapidly expanding cities. Manchester has had a particularly unfortunate record in this, and its plans to take water in very large quantities from the Lake District, using the valleys as cheap reservoirs, has been unwarrantable and damaging. The plan for Thirlmere, which had been brought out in 1878, not only involved the destruction of the valley itself but the enclosure of a wide area of common land in the catchment area. It was fought by Rawnsley, and by the Commons Society, the latter at least securing a right of access for the public to the commons of the catchment. Otherwise this was a major defeat and it is sad indeed to follow Hardie's desperate efforts to save the 'Rock of Names' – that hallowed spot where William Wordsworth and Dorothy, Coleridge and Sarah and Mary Hutchinson had met to picnic halfway between their homes, and had carved their names. When inundation became inevitable Hardie engaged masons to move it to safety. This proved, because of the nature of the stone, impracticable and later, when it had been dynamited in the course of the engineering work he and his wife gathered up the fragments to build a cairn high above the site.

> Farewell! the dear irrevocable shore
> Dark firs, and bluebell copse, and shallowing bight!
>
> Stern Raven Crag is cheated of its height,
> Gone is the bridge the Romans crossed of yore.
> The 'Rock of Names' has lost its guardian right –
> Where poets met for tryst, they meet no more!

Thus Hardwicke's elegiac 'Thirlmere – Loss and Gain'.

A new force in the preservation field took shape in the late 1870s. The philosophy behind it owed much to the preachings of Ruskin, but it was the creation of the Pre-Raphaelite, William Morris. The Society for the Preservation of Ancient Buildings, which held its first Annual General Meeting on 21 June 1878, was not as influential in forming the ideas of the Quartet as had been the Commons Society, but it did make a major contribution to the subsequent scope of their work. None of the Quartet were members, although Harriot Yorke, Octavia's friend, was to join in 1891 and Octavia herself was given Honorary Membership in 1897. There were, however, links, the strongest of which was formed by John Ruskin, a founder member of the Society's Committee. The Grosvenor family was well represented by Hugh Lupus Grosvenor's cousins, Robert and Norman, sons of Lord Ebury (the former becoming later an Honorary Secretary) while Thomas Hughes, both his friend and Octavia's, was a member.

The society's objectives and interests were at first too narrow to have much common ground with the Open Spaces movement. The Society of Antiquaries of London had found itself at odds with builders and architects on archaeological and historical grounds. They rightly regarded the removal or rebuilding of surviving structures as the destruction of evidence. Ruskin in his *Seven Lamps of Architecture* lifted this dispute onto a moral and aesthetic plane. Restoration was desperately needed in many churches throughout the country. However, a religious movement to revert to what was imagined to be the high point of Christian expression, the fourteenth and fifteenth centuries, demanded that a revival of faith should be matched by a revival in building style. This argument of the Ecclesiologists, as they were known, drove the Gothic perfectionist Augustus Pugin into the Church of Rome, but High Anglicanism embraced the movement and in its name there followed a spate of 'restorations' which, in fact, were destructions.

Roused first by Ruskin to whom restoration was 'a lie from beginning to end', the practical and brilliant William Morris began a campaign which culminated in the founding of the SPAB which was supported by many artists and writers. Out of the very large Committee of 1877 (it totalled fifty-six!) – more than a quarter were artists and only three were architects.

Although constituted to have the interests of all old buildings at heart, the Society in its early years was overwhelmingly concerned with ecclesiastical buildings. The first resolution moved by Lord Houghton illustrates very clearly its primary motive: 'In view of the deplorable falsification that has for long been going on to ancient buildings in the name of restoration, this Society deserves the support of all those who are interested in art, archaeology, and history.'

In 1881, for example, out of fifty-nine buildings with which the Society concerned itself only nine were secular, including Westminster Hall and the Tower of London. In the first ten years of its existence the Society seems to have concerned itself with only two properties which eventually came into the possession of the National Trust: Blundells School, Tavistock in 1883 and Lavenham Guildhall, Suffolk in 1887.

Meanwhile Octavia Hill's 'small central open spaces' campaign had suddenly taken off. The Kyrle Society had formed a special Open Spaces Sub-Committee in 1879, with Robert Hunter as its honorary legal adviser. One branch of the work was taken on by a new organisation, the Metropolitan Public Gardens Association, founded in 1885, which made the care of disused burial grounds its special concern. Government – if not as yet Parliament as a whole – had come alive to at least some of the needs and problems and Ministers allowed themselves to be guided by the pioneers in some of the details of legislation which began to find its way on to the statute book.

To look ahead a little, there were several successes such as securing the forty-five acres of Hilly Fields at Lewisham from development. This involved raising nearly £45,000 partly by private subscription, the rest coming from a reluctant Metropolitan Board of Works. In 1887 Octavia secured the Lawns in Lambeth (now known as Vauxhall Park) and royal recognition too, when in 1890 it was opened by his Royal Highness the Prince of Wales. It must have given Octavia extra pleasure that another member of the royal family, Princess Louise, was present too, because she had been a friend and supporter ever since the very early days.

Meanwhile there had been an event which, in itself, was no more than another of Octavia's enterprises, but which set in motion the train of thought which was to lead Octavia to the idea of founding the National Trust. In 1884 Mr Evelyn, described by Octavia as 'an old man, and I should think an eccentric one' had promised to give land at Sayes Court, Deptford to the Metropolitan authority, but there was a snag about which Octavia consulted Robert. There was no legal means of vesting the land in the authority, subject to the necessary trusts for its future use. Robert suggested the creation of a corporate company under the Joint Stock Companies Act, because the appointment of individual trustees would be unsatisfactory. Octavia replying on 27 August said, 'I think such a company as you suggest would be valuable and that Sayes Court might well be handed over to it.' However in view of Mr Evelyn's age and character she was unwilling to wait and wanted to clinch the deal at once.

Nevertheless, neither she nor Robert let go of the idea. Later in the same year he read a paper at Birmingham to the Association for the Promotion of Social Science, putting the idea forward as being capable of a general application.

How long the gestation period would have been had not more problems been brewing in the Lake District it is hard to say. Certainly there was plenty of activity in the south. By this time Harriot Yorke and Octavia had set up a home together in the country at Crockham Hill, in Kent, close to her married sister, Gertrude Lewis. Together Octavia and Robert, now established at Meadfields near Haslemere, founded the Kent and Sussex branch of the Commons Society in 1888 with the preservation of footpaths specially included in its responsibilities. This lead them into local activities which were to produce practical and permanent results early in the life of the Trust.

But it was trouble in 1893 at the Lodore Falls, south of Keswick, which brought matters to a head. Hardwicke Rawnsley, fearful that the sale of that romantic spot would lead to its spoliation, and yet not knowing how and by whom it should be cared for even were the financial means available, turned to the Commons Society. Octavia put the idea of a public trust to the Duke of Westminster who took it up at once: 'Mark my words Miss Hill, this is going to be a very big thing.'

The groundwork laid in the succeeding twelve months bears all the hallmarks of Hunter's work. Curiously enough the precedents had already been established in the United States. An American Act of 1891 to establish the Trustees of Public Reservations, Massachusetts, formed the basis for a constitution first considered at a meeting in the offices of the Commons Society on 16 November 1893. The proposals Robert Hunter put before that meeting have scarcely changed, although they have been greatly enlarged over the years. *The Times*'s leading article the following day, based no doubt on detailed information from the Society, is a clear, if lengthy, exposition of the methods to be employed and the long-term objectives.

There was to be a Provisional Council which would present the proposal to a public meeting and the members were to include the Duke of Westminster, Lords Dufferin and Rosebery, Professor Huxley, the Provost of Eton, the Master of Trinity and Mr Shaw-Lefevre. An association would be incorporated under the Joint Stock Companies Act, non profit-making 'and having no right to divide their property among the members in the event of a winding up. It is clearly indispensable that a trust of the kind now proposed should be subject to these limitations.' The writer looked ahead to a Royal Charter or special Act of Parliament and powers to make bye-laws.

'The scheme appears to be highly commendable,' said *The Times*. 'The association will at first have no other function than to facilitate the bestowal of gifts upon the public', but it looked forward to an enlargement of its scope with appeals for money to buy property.

The *Daily News* ran the story on the same day, saying that 'the new Trust is primarily a caretaker and it may roughly be described as the Commons Preservation in active rather than in merely advisory functions.'

On 16 July 1894, a meeting was held at Grosvenor House, presided over by the Duke of Westminster. It was proposed that a society be set up under the Joint Stock Companies Act. This original suggestion was subsequently altered to make the society into a Trust, as it was felt that the public would not like an unsuccessful commercial venture, but would be sympathetic to a trust.

Six months later, on 12 January 1895, the Duke again played host at Grosvenor House to a public meeting when the formation of the association, already entitled The National Trust for Places of Historic Interest or Natural Beauty, was formally agreed, and registered with the Board of Trade.

It is interesting to note that *The Times* had been right to look forward to the promotion of a private Bill. Within twelve years matters had progressed sufficiently to make this desirable and possible, and 'an Act to incorporate and confer powers upon the National Trust' received Royal Assent on 21 August 1907. The First Schedule listed twenty-six freehold properties and three others.

Robert Hunter's original constitution passed to all intents and purposes unchanged into statute, the process guided wholly by his hand. There have had to be changes, as the scope of the Trust's work has grown, but Robert Hunter's Act remains after some eighty years as sound a framework for organisation as it had been from the start.

CHAPTER III

First Fruits

As experienced campaigners, the Quartet knew that they must show immediate results for their new Trust. It fell to Hardwicke Rawnsley to make the first strike. Writing about it more than twenty years later he recalled that in 1895 he had been staying at Barmouth on the Welsh coast with Mrs Fannie Talbot. She was an old friend of Ruskin and had been an early benefactor of his Guild of St George. Horne and Birkett – now solicitors to the National Trust – sent the draft articles of association to Rawnsley for comment and Mrs Talbot read them out of general interest and 'a natural love of law'. At the end she said, 'I am so grateful for this chance, for I perceive your National Trust will be of the greatest use to me. I have long wanted to secure for the public for ever the enjoyment of Dinas Oleu, but I wish to put it into the custody of some society that will never vulgarise it, or prevent wild Nature from having its own way ... I wish to avoid the abomination of asphalt paths and the cast iron seats of serpent design ...'

This land was – and is – a steep, gorse-clad, rocky fell of less than five acres above 'unbeautiful Barmouth' but with splendid views over Cardigan Bay. The name has been interpreted as 'Fortress of Light'. What endeared it to Hardwicke was surely the happiness of the children he saw there: 'a group of children as spectators of the dancing of one of their number, with ribbons cross-gartered on her bare legs and an ivy chaplet on her head.

'"Dance for us then" we said, and at once the child with most graceful gesture of arms and legs danced what she called "the Song of the Flowers". – Two other children wearing chaplets of flowers came up the steep path ... When they emerged they had doffed their ragged petticoats and appeared with short skirts and bare legs. Four children joined hands and danced a pretty dance. Then a dark, handsome girl, selecting a smooth slab of stone, began a dance of the Scotch-reel type. Another child appeared with her hands full of foxgloves which she distributed to the dancers who waved them as they danced.'

So Mrs Talbot's generosity was not the only spur to providing the Trust with its first open space!

We know the full story of the Trust's first acquisition of a building through the persistent enquiries of Mr Leslie Millard. Upon retirement from the Trust's Head Office, he took charge of this property as recently as 1978. The Clergy House at

Alfriston in Sussex had come to the attention of the Society for the Preservation of Ancient Buildings in 1891. For years before that it had been a worry to incumbents and, in 1879, the Bishop and the patron of the living authorised demolition. However, before that happened the living passed into the hands of the Rev. F.W. Beynon who was anxious to preserve it. He failed to get support from his churchwardens and parishioners and, probably after contact with the SPAB, launched an appeal which also failed. Eventually someone seems to have advised him to write to Canon Rawnsley and this he did on 26 July 1894, just ten days after the formal incorporation of the National Trust.

The house had all the qualities which made it the sort of building which the National Trust hoped to preserve. As a pre-Reformation house, certainly fourteenth century and not much altered, it was of prime antiquarian importance. It was in a charming village in an unspoiled district and capable of being itself quite lovely. It was in the last stages of dilapidation. There were difficulties: money had to be raised for repair and the Ecclesiastical Commissioners had to be persuaded to authorise its sale to the Trust for the nominal sum of £10. However, with the appeal fund still well short of what was needed, on 16 April 1896 the house was conveyed to the Trust.

Octavia Hill seems to have been in charge of overseeing liaison with the SPAB on repairs. Letters flew between her and Thackeray Turner, the Society's Secretary, and she was often anxious. To her colleagues she wrote 'a much more difficult problem (than an open space) – still, into a safe state it must be got.' The unusual use of words seems to underline her determination. When things did not move as rapidly as she wished she switched to more informal letters to young Sydney Cockerell who, as her disciple and SPAB committee member might by-pass his Secretary. She was clear on the obligations of the Trust: 'We should very naturally be asked to "restore" it, in so far as that odious word means preservation from decay.' She was a true disciple of Ruskin in her attitude towards restoration.

The SPAB report in 1897 details the work done for the £170 then available: bolting the timber frame – which was loose – on to a lighter duplicate frame inside; repairing the clay pugging between the framing; temporary straw thatch over the two rooms being made habitable for a caretaker. The rest of the work, mainly re-thatching with reed, was then put in hand but a further £150 was needed by the Trust. The sums involved seem trivial but the Quartet unanimously believed that in all their concerns they must live within income. Even by 1900 the Trust's income was only £300 a year and each new acquisition and its subsequent maintenance meant raising money specially for that purpose. This good housekeeping principle has been a consistent element of policy ever since. In the end, however, the restoration was a complete success.

All the Quartet was continuously active in the affairs of their new National Trust. Robert Hunter engaged in a protracted but unsuccessful correspondence with the agents for Lord Harlech over difficulties in acquiring more land at Barmouth, which had been promised, and by 1899 had drafted three Bills to improve preservation in ways which would complement the work of the Trust. These were aimed at easing the methods for protecting ancient monuments, facilitating the dedication of land for public enjoyment, and the protection of place of natural, scientific or historic interest. They are notable because they anticipate matters which did not become generally acknowledged public issues until much later. Dedicated land, for example, was to be rated only on its value for letting subject to public use, and to be eligible for remission of estate duty on the owners' death, while the terms were binding upon all successors, including the remainderman under a settlement. The third Bill gave Government power to exercise protection through an order in Council, with compensation to the owner, but a sanction of a fine (£50 maximum was quite a high figure) for any who transgressed the order.

Hardwicke Rawnsley was very busy with his job as Honorary Secretary and it was largely he who conducted the Trust's vociferous objections to various schemes of development – often railways. One, an extension from Henley to Great Marlow, must have particularly enraged him since this was the Thames Valley of his earliest remembered youth. In the Annual Reports (which were of Hardwicke's authorship) over the years 1897 – 1900 there were no less than nineteen matters listed in which the Trust had sought either to prevent some offensive scheme or to promote some necessary intervention. There was a joint effort with the SPAB in 1898 to raise funds for the restoration of the church of St Mary-le-Bow in London's Cheapside. This involved the very large sum of £4,700 and it is interesting that the National Trust was, at that stage when every pound was important to its central work, prepared to devote its energies and possibly divert money which it could have used to advance its own interests, to a field which had previously been quite outside its concerns.

At the same time the Trust mounted a campaign which would be regarded even now as extremely ambitious. Urged on by the Marquess of Dufferin, the Annual General Meeting in 1900 resolved that 'were the Lakes of Killarney, perhaps more widely celebrated for their beauty than any other spot in the British Isles, to be closed against the public, or marred by vulgarising or incongruous treatment' it would be deeply deplorable. This was provoked by the sale of the 13,000-acre Mackross Estate, and was seen as a chance to create 'a great National Park after the manner of the Yellowstone region in America'. The Council of the Trust formed a joint committee with Irish interests, including the Lord Mayor of Dublin, and went so far as to seek an option to buy for £40,000. In the event it was bought for half as much again by the Guinness family, on whose good intentions the Trust was prepared to rely.

With all this going on, it is hardly surprising that the Duke of Westminster should add his entreaties to Canon Rawnsley not to go as Bishop to Madagascar. 'I quite agree with those of your friends who hope that you will not undertake the Bishopric as we want you at home!' This was an aside in a letter – in the Duke's own hand – on the subject of footpaths. He and Rawnsley had been corresponding on the subject since 1896, the Duke then rejecting the appointment of a Commission to regulate use and abate obstructions, in favour of an association which could raise funds for legal action. This was to culminate in the amalgamation of the Commons Society with the Footpaths Society in 1898.

Sadly Hugh Lupus Grosvenor, Duke of Westminster, was to be the first of the Quartet to die, and the short tribute to him in the National Trust's Annual Report for 1899–1900 rings with absolute sincerity: They put on record:

> their deep sense of loss … and their recognition of the invaluable services which he rendered to the Trust from the day of its inception to the day of his death.

They wish it to be remembered that it was largely owing to his constant kindly personal care for the success of the Trust, and his keen interest in its objects, that the Trust has been able to carry on its work for the nation, and to commend itself to the public as worthy of support. The Duke did much more than lend his name to the Trust. He took the keenest interest in its work, he presided at every Annual Meeting, ... and he was always accessible to the officers of the Trust, and ready to give his personal support to any project which the Society had at heart.

Hardwicke Rawnsley was one of the honorary secretaries of the memorial committee, which eventually replaced the 1840 stained glass in the windows of the south transept of Westminster Abbey as a memorial to the Duke:

> Gleam on, thou rich rose-window, gleam and show
> With angel petals how all good and great
> Were glad forerunners of the Christ to be.
> Still God's way needs a herald; such was he
> Who kept a humble heart in proud estate,
> Who helped the high and lifted up the low.

Hugh Lupus Grosvenor might well have been satisfied with the remembrance of his achievements, including the creation of the National Trust.

By 1913 the list of Trust acquisitions had grown to fifty-nine and the report could have a map of England and Wales on the back cover with a fine showing of possessions scattered over its length and breadth. The ways in which they were acquired were varied, always interesting, often curious. A few need immediate notice, more will appear later, as they come to represent early examples of developing concerns.

It was Octavia who made the first personal gift, albeit a small one. At Toys Hill, not far from her Crockham Hill home, Mr and Mrs Freeman made the gift of a spur of land which juts from the sandstone ridge overlooking the Weald (the first, incidentally, of many gifts *in memoriam*). Octavia added a neighbouring plot. The report emphasises that 'these promontories are being rapidly purchased for building and enclosed.'

Miranda chipped in next, securing an option to buy Ide Hill in 1899 and the greater part of Mariners Hill was finally secured in 1908 by Octavia's efforts over four years, probably helped financially by an old associate in housing work, Lady Ducie. There, looking west towards Crockham, she placed a stone seat in memory of her mother, Caroline Southwood Hill, who died in 1904.

Octavia was involved in the acquisition of more land near Toys Hill, the solicitors Horne and Birkett sending her a map of Parson's Marsh for her to check. These 18½ acres came to the Trust in 1911 under the will of Mrs Fleming, whose widower wrote to Nigel Bond that, 'My wife always had the highest opinion of the work being done by the National Trust.' From this patchwork of tiny areas there has now developed an estate of over 1,500 acres, spread from Limpsfield eastwards to Ightham, eleven miles away. The balance needed for the Mariners Hill purchase, £500, came from an old friend on the last day of Octavia's life, and a plain stone on the hill not many hundred yards from her mother's seat commemorates her work. There were to be other memorials, but none better.

It was to be 1902 before there was any acquisition in the Lakes, but when it came it was a notable occasion. The 108 acres of woods and parkland of Brandelhow lie on the west side of Derwentwater below the great hill of Catbells. Beautiful in themselves and surrounded by beauty they served to secure access on the lake shore, where public rights were far from certain. Most of the shore was in private ownership and there were only three or four public landings. Hardwicke Rawnsley applied all his immense store of energy to convincing the public that this was an opportunity of 'incalculable value' and, within five months, raised the purchase price of £6,500.

Octavia secured the presence of Princess Louise, Duchess of Argyll, for the opening ceremony and in October that year wrote to her mother:

> I have just come back from the great opening, and I want to tell you about it. It was very successful, very simple, real and unconventional. The place was looking very lovely. I never saw the light more beautiful, it was not what people call fine, but it was *very* beautiful and did not rain. The wind was high and tore the tent to ribbons when it was being put up, but I think it really did better because the simple little red däis was out under the free sky, with the great lake lying below, and the golden fern clad slopes of Catbells above. It was very funny and primitive and the nice North country folk were quite near and saw and heard all. The Princess was most friendly and kind, and really did show deep and intelligent interest in the National Trust work. She asked me whom we were going to make President and added 'I hoped you would ask me, I should really like to do more for the work, and I should like Lord Carlisle as Vice-President.' She then went on to tell me of some beautiful old houses she wants us to try to save. She really does care and know, I think ...

Events of that sort give impetus both to fresh endeavour and public recognition and the further progress of the Trust in the Lakes was characterised by the size and significance of the properties. Only four years later the 750 acres of Gowbarrow Park, with 'the exquisite glen through which the Aira tumbles and leaps to the lake [Ullswater] below' was bought. Further land around Derwentwater followed, with land and part of the lake bed (important now, even more than then) and, in 1910, Borrowdale with the Bowder Stone and Grange Fell came on the market. With a new ally, the solicitor Birkett, Hardwicke snapped this up just in time. The National Trust was given a five-year option to buy all except a farm, which did not seem important for preservation. This Hardwicke kept and later used it to endow a scholarship for his Keswick School. The £2,200 for the 310 acres was quickly subscribed, Princess Louise paying for Grange Fell itself as a memorial to her brother, Edward VII. Just below the summit is a stone let into the rock face and inscribed, in lettering designed by Edith Rawnsley, with the Princess's dedication: '... as a sanctuary of rest and peace. Here may all beings gather strength, and find in scenes of beautiful nature a cause for gratitude and love for God, giving them courage and vigour to carry on his work.'

The quest for access to lake shores brought a further success, this time by the increasingly built-up Windermere. Queen Adelaide, widow of William IV, seems not only to have been the only English Queen to have visited the Lakes, in 1840, but also contrived to have her name attached to a wooded hill with a frontage to the lake. The development value of sites such as this, just twenty acres with a cottage, can be judged from the fact that Rawnsley had to raise £5,000, a figure which would have been regarded as expensive fifty years later. A further mark of success was that those who attended the opening were invited to tea and a lecture by Professor Hoverfield on the Roman Galava fort in Borrans Field, Ambleside. Plans to acquire this critical spot at Waterhead had fallen through in 1898 and eventual success fifteen years later was all the more sweet.

In retrospect these achievements may seem modest in comparison with the essential importance of the English Lakes in inspiring the whole movement. Against this we must set the high value for development of land around the lakes and the large scale of the operations imposed by the character of the landscape. However, there was a lot more to happen later.

Robert Hunter (Sir Robert since 1894) also produced a direct contribution in his own district, though the fruits of his work did not appear until more than ten years had passed. From his home near Haslemere he began to marshal local interests to preserve in Surrey the same greensand ridge that Octavia was protecting thirty miles to the east, and along the south-facing scarp of the North Downs. This was, and had been for 150 years, Londoners' country. Nelson had spent an idyllic holiday at Burford Bridge; Jorrocks had put up at the Swan to pursue the fox; Robert himself had spent his formative holidays there; and, to London south of the Thames, Box Hill was the more distant counterpart of Hampstead Heath.

With customary thoroughness he nursed a Hindhead Preservation Society which in 1906 gave no less than 750 acres at Hindhead, astride the Portsmouth Road and embracing the great amphitheatre of the Devil's Punchbowl. This was followed two years later by 550 acres at Ludshott Common, and by other patches of land. In that and later years these served as a framework for later acquisitions which have succeeded against all odds in limiting the suburbanisation of the area.

The eighty acres of Marley Common were bought by the Haslemere Commons Society in 1911. The owners of land adjoining the west side of the common, woodland of Scots Pine trees exceptionally straight and tall, wanted an access across the common, to which Sir Robert agreed on condition that they gave to the Trust a broad strip of the wood. Not only did this form a screen against the housing development beyond, but it became a cherished walk, the columns of the trees earning it the name of 'The Cathedral Pines'.

It was to the preservation of Box Hill, the eastern buttress of the Mickleham Gap in the North Downs above Dorking, that Sir Robert turned his attention in his last years. The district had been dear to him since his school holidays, but it had been associated with many other people of distinction, amongst them the poet, George Meredith, whose cottage looked up across its slopes from the valley called Little Switzerland. Nearly a hundred years earlier Talleyrand had taken temporary refuge at Juniper Hall. Distinguished naturalists had found in its unmodified ecology and its accessibility from London such a rich hunting ground that its insects and plants are probably better and more continuously documented than anywhere else. There was a railway line from Leatherhead to Dorking down the Mole valley and another following the foot of the downs from east to west, linking with main lines to London. Not only was it all ripe for suburban growth but the downland behind was already spattered with the villa-mansions of the rich. It was high time for urgent intervention.

The whole price of the 230 acres was found by Leopold Salomons and this Robert Hunter knew before he died in 1913. Robert's death had come hard upon that of Octavia Hill's, in the previous year. During the last year of her life Miss Hill was living at Crockham Hill and coming up to London during the week, where a Miss Sims kept house for her and acted as manager. Despite Miss Hill's long affliction with cancer, Janet Upcott (whose role in the Trust's affairs will be discussed later) remembers that she 'never gave up and worked until the last week of her life'.

The loss of two such dedicated and inspiring leaders in successive years was devastating for the National Trust. It was this, as much as the outbreak of war in 1914, which slowed down progress. Lord Plymouth was chosen to succeed Hunter as Chairman and in the circumstances he may have been a good choice. An artist in his own right, he was prominent and active in the national collections, being a Trustee of the National Gallery and Chairman of the Trustees of the Tate Gallery. He was also practically involved with preservation in his capacity as First Commissioner of Works (a post later to be styled Minister of Works). It was under his aegis that the Mall had been laid out, and he was responsible for the fact that the Crystal Palace was preserved, sadly much later to be destroyed by fire. Lord Plymouth's great achievement as Chairman was to keep the organisation together during the First World War and to bring it through ready to take the opportunities which were to arise afterwards.

Hardwicke Rawnsley was now in his sixties, suffering the loss of his wife in 1916, and himself very ill indeed in that year, there was not the same vigour in his work for the Trust. He had, to be sure, secured land in Borrowdale which he gave to the Trust in 1915, optimistically calling it Peace How, as a commemoration of the peace which he hoped would succeed conflict. In July 1918 he made a tour of the Trust's West Country properties. It is hard to imagine that in that month when Ludendorf's offensive was still not finally checked, and the Germans once more across the Marne, that an elderly cleric could spend weeks travelling the country, grumbling about the trains, hiring motor cars and being very choosy about hotels, with seemingly no thought for anything but the properties of the National Trust. Yet that is how his account, *A Nation's Heritage*, reads.

It is significant in trying to understand an attitude to the Trust's work which, judging by reports, guide books and correspondence, was then quite general, to discover that Hardwicke was as much interested in associations as in the places. At Minchinhampton Common the church, 'savagely restored at the worst time, i.e. 1842', and the picturesque sexton's house, have equal prominence with the views over the Severn to the Welsh hills and the recollection 'that hereabouts, in 628, Penda King of Mercia fought a bloody fight against his two rebellious sons, Cynegills and Cwichelm.' At Glastonbury his mind is not so much on the Trust's property of the Tor but upon the marshmen who once dwelt at its feet, and he recognises with apparent certainty the Island Valley of Avalon, whither King Arthur went 'to heal him of his grievous wound', and quotes his hero Tennyson. What with Glastonbury Abbey and Kelways still-famous nurseries it is surprising that on the same day he did reach Muchelney, sat on the steps of the old village cross and went 'back in dream to the time when this village was so surrounded by marshes ... as to be called, what its name implies, the Great or Muckle Island.' He does however record his appreciation of the careful work of the SPAB in doing the repairs to the Priest's House for the small sum of £200.

He marked Camelford as the site of Arthur's last battle, and the occasion of his mortal wound. On Tintagel's Barras Head he recorded 'soft grass, enamelled with great patches of thyme ... and golden with anthyllis'. The fourteenth-century house, known then and today as the Old Post Office, got a polite nod. He met Miss Johns, who had bought the house for preservation in 1893, but finding it beyond her means, secured the help of the National Trust and the SPAB ten years later. In fact both those Tintagel properties are interesting illustrations of the ways in which acquisitions were made. Miss Johns made a gift to the Trust which, with the SPAB, raised the money to repair the building and Miss Johns reserved the right to remain in occupation. She had to keep the tiny garden and open it to visitors. Later she became something of a thorn in the side of the Secretary, always promising to cut back the invading shrubs but never quite getting round to doing so. Barras Head was bought at auction by the Earl of Wharncliffe with the idea of developing it as an hotel garden. However, in his letter of 2 June 1896 to Canon Rawnsley he agreed to resell to the Trust for the price he gave for it, only reserving a right of pre-emption if the Trust were to sell.

Hardwicke Drummond Rawnsley died on 28 May 1920, at home in the Lakes. His epitaph he himself had written eight years before:

> Here rests at last a man whose best
> Was done because he could not rest.
> His wish to work his will to serve
> Were things from which he could not swerve.

There can be no quarrel with this self-assessment. His marriage to Eleanor Simpson, a close friend of his late wife, had taken place just before his West Country trip. With her and her sister he had, back in 1905, set off at midnight after a full day's work to climb Helvellyn, where they watched the sun rise, then, home by seven in the morning and after three hours sleep, off again to address the British Women's Temperance Association, give an afternoon lecture at Dove Cottage and take the train to reach London by midnight again! With them ten years later he had crossed the sands of Morecambe Bay, a ten-mile, barefoot tramp over ribbed sands. In her biography of Hardwicke written in 1923, in explanation of his decision to marry again, Eleanor writes that 'Hardwicke's nature had more than its full share of the universal need for sympathy.' Insofar as it is possible to see from the outside the inner workings of others, this seems likely not only to be true but to be an element of his dynamic concern for everything and everybody.

The common denominator of the members of the Quartet was that over and above everything else they cared for people:

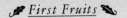

I pray thee then
Write me as one who loved his fellow men.

Janet Upcott, who trained as a housing manager in the early days and worked for Octavia for two years, remembers an occasion when Octavia and Harriot Yorke had been to visit the property on the River Wandle. South London was already engulfing the area, and now it is, of course, a tiny oasis in a desert of development. Her sister Miranda had died in 1910 and in personal memory, and in recognition of the work done by her Kyrle Society, eleven acres had been bought for the National Trust. Octavia was pleased with what was a new feature of her small central open spaces – a riverside walk where families could come and play and picnic away from the cramped enclosure of their homes. No wonder that Janet Upcott remembers Octavia's reward that day was the sight of children playing joyfully on the bank and paddling and splashing in the water.

A happy thought was to add land on the Wandle as a memorial to Octavia, as well as to dedicate to her memory Hydon Heath and the Ball, a 600-foot greensand hill, near Godalming. This was already under negotiation at her death and her sister Emily and Harriot Yorke put down the money to secure it until the Memorial Committee should have assembled its resources.

For Robert Hunter a Memorial Fund was opened and over fifty years it contributed to a large number of purchases. Hardwicke Rawnsley's memorial is possibly the most appropriate. Derwentwater was perhaps as dear to him as any place and that romantic promontory of Friar's Crag on which he himself had placed a memorial to Ruskin, formed the principal part, with Lord's Island which lies full in view and a stretch of the lake shore in Great Wood. Of all the Quartet only Hugh Lupus Grosvenor is without a memorial in the form of National Trust property.

Lord Plymouth remained Chairman until his death in 1924, and with him it is possible to close the first chapter of the life of the Trust. By that time the number of properties had increased to 108, and the pattern had been set for all the main lines of the future development of the work. Perhaps more importantly a second generation of devoted workers had already been recruited who, with the leaven of those who remained from early days, were to see the Trust through to the second half of the century and beyond.

CHAPTER IV

Into a New Century

Thanks to the example of the Quartet, the Trust was business-like from the word go, and the framework of the organisation has changed remarkably little in the succeeding ninety years. (For those who are interested in the minutiae of such things a diagram of the pattern of Council and Committees forms Appendix I.) The Council fairly soon entrusted much of the work to its Executive Committee; very soon (1899) there was also a Finance and General Purposes Committee, and a year later an Estates Committee. When one considers how small the Trust's estate then was, this early provision for management was remarkably optimistic and far-sighted.

Matters of administration were dealt with by Canon Rawnsley as Honorary Secretary, and all the early reports are in his hand. He was assisted for the first two years by Lawrence Chubb, who then became a very notable and influential Secretary to the Commons Society, and to whom the Trust was to owe a great deal. After two short-term office holders, Nigel Bond took the office of Secretary and held it for an important ten years, to 1911, after which he was co-opted on to the Executive Committee.

A quiet and retiring man, John Bailey, became a member of the Council and the Executive Committee in 1898. He was appointed Vice-Chairman in 1913 and became Chairman in 1922 It is not possible to point to any dramatic consequences of his participation in the organisation, but he is important because of the sort of man he was, his interests and his friends. Without the consistent effort that he and others like him were to devote to the cause, the National Trust would not have developed so surely along the lines laid down by the founders.

Born in Norwich in 1864 and brought up with a deep love of Norfolk, he went up to New College, Oxford. He was in time to hear Jowett preach, although he seems to have had somewhat stuffy ideas about the congregation which, in his diary, he describes as 'dishevelled Balliol men and higher education ladies'. English literature and poetry were his passion and Matthew Arnold's death left him 'shocked and startled terribly. He was nearer to our true hearts than any other author.' It was possibly because of its literary connections that he noticed, rather coolly, the Pre-Raphaelite school: 'it was most necessary, but only as a passing phase, to correct the vagueness and insincerity of previous art.'

As a young man, Bailey taught regularly at Toynbee Hall, and later at the Working Men's College, and kept up his links with them all his life, feeling humble at the effort towards self-improvement made by those who had to spend a hard day at manual labour: 'These working men put us men of leisure to horrible shame by the amount they manage to read.' Politically he was a Conservative. In the light of his convictions, the evidence of his sensitivity to human condition is all the more impressive. He read, in 1894, 'a horrid Socialist book which has made me very uncomfortable. Nothing else depresses me but this hideous doubt..., of whether one is justified in living on rents and interest at all ... the awful inequality of our social conditions is enough to give one pause, and certainly is responsible, in my case, for more hours discomfort and uneasiness than anything else.' It is also an indication of his moderate, commonsensical nature that he concluded 'that it is better to accept the amazingly rapid improvement that is going on than to plunge into any Socialistic Medea's cauldron!' His views were much the same more than twenty years later, during the Great War. Over dinner, with H.A.L. Fisher, the historian and one of his Lyttleton in-laws, they spoke of 'the extraordinary selfishness and folly of northern (in this case Lancashire) employers ... Every workman is made a Socialist by their stupidity and their "damn them, shoot them" attitude.'

John Bailey soon became an unobtrusive worker, though the official records have but sparse indications of that. Writing to his wife while away on a walking tour of the English Lakes in 1902, he gives an interesting glimpse of his role. 'Here we are – and I have had to write a long letter to Octavia Hill in reply to one I had from her this morning about various matters. I enclose it so that you may see her curious modesty and her ridiculous deference to your superior husband! It is odd that she should be so very polite. But the result of it is bad – for I had to give her my views on all these subjects.'

Three years later he was writing to Octavia with commendable firmness: Sir Robert Hunter was being cautious about spending so much money on such a large area, over 700 acres at Gowbarrow, and wanted to see 'whether in many cases we cannot secure our purpose of "preservation" without the vast expense of buying, which must limit our operations so seriously.' John Bailey is insistent that Sir Robert's point must be discussed. One suspects pressure from Hardwicke Rawnsley for immediate action, because in a postscript he reassured Octavia that he 'had not the very slightest fear of any other buyer'.

Bailey was close enough to Octavia Hill to be forewarned of her last – and very long – illness. Writing to Nigel Bond in August 1909 (about what is still a perennial problem, local councils and others wishing to put seats on the Trust's property, this time Tintagel!), 'Have you heard how Miss Hill is? I dread to think it but I am afraid that she will not be with us very much longer. Do not quote me as saying she is seriously ill as I hear she objects to it being known.'

The same letter contains a sincere tribute to Bond's work as Secretary. 'I have just been reading the Report. It is quite excellent and the whole thing is very encouraging and you certainly deserve many feathers in your cap for the progress of the Trust.'

By 1914 he had been appointed Vice-Chairman, possibly with the intention of providing help for Lord Plymouth, and was closely involved in helping to direct the day-to-day work. S.H. Hamer had succeeded Bond as Secretary in 1911 and was at the receiving end of a succession of sharp if courteous letters from Bailey on the subject of a set of intolerably restrictive covenants which the vendor of land at Reigate was seeking to impose. Here is a small taste of his style:

> I think you went a little too far in saying that the Trust would not desire to do any of the things Lord Monson desires to forbid. It is because we *might* do so that we object to the restrictions ... our whole record and *raison d'être* show that we should aim at carrying out the spirit and main intention of their restrictions but that we decline to be treated as children and hampered in detail by the control of persons unborn who may be wholly unreasonable.

Another of Bailey's friends, active in National Trust affairs, was George Macaulay Trevelyan, the historian, but their friendship originated in their mutual passion for literature. Trevelyan writing to Bailey in 1911 about dedicating to him an anthology called *English Songs of Italian Freedom* says that 'there is a particular propriety in dedicating this little volume ... to you, because the sort of attitude to literature and life that it represents, the love of poetry in particular, not as unrelated to ethics, to history, and to public affairs, is the thing that binds you and me together.' That statement could perhaps be extended to embrace the common sentiments of many of those active in the work of the Trust from the beginning.

Since he was so highly regarded by at least two such wise and eminent people as R.C. Norman and Trevelyan it is odd that Bailey has not left behind him a more vivid impression. Notes on the Trust made in 1981 by the first Lord Chorley who served on the Executive Committee for forty-five years remembered his kindness.

> He was clearly sensitive to natural beauty and conducted the business of the meetings in a competent and sensible way if not with outstanding vigour or ability. During the period I first knew him he would be in the early sixties, but was already somewhat lacking in energy, and certainly not the man to arouse Hamer to any excess of activity.

Despite this he concludes that 'after the founders the Trust in its early years owed more to his work than any other single person.' It is even odder that John Bailey should have left so slight a reputation because the period of his offices, firstly as Vice-Chairman and then Chairman till his death in 1931, was one in which some of the main lines of the Trust's work were developed with dramatic success.

Chorley says that in the late 'twenties 'the Trust was not a very go-ahead institution,' and he attributes this to the character of the Secretary, Hamer. Chorley, himself an energetic member of the Executive Committee for 45 years, gives an entertaining and wholly unmalicious account of Hamer's approach to work. He had first met him when representing the Fell and Rock Climbing Club which was proposing to give land as a war memorial. 'We had then sized him up as being far from a go-getter.' The day's work was said to begin by reaching the office – then at 7 Buckingham Palace Gardens – at eleven to half-past, reading the day's letters, drafting Committee papers 'and then dictating the results of these activities to his secretary Miss Wilkinson, a charming and capable young woman .... Then across the park to his club, lunch, read the papers, back about 3 p.m. to sign his letters and get himself through his day's work by about 3.30 p.m.' Exaggerated though this account must be – and we know that Hamer was obliged to travel a lot and had some fearful correspondents to cope with! – it must be allowed to reflect a fairly relaxed attitude.

Victoria Spencer-Wilkinson, daughter of an Oxford academic, was Assistant Secretary in the mid-1920s. She was by no means simply a clerical assistant, but deputised for the Secretary in visiting properties. She and Snooks, (Florence Paterson, more respectfully known to later generations as 'Miss P') were the only staff Hamer had, but they seem to have coped remarkably well, and some clue to his apparently leisured approach to work may have been derived from an ability to delegate. For example, Miss Spencer-Wilkinson, then about thirty, was given the important job of drafting the Ashridge appeal leaflet. As a reward she was able to bank Miss Courtauld's cheque for £20,000 at the branch of Barclays in Belgravia which still has the Trust's account, and had the reflected glory of all the staff crowding round to see for themselves this exceptional item.

Miss Spencer-Wilkinson's adventures into the country – she was a town girl – must have needed a degree of resourcefulness. Sent to meet and advise the Ide Hill Committee on a hedging problem, she was obliged to discover from them what sort of a hedge they wanted – a wattle hedge – and then, without knowing in the least what it was, advise them that it was the correct solution. She also had to cope with being confronted with those whose way of life had changed little since before the Great War. Lord Coleridge, for example, who looked after the Trust's interests at the little property of Rockbeare Hill in Devon, sent his electric brougham, with chauffeur *and* footman to meet her at the station. All the luggage she had to hand over was an ancient Burberry and a case so small that, on her departure, the maid was unable to persuade it to accommodate her belongings.

Her recollection of Ronnie Norman, 'that beautiful man', illustrates the cosy, family atmosphere of the office. With Mr Hamer away one day, Victoria and Snooks decided to have hot buttered toast for tea, but in the midst of their preparations who should come in but the Chairman of the Finance Committee, Mr R.C. Norman. The girls were clearly dismayed at being caught but the outcome was a tea party for three instead of two.

Victoria's description of Ronnie Norman was not as extravagant as it may seem. He was good looking, bright eyed, slim and quick moving, and with a ready sense of humour. He had early been a member of the London County Council and became its chairman, as he was of the BBC later. Chorley wrote of him that 'his quick decisive mind, grasped the essentials of a problem easily and clearly, acted promptly and without hesitation, and could put his point of view with vigorous eloquence with the conviction that carries opinion with it.' Right into old age the handsome, keen features under white unruly hair, and a manner of immense but effortless charm, cast the same spell over the next generation. In committee, although perhaps leading less obviously than some twenty years earlier, his was often the last word and the one which was acted upon.

George Macaulay Trevelyan was a very different man who was, appropriately, a force of a very different kind in the affairs of the Trust, but perhaps of almost equal importance. Born in 1876, youngest son of Sir George Otto Trevelyan, a distinguished Liberal politician and historian, he went like his father to Harrow and Trinity College, Cambridge. His family had estates in Cornwall and Northumberland and he had a thoroughly country upbringing, but like his father and also, and more especially, his mother's brother Lord Macaulay, he became an historian of great eminence. He inherited his father's Liberal politics but without the unattractive righteous republicanism of his uncle. During the Great War he commanded the First British Ambulance Unit in Italy and was awarded the silver medal for valour. His work brought him a CBE in 1920 and ten years later the highly prized Order of Merit. In 1927 he took the chair of Regius Professor of Modern History at Cambridge and later became a distinguished Master of his old college. In the period between the wars his reputation was of international proportion.

It is necessary to recall his contemporary fame because as Norman put it 'his great distinction, gave us distinction'. The Trust owes to John Bailey Trevelyan's active participation, but he was independently concerned with its cause, writing in 1929 an essay, 'Must England's Beauty Perish?' which began the spate of publications on that subject which were to mark the next decade. Chorley, looking back at the Executive Committee of the time, cannot remember him as impressive or noticeable, though he recognises the importance of his work for the Trust. It is perhaps because the most significant part of his work was done as Chairman of the Estates Committee, a role in which Chorley would not have seen him until he himself joined that Committee in 1943. He was never a good chairman in the technical sense, but his authority, wisdom and foresight were more than enough to offset that deficiency. There are several stories of Trevelyan falling asleep while presiding over meetings when he was in his seventies.

Another valuable Trust Committee member was Dorothy Hunter, the youngest of Sir Robert's daughters and perhaps the most like her father in her mental equipment. Clear-minded and precise, she had both his ability to get to the heart of a subject and to master detail, and at the same time to give her views clearly, briefly and persuasively. She was born in 1881 and in her early twenties became notable as a 'girl orator', speaking on behalf of the Liberal party, mainly on the subjects of women's suffrage and free trade.

C.E. Mallet, MP, one of the Honorary Secretaries of the Free Trade Union, took the trouble to write to Lady Hunter at Christmastime, 1910, recording an unsolicited testimonial to Dorothy's powers of persuasion. A rough-looking labourer explaining to a cynical young clerk why he had come to hear Dorothy speak:

> I tell you what it is; I have heard a lot of men politicians talk by the yard but all the lot of them put together never put it as she put it last night! She made it quite plain to me; I see what Free Trade means now; I didn't before. They ought to put her up to speak everywhere and Tariff Reform would be killed stone dead.

It may have been her father's death in 1913 and her co-option onto the Executive Committee of the Trust which distracted Dorothy from politics. She did become for eighteen years a member of the Haslemere UDC and was Chairman of its Planning Committee, and was active in many local organisations, but it was to the National Trust that she gave her principal services. She is remembered for her remarkable qualities by fellow committee members and by the staff of the Trust right up to, and indeed after her retirement from the Executive in 1964.

Harriot Yorke, who gave up the Treasurership in 1925, continued to sit on the Executive until Chorley's time. He describes her as 'a big rather overflowing woman with a gruff voice', but he recognised what was important to the continuity of the direction of the Trust, that she represented to others on the Committee the authority of Octavia Hill. Not for nothing had Octavia been known as 'The Lion' and Harriot as 'The Keeper'!

In direct line of descent from the founders were two people who were to span the whole of the period from before the Great War until after the Second. Janet Upcott, who worked for Octavia Hill has already been mentioned. Born in 1889 she was one of what was almost the first generation of working gentlewomen; she went to the School of Sociology at Denison House and to the London School of Economics. As part of her training in housing management she was required to do a period of practical work – she speaks of it as 'skilled apprenticeship' – and applied for a job to Miss Lumsden who managed the Church Commissioners' estate at Walworth, a post she had been given on the suggestion of Octavia Hill. Here she was unsuccessful but was referred to Miss Hill. On going for interview she found herself placed at some disadvantage in a very low chair which she was told had once belonged to George Eliot, and had to account for herself to Octavia and her sister Emily Maurice. So it was that in 1910 she came to work with Octavia Hill.

> She was obviously a great woman. She was very dominant: I rather shrink from that. She sat facing the window with her portrait by Sargent behind her. I was set to copy the rent sheets. At first she was rather cautious about my ability saying 'What is Miss Upcott doing? Isn't that rather a responsible job for her?' but when it came to the next quarter, and having satisfied herself about me, – 'Isn't that rather a waste of her time?'

Janet Upcott also did some work on the National Trust, keeping a ledger for the Estates Committee and being regularly reminded by Octavia: 'Every property should pay for itself.' That was precisely the way in which she herself had started, and succeeded, in housing.

It was immediately after Octavia Hill died that Janet Upcott joined the Trust's Finance and General Purposes Committee in direct succession to her, and also the Estates Committee. She was to serve fifteen years on the former and fifty-six years on the latter, as well as becoming, and remaining, Honorary Adviser on Housing. This was a subject in which she really was an expert and had learned not only from its pioneer exponent but also in the hard school of reality. During the Great War she was employed by the Ministry of Munitions to re-organise its housing estate at Dudley in Worcestershire. There she found the manager permanently drunk and three hundred tenancies most of them with rents in arrear. In the event, having evicted the drunk and straightened out the tenancies, she stayed on for nearly four years before taking up the Cumberland Market estate management for the Commissioners of Crown Lands. She had been a founder member of the Association of Women Housing Managers in 1916 and was to write a number of important papers over the succeeding twenty years.

She disclaims having contributed much to the work of the Trust, and indeed is remembered by those who saw her at committee meetings as saying very little, but being attentive and closely interested. It is true, however, that her presence and her direct link with the origins of the organisation maintained a tradition of continuity in the proceedings.

It is difficult to place Benny Horne in the affairs of the Trust because he played a dual role. The firm of solicitors in which Robert Hunter took his first partnership underwent several changes of name: it started as Fawcett, Horne and Hunter, then Horne, Hunter and Birkett and finally just Horne and Birkett. H.P. Horne, one of the three original partners continued in it, taking Mr Birkett as a partner and the firm became Honorary Solicitors to the Trust immediately upon its incorporation. Mr Horne's son Benjamin succeeded his father and took up the Trust's work. The term Honorary is curious, because the firm was paid for the work which it did, such as reporting and conveyancing; presumably it was the partners' time which was given freely. Certainly by 1920 the term had been dropped from the Annual Report.

Young Benny Horne was from the beginning very keen on the work of the Trust and was a great favourite of both Robert Hunter and his wife. After Margaret Hunter married Mr Mason, Benny became godfather to their first child, Bunty. She paints a picture of a kind and lively man who was clearly very fond of her and of her two sisters and her brother. She believes that in other circumstances he would have liked to have married her mother, but her sister Ruth disputes that, and since Bunty was as fond of him as he was of her, there may be some element of wishful thinking. Be that as it may, Benny did spend a lot of time with the family, especially when they were living at Headley in Surrey between the wars, when he would often come for weekends. He loved riding and as the Masons had two or three ponies he used to hire others so that they could all go out together. This was, of course, Robert Hunter country, with Box Hill nearby and 500 acres of Headley Heath and the mile long gallop on the ridge of Mickleham Down, both of which were to come later into the Trust's ownership.

Benny's other hobby or recreation was the National Trust and quite apart from the formal legal work that the firm did, he took every opportunity to go and look at properties either owned already or under negotiation. His formal reports, generally made when he was either on holiday or in the district for other reasons, are clear and practical and full of useful information for a desk-bound Secretary. He called at Watersmeet, Devon, in the late summer of 1931. The miniature Victorian resorts of Lynton and Lynmouth were threatening to expand and there was a local preservation movement starting. Horne writes that it is a very desirable acquisition, notes its popularity – 'Five charabancs of visitors' and advises that 'arrangements should be made for making a suitable car park.' In the autumn of 1932, after the Trust had launched an appeal, he was back again and wrote to the Secretary with a number of businesslike comments and suggestions. Incidentally, because of the steepness of the valley it was thirty years before there was any car park and that one hardly 'suitable'.

It is probable that Hamer valued this legal adviser with his roving commission, and certainly his reports when read today are informative and thoughtful. It may not have been so in his successor's time when administration became more methodical, for Christopher Gibbs, who joined the staff in 1935, says that he infuriated the new Secretary by going off on his own and negotiating direct with prospective donors! However, he too describes a clever and dedicated man, and a kind one, for he once took young Gibbs, for 'a splendid evening on a launch, with supper, from Westminster Bridge to Barking and back'.

Presumably because of his position as Solicitor to the Trust, Horne did not join its Council and Executive Committee until 1945, three years after the Trust had appointed a solicitor to the staff and the firm no longer acted directly for the Trust. He was, however, co-opted on to the Publicity Committee when it was formed in 1927 and remained a member until it was disbanded in 1939. His background knowledge of the Trust and its workings must have been of great benefit to a new and difficult venture. The three years he spent on the Executive were valuable mainly for the extent of his knowledge of past history. Heavily moustached, bowed with his years and, one may guess, tiring somewhat, he too like Janet Upcott was a symbol of the continuity of the Trust's work.

The last member of the second wave of workers for the Trust to be mentioned here is Professor (later Lord) Chorley, and only then in an introductory way, since he will appear regularly over the next half century. I have already quoted from the detailed memoir which makes him a good and reliable source of information about people and events from 1920 onwards. His introduction to the Trust was through the Fell and Rock Climbing Club. His home was Kendal, and his recollection of the National Trust went back to the appeal for the purchase of Queen Adelaide's Hill shortly before the Great War; he would have been about seventeen, and he cycled off to inspect the place, approved of it and sent off his subscription. After the war, called to the Bar and practising in London yet with roots in the Lakes, Chorley became at once a very useful person to the National Trust. Although Speaker Lowther (by then Lord Ullswater) was a member, he rarely came and there was no-one else on the Executive other than G.M. Trevelyan who knew the Lake District really well.

Moreover, Chorley was not the sort of member to take years playing himself in. In his own words, 'Although shy in personal contacts I have never had any particular difficulty in taking part in Committee discussions', and he is remembered for his tendency to address his colleagues in a somewhat formalised way, at times giving the impression of speaking from a prepared brief. This made him stand out in a group of people whose business was always conducted in the most informal round-the-table manner. He, like Benny Horne, became a member of the newly formed Publicity Committee. That, with his position as the Trust's representative on the Council for the Preservation of Rural England (which will be discussed later), put him right in the centre of the Trust's work. Tall, spare with, later in life, thick-lensed spectacles, he had the slight awkwardness, both physically and in manner, that can be associated with shyness, but that was never reflected in his mental processes, and he became a great force in keeping the Trust in line with its origins.

While these members and others were carrying on the government of the Trust at the centre, the accumulated properties were being looked after mainly by one system, but a system which took many forms. From early on it had been both practical and politic to appoint a local committee which would have the responsibility of management. These committees usually included those who had been involved in promoting acquisition by the Trust and others either prominent in local affairs or having some special expertise.

A more general representation throughout the country was achieved in some degree by the appointment of Local Corresponding Members who 'without pecuniary contribution undertake to further the objects of the Trust in any parish, district or place in such a manner as to the Council may seem meet.' There was never full coverage and the usefulness of the system varied very much but it did serve to give the Secretary some form of communication with the provinces.

The earliest of the local committees to be formed was at Hindhead in Surrey. As mentioned earlier the Hindhead Preservation Society was the creation of Robert Hunter and its conversion into a management committee was a logical progression from that. Later, on the acquisition of Box Hill, a management committee was set up under the chairmanship of Leopold Salomons, the donor. This time the committee was formally constituted by deed in terms which subsequently led the members to consider themselves virtually independent of the National Trust as such. Sir Robert must have died before the document was drafted because it would have been most unlike him to have allowed that to happen.

Along the ridge of the Downs east from Box Hill the Reigate and Redhill Open Spaces and Footpaths Preservation Society was working hard to stop suburbia from creeping up over the face of the hill. The Society had a good pedigree, being derived from the branch of the Commons Society which Octavia and Robert had founded. They succeeded in securing sixty acres at Colley Hill and in 1913 Marquis Curzon of Kedleston 'opened' it.

The Marquis was a great catch, and was perhaps persuaded to become involved because he was then living nearby at Reigate Abbey. In his address he identified London as the menace; 'Like a great octopus stretching out its tentacles in order to lay hold of the rich pastures and leafy lanes of the countryside.' He too was conscious of the contrast between economic prosperity and deprivation:

> behind it [prosperity] there is a background of misery, squalor and gloom...
> the soul of the nation is to be found far more in the countryside than in the
> dark and crowded cities and it is because we want to preserve the soul of the
> nation... that we attach such importance to the preservation of open spaces
> such as Colley Hill.

The Purchase Committee, of course, continued to look after the property and this provided a continuing effort, so that they were able to add to the piecemeal accumulation of protection. Just over ten years later they were able to send out invitation cards for Monday 16 June 1924 at 5.20 p.m. 'when the land recently purchased by subscription for the enjoyment of the public will be formally dedicated to the Nation by Sir Jeremiah Colman, Bart., D.L., J.P. (Tea may be obtained on the ground from 4 p.m. onwards).'

Sir Jeremiah was to give, in 1952, 102 acres of woodland at Gatton Park and the Trust bought then a slightly larger area nearby. By 1980 the total stood at 150 acres at Reigate and 212 at Gatton, precious elements preserved by perseverance.

By contrast the preservation of the 'Long Barrow' at Coldrum in Kent did not go so well. The village grocer at Ightham, Benjamin Harrison, had died in 1926 at the age of eighty-nine. Besides being an unassuming and charming man he had, self-taught, become well informed about natural history and archaeology in the way of so many nineteenth-century amateurs. But in one branch he excelled: palaeontology. Knowledge of early man was in its infancy, and by an exhaustive study of flints and flint tools he not only expanded this but formulated a new early classification, that of eoliths ('dawn stones'). His friends decided that they would buy in his memory and give to the National Trust the megalithic remains at Coldrum. A Committee was formed but 'owing to the deaths of ... the Honorary Secretary and Treasurer and several other members of the Executive Committee there has been some delay.' However, a new appeal was launched and succeeded, the deeds being handed to the Trust in July 1926.

However, no-one seems to have thought about looking after the place. Fifteen months later there were complaints of neglect, the Rev. Gilbert, Vicar of Ightham and Mr A.F. Buxton citing broken fences, erosion and loosening of the stones. Under pressure, and in recoil from the suggestion that the Kent Archaeological Society would be better custodians, the Trust belatedly reverted to its usual custom and set up a local committee under the chairmanship of Professor Newberry, who had been Treasurer for the appeal.

Local committees played so dominant a role from the beginning indeed – and perhaps increasingly from the 'twenties – that many feature in subsequent chapters, but it is worth following the formation and progress of one which started in 1922. The Isle of Wight had been spared much of the degradation of nineteenth-century development until Queen Victoria's long residence at Osborne made its mark on the national consciousness and the railway and steamboat enabled access. This produced holiday resort development which straddled the east of the Island from Ryde to Ventnor. The emergence of yachting as a pastime of the wealthy under royal patronage made Cowes, briefly but annually, the hub of Society.

It says much for the status that the National Trust had achieved in twenty-seven years that, without prompting, a Mr M. Llewellyn Evans turned to it for help. Out of the blue S.H. Hamer received a letter from a London solicitor in which he intimated that he had a client who owned St Boniface and Bonchurch Downs behind Ventnor and 'was desirous of vesting them in some public authority with a view to their being enjoyed by the public in perpetuity.' In a letter to *The Times* on 18 August 1922 Lord Plymouth announced this gift of 221 acres, adding that 'a strong Local Committee of management will be set up immediately.'

It cannot have been easy to form such committees without good local contacts and Hamer wisely relied on an Oxford professor, Edward Poulton, whose home was on the Island. He produced a few eminent people, Major General Jack Seeley, for example, (who became CIGS and 1st Lord Mottistone) and two stalwarts Frank Morey and George Colenutt. Their provenance shows the important contribution made by local societies to the Trust's growth: the former was Hon. Secretary of the Island Natural History Society and Hon. Curator of Carisbrooke Museum, while the latter was the local Hon. Secretary of the Hampshire Field Club and Archaeological Society. The first meeting was held in Ryde on 21 December 1922, and George Colenutt became Secretary. Hamer was there, with a letter of congratulations from Princess Louise, whose family connection with the Island enabled her to write with authority on the advantages to the inhabitants of Ventnor and Bonchurch.

The Committee's job was to manage the property, but its very existence at once promoted the work of the Trust in a place where otherwise its influence might not have been felt for decades. A well-wisher was quick to warn them that Arreton Down was in danger. Within a month Colenutt was seeking to persuade the Ward Estate to sell Alum Bay (where the cliffs are striped with coloured sands) and Headon Warren which looks over the Solent to Hurst Castle. Alum Bay was never to come to the Trust but Headon Warren was eventually acquired in 1971.

Meanwhile there was an active pressure group to harass the Ventnor UDC about litter dumping and to stop the Southern Railway Company from building a funicular to the top of St Boniface.

However, more property came in 1925 in the form of a gift from their Chairman, now Sir Edward Poulton, of St Helens Common and in the same year Frank Morey died and left Borthwood Copse to the Trust. But a third addition the next year irritated George Colenutt. The 2nd Lord Tennyson wished to give East Highdown, one of the series of great whale backs which reach across the Island to drop into the sea at the Needles, in memory of his father, the Laureate. The hill lies just above Farringford, the poet's home for many years. The offer was made to the mainland (that is to the Trust's Headquarters) and under the seal of strict confidentiality. This combination irritated the peppery Colenutt almost beyond measure. Later he was to write to Hamer's successor, 'if people from the mainland would only leave the Island alone it would … be better for everybody!'

Indeed Lord Tennyson's approach was both somewhat dictatorial and he wished to reserve so much – minerals, grazing, turf cutting – that the Trust's Solicitor doubted whether the transfer would be legal. However, the connection with the poet was irresistible. 'You will say it is given in memory of my father who used to walk there almost daily in his later years,' – the donor wrote, and to *The Times*: '… the land is now secure for ever from the danger of being spoilt by building as so many downs elsewhere have been.

> Where far from noise and smoke of town
> I watch the twilight falling brown
> around a careless ordered garden
> Close to the ridge of a noble down.

Hardwicke Rawnsley, with his Tennyson connections, would have been overjoyed to know of this gift. His sister, Frances Ann, had written about the Downs some thirty years before: '– at 12 o'clock he [Tennyson] would come out – (from the room in which he had been writing) – for a walk on the Downs till lunch time … would suddenly stop and point with his stick to a flower and would say to me "do you know what that is?" He knew the name of every flower that grew.' She remembered on one occasion 'Tennyson repeating "Oh Waly, waly up the bank, and waly, waly down" saying it was one of the sweetest poems ever written.'

There is a long pause in the Trust's activities after this: no doubt the slump and the war which followed soon after partly contributed. But there was just one event of real importance. There was to be a new Secretary at Head Office, Donald Matherson, and he wanted to visit the Island to familiarise himself with it. He was met and taken round by a young chartered accountant who was Branch Honorary Secretary to the Council for the Preservation of Rural England. His 'thank you' letter of 14 December 1934 expresses 'thanks for giving up so much of your time to taking me round the Island. I was very much interested to go to St Catherine's Hill and hope that the Island Branch of the CPRE may be able to do something about it.'

Francis Wadham Bright was then twenty-five. Island-born, he had returned two years earlier after some ten years away at school and serving articles, and had been appalled with what he described as low standards of building which were destroying the countryside of the Island. There were to be other notable characters on that Committee, but it was he who provided the continuing impulse through a long period as Honorary Secretary and later as Chairman until his retirement in 1984. Of a Pickwickian rubicund appearance, he was the most patient of men in the pursuit of an objective. He would never let go of any thread, no matter how remote the possibility might be of it serving any useful purpose. His perseverance is illustrated in the fact that, thirty-three years after that visit to St Catherine's Hill, he finally secured its preservation by the Trust.

The importance of the Committee was, as we have seen from the beginning, that it constituted a presence for the Trust on the Island. It attracted to it substantial Island landowners, lawyers, auctioneers and those retired or otherwise leisured people who can contribute so much to local effort. Sir Vere Hobart, descendant of the Lord Chief Justice who built Blickling Hall in Norfolk, was Chairman during the war and thought well enough of the Trust to place restrictive covenants in its favour over 1,000 acres of his Gatcombe property in the centre of the Island. Later Sammy Watson took the chair, a major departure from the principle of looking for orthodoxly eminent chairmen. He had been an agricultural valuer and auctioneer on the Island since before the Great War, knew and was known by everyone, high and low. Eminently practical, shrewd and purposeful, he had a deeply impressed love of the country, and a manner in which innate courtesy controlled a brisk temper.

It was this clear identity of the Trust on the Island which brought it material success. Starting in the late 1950s, its holdings by 1983 grew to 3,240 acres: the Needles Headland on the western tip and Headon Warren which George Colenutt had tried for sixty years before; St Catherine's Point, the southern-most tip, with the cottage from which Marconi had experimented in wireless telegraphy; the last remaining windmill at Bembridge; the harbour and much of the burgage plots at Newtown as well as the Town Hall and long stretches of the still unspoiled Downs of the West Wight, its coastline and the stone built manor house of Mottistone; these and more sprang from the existence of the Committee.

After the second war the Committee threw up a man of very special qualities. Tom Parsons joined as an ordinary member but was given the job of Field Officer, to deal with day to day management. He had been severely wounded in 1944 but had supported his family by the exercise of a combination of artistic and practical talents. These he brought to the service of the Trust, but beyond that his dealings with people of all sorts whose lives were touched by the Trust's activities established the organisation as humane and acceptable. Energetic, though quiet and sensitive, he was largely responsible for ensuring that the Committee secured general support on the Island throughout the period of growth.

The importance of individuals is a common denominator in the history of all local committees and a similar story could be told of many another. By 1949, the total number had grown to 103 but with subsequent changes in structure and administration they were reduced to 72 in 1984. It is certain that without them the conduct and growth of the Trust would not have been so successful.

CHAPTER V

England
and the
Octopus

The tide of public opinion began to run very strongly in favour of preservation from the mid-1920s. This was exemplified in a large number of popular writings, ranging from newspaper articles and essays in periodical magazines, to full-scale works of propaganda. The causes were no doubt complex but were probably rooted in the speed and extent of unregulated change after the end of the First World War. There was no really effective planning legislation. Even when the Town and Country Planning Act was passed in 1932, it was born into the most disastrous economic slump and many of its provisions were frustrated in practice by lack of money with which to pay the neccessary compensation. This was the age of the jerry-builder whose shoddy houses and bungalows of bad design and materials spattered the landscape wherever there was cheap land and available road frontage. Some areas of bungaloid growth eventually matured into fully developed urban areas. The best known instance is Peacehaven perched high on the open downland cliffs east of Brighton, covering by the end of the 1930s several hundred acres with a sparse rash of ugly buildings.

G.M. Trevelyan's 1929 essay, 'Must England's Beauty Perish?', set the pattern for much that was to be said and written. It was sub-titled 'A Plea on Behalf of the National Trust' but it was wide-ranging in its review of the dangers to the countryside and specific in its opinions on preservation. Trevelyan attributed the current mood in favour of preservation to the fact that, 'In an age when beauty, especially the beauty of nature and the landscape, is being destroyed with unexampled rapidity by modern inventions and economic and residential developments, the desire to save beloved places from the ruin is much more widely and intensely felt than ever before.' He traced the causes to the State which would do little or nothing to preserve the countryside but whose system of taxation contributed to the trouble. In a later essay he was to develop the theme: 'The State is socialist enough to destroy by taxation the classes that used to preserve rural amenity; but it is still too Conservative to interfere in the purposes to which land is put by speculators to whom the land is sold.' He considered the work done by municipal bodies but concluded that because of political changes 'there is no security for the continuity of municipal policy.'

His assessment of landscape beauty was interesting:

In 1829 ... It was all good to look at, not least the 'improvements' of the eighteenth century: the thatched and gabled houses, the cornfields, hedges, lanes, stone bridges, new plantations of oak and beech all harmonized well together, and harmonized with the wilder parts of the nature in which they were set, the still remaining wrecks of the old English forest, thicket, moorland and marsh.

He emphasised the small scale of the landscape – as against that of the Alps. 'Common English scenery ... has a delicate and fugitive beauty made up of small touches, a combination of nature with the older arts of man ... easily destroyed by a few rash strokes of the crude levelling machinery of modern life.'

Trevelyan must have come upon the beginnings of what has now become something of a cult, the preservation of plants and animals for their own sake. He was categoric about his own attitude: 'The preservation of natural scenery and the wildlife of English flora and fauna may be based on motives that regard the welfare of human beings alone.'

An exposition in summary of National Trust policy followed. Buildings must be maintained and repaired in accordance with the tenets of the SPAB, and if habitable they should be inhabited. Lands, being mostly uncultivated, could be left to nature, but grazing was important to downs and fells. Woods were the greatest problem, requiring the most active intervention by the Trust to 'preserve in perpetuity the woodland character of the places we own ... and to prevent the substitution of conifers for old English hardwoods.' Significantly, for a statement made in 1929, he recognised the contribution to be made by the Trust's ownership of enclosed and cultivated agricultural land and the value of its rents to the management of less productive land.

Money – or the lack of it – was a recurrent element of the essay: the immense amount of benefit that a millionaire's gift of £100,000 would bring; the ease with which a critic could bring about change by the provision of £1,000 or even £100. He pleaded for help in two ways:

(1) To secure for us beautiful places before the attack of the exploiter threatens.
(2) To give us a central endowment ... and by enlarging by several thousand the number of our subscribing members ...

A little book produced in 1930 by the Trust's Assistant Secretary, Bruce Logan Thompson, dealt specifically with the preservation of the Lake District. Trevelyan wrote a short foreword, stressing the author's origins in that area and his knowledge of the local traditions and literary associations. Thompson faithfully traced the beginnings of the mystique of the Lakes, invoking the authority of the Patron Saint, detailing the erosion of its wilderness by water-supply undertakings, road improvements, railway building and what he then described as 'the first serious outburst of building on the shores of the greatest standing water in all England' [Windermere]. He identified new threats: 'the planting of spiky foreign conifers ... placed in military rank upon the hillside,' and 'overhead cables on enormous pylons' and he foresaw 'that the transmission of cheap electricity ... will necessitate a regrettable disfigurement unless the cables are placed underground.' He felt, however, that, thanks to the preservationists, the development had been fairly inoffensive and concentrated. But he warned that 'there is a pressing need and urgency that the rural aspect and the rural spirit of the remoter dales should not be marred now by incongruous building in out-of-the-way places made newly accessible by motor.'

He also recorded the view that public access had now been sufficiently provided and protected, mentioned the Trust's 'new' policy of accepting farmland 'where public use must of necessity be limited. The first need is to safeguard the landscape, and the second is to provide a reasonable amount of public access.' This was an expression of a problem not particularly apparent to the founders, but one which had become serious by the 1920s and one that still recurs.

Perhaps the work which most comprehensively dealt with preservation – in its widest sense – and best reflected the opinions of the time was *Britain and the Beast*, edited by Clough Williams-Ellis and published in 1937. It was a collection of twenty-five essays, the authors of which had in common only their own eminence and a love of the buildings and countryside of England. The editor was an architect and publicist. In the former role he is probably best remembered for Portmerion which he developed – created would be a better word – as an ideal village inspired by Portofino. It was at once a natural growth from the soil of Wales, at once an Italianate *jeu d'esprit* and a serious business venture. As a publicist he had a ready wit and an equally ready pen. He had already written *England and the Octopus* (echoing Curzon's phrase about the tentacles of London reaching out into the country).

The book was prefaced by commendations from ten people of position – David Lloyd George, George Lansbury, Stafford Cripps, J.B. Priestley and Robert Baden-Powell among them; and the first essay was by John Maynard Keynes. A brilliant scholar at Eton, and again at Kings, Cambridge (where he was a member of The Apostles, of which Hugh Lupus Grosvenor would have approved), his aesthetic tastes influenced by the Bloomsbury group, Keynes was involved with art in many forms. In his work at the Treasury he was able to develop the State's involvement with the arts, and this theme is the one that he pursued in his essay. He gave two examples of what might be done 'one for the preservation of what we have inherited, the other for the enlargement of what we shall transmit.'

1. There should be established a Commission of Public Places with power to issue an injunction against any act of exploitation and development of land or any change or demoliton of an existing building ... contrary to the general interest.

   The Commission would be obliged to pay compensation and would be able to meet any part of maintenance costs.

2. Initial preparation should be made, so that some plans will be ready and available to ward off the next slump for the embellishment and comprehensive rebuilding at the public expense ... [of whatever seemed necessary].

The area he gave as an example was the South Bank of the Thames downstream from County Hall!

Keynes was, of course, writing at a time when he was also advocating the relief of unemployment by Government spending and his words find many echoes today. However, in the context of this story his essay was important for its prescription for preservation by the State.

Other authors were pessimistic about the destruction of rural life although W.A. Eden backed Trevelyan in crediting the landowner down the years with both the creation and the good stewardship of beauty in the countryside. '... since such bodies as the National Trust can only, by their nature, act as stewards for comparatively small areas' he suggested that the community should take up the work which was passing from the landowners' grasp.

C.E.M. Joad, an academic who achieved popular national recognition with impish teases on radio's 'Brains Trust' programme, abused almost everyone without reserve, but he found it difficult to deal with the preservation of the countryside without taking account of the position of agriculture. He derided a subsidised agriculture but desired to maintain it in being. He went full tilt at game preservation '... totally unable to see any reason why the gratification of the tastes of a few rich men should be allowed to obstruct the pursuits of the many ...'. His prescriptions for improvement were sufficiently orthodox to have been by now realised at least in part. Cars were to be confined to motorways; there was to be restraint of unplanned building; National Parks must be set up under a Ministry of National Amenities. 'Some of these proposals may seem socialistic ... Well, what do you expect? I am a Socialist ...' However, he gave the landowner the familiar pat on the back and 'if ... an impoverished country gentleman declares himself unable to afford the upkeep of his house ... I would make him a grant for the purpose.'

The agriculturalists were remarkably unbiased in their approach. Professor Stapleton, whose work at Aberystwyth on plant breeding and grassland management had been a major factor in farming progress, looked to a Commission of Land Use embracing farming, forestry and recreation with a budget of a million pounds a year to be spent equally on the three. (The Strutt Report of 1979 put forward very similar ideas.) A.G. Street plainly stated the problem which is still with us: 'Generally speaking the former (the countrymen) value it as a business premises, the latter (the townsmen) as a free playground. Under existing conditions neither class is willing to pay for its preservation as a national asset and, while these conditions remain, all this talk ... of preserving rural England is so much eyewash.'

It is not surprising that Professor Patrick Abercrombie, himself the greatest exponent at the time of town and country planning, should find the failure of planning control to be caused by lack of a National Plan and he too looked to some form of co-ordination. He also looked to the creation of National Parks to operate on a scale which he saw as being beyond that of the Trust. (The Government National Park Committee had reported in 1931 and there was widespread irritation at the failure to implement its recommendations). Like other contributors, and like Strutt forty years later, he deplored the separation of the Minister of Agriculture from involvement with the wider problems of the countryside.

G.M. Trevelyan's contribution was entitled 'Amenities and the State'. It is of special interest because he was not by any means a Socialist in the modern political sense, but a sturdy and radical Liberal.

I am not a fanatic in these matters. I fully realise that ... the prime needs of industry, housing and defence have to be met, often at the expense of natural beauty. But in disputes ... the interest of amenity is unduly handicapped. It is not officially represented in Government departments; it is only when protest is raised in the newspapers that the departments occasionally throw it a bone.

The State, he stressed, must take upon itself the overall duty. 'Lay not the flattering unction on your souls that the National Trust is solving the problem of rural amenity.'

The editor himself – an individualist if ever there was one – inclined to the necessity for the State to take action, and the whole tone of the book, despite the fact that it was compiled by twenty-five different hands, is unmistakeably one which recognised that the time had come for the country as a whole to address itself to the problem. These opinions had been evolving for at least ten years before, and much of what was then advocated has taken shape in one form or another since. They should enable us therefore to see the work of the Trust in its middle years against a background of general sentiment. The interruption of the Second World War and its aftermath created an apparent gap in the evolution of national attitudes to what Trevelyan called 'the amenities'. In fact the trend continued to develop both in and out of Parliament, with the National Trust playing a leading role in some aspects, and it was to be expressed both in national policy as legislation and in the Trust's conduct of its own interests in the ten years which followed the end of the war.

As well as the campaigns for the acquisition of land and buildings, the Trust had from the beginning taken part in all the general crusades against damage to what has become known as the environment. This, indeed, had in some measure been a principal activity of many of its early leaders, and certainly of its god-parent, the Commons Society, and of some of the other organisations who appointed members to the Council, especially the SPAB. Early reports deal, as we have seen, with threats of railways, with threats to the surroundings of the Palace of Westminster, with the listing of churchyard yew trees, with the Highland Water Power Bill which 'would ruin the tender beauty of Scotch hillsides', with worries about the effect of coal mining in Kent and with the creation of a public footpath around the coast of Cornwall. By the 1920s the Executive Committee had begun to find that the care of its own properties and the acquisition of more presented as much work as the organisation could manage. It formally decided to limit its public intervention to matters which affected either what it already owned or expected to acquire.

There was a general feeling abroad in 1925 that an organisation combining the interests of all the amenity societies was needed. This would keep watch on the activities of both private enterprise and public authorities, which constantly threatened all parts of the country, and also apply pressure on Government for legislation to promote better controls. There was a well arranged campaign which started with a letter to *The Times*, on 19 December 1929, from the President of the Royal Institute of British Architects, Guy Dawber. He suggested that the Minister of Health, (whose department at that time held such responsibility for the environment as existed in Government) or 'some other body' should summon a conference of all interested organisations. *The Times* ran a leader on the subject which can at best be described as lukewarm. On the same day the Earl of Crawford, Chairman of the Society of Antiquaries, wrote to Professor Patrick Abercrombie suggesting that a list of organisations should be sent to Dawber. The following month the latter sent out invitations to a conference to be held on 24 February 1926. Those attending included two representatives from the National Trust, John Bailey, and Colonel Buxton, from the Commons Society, Lawrence Chubb, and from the National Federation of Women's Institutes, Mrs E. Holland-Martin. Abercrombie had produced a proposal for the formation of a League for the Preservation of Rural England with six main objects: 1. To focus attention on the need; 2. to explore existing powers of control; 3. to use existing powers; 4. to consider new legislation for rural planning; 5. to promote understanding of rural interests through education; 6. to prepare a plan for areas of no development and to preserve them either through the National Trust or by means of national parks.

At this first meeting Lord Crawford spoke in enthusiastic terms, and Edwy Buxton likewise, though he preferred the device of a Standing Conference. Perhaps typically, John Bailey did not think it necessary to intervene. The upshot was the formal constitution of a Council for the Preservation of Rural England with Lord Crawford as President, Mrs Holland-Martin as Honorary Treasurer and, among others on its Executive Committee, Professor R.S.T. Chorley, Clough Williams-Ellis, Edward Salisbury, George Langley-Taylor, Lady Trevelyan (George Trevelyan's sister-in-law) and Sir Henry Fairfax-Lucy (whose successor was to give Charlecote Park, Warwickshire, to the Trust twenty years later). A sub-committee was set up which published the constitution and the rules of the Council in July the same year. Lawrence Chubb drafted them with thirty years experience of the movement behind him.

It is difficult to know how big a part was played by the National Trust in founding the CPRE. Certainly there exists a tradition which goes back as far at least as the late 1940s that it was virtually the Trust's creation. That must certainly be wrong, but there was some basis for the idea. Patrick Abercrombie refers in a 1926 pamphlet to a move promoted by SCAPA (Society for Checking Abuse of Public Advertising) in 1898 to combine the then major amenity societies, the Commons Society, the SPAB, the National Trust and itself. So the idea of joint action was not new. John Bailey was an especially enthusiastic member of SCAPA and his daughter remembers that he so hated the flashing lights of the Piccadilly Circus advertisements that he shut his eyes as he passed by! Herbert Griffin, the Council's first General Secretary, referred in correspondence to a meeting held at the headquarters of the National Trust at 7 Buckingham Palace Gardens prior to the formation of the CPRE at which the name for the new organisation was discussed. Nevertheless, no National Trust representative sat on the all-important sub-committee which framed the rules.

The new organisation was well received in influential circles. Neville Chamberlain, as Minister of Health, addressed the inaugural meeting and there was an immediate spread of branches across the country, including a Cambridge one formed by Trevelyan. There was immediate business of all kinds, Lord Astor trying to interest the President in the preservation of the Thames Valley and the Bursar of Magdalen, Oxford, Michael Holland-Hibbert (whose son was later to be a Regional Chairman of the Trust) lobbying on behalf of the Oxford Trust. Education was promoted by the distribution to schools of Clough Williams-Ellis's *England and the Octopus* (paid for by Mr Boies Penrose). When an appeal for funds was made a few years later it attracted the public support of the Prime Minister, Stanley Baldwin.

The appointment of Professor Chorley as the Trust's representative on the CPRE was a masterstroke. He cultivated as strong an interest in the new body – of which he later became an Honorary Secretary – as in the Trust, and kept a secure and lively link between the two.

CHAPTER VI

Open Spaces
and
Nature Conservancy

Although the present extent of the property preserved by the National Trust and its variety are enormous, the lines of much of its work were set early on. Four main areas of concern: open spaces, nature conservancy, the preservation of archaeological sites and the fate of historical buildings all emerged during the first quarter of this century.

The open space was, and largely still is, the principal target for preservation by the Trust. It meant any area of unenclosed land to which people could freely resort. It could be small – Dinas Oleu, or the banks of the Wandle; or extensive – Hindhead or Brandelhow; it could be a hilltop, or a cliff, a viewpoint or a wood. Although all was grist that came to the Trust's mill, much of the effort was expended where the risks were greatest and the Peak District of Derbyshire, an island in a vast sea of industrial development, was a natural field for the work of preservation.

The valleys of the Dove and Manifold have been famous for three hundred years or more. Charles Cotton lived by the Dove at Beresford Hall, and there he and his friend Izaak Walton built their fishing temple and Izaak immortalised the rivers and the surrounding country in *The Compleat Angler*. It was well known later to Jane Austen: in *Pride and Prejudice* Elizabeth Bennet visits Dovedale as a tourist before encountering Mr Darcy, whose estate was nearby. Before 1914, after the railway had come to nearby Thorpe, more than sixty donkeys stood by to carry trippers to the Gorge.

The Trust showed concern as early as 1910 when Nigel Bond tried to get the Co-operative Holidays Association – (whose Vice-President was Canon Rawnsley!) – interested in Ilam Hall. That extraordinary example of Victorian Gothic stood in an exceptionally lovely spot where those curious and partly subterranean rivers the Hamps and the Manifold finally emerge before joining with the Dove a mile or so below. It was for sale. This came to nothing for lack of funds, although the estate failed to sell at auction. The agents, Knight, Frank and Rutley tried to salvage something by offering the Izaak Walton Hotel and Dovedale Hill for £1,500. Many later problems could have been avoided had the money been forthcoming.

As so often was the way, the cause of Dovedale needed a champion and it found one six years later in F.A. Holmes, a Buxton businessman. His knowledge of the countryside, in particular the White Peak, south of his home town, was reinforced · by his passion for archaeology and geology. Like Benjamin Harrison of Ightham, he was largely self-taught in these subjects, to which he was to make a direct contribution in several ways. He was active also in local work, the Devonshire Hospital Management Committee, the Buxton and the Derbyshire Probation Committees and, from 1918, as a County Magistrate. He cared very much throughout his life, too, for the welfare of others. His diary entry for 7 January 1892 reads, '21 years old today, probably a third of my lifetime, yet what have I done for my fellow men?' The story goes that Holmes was walking through the Dovedale gorge in 1916 when he heard the sound of axes. There and then he conceived a determination that, regardless of the war, those trees should not be felled and that the whole of the valley should be preserved for public enjoyment.

Why he turned for help to Sir Geoffrey Mander, MP for Wolverhampton, is not clear, but he did and, after questions in the House, the felling was stopped. It was remarkable that in the year which was to see the casualties on the Somme reach more than 400,000 that authority was prepared to listen and to act in such a case. F.A. Holmes must have known of the Trust's earlier interests because, by 1919, he was stirring Hamer up with enquiries on progress, only to be told that 'during the War such matters have been in abeyance'. Despite that, Hamer was not left in peace. Others wrote on the same subject, notably Ethel Gallimore from Sheffield, the Peak District and Northern Counties Footpaths Preservation Society, the North Staffordshire Field Club and the Ramblers Association. Fifteen years were to go by without success: Ilam Hall Estate was up for sale again in 1926, the Hall and 157 acres being withdrawn at £8,000 but the Izaak Walton Hotel and 268 acres did this time sell, at a price of £8,000.

F.A. Holmes persisted in his efforts, embracing especially the alternative strategy of putting Dovedale forward to be the first National Park, a strategy which he and others besides never entirely abandoned. Their concept of such parks was one in which some form of state ownership preserved, managed and opened the countryside to the people. In this cause he wrote and spoke wherever opportunity offered, and gave evidence before the National Parks Committee which, under the Chairmanship of Dr (later Viscount) Addison reported in 1931. In the course of all this he came into contact with a Manchester businessman of considerable means, Mr (later Sir) Robert McDougall who became his supporter and financial backer.

The piecemeal building up of landed estates is a tiresome and tortuous business and calls for constant application and careful ground work. This Holmes encompassed with maps, records of ownership, acreages, and rents over seven miles of the valley, supported with photographs and descriptive notes. So, when land at the upper end of the Gorge on the Staffordshire side came up for sale he was in a position to alert McDougall and the Trust. The first 120 acres, including Hurt's Wood from which the warning axe strokes had rung out, were bought amid a fanfare of free publicity engineered by Holmes and valued by McDougall at above £4,000 'at 'at ordinary Press Advertising rates.' That was accomplished in the last month of 1933, but poor Mr Hamer's trials continued until his retirement the next year. He was repeatedly berated by letter, summoned to conferences by telegram, and must have been thankful that Mr Holmes did not seem to think the telephone a proper means of communication.

However, the ball was now rolling and new acquisitions built up at such a rate that by 1938 the total area protected, according to a graph compiled by Wendell (Mr

Holmes's son and later a long serving member of the Committee), had risen to a total of 6,200 acres. Of this 2,200 were freehold and the balance under restrictive covenant. The latter needs an explanation: generous though McDougall and other benefactors were, the protection of the wide open, limestone plateaux through which the rivers had carved their way was too expensive to contemplate, even at that period when land prices were at rock bottom. The policy adopted was either to buy land and re-sell a part subject to restrictions or to buy direct the benefit of covenants. Owner occupiers at that time were desperately short of money and could see little disadvantage in binding themselves not to do things with their land that they could not see themselves wanting to do anyhow. The land retained on re-sale was generally the valley itself and the steep slopes of its flanks, this being both the least valuable in cash and the most beautiful. Forty years later the problems of finance and management were to bring regrets that a wider view had not been taken, and efforts were made to broaden this linear estate.

In the dozens of transactions that were to result from this campaign there was one of particular interest. Ilam Hall was in 1934 at last secured for the Trust by Robert McDougall. It was a somewhat complex business because there was no way of avoiding the problem posed by the Hall, for which the National Trust could not accept responsibility. The solution was provided by the Organising Secretary of the Derbyshire Rural Community Council, Laurence Ramsbotham, who was involved with the Youth Hostels Association. It was in August 1934 that he wrote suggesting partial demolition and the conversion of the remaining part into a Youth Hostel:

> The present building is absolutely useless for Youth Hostel purposes, but certain minor portions could be adapted. Our architects estimate this adaption will cost £2,000. My own feeling is that this estimate is too high, and we are prepared to take the risk if we can see £1,000 from the sale of the major building. If you think a better method could be arranged on the lines of the National Trust taking over all the property and renting a portion to us, we shall be very happy to explore the possibilities.

That is what happened: the YHA had a lease which covered only the area of the Hall to be left and the demolition rights were sold to Twigg of Matlock who began work in January 1935. This co-operation between the so-called 'kindred bodies' was characteristic of Trust policy.

There was, as so often happened, a ripple effect from F.A. Holmes' activities. A large wood at Taddington on the steep side of the Derbyshire Wye was given anonymously in 1933 and another above the Derwent, the 200-acre Shining Cliff Wood, the following year. Holmes in this case acted as intermediary between the Trust and the donor, the Sheffield philanthropist Alderman Groves. Holmes himself added to the ripple effect by buying and giving to the Trust a small but crucial area on the very edge of Stanton Moor which looks down on the same valley.

Additions went steadily on with an appeal in 1938 which Holmes promoted with his usual vigour and which produced enough to bring off a major coup in the purchase of two great hills Ossums and Wetton which lie astride the River Manifold. Nearly 900 acres in a critically strategic spot lying just to the south of the Staffordshire moorlands were an outstandingly important acquisition. The area lies easily accessible from the Potteries and being less famous than Dovedale was likely to lack the same protection, though it was in its way no less beautiful and interesting.

Fifty years after the first property was acquired, the National Trust had come to own 2,449 acres and protected 2,966 by means of restrictive covenant. What, to employ the words of the 1907 Act, was the benefit to the nation? It is necessary to remember that the area had been for a long time a place of public resort and so it was less to obtain public access than to secure it for the future that the Trust was seeking. The result is that for over six miles of the Dove visitors can walk on one bank or another (with a short break at Milldale) through a wholly unspoiled valley, and this they do in their thousands and tens of thousands. The geological and botanical curiosities of the place are also secure. The three valleys are honeycombed with caves and swallow holes and subterranean river courses while, especially in Dovedale Gorge, the great limestone stacks not only provide a dramatic scene but harbour a remarkable flora. The Victorians gave vivid names to these stacks: the Twelve Apostles; Lovers' Leap; Jacob's Ladder; Ilam Church; Reynard's Cave; Tissington Spires; Ilam Rock. This last was the scene of an exploit by Holmes when as a young man he succeeded in climbing to the very top of the 100 foot stack, and having reached it celebrated by standing on his head. Fred Smith can still point to the tree to which the suicide tied himself by one ankle before plunging in to dangle head first in the Dove. Victorian ideas of enjoyment lingered a long time. There was a refreshment hut on the west bank of the Gorge to which the ginger beer and lemonade had to be lowered by rope down the scarp of Jacob's Ladder from the crest nearly 500 feet above. Mrs Bettendon had her own devices for increasing the enjoyment of visitors. Reynard's Cave is approached by a very steep climb through a rock arch, and this resourceful local lady fixed a rope by which one could pull oneself up – for a penny a time. Those who were by that time thirsty were allowed for a similar sum to drink the pure spring water nearby, using one of her not so pure drinking vessels with a ration of lemonade powder. There are still stalls by the Stepping Stones which the pure in thought would like to banish: it is to be hoped that they may not succeed.

Ilam Hall and its surroundings form a focus of interest which would have delighted the Quartet, but embarrass those in the modern government of the Trust who have accustomed themselves to think of country houses as acceptable only when restored to their original form. The poor truncated remains of the Hall, the vestiges of its garden and pleasure grounds, overrun with hostellers and school children seem not to accord with the Trust's standards. However, the park is still furnished with splendid trees and the ridge and furrow of the mediaeval open field remains clear and un-'improved', the well of St Bertram is only occasionally full of beer cans, and the Boil Holes, where the Manifold emerges after four underground miles, still form the target of zig-zag paths down through the shrubbery. In the towering amphitheatre of Hinckley Wood across the water the small-leaved lime still perpetuates the ancient forest. In all its parts the Trust's properties in the valleys of the Dove, Manifold and Hamps remain true to the ideals of the founders and are a fitting memorial to F.A. Holmes and Robert McDougall and their friends, co-workers and successors.

We have already met Ethel Gallimore. She was born in 1904, the daughter of

Thomas W. Ward of Sheffield, a dealer in scrap metal. Ethel married very young and her husband went to war as a gunner and was killed. Sad and lonely, Ethel occupied herself by walking in the Peak District with her sister Gertrude and, when he could spare the time, her brother Alan. They went generally by train, rain or shine. 'I can't think why you want to go'; (Mother). 'You can't see anything! What can you see?' (Father). 'Mist'. (Gertrude). This hardihood in the face of Peak District weather is an essential quality in those who love the place. 'One day, when the rain was piling down I arrived at the Fox House Inn at tea. The Landlord said "Oh it's you! I might have known it was your weather!"' She expressed her love of this country in poems published as *The Pride of the Peak*. Ethel was distressed by the damage being done to the countryside by building which was inappropriate both in design and siting and by that especial bogey, the petrol station. It was her own idea to start the Sheffield Association for the Protection of Local Scenery. She achieved this in 1924, but there was little positive work until 1927, when the Trustees of the Duke of Rutland put some 10,000 acres on the market to meet Estate Duty. Then it was that the Association formed an Appeal Committee with Dr R. Abercrombie (a distinguished orthopaedic surgeon and brother of Professor Patrick Abercrombie), J.H. Doncaster, a Quaker, as Chairman and Elliot Dixon as Honorary Secretary.

There was no prospect of buying more than a part and the question was which area to go for. Elliot Dixon homed in on the Fox House Inn. It is at this point on the boundary of the City of Sheffield that the road into Derbyshire forks into three, giving building frontages in plenty and a bus route into the City. The appeal succeeded, although it took time to raise the money. Much of it came from prosperous Sheffield businessmen, but the supporters of the Association, rich or poor, tended to be of Liberal sympathies, and this was enough to raise suspicions among contributors. Miss Tozer, when approached by Ethel to give the last £1,000 exclaimed, 'Mr Sandford says you are all Bolsheviks – are you?' Ethel herself was 'inclined to the left', the founder Chairman of the *Clarion* Rambling Club and a convinced socialist, as was Phil Barnes, later an assistant secretary to the Association. His book *Trespassers will be Prosecuted* was, and perhaps still is, the classic work on public access to open country.

The thousand-odd acres bought for the Trust effectively sealed off from city development the most vulnerable part of the Derwent valley. The villages of Hathersage and Grindleford which lie beyond it show all the signs of suburban development: had they been linked with Sheffield the destruction would have been unstoppable.

The area owned has grown today to 1,600 acres, with a further 425 protected by restrictive covenant. To almost all of this there is access for visitors, subject only to the safety of the sheep and their lambs. There is the heather playground of Lawrence Field, bounded by the Burbage Brook which drops down through the rocky oakwoods of Padley Gorge, perhaps a survival of aboriginal forest. There are the great quarries from which the stone was cut seventy-five years ago for Howden Dam on the Derwent and where partly-cut millstones for the steel tool industry lie in clusters in what is now a giant natural rock garden. All this, just nine miles from the centre of the nineteenth century's greatest steel town, is true open space.

This venture was approaching success when F.A. Holmes was still struggling to start in Dovedale. Ethel herself supported his appeals and he later put in a good

67

word with the press when her Association secured the Winnats Pass on the road to Buxton. However, there was certainly a schism between the two centres working for the National Trust. It was probably more to do with the fact that there is no social or economic unity in the Peak District: the area divides into three separate and outward-looking sectors. The Trust was lucky to find champions for at least two.

Mrs Gallimore is now better known as Ethel Haythornethwaite. She married Lieutenant-Colonel Gerald Haythornethwaite and the two have devoted themselves to the management of Longshaw and the promotion of the Council for the Preservation of Rural England (which succeeded the Association). Gerald was a founder member of the Board of the Peak District National Park, and for a long time was chairman of what has become the Council for National Parks. Despite these wider interests they have both continued with benefactions to the National Trust, and in their view the Trust's work has come up to their expectations. A particular feature of the Longshaw Estate was the institution of a club of voluntary wardens. These, drawn mainly from the rambling fraternity, not only exercised a custodial role but formed working parties to maintain paths and fences, dig drains and plant trees. This club still endures, and has been the pattern for other similar voluntary efforts elsewhere. Amongst other successes they raised £400 towards the original appeal by collections from visitors.

The work of the Trust in the Lake District, in relation to its long-established reputation and its present magnitude, was slow to start; all the more surprising that it should have been so with Hardwicke Rawnsley there. It was, however, one of his many proposals to extend the work of the Trust which was to establish the dominance of the Trust in the district. We have already noted his gift of Peace How, and about that time he persuaded the Trust to adopt the idea that gifts of land should after the war be accepted as memorials to the dead. In this way the crest of Scafell Pike was in 1920 given by Lord Leconfield, 'In perpetual memory of the men of the Lake District who fell for God and King, for freedom, peace and right in the Great War 1914 – 1918.'

This gift prompted, so Chorley believed, a similar but far more extensive gift by the Fell and Rock Climbing Club. He describes a meeting of the Club to discuss the form their memorial should take and, 'Herbert Cain, the most dynamic personality among us, at once exclaimed "A Fell!"' Nearly 1,200 acres either side of Styhead Pass, all above 1,500 feet and rising to the tops of Great Gable and Broad End, each in the neighbourhood of 3,000 feet, passed as another memorial into the hands of the Trust. It was as a direct result of this splendid initiative that Cain was invited to join the Executive Committee of the Trust as an unofficial representative of the Club. On his sudden death a few years later Chorley became an automatic choice as his successor. So it was that the Lakes had in him an informed and determined representative within the Trust for more than forty years.

This particular area attracted a further major gift in 1925 when Gordon Wordsworth, grandson of the poet, and A.C. Benson gave the rest of Scafell, 1,300 acres, so that a more or less continuous holding of over 2,500 acres was formed. The consequences in terms of prestige nationally and involvement locally were tremendous.

Bruce Thompson's *National Trust Properties in the Lake District*, published in

1930, was able to list sixty-three individual properties. Although his acreages are not exact, he lists in round figures property which totalled nearly 11,700 acres, of which all but 1,656 acres had been acquired since 1920. It included another memorial – Castle Head, the romantic rock fort which is one side of the Jaws of Borrowdale, given by the father of Lieutenant John Hamer, killed in action 22 March 1918. With him, and listed on slate let into the living rock, are those men of Borrowdale who also died in the war.

By far the greater number of properties were gifts by individuals or groups. Two were gifts from Oliver Brett, who as Lord Esher was soon to play a major role in the Trust's affairs. G.M. Trevelyan gave 400 acres, which comprised nearly all the farmland at the head of Langdale, at once one of the finest and most threatened of all the dales. An unusual form of protection was a lease of over 3,000 acres in Ennerdale bought from the Forestry Commission. It was in fact that part of the Gillerthwaite Estate bought by the Commission but unsuitable for planting. Its details form part of an important story to be told later, as are the circumstances in which the Monk Coniston property was acquired. Progress around Derwentwater had early on been good, and by 1930 Thompson reckoned that one third of the shoreline was protected. At Windermere, already the most damaged and most at risk, there was but 146 acres. Good buildings were few but there were some on the farms, including Yew Tree Farm with its wool gallery, and the extraordinary little Bridge House at Ambleside. Wray Castle, too, that mock Gothic mansion which had played a part in Hardwicke Rawnsley's career, came as a gift with its lakeside parkland.

Herbert Marshall, in his contribution to *Britain and the Beast* in 1937, was able to write that in the Lake District, 'the forces of sanity and protection are strongly mobilised. The National Trust is firmly entrenched.' There was more, much more, to be done but in essence it was to be an extension and expansion of the valuable pioneer work. We have already mentioned the great trial of strength over Berkhamsted Common staged between Lord Brownlow and Augustus Smith. On the death of Lord Brownlow's successor in 1921 it was decided to sell the whole property. The Berkhamsted estate lay well beyond the north-west London suburbia of that time but the district was already drifting into the character unkindly known as the 'stockbroker belt'. There was a very real prospect that upon sale there would be such extensive house development that the whole stretch of countryside would be ruined. There was a long delay, possibly because the Trustees were not all of the same mind, Humphrey Talbot probably searching for a method of disposal which would be least damaging to local interests. Be that as it may, when the final date for payment of estate duty loomed near, the Trustees plumped for a sale of the property as a whole to a land speculation syndicate. It was this postponement of a decision which produced the crisis, for the Trustees left themselves little time to negotiate any compromise.

The news broke in the autumn of 1925 and it is virtually certain that the National Trust's immediate and complete involvement was due to the fact that G.M. Trevelyan then lived at Berkhamsted. He was a great walker and knew in detail the commons and woods, the parkland round the house, and the ridge of hills which rises to Ivinghoe Beacon. The master-stroke of the operation was certainly his: he first secured from another Berkhamsted resident, Renée Courtauld, the promise of

£20,000 to prime an appeal. This act of retiring generosity (the gift was at the time anonymous) was by no means the only benefaction to the Trust by Miss Courtauld, but it was critical. It enabled Trevelyan to secure a remarkable letter urging that Ashridge be saved for the nation by public subscription to the National Trust over the signatures of Stanley Baldwin, then Prime Minister, Ramsay MacDonald, the Earl of Oxford and Asquith, and Viscount Grey of Falloden. It was published in *The Times* on 20 October 1925.

Who secured the Prime Minister's agreement to this is not clear. Trevelyan's daughter says in her biography of her father that it was Humphrey Ward, her grandfather. However, Trevelyan himself may have done so because he knew Baldwin well. Indeed, in 1927, it was Baldwin who appointed George Trevelyan Regius Professor of History at Cambridge.

There is another version of the story. Miss Bridget Talbot, who at the time lived at Little Gaddesden House, set her recollections down in 1957 in such vivid terms that they deserve recording. She and two others drafted a letter, she says, asking for a fortnight's delay in the sale. 'Next day the letter was taken up to the National Trust in London to see if they could get some distinguished names to sign it and send it to *The Times*. The National Trust Secretary (sic) Mr Bailey, seemed very doubtful owing to shortness of time. However it was settled that they would meet at 4 p.m. the same day and consolidate any results they could obtain. On returning to the office Miss Talbot asked Mr Bailey what names he had been able to collect. The answer was "none". Miss Talbot then produced her copy of the letter signed by three Prime Ministers .... On hearing this Mr Bailey sprang from his seat like a shot rabbit, so great was his surprise!'

The letter did the trick and a month later John Bailey and Ronnie Norman wrote to *The Times* to report that they had made a deal with the Trustees to set aside for purchase by the National Trust 'the lands which we regard as most essential of all for the enjoyment of the public ...' A minimum of £60,000 was needed, but this would not buy all the land that the Prime Minister had hoped would be secured and they raised their sights to £80,000.

George Trevelyan had been the Trust's adviser on which parts to go for and it was not easy. 'We were near shipwrecked, but saved by (I think) skilful steering,' he wrote afterwards, giving John Bailey the credit for that. By the end of February 1926 Bailey again wrote to *The Times* to report that, 1,600 acres had been secured, mainly the commons of Berkhamsted and Aldbury and the Ivinghoe Hills. Local opinion had been aroused by a packed meeting in Berkhamsted Town Hall on 6 November 1925. It was addressed by both Trevelyan and Hamer on behalf of the National Trust and it brought together several of those who would soon become leading members of a Local Management Committee, which continues today, after sixty years, to look after the property.

The complexity of the subsequent disposal of the Ashridge Estate is such that it is very difficult to unravel. The Gothic house was bought through the first Lord Fairhaven and endowed to become the Bonar Law Memorial College, with the intention that it should provide training for party workers. On an outlying ridge of the hills the Royal Zoological Society bought land near the hamlet of Whipsnade on which was established the first country zoo. Miss Talbot claims that the idea for this came from Humphrey Talbot. She also says that she put forward an idea that

Ashridge House should become an 'Empire Centre where Commonwealth Prime Ministers and Foreign Ministers could meet ... and where visitors from the Dominions could come on arrival instead of going to hotels and lodgings.' She blames Sir (later Viscount) John Davidson, then Conservative Party Chairman, for frustrating this idea: 'He said he could gain a peerage by getting someone to save the house as a Conservative college.' Davidson wrote in 1963 to Major Hopkins (they had both been on the Ashridge Local Committee) about this: 'Although Bridget Talbot was in favour of the Appeal in 1925, I did the work for it ... I had considerable trouble with her later with regard to what use would be made of the College.'

Development for housing began at once wherever road frontages were available on those parts not bought by the Trust and virtually the whole of the northern corner of the park was destroyed. It is remarkable that local effort on the part of the Trust did not slacken and a continuing campaign of acquisition was pursued by negotiation and appeal. Among the original supporters of the Trust's first appeal were the partners of a firm of land agents, Brown and Merry, who were subsequently employed as agents for the Estate. One of them, Mr MacDonald (formerly MacDonald Brown, the second part of the name being dropped later) formed a Trust, the objects of which were to buy parcels of the estate, hold them until finance was available and then convey them to the National Trust. This process was inevitably prolonged and complicated, and at one point was made possible by the sale of building plots where it was thought to be acceptable.

This illustrates a major difference in standards and by 1937 Trevelyan and Miss Courtauld felt obliged to step in and buy the rest of Frithsden Copse from the MacDonald Trust to prevent further building. Today a little colony of up-market villas ranged along either side of a tidy roadway, sitting isolated in a still rural setting, exemplifies the incongruous character of that kind of housing development which contributors to *Britain and the Beast* so much deplored. Much of the park with the house had come into the hands of Thomas Place, who sold the house as has been described and laid out a golf course in the park. He sold this to the National Trust in 1929, having reserved to himself the right to maintain and use the golf course. The gain for the Trust was the prevention of further building, but the damage done to the landscape of the park is sad.

By such steps the original 1,600 acres have by now grown to more than 4,000 and their diverse character offers both space for the enjoyment of large numbers of people on a summer Sunday afternoon, and privacy for the solitary walker and the naturalist. The vicissitudes to which the one time unity of the Ashridge Estate was subjected have been reviewed in some detail because they illustrate so well the problems and effort demanded in solving long-drawn out problems associated with land preservation and development.

It is remarkable that from its very beginning the National Trust has been formally committed to nature conservation. The words of the 1907 Act repeat those of the 1894 Articles of Association: 'The National Trust shall be established for the purposes of promoting the permanent preservation – (of lands of natural beauty) – and as regards lands for the preservation (so far as is practicable) of their natural aspect features and animal and plant life.' Among the organisations originally nominating a member to the Council were the Linnean Society, the Entomological Society and the Royal Botanic Society.

The first step towards the acquisition of a nature reserve was recorded by the Honorary Secretary in the Report 1898–9. Herbert Goss, a Fellow of the Linnean Society and a member of the Trust's Council nominated by the Entomological Society, reported at a meeting on 26 April 1895, on the subject of Wicken Fen in Cambridgeshire, that 'this was the only undrained portion of the old Fen, that it was the haunt of much wild life and of the rare swallow-tailed butterfly, and urged the desirability of acquiring some portion of it.'

Goss knew an entomologist, J.C. Moberly of Southampton, who owned a two-acre strip which he sold to the Trust for the nominal sum of £10,

> and added a donation to the Trust which covered half the purchase money. It is hoped that when other portions of the Fen come into the market, the Trust will be able to considerably enlarge this small property. This being the first instance in which a property has been acquired partly on the ground of its scientific interest, the Council wish to point out the value of the work of the National Trust to all lovers of natural science ...

This was followed by a further strip as a gift from Charles Rothschild, an ardent entomologist, who added an entomological wing to his brother's museum at Tring some ten years later. It was, however, another expert in the same field, C.H. Verrall, whose gift in 1911 of 239 acres really established the Fen as a major nature reserve. Since then there have been a dozen other donors, some backed by subscriptions from their friends so that the Trust's Wicken Fen property now covers 600 acres.

While the Fen as a nature reserve of the highest importance is a success in itself, it may be that its emergence so early in the life of the Trust has had an even greater significance. F.W. Oliver, a botanist from University College, London, obtained from Nigel Bond details of the Trust's constitution and wrote enthusiastically on 1 May 1908, '... it looks to me from the Act as though the National Trust were fully authorised and competent to preserve natural scenery not only on the grounds of beauty but of scientific interest. Indeed the case of Wicken Fen seems to show that this is the view of the Trust.'

The inference is that the natural history world had been looking for some organisation of this kind. Indeed, in 1904, Charles Rothschild had founded the Society for the Promotion of Nature Reserves, being, his daughter Dr Miriam Rothschild thinks, disappointed in the way in which the Trust had not come up to his expectations. However, the Trust must have still seemed the best bet because both Robert Hunter and the Earl of Plymouth were appointed members of its Council, and its objects were essentially to identify areas of land 'which retain their primitive conditions', to prepare a scheme to secure them, then – Object III – 'To obtain these areas and hand them over to the National Trust under such conditions as may be necessary.'

It was in conformity with these principles that Professor Oliver contrived the acquisition of Blakeney Point in Norfolk. Lord Calthorpe, in 1910, had granted him a lease of the Point for purposes which were described as 'marine horticulture' – in fact a vegetation survey. When two years later Lord Calthorpe died, Oliver secured the support of the National Trust and with money from the Fishmongers' Company and an anonymous benefactor, the 1,100 acres of the Point were bought and vested in the National Trust, on condition that the natural fauna and flora should be preserved.

As was its practice, the Trust instituted a Local Management Committee which held its first meeting on 3 January 1913, but its work was to be interrupted by the outbreak of war, and it met only four times during that time. Peace brought renewed activity, with Professor Oliver as chairman. In 1922 the Lifeboat House was for sale, and when writing to the Fishmongers' Company for help to buy it, Oliver reveals that their co-benefactor in 1912 had been Charles Rothschild. Indeed he was wholly instrumental in the purchase because, as Benny Horne explained in a letter to Hamer in 1929, the Trustees of Lord Calthorpe's will sold first to a Mr Crundall who re-sold to Rothschild. The Fishmongers' Company made a grant of £25 towards the cost of purchase and the Lifeboat House became the working base for the Point.

Dr D.J.B. White wrote of Oliver that: '... he saw the function of a nature reserve as composed of three strands; Education, Conservation, and Amenity. Education included basic research into the relationship between the living organisms and their environment, and the teaching and training in such matters of young people from school to university level.' He certainly practised this doctrine, bringing parties of students from University College, London and interested people such as the botanist, Edward Salisbury, who joined him in writing a *Topography and Vegetation of Blakeney Point*. Perhaps the best record of his work is the degree to which it features in A.G. Tansley's *British Islands and Their Vegetation*.

Management was not without its problems and, in a long and very well informed letter of 7 June 1922 to Hamer, Professor Oliver allows himself an outburst which today would earn him a lynching by the progressives:

> The seals which guard the entrance to the harbour have multiplied and are a perfect nuisance as they drive away all the fish they don't consume and prevent fish entering the harbour. Practically they have destroyed the industry ... The job of killing them is beyond the locals. The way to do it is by air bombing, trench mortars, or possibly laying a mine and exploding it from a distance.

Not only did this tongue-in-cheek tirade graphically illustrate the problems of balance in managing reserves, but also the fact that the smooth running of the property was dependent on the goodwill of the fisher families of the village. The 'harbour' incidentally is the very long sheltered inlet between the Point and the mainland at the head of which is the village.

John Bailey, himself a Norfolk man, visited the Point in August 1923 and expressed himself '... much impressed with Pinchin, an excellent man who seems to know everything and unlike many of the learned can instruct the ignorant.' This was the Watcher, employed by the Local Committee to prevent poaching, illegal shooting and egg stealing, and to do such work as extending the area suitable for terns to nest. Oliver had earlier written of him, 'Pinchin cares for all these birds as though they were his own family.' There was trouble in store for everyone, though, when a particularly vicious campaign was mounted against Pinchin and the Trust which alleged that 'collectors' were being allowed to shoot protected species of migrant birds, that the Watcher was taking bribes and even joining in. Hamer had to come down and form his own opinion which seems to have been that the attacks were sparked off by false or at least exaggerated claims by collectors which enraged some holiday visitors, who resented the shooting of wild fowl which was the winter occupation of the fishermen.

The Local Committee had, however, to write a very carefully worded letter to Pinchin instructing him that he was not to shoot anything except geese, duck and vermin, not to ferry visitors in the breeding season. Just a year later Pinchin retired and the following testimonial reveals nothing but praise for his record:

> The expansion of the ternery in recent years is in our view largely due to Pinchin's unfailing zeal and resource; as a guide to the nesting grounds thousands of visitors will agree that he was unrivalled for his powers of observation, bird mimicry and humorous exposition. Ornithologists of the highest standing gratefully admit their indebtedness to him ...

By 1927 Professor Oliver had somewhat changed his view from the single minded enthusiasm of 1908. There had clearly been some divergence in the relationship between the Trust and the SPNR for, in 1925, a joint meeting was held at which it was decided to liaise informally and exchange proposals for new acquisitions, and if the Trust thought that a proposed reserve 'did not appear to be of historic interest or natural beauty' there would be no objection to the SPNR acquiring it.

Oliver went much further: in an address to the British Association he said:

> As regards the National Trust itself there seems no reason why it should not welcome the devolution which County (Naturalists) Trusts would mean. Already in very many cases it gives to its Local Committees of management a very large measure of independence, and one might even look forward to a time when many of the properties now held by the National Trust could be handed over (or at any rate leased) to the County Trusts, so soon as they qualify by work done and financial stability. This delegation of functions would leave the National Trust more free to act as a correlating and advisory body and to represent the movement in the metropolis. Ultimately the relationship between the parent body and the County Trust would have to be defined, and this perhaps might include a right of veto for the National Trust.

It was to be another thirty years before the county naturalist trust movement really took off, and it was preceded by the formation of a government agency in the shape of the Nature Conservancy Council. Even so, that devolution to which he looked forward came to be tried out by the Trust with varying degrees of success after the Second War.

The view expressed at the joint meeting in 1925 that there were some potential reserves which were outside of the Trust's proper sphere, may have been prompted by a cooler look at the Ruskin Reserve, Cothill, four acres of marshy woodland between Abingdon and Oxford. This had been given in 1917, nominally by the Ashmolean Society, but actually by Dr Claridge Druce and Professor Poulton (the same to whom Hamer later came for advice on the formation of the Isle of Wight Committee and who was to give another somewhat wet and difficult area, St.

Helen's Common). There was for a time a local committee but this faded out after Dr Druce died. In 1948, the Chief Agent was to write, 'The National Trust should never have taken it', on the ground that there was no public access and that by itself it made no contribution to the beauty of the landscape. Now ill-drained land and its associated wild life has so much diminished that there is real scientific value in its survival, and this is acknowledged by the present lessees, the Nature Conservancy Council. It is nevertheless an excellent example of the nature reserve which falls outside the scope of the Trust's work.

A very different proposition cropped up in the early 1920s: the Farne Islands, off the Northumberland coast. These rugged extensions in to the North Sea of the basalt whin sill lie opposite Bamburgh and about four miles from the little harbour of Seahouses. The seas around them can be desperately rough and landing depends on the direction of the wind. When it blows from the north the underwater ridge that links the visible rocks above forms at low tide a natural breakwater south of which the sea moderates, and it was in such circumstances that Darling, the lighthouse keeper on the Brownsman, was able, with his daughter Grace, to row across to the outer rocks to rescue the survivors of the *Forfarshire* which had struck and foundered one murderous night in 1838.

The islands had long been notable both for the number and species of birds breeding there. The inner group of islands had been in the ownership of Archdeacon Thorp who had been at pains to protect the birds, and the outer group was bought in 1894 by the armament manufacturer, Lord Armstrong, himself a keen naturalist, and whose castle, Bamburgh, perched on its own basalt rock by the sea's edge looked out to the Farnes. Despite the employment of a watcher in the summer, protection seems to have been increasingly ineffective. Mrs Hickling, who has supplied much of this information, writes of 'some dreadful incidents, including the burning alive of large numbers of Sandwich terns.' (The nesting sites are among low vegetation which must have been set on fire late in the breeding season.) She believes that the passing of the first Bird Protection Act in 1880 stimulated the formation of a Farne Islands Association to which members subscribed and which then, with the consent of the owners, attempted to prevent disturbance and damage. So matters went on until, in 1922, the Archdeacon's descendant decided to sell the inner group of islands. These included the comparatively sizeable Inner Farne, where there was a lighthouse, and St Cuthbert's Tower and Chapel, which might conceivably have been developed for some sort of tourism.

How real such fears were is difficult to know but it is quite certain that all those who were interested in safeguarding the islands – including Lord Armstrong – wished to achieve a permanent solution so that matters would not be dependent on the goodwill of an owner whose proprietorship might end at any time. It is this desire for an assured future, rather than any disapproval of private ownership *per se*, which has time and again prompted people to turn to the National Trust, and that is just what happened in this case.

The Ornithological Section of the Northumberland Natural History Society convened a meeting on 18 January 1923 at which the whole ornithological establishment was represented. There was a five-strong contingent from the Farne Islands Association – including Lord Armstrong who was voted into the chair – and two others represented the National Trust as well as other societies. The issue of law and order was in their minds and the Chief Constable of the County was there too. Speakers rehearsed in considerable detail the problems of protection which revolved mainly around the stealing of eggs. Professor Meek 'advocated better Watchers and greater restrictions on visitors. He mentioned that when his motor launch was lying at anchor in the "Kettle" last year he had repeatedly seen fishermen landing on the islands at daybreak. This was long before the watchers were astir, and the speaker advocated the engagement of more active and energetic men.'

The Chief Constable turned out to be somewhat unhelpful, pointing out that 'as the islands were not rated the owners could not call upon police protection.'

The decision on action was not much debated and it was resolved to try to buy the islands (Lord Armstrong having there and then agreed to part with the outer group for £1,000) and to vest them in the National Trust.

Viscount Grey of Falloden, the former Foreign Secretary and a native of Northumbria, had sent his apologies for being unable to attend the meeting, but he wrote to *The Times* on 6 February 1924 to try to bring the project to a successful conclusion. In the course of explaining the importance of the islands he wrote, 'In one respect they are I believe unique. They are the northernmost breeding place of the Sandwich tern and the southernmost breeding place of the eider duck. Without organised protection the islands would, under modern conditions, be destroyed as a breeding place for the rarer species.'

He went on to say of the £2,200 needed £1,800 had now been raised and that he hoped the balance would be subscribed. It was, and in 1925 the islands were vested in the Trust. The Association continued to manage the islands for more than twenty years before various pressures gradually changed it into a Local Management Committee of the National Trust. Even after its name had been changed, in 1947, its records continued unaltered, giving the impression of dual personality, until 1965. This underlines still further the way in which the role of the Trust was seen to be that of continuity of ownership rather than one of executive management.

Whatever others may have thought, the Trust itself began to realise that it was becoming responsible for properties with a range of important natural history features, and that these would need special care and management. The Estates Committee, whose chairman from 1926 to 1949 was George Trevelyan, increasingly equipped itself to deal with its specialist problems. For example, Arthur Tansley, whose name had been tentatively put forward in 1908 by Professor Oliver, became Honorary Adviser on Ecology thirty-nine years later. By that time he was a professor, had received a knighthood, and had brought the science of ecology and its understanding and acceptance by both academics and laity, to a pitch which has not been rivalled since. Tall, kindly and unassuming, with a great depth and breadth of knowledge, he had the gift of making complex matters at once interesting and simple to comprehend. He became a member of the Estates Committee and its Forestry Sub-Committee and was for four years also an elected member of the Council until his death in 1955. Another young associate of Oliver's, Edward Salisbury, also became involved with the Trust as an Honorary Adviser on Botany and Zoology, in which role he continued long after his retirement from the Directorship of the Royal Botanic Gardens at Kew.

A Sub-Committee for Nature Conservation was formed in 1944 and after the war produced a ten-page booklet written as *Notes for the Guidance of Local Committees who are responsible for the Management of Properties of Nature Conservation Importance*. It illustrates usefully the extent to which the Trust had recognised the pressures and priorities involved. The first task was 'that of reconciling the maximum enjoyment of the public with the preservation of the very objects upon which that enjoyment so largely depends ... The recreational and scientific aspects are not antagonistic but are corollaries the one of the other.'

Then there follow three pages illustrating the facts of ecological succession: 'If we enclose ungrazed an area of chalk downland this will become covered with bushes of hawthorn. ... Even reed swamps will eventually become alder-willow woods and these in turn give place to a swampy type of oak wood.' These examples are used to underline the message that, 'Active and vigilant management can alone prevent the progressive change that accompanies the passage of time. ... Our policy of control must therefore consider whether we do or do not desire change with its accompaniment of gains and losses and what our funds will permit.' Sanctuaries 'to which all forego access' are said to be seldom necessary except for breeding birds, and there is special emphasis on the propriety of keeping down 'or perhaps even exterminating what may be a pest or a nuisance to neighbours or the community at large'.

With the emergence of the country from the Second World War and the creation in 1949 of the Nature Conservancy as a government agency both for research and practical conservation, the Trust found itself operating in a field in which other organisations – the Field Studies Council and the County Naturalists Trusts, the Royal Society for the Protection of Birds – were playing an increasingly important part, and it is likely that the Trust's own position would have been very different had its early life not involved it so closely with nature conservation.

CHAPTER VII

Archaeological Sites
and
Historic Buildings

Archaeological remains are patently 'places of historic interest' and it was to be expected that the National Trust should seek to protect them. Moreover, despite the Historic Monuments Act of 1882, protection was far from secure. It was to improve this that Lord Avebury, and Lord Crawford and Balcarres on behalf of the Trust promoted the Ancient Monuments Bill, drafted by Sir Robert Hunter. Also in order to whip up interest and support the Trust sent out a letter in 1899 signed by the Duke of Westminster, the Earl of Rosse and Sir Robert Hunter to archaeological and other learned societies urging co-operation, and putting forward the outlines of an organisation in which affiliation of clubs to the National Trust would secure an interchange of information and a means whereby local authorities might be influenced to help in preventing 'wanton and careless disfigurement to interesting features'.

With such early concern it is surprising that there was only a trickle of such properties to start with. Duffield Castle which once overhung the Derwent just north of Derby was the first to come, in 1899. Little more than a great mound above the river, with only the foundations of its immense keep easily identifiable, it was as important to the Trust as an 'open space' for the village as for its remnants of mediaeval fortification. The White Barrow near Tilshead in Wiltshire, a well-preserved earthern barrow of Neolithic origin, may more properly be regarded as the Trust's first archaeological property, bought by subscription in 1909. As with the nature reserves, there was a tacit feeling that such places should be beautiful or romantic as well as being of historical importance. The two 1913 acquisitions in the Lakes – Borrans Field at Ambleside with its Roman fort, Galava, and the circle of standing stones at Castlerigg near Keswick – both qualified as much on these grounds as on grounds of historic importance. They were both, of course, promotions of Hardwicke Rawnsley, and he was a joint donor of the latter.

It was as early as 1907 that the attention of the Trust was drawn to the condition of the Cerne Giant. This immense figure of a naked man is cut into the chalk of a hillside above the village of Cerne Abbas in Dorset, and was at that time a part of the Pitt-Rivers estates. (General Pitt-Rivers, who had died in 1900, had been an amateur-expert in ethnology and had conducted extensive archaeological excavations elsewhere on his property.) Nigel Bond who had connections with Dorset was

78

able to arrange with the Reverend Pontin through the Dorset Natural History and Antiquarian Field Club to have the figure cleaned up.

Thomas Hardy wrote on 21 September 1925 a succinct memorandum which explains the process: 'The Cerne Giant's figure was never all over white like that of King George's near Weymouth, but only the trenches forming his outline. These are fairly deep and all that can be done is to keep the trenches cleaned out and spread white chalk over the bottom of them. This will remain white many years if raked over and weeded now and then. The interior of the Giant's figure was always green.'

So as far as the Trust was concerned matters were left like that until 1919 when George Pitt-Rivers put the Cerne Abbas Estate on the market. His agent Mr M. Wood contacted the National Trust through Albert Pope of Wracklewood House near Dorchester, because of the interest shown locally in the preservation of the Gate House and Guest House which were the principal, and very fine, remains of the Abbey. This project fell through but Mr Pope wrote to Hamer that the Giant had been reserved out of the sale and asked whether the Trust would accept it as a gift. Three weeks later Hamer's answer was 'Yes' and he must have been reassured by Pope's further letter: 'The costs of maintenance should be trifling. There is a fence round that would have to be kept up and the gutters would have to be taken out occasionally.'

So it was that in 1920 this supposedly Romano-British figure, said to be a fertility symbol, was conveyed as a gift by Mr Pitt-Rivers to the Trust. It was to be supported financially four years later by an endowment given by Sir Henry Hoare, who was to become one of the Trust's great benefactors. It was not until twelve years later that the storm blew up over the undisguised masculinity of the Giant. Shocked letters to the papers and reproachful ones to the Trust were summed up in one dated 12 July 1932 from a W.L. Long, purporting to be writing on behalf of the Bishop of Salisbury but giving no address. After saying that 'such a figure, 27,000 times life size ...' would, if a similar subject half a million part of its size were exhibited in a shop window, immediately receive attention from the police, and that antiquity was no defence – winds up as follows: 'I trust that after due consideration you may see your way to so altering a portion of this figure (by adding the leaf or turning it into the simple nude) that it may conform to the moral and legal standards of a Christian country.'

The Giant survived this onslaught on his reputation and the next thirty years passed quietly. The Trust missed the chance, in 1937, of securing ownership of the hill on which the figure is cut, when on the death of the Pitt-Rivers successor, Miss S.J. Rolle, 500 acres of the Abbey Estate was up for sale. The inability of the Trust – because of its fragile financial base – to react effectively to opportunities such as this was to remain a handicap until the 1960s. Fortunately the Trustees of the Minterne Estate stepped in on behalf of Lord Digby, but minor problems such as access to the site, fencing to prevent damage by cattle and horses (the hill in the hands of the Trust could have run with sheep only) could well have been eliminated. Hardy's prescription for maintenance seriously under-estimated the frequency, cost and general difficulty of the operation, and the Giant during and after the Second World War became almost invisible, needing two major restorations in twenty years.

In 1968 the Giant underwent a traumatic experience which is best described by quotation from Richard Philips, the Clerk of Works to the Trust in Wessex:

Police Sergeant Bartlett, Dorchester Police, reported to this office that the Cerne Giant had been subjected to a sex change by vandals on the night of the 4th/5th September. The change had been made by the use of either lime white or Snowcem (at the moment I am not sure which) and a green solution, possibly emulsion paint. The change was very complete and had been carried out with expertise and fine finesse .... The incident caused quite a stir and I learned from the police that Lady Digby was getting rather excited (national and local press and radio reporters were massing in the area).

The Ministry of Works refused to allow this Scheduled Ancient Monument to be touched without an inspection by a Superintendent and so the sad state continued for five days before cleaning down started. 'This was done by Dennis Chapple (the Trust's Head Forester) and his staff; the whitened areas being removed, and as a result of this there was considerably less intensity to the "greened" areas.' The perpetrators of this outrage upon the Giant were never identified.

The 1920s was a great period for growth in the Trust's archaeological work. The Roman villa at Chedworth, north of Cirencester, had been discovered by a gamekeeper on Lord Eldon's estate, digging in a rabbit warren for his ferret. On excavation it turned out to be very fine and with several survivals of high-quality mosaic floors. Its setting was, and still is, remote from more modern habitations, amid woodlands in the valley of the Coln. The surviving masonry was carefully – if somewhat comically – capped with little roofs, and the mosaics enclosed to preserve them from the elements, and there was no real danger of neglect or ill-treatment. It was another instance of looking for the long-term security that the Trust offered when, in 1924, money was raised to buy it.

Norman Irvine, who was for many years the Trust's custodian at the villa, compiled a list of the number of visitors year by year for fifty-eight years. In 1924 there were 2,270 and this number grew steadily rising to 12,879 in 1938. This increase almost certainly reflects the growth in the use of motor transport. Of the total number only 56 were National Trust members, which measures the tiny body of membership at that time. Throughout the Second War the numbers fell to around or even less than at the start, but it is remarkable that with transport problems and petrol shortage that anyone should visit at all. These conditions were prolonged well beyond the war's end and not until 1951 did the figures top 20,000. It took another ten years to double that (members then numbering 1,266 or 3.1%) and by 1978 it nearly recorded another doubling with 78,297 of which members made up 15%. From then until 1982 the economic recession brought a similar trend in numbers but the visiting members continued to increase until they constituted a quarter of the total.

These figures illustrate, of course, the growth in public support in terms of membership to which reference in more general terms will be made later. In the present context they are more noteworthy for the way in which the Trust as a minority group in the 1920s accumulated unregarded treasures which later became of general interest and value, rather like the man who buys works of contemporary art for modest sums and whose descendants suddenly find themselves possessed of a fortune.

1924 also saw an appeal for £2,000 to buy Cissbury Ring on the South Downs inland from Worthing. The leaflet says, 'it is earnestly hoped that members of Archaeological Societies will contribute to the funds required for purchase of this most interesting resort, so that it may be preserved for the public benefit for ever.' There followed an account of General Pitt-Rivers' excavations of what turned out to be a very complex site and calculated to have great appeal to specialists. But the Trust then broadened its appeal: '… apart from its unique value as a prehistoric earthwork, it is beyond all question worthy of preservation as a place of natural beauty. The views to be obtained from the camp on a clear day are wonderfully fine: Chanctonbury Ring is but 2½ miles away, Beachy Head and the Isle of Wight may readily be discerned, and the long stretches of the South Downs on either side make up a prospect of almost unsurpassable beauty.' Well, one way or another, it worked, and in 1925 the Ring was the Trust's.

The acquisition in 1926 of the Megalithic long barrow at Coldrum in Kent has already been mentioned. That indeed, although set in pleasant country, was essentially an archaeological site. The great event of 1927 – an appeal for money to buy over 1,400 acres of downland around Stonehenge – was typically rooted as much in access and landscape preservation as in the incomparably valuable prehistoric relics which pattern the surrounding countryside.

As so often, it had started with an effort in 1882 by the Commons Society in the person of Shaw-Lefevre to get the owner, Sir Edmund Antrobus, to place the stones under the protection of the then brand new Ancient Monuments Act. This was unsuccessful, but point was given to the suggestion when in the closing hours of the century a trilithon fell, possibly dislodged by New Year revellers, and the cap stone was broken. There was a general public alarm and Sir Edmund's son and successor, also Edmund, responded by fencing in a large area around the stones, erecting a hut and turnstiles and charging for admission. In this he had the approval of what the Society's report terms 'certain learned societies'.

Since it had been established that an owner might be held to have 'dedicated' a right of way to an object of general interest (in that instance a judgement by the Lord Chancellor of Ireland as to access to the Giant's Causeway) the Society, with the National Trust and the Kyrle Society, first petitioned the Wiltshire County Council for action to assert such a right. This bore no fruit, and an attempt to get the Government to buy the stones was frustrated by Sir Edmund's price – £50,000. 'Outrageous', said the Minister. The Commons Society decided to go to the Courts, and Robert Hunter drafted a letter to *The Times* which was published on 15 July 1903 over the signatures of Shaw-Lefevre, Buxton, Hunter and Rawnsley. All in vain, because Mr Justice Farwell declined to presume from the overwhelming evidence of unrestricted passage that the tracks had ever been dedicated. He declared that 'there cannot be a *prima facie* case for the public to go to a place where the public have no right to be.' Despite expressions of anger and downright disbelief in the validity of the judgement, it was thought impossibly expensive to appeal, and there the matter rested until, in 1918, Sir Cecil Chubb was able to buy the stones and give them to the nation. (It is interesting that in this case the word meant 'state' whereas for many years in this context it has been used to describe gifts to the Trust).

There was still great concern that the surroundings of Stonehenge would be disfigured and on 5 August 1927 *The Times* printed another letter of which Stanley

Baldwin was the principal signatory, backed this time by J. Ramsay MacDonald, the Earl of Crawford and Balcarres, (President of the Society of Antiquaries), Viscount Grey of Falloden (Vice-President of the National Trust) and the Earl of Radnor, as Lord Lieutenant of Wiltshire. David Lloyd George also signed a copy of the letter but he was away from London and his signature arrived too late to be added to the publication. The letter sets out some of the worries: '... there is an obvious danger that the setting of Stonehenge may be ruined and the stones dwarfed by the erection of unsightly buildings on the Plain.' The huts of the wartime aerodrome were still standing, close to the stones; 'an enterprising restaurateur has built a bungalow, the Stonehenge Cafe, within hail of the stones .... The conditions of modern transport make it extremely likely that this structure ... will be the first of many .... Projects are already in existence which would involve extensive building and the laying of water mains.'

An appeal leaflet issued later was more explicit. The land was on sale in three plots, on which, in August, the Trust had secured short options. The derelict aerodrome was plot A, 389 acres, and this had been bought for £8,000 and the demolition of the buildings already begun – a splendid spur for an appeal. Plot B, with a frontage to the Amesbury road, was already planned for development and covered 404 acres, and this too had been bought although £1,500 of the £8,000 price was still outstanding. Of Plot C the leaflet says: 'There remains, therefore, the third plot: 650 acres to the north of the Devizes road. This tract, which includes the southward facing road frontage immediately opposite the stones, is in immediate and obvious danger of building and the price asked is £16,000. UNLESS IT IS SAVED THE WHOLE WORK OF THE COMMITTEE AND THE SUBSCRIBERS WILL HAVE BEEN IN VAIN AND STONEHENGE WILL HAVE A SOLITUDE TO THE SOUTH AND A STREET TO THE NORTH.'

A long list of subscribers up to 17 November followed, headed by HM King George V, with twenty guineas, followed by Anonymous with £6,000, and totalling £14,810. 11s. 2d. The appeal caught the national interest and the *Illustrated London News* published sketches, including a fantasy of Piccadilly Circus at Stonehenge. Money enough was raised for the purchase to go ahead, although the last bit took a while to raise. Indeed the property had to be vested in Lord Zetland and Mr R.C. Norman as trustees for the Trust until the last part of a loan was repaid on 27 February 1934, £2,300 plus 5% interest. One of the contributors had been the Vicar of Amesbury, Mr Moxon, who, enterprisingly, took a collection in his church for the fund.

Baldwin's appeal letter had included a number of promises explicit or inferred:

> The solitude of Stonehenge should be restored and precautions taken to ensure that our posterity will see it against the sky in lonely majesty before which our ancestors have stood in awe throughout all our recorded history ....
>
> Further building will be prevented, and the valuable archaeological remains of the site permanently protected from the plough ....
>
> Part at least of the revenues derived from the rents of grazing etc. will, it is hoped, be available for the further protection of the archaeological treasures and amenities of Salisbury Plain.

At that time the sheep and the rabbit were the principal denizens of Stonehenge

Down. A farming company, Messrs Wort and Way, were the tenants. Good farmers, they had their own farmstead distant from the Down and where the main centre of operations was located. In the late 1930s they were the proud owners of Cherry, a little red Irish cow who had given more milk in one lactation than any other recorded at that time. But the Down was unfenced and there they grazed a big flock of sheep, tended day by day by a shepherd, tall, bearded with the pale blue eyes of the outdoor man, who with his smock and his crook might have come straight from a Thomas Hardy novel. The land was faintly marked with the remains of the prehistoric tracks – the 'Avenue' which winds up to approach the stones from the north and the 'Cursus', that broad straight band running roughly west/east across the northern down – and liberally peppered with tumuli singly and in groups. Even more barrows lay close to, but not on, the Trust's newly acquired property. Their greatest danger was from the rabbit for whose burrows they might have been purpose made. It must have seemed that there would be little required of the Trust beyond masterly inactivity.

How wrong! Just as Hamer was about to retire from the Secretaryship a blast arrived from Howard Cunnington who was Honorary Curator of the Wiltshire Archaeological Society, one of the main initiators of the appeal. The Trust had agreed to provide land for a car park for visitors to the stones and Hamer's efforts to placate Cunnington's wrath were wholly ineffectual, the latter replying, on 14 December 1934:

> Your statement that cars or charabancs on the road obstruct the view looking toward the point of sunrise is quite untenable, as those who have any knowledge of the site must know.
>
> The Local Authority cannot insist that a car park should be made and even so it would not be the responsibility of the National Trust to do so.
>
> The whole point is that if the National Trust yield to the blandishments of the Office of Works, and hand over land that was entrusted to its care, solely for the purpose that it should be safe from further encroachment and vulgarisation, what guarantee has the subscribing public that further encroachments, perhaps of even more objectionable character, will not be made?
>
> It is certain that if this possibility had been foreseen by those originally responsible for the purchase of the land it would never have been made over to the National Trust.

Cunnington was by no means unsupported in his opinion. The *Wiltshire Gazette*, in January 1935, printed a long leading article which did acknowledge some redeeming features of the scheme which had been hatched jointly by the Office of Works and the Trust. This involved the demolition of the two cottages which stood in the fork of the road below the stones (and which were occupied by the toll-takers and caretakers of the monument) and the removal of the ticket hut from near the stones to the new car park. There was credit also for the Trust's intended removal of the café when its lease expired. However, the car park would be 'repugnant to many', and 'there is in principle no reason why other conveniences should not be made and other facilities provided for the trippers who swarm round the stones and gawk at them with uncomprehending gaze.' As far as the Trust was concerned, allowing a portion of its land to be used for the purpose – 'is not morally defensible. This area around Stonehenge was handed over in the belief that it would be reserved for ever for agricultural purposes only.'

There followed a good deal of wriggling on the part of the Trust, Hamer's successor finding that there was a covenant against any building within 400 yards of the stones only to discover to his chagrin that the only enforcement of its terms lay with the Office of Works. Another ploy, the object of which is unclear, but which came from the Trust's Estates Committee, was to try to renege on the promise to demolish the café. This time on the other side pressure from the Office of Works obliged the Trust to adhere to its bargain.

So with the Second War approaching the whole business settled down and the complaints died away, no one foreseeing that a much more far reaching change was a few years away. The agricultural revolution which accompanied the war resulted in virtually the whole of the down being cropped in corn and that was followed by enclosure and division by barbed wire fences and the introduction of cattle grazing.

Worse was to come when in 1960 the then Minister of Works, Lord John Hope, decided that there must be massive provision for tourists and demanded – that is not too strong a word – the co-operation of the Trust. Lord Crawford – son of the signatory of the Appeal letter – was dismayed. Writing to the Minister on 13 January 1961 he recalled that 'one of the objects of the original Stonehenge Appeal signed by Baldwin, Ramsay MacDonald, Grey, Radnor and my father was that further building should be prevented.' He told the Trust's Executive Committee that he could make no impression and he understood that Lord John Hope, having been to France and enjoyed a meal in a restaurant overlooking an historic monument, had decided that every major monument in England should have such a restaurant too. It was no joke, because the threat of compulsory purchase, from which the Trust has never been wholly immune, was in the prevailing circumstances quite real. After long and bitter opposition the Trust compromised with a lease for a large car park served by 'amenities' – shop, refreshments, lavatories, ticket office – below ground with an underground passage to the stones. Although the impression made on a visitor is that he is in an Underground Station on the Maginot Line, it must be admitted that special provision had to be made for visitors, who increased in numbers from 120,000 in 1951 to nearly a million thirty years later. That it was the wrong solution was the consensus in 1979 of a working party set up by the Department of the Environment.

A new element appeared with flower power and hippies at the end of the 1960s when the esoteric cult of witnessing dawn at the stones at the mid-summer solstice developed, accompanied by a pop festival and the monument was invaded by thousands of people who camped for days and sometimes weeks. Fearing for the stones, the Department of the Environment took legal action against the organising group, the Wallies, who, rather endearingly, changed their name by deed poll so that when the case came for trial it had to be cited as the Department of the Environment v. the Department of the Environment. For the Trust the result was that the camp shifted from the monument to a field a few hundred yards away and there it has been held, year by year, with allegations of all sorts of illegalities and undesirable activities, and undeniable mess and damage, until in 1985 the Trust and the Department, with the authority of a court injunction and the co-operation of the police to enforce it, finally put an end to the practice.

In order to protect the stones and prevent the site becoming a quagmire, they are now roped off during the summer season and have to ve viewed from a distance by as many as 7,000 tourists a day. However, the barriers are removed in the winter when visitors can enter the stones. On a grey January day, when flakes of snow are being driven by icy winds, Stonehenge comes into its own.

This long tale of the Trust and Stonehenge has seemed to be worth the telling for three reasons: first, there is the confusion in the collective mind of the Trust between its romantic, aesthetic and scientific objectives, which has its parallels in other elements of its work; secondly, there is the failure – more common before the Second World War than after – to appreciate that circumstances might arise in which it could not keep its promises; thirdly, there is the emergence of Government as potentially one of the most dangerous enemies of preservation.*

It has been necessary to by-pass a major event in the archaeological work of the Trust which occurred in 1930 when J.M. Clayton gave five and a half acres on Hadrian's Wall in Northumberland. It included the fort at Housesteads, Vercovicium, then not wholly excavated but already known as the best preserved on the Wall. The fort lies high on the ridge which the defences follow and the views all round over a wide and sparsely populated rolling countryside give an immense feeling of freedom.

This was to grow by 1982 into an estate of 1,700 acres containing some three and a quarter miles of the Wall. George Trevelyan was instrumental in beginning the extension by the acquisition of 913 acres of Hotbank Farm in 1942, and the whole property is now one of superb scenery and romantic association, as well as the repository of archaeological relics of exceptional importance. There are very large numbers of visitors, about a quarter of a million people using the car park below the fort each year and uncounted numbers walking the length of the Wall. Much of the extension of the estate since 1972 has been acquired with the help of grants from the Countryside Commission.

The archaeological world, however, has not been pleased with the National Trust. Its Local Committee of Management, formed at the time of the first gift, believed that its duty consisted in maintaining things as they were. Educational interests had been catered for by the building of a museum close to the fort to house the finds from previous diggings, but the Committee was not prepared after the Second War to institute a major programme of further excavation, nor was it inclined to treat the

---

*Stonehenge and the small triangle of land on which it stands, is now under the protection of English Heritage who lease the site of the present car park and bunker from the National Trust. Both organisations are determined to remove all these eye-sores together with the section of the A360 which separates the stones from the Trust's land to the North. Ably led by its Chairman, Lord Montagu, English Heritage have negotiated with the Ministry of Defence to acquire land near Larkhill Camp on which to build new car parks and a reception centre. A special access road will have to be built from the A345 and visitors will approach the Henge on foot from the north. Arrangements will be made to bring the elderly and disabled by vehicle. The new buildings will not be seen from Stonehenge, which will eventually regain a little of the 'lonely majesty' described by Baldwin.

maintenance of the Wall in the way then approved by the Ministry of Works –
consolidation and capping with mortar. The Committee regarded it more as a
romantic walk-way, topped with turf, its unmortared facing stones being replaced
from time to time as they fell out.

This was in no way acceptable to such people as Professor I.A. Richmond, who
had devoted a large part of his life's work to studies of the whole Roman defensive
system and what would now be termed its infrastructure. The Trust's Executive
Committee went so far as to abandon its policy of private deliberation and on 14
October 1949 allowed the Professor to appear before them to put in person his plea
that all the Roman remains in the ownership of the Trust should be put into
guardianship of the Ministry of Works. Only in that way, he pleaded – his feelings
so strong that he was on the verge of tears – could the remains be fully explored and
permanently protected.

The decision of the Executive Committee was to agree to place the fort only under
guardianship, and to retain full control of all the rest, undoubtedly influenced in the
latter case by the strong feeling that the Trust must above all try to protect the
romantic ambience of the place. They felt able to hand over the fort to the Ministry
on purely financial grounds: the numbers visiting had, of course, plummetted with
the war and because of petrol rationing had not recovered since. There was no
prospect, the Committee thought, that there would ever again be enough visitors
paying to see the fort to make ownership profitable.

The 120,000 who were yearly paying for entry by 1980, brought unimagined
problems: they began to trample the genuinely original footings of the Roman Wall
out of existence and the Ancient Monuments Department of what had become the
Department of the Environment was reasonably concerned. It had the good fortune
at that time to be responsible to a senior Civil Servant, one Maurice Mendoza, no less
pugilistic than his great forebear the bare-fist fighter and Champion of England.
Mendoza's attack on the Trust was precisely what was needed to revive its
realisation of where its duty to archaeology lay. He not only arraigned the Trust for
ignorance and neglect, but he followed up with a grant of Government money to
enable the Trust to do what was needed.

The confusion that existed between the Trust's scientific and aesthetic responsibilities might have resulted in its concern for archaeology becoming wholly
extinguished were it not for the accident that so many of the properties it acquired
were encumbered with archaeological remains. The current List of Properties
summarises over 125 with Roman and pre-Roman remains, and the mediaeval
element is also massive.

In the March 1930 issue of *Antiquity*, R.C.C. Clay had written 'The Trust is
becoming the possessor of places of archaeological interest, and therefore
archaeology should be more adequately represented on its councils. Furthermore the
funds accruing from the ownership of places of archaeological interest ... should not
be engulfed in the common fund, but should go to form the nucleus of a fund for
purchasing and preserving other sites of archaeological interest. In short there
should be a separate archaeological branch of the Trust with its own control
committee with separate sub-committees for individual sites and its own special
fund .... The Trust out of small beginnings, has grown to be a great landlord with

high responsibilities, and if it is to continue to act with efficiency it must adapt itself to new conditions.'

For reasons which are obscure, the Trust kept the science of archaeology at arm's length for a very long time. Perhaps it was because the only visible practitioner, the Ancient Monuments Department, produced so arid and unromantic a result that those whose preservationist ideals were born of the poetry of Gray, Wordsworth and Tennyson were repelled. The Trust did seek to protect itself with Honorary Advisers on archaeology – the first was Sir Cyril Fox and later Sir Mortimer Wheeler, whose bluff charm and practical commonsense ironed out a lot of problems. He shared the work with Professor Richmond in the north and Sir Cyril Fox in the south-west. It was really left to Phyllis Ireland, in the 1960s, to compel the Trust, by force of her own personality, to accept archaeology as one of its basic responsibilities and to appoint her – for a pittance – to do the spade work which was necessary to identify the archaeological remains on the Trust's properties and to ensure that the minimum care needed for their survival was provided. In 1971 Phyllis Ireland produced a little booklet on the *Prehistoric Properties of the Trust*. This was the first publication by the Trust on the subject other than guide books to specific properties. It featured a plan of a causewayed Neolithic fort at Barkhale on the Sussex Downs, part of a property owned by the Trust for more than twenty years before it became aware of the fort's existence.

Details of the way in which during the last ten years the Trust has got its archaeological house in order must come later. At this point its early perception of its task and its later confusion need to be seen against the major place which archaeology has come to take among its preservation achievements.

The preservation of buildings seems to have been almost a last-minute inclusion in the self-prescribed role of the Trust, and it is not easy to see who initiated it. Octavia Hill was certainly interested and perhaps the younger Sydney Cockerell may have influenced her here. It is also true that Robert Hunter was an admirer of Morris: the idea may have come from there. However, the Society for the Preservation of Ancient Buildings did not feature in the original list of nominating bodies and was not introduced as such until the first Annual General Meeting. Once involved in buildings, the main source of interest did come from the SPAB and they supplied a series of suggestions which sometimes bore fruit. The buildings were almost all mediaeval and small: the Clergy House at Alfriston; the Joiners' Hall, Salisbury; the 'Old Post Office' at Tintagel; the bridges over the Wey at Eashing; the Courthouse at Long Crendon; all these came in one way or another via the Society. Other early acquisitions of a similar nature are the Market House of Winster; Keld Chapel near Shap; the gate house of Westbury College; another Priest's House at Muchelney; and the Chantry Chapel in Buckingham.

Inspired again by the Society, the Trust made a departure from the small to the large in 1904, when Barrington Court in Somerset with 220 acres of land came on to the market. Although, like other early possessions, it was mid-sixteenth century or earlier, it had been a very grand house, its traditional architecture enlivened by spiral chimneys and finialled gables. It had been dreadfully ill-treated, the greater part of the interior gutted and the staircase with its oak panelling and the balustrading removed. A benefactor came forward in the person of Miss J.L. Woodward who put up £10,000, provided the Trust would find the balance, £500 only, and another £1,000 for restoration. Even then the amount for 'restoration' was hopelessly inadequate, and the problem made such an impression on Nigel Bond that thirty years later he greeted any suggestion of preserving a house with, 'We cannot possibly afford to take it on: remember Barrington!' When Hardwicke Rawnsley went there on his West Country tour in 1918 it was still in use as a farmhouse. Externally it had been made wind and water tight, but it was still far from secure until another benefactor emerged in the person of Colonel Lyle. In return for a very long lease he undertook the renovation of the building and laid out a new garden, the plans of which were approved, if not made, by Gertrude Jekyll. The stable block, built late in the seventeenth century by the Strode family, was converted into a family house, new farm buildings were put up, and the whole property took again the form and substance of a country house, the first of its kind to come into the care of the Trust.

Otherwise the pattern of acquisition was maintained right through to the early 1930s. Such houses as Eastbury Manor – another SPAB project – at Barking, Paycockes in Coggeshall, Stoneacre near Maidstone, with its high hall and complex kingpost roof, were all mediaeval to Tudor, and smallish in size. Quebec House in Westerham had its origins in that time too, though it had assumed a seventeenth century appearance, and the substantial manor house at Princes Risborough was properly of that later period, both being slightly less modest than the average run of houses protected by that time.

A benefaction in 1926 stands out as something quite new in the history of the Trust and with few if any repetitions in later years. It introduced a wholly new sort of property into the care of the Trust, and it linked the organisation with the name of a man who had been exceptionally prominent in the affairs of the British Empire. He is probably best remembered now in the rhyming couplets composed for the Masque of Balliol in 1881:

> My name is George Nathaniel Curzon
> I am a most superior person,
> My cheek is pink, my hair is sleek,
> I dine at Blenheim once a week.

Curzon was born in 1859 into an old family which had been possessed of property near Derby for some eight hundred years, who in the eighteenth century built themselves an exceptionally beautiful house at Kedleston.

For a number of years Curzon travelled the world. He began to concentrate especially on the Indo-Russian borders, and his journeys through the mountains of north-west India and into Afghanistan were remarkable for the physical effort and endurance required, as well as for the depth of knowledge that he gained of place and people. It was in part the detailed knowledge that his travels brought him that led to his being appointed Viceroy of India in 1898 and which, in turn, brought him his first peerage. Because his titles are so confusing it is perhaps helpful to explain them here. His father, the fourth Lord Scarsdale, lived on well beyond the end of the nineteenth century. Curzon had to have a peerage to enable him to take on the vice-

ABOVE LEFT Henry Lupus Grosvenor, 1st Duke of Westminster (1825–99). He was to play host at his London home, Grosvenor House in Park Lane, at the meeting on 12 January 1894 that saw the formation of The National Trust for Places of Historic Interest or Natural Beauty.

ABOVE RIGHT Robert Hunter (1844–1913). At the age of 24 he became solicitor to the Commons Preservation Society, winning key battles to save, among others, Epping Forest, Hampstead Heath and the Commons of Wimbledon and Wandsworth.

ABOVE LEFT Octavia Hill (1838–1912), tireless fighter for social and housing reform. Her determination to preserve open spaces as 'sitting rooms' for the urban poor led her to become one of the founders of the National Trust.

ABOVE RIGHT Hardwicke Rawnsley (1851–1920). In 1877 he was given the living of Wray on Windermere, the beginning of his devoted relationship with the Lake District. From 'Guardian of the Lakes' he became Honorary Secretary of the National Trust in 1895.

OPPOSITE It was through her friendship with Canon Rawnsley that Beatrix Potter came to know of the National Trust, and at her death in 1944 she left her Lakeland hill farms with their Herdwick sheep to the Trust. In this photograph, taken at the Eskdale Woolpack Show in 1931 by M. C. Farr, she is shown with Harry Lamb.

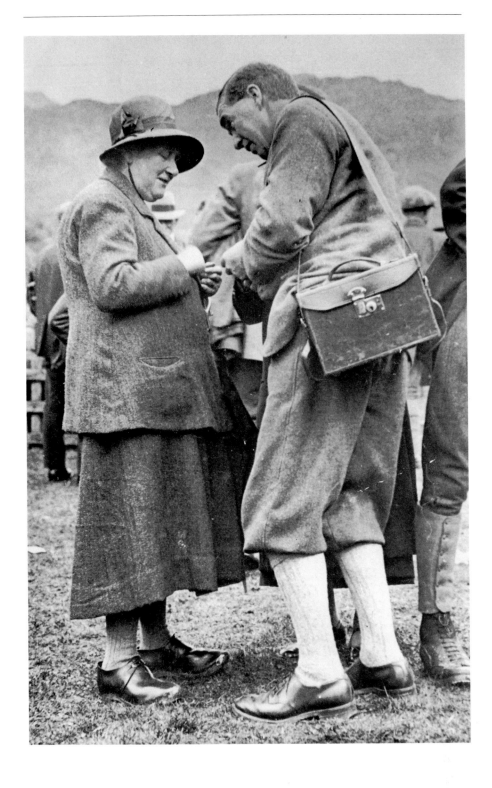

ABOVE The promontory of Frair's Crag, Derwentwater, bought by public subscription in 1922 as a memorial to Hardwicke Rawnsley.

OPPOSITE Pickering Tor, Dovedale in the Peak District. Dovedale's champion was a Buxton businessman, F. A. Holmes, who resolved in 1916 to preserve the valley from destruction.

ABOVE The 14th-century Clergy House at Alfriston in Sussex, 1894. The house, the first to be purchased by the Trust, was bought for £10 in 1896.

OPPOSITE ABOVE Barrington Court, Somerset, the first large country house to come to the Trust, in 1904. Two generous benefactors, Miss J. L. Woodward and Colonel Lyle, saved the dilapidated house and restored it to its former grandeur.

OPPOSITE BELOW HRH Queen Elizabeth, the Queen Mother has been President of the National Trust since 1953. This photograph was taken at Polesden Lacey in 1923 with Albert Duke of York, later George VI, on their honeymoon. In 1944 Mrs Ronnie Greville gave Polesden Lacey, in Surrey, to the National Trust.

Elizabeth   Albert
April 26th – May 7th

ABOVE Hadrian's Wall, Northumberland. In 1930 J. M. Clayton gave the Trust $5\frac{1}{2}$ acres of the Northumberland section of the Roman wall, including the fort of Housesteads. By 1982 the estate covered 1,700 acres, including $3\frac{1}{2}$ miles of Wall.

regal post and he was accommodated in the Irish peerage as Baron Curzon of Kedleston. In 1911, while his father was still living, he was created Earl Curzon in the English Peerage, becoming Marquess in 1921 and also having inherited the Scarsdale title on his father's death. He had no direct heirs and so his Kedleston titles died with him and his successors have again the barony of Scarsdale.

Curzon, a member of the National Trust himself, took an intense and informal interest in all forms of architecture, especially although not exclusively, ancient and mediaeval. Kedleston must have informed his mind from the beginning but he attributes his first awareness of ancient architecture to a visit to Egypt when he was twenty-four. He found the Viceroy's Lodge in Calcutta to be a pastiche of Kedleston which not only amused him but provoked one of those remarks which are remembered when matters of real importance are long forgotten. 'Kedleston,' he is reported as saying, 'is built of stone and alabaster, while this is only lath and plaster.' His short flat Derbyshire 'a', which he always retained and for which he was often teased, had in that comment a splendid run of five repetitions. He was to use his position in India to ensure the preservation of the great monuments of the country's past to such good purpose that Pandit Nehru, the first Prime Minister of India after independence, was to say to the Secretary of State for Commonwealth Relations, the Earl of Swinton, 'After every other Viceroy has been forgotten Curzon will be remembered because he restored all that was beautiful in India.'

Curzon had been re-established in England for a good many years when the Trust got itself into a serious muddle over the welfare of the ruins of Tattershall Castle on the edge of the Lincolnshire fens. It had been built in the mid-fifteenth century by Ralph Cromwell, Lord Treasurer to Henry VI. It followed elaborate requirements of much earlier defensive fortifications but was in fact a mansion house of superb and splendid scale and ornament.

In a county where there was no easily obtainable stone, the whole edifice was of brick, and though a ruin for more than two hundred years the great Tower still stood a most remarkable and beautiful example of the precision of East Anglian brick building. Within the tower on each floor were fine Gothic ornamented fireplaces of imported stone. Apart from their intrinsic merit they had become famous when Pugin used them to provide designs for the new Houses of Parliament. No one seems to have bothered much about the property. It had been in the ownership of Lord Fortescue who had sold it along with his Lincolnshire Estate in about 1906. Then, in 1911, all hell broke loose when it was discovered that the treasured fireplaces were being removed for shipment to the United States.

Canon Rawnsley was immediately in action making an appeal, on Thursday 14 September, in the columns of the *Daily News*, having secured a stop on the work until the following day. He also appealed to the Lord Lieutenant, Lord Brownlow, and to Captain Weigall of Petwood, Woodhall Spa for their assistance. He even approached Lord Stamfordham who was then with the King at Balmoral, to try to secure Royal intervention in the matter, but without success. Nor did he have any more luck with the Ambassador of the United States, who replied that there was no reason to presume that the purchaser was an American. The Prime Minister, Mr Asquith, did at least reply to Rawnsley, and in his own hand, but the substance of his letter was equivalent to his famous 'Wait and see'.

A telegram to Robert Hunter did get a very positive reply written on 23

September. 'I have just received your telegram and I have shown it to Lord Eversleigh ... and to Briscoe Eyre. We all think no good can result from appealing to the American Minister. .... We have failed through the cupidity and want of scruple of the people who have temporary control of the castle and we had better let the whole matter drop now. I utterly mistrust the gang who have the matter in hand now, including Trippel.' He went on to say that, 'We ought to bend our energies to getting an alteration in the law which shall prevent this sort of thing in the future.'

As we have seen, this did not prevent Rawnsley writing to the Ambassador the following day, when Hunter again put pen to paper too. '*The Times* comes here [Bromshaw] a day late and I had not seen your communication in Saturday's when I wrote yesterday. I must frankly say that I wish you would let the subject of Tattershall Castle alone now. You are only playing into the hands of speculators.'

Three days later *The Times* printed several letters on the subject. There was a long one from Sir Francis Trippel, who appears to have been trying to play the part of go-between, and recounts various efforts on his part to secure the property which are too complicated and obscure to repeat here. The really important one was a statement on behalf of Albert Ball, formerly Mayor of Nottingham, who had been cast as villain of the piece. He had bought the Castle in the middle of 1910 as 'an interesting speculation' and had thought of making the castle habitable but friends interested in archaeology had urged him to allow it to become a national property. He agreed, and through the Curator of Nottingham Castle Nigel Bond, then also the Trust's Secretary, was told that Ball would sell for £2,000 and make a donation of £100 towards the cost. Bond replied that the price was too high and in response Ball wrote, 'I have had a very considerable sum offered for the mantelpieces and I am sure I shall get more for them if I break them up, which is my intention unless I dispose of it [the castle].'

That was in November 1910 and after a bit more inconclusive correspondence the matter died. Three months later Mr Ball sold the castle. He wound up his statement – 'I greatly regret that this interesting building should be lost to the nation, but the fault is entirely that of the National Trust.' The same page of *The Times* carried a footnote, 'The famous mantelpieces removed from the Castle were brought to London yesterday by Messrs MacNamara (Limited) by steam wagon.'

Poor Hardwicke Rawnsley, chastened for once, read it all and wrote the same day to the paper: 'It is easy to be wise after the event. I am quite willing to bear my share of the blame for the fact that the negotiations failed in the first instance with Mr Ball .... It is quite true we did not realise the unique interest attaching to the fireplaces nor their inflated marketable value.'

There was, however, a God in the Machine: George Nathaniel Curzon became aware of the rumpus. Curzon explained, 'The Castle was presently acquired by an American Syndicate of Speculators, who looked only for profit. The fireplaces were sold separately from the Castle and were bought by a London firm of art dealers and again disposed of there by them to a German dealer with partners in America, where it has all along been intended to offer them for sale.' Despite these complications he was determined to intervene and wrote on 29 October 1911 to the Rev. Yglesias, Vicar of Tattershall, who was to become his adviser and representative. 'When I got back to Town last Friday [from Tattershall] I found that negotiations were proceeding for the acquisition of the Castle for purposes of vandalism, if not of demolition. I therefore cut the Gordian Knot by buying it myself and it is now mine ... I have not abandoned all hope about the fireplaces.'

That was to take a lot longer but on 15 May 1912 he told the Vicar, 'The recovery of the fireplaces will be accomplished and announced next week.'

That done, Curzon set about the study and restoration of the ruins, in which he was assisted by Professor Hamilton Thompson, an archaeologist with specialist interest in the castle, and the SPAB stalwart, William Weir. Their work was a model of scholarly research and practical skill. Perhaps the most interesting aspect was to find remnants of a stone-built castle dating from the thirteenth century partly incorporated in the work of Ralph Cromwell some two hundred years later.

Tattershall was not the place which first awakened Curzon's interest in occupying himself with the restoration of a romantic mediaeval ruin. '... on the first occasion that I ever saw Bodiam (I fell) an immediate victim to its charm, and to desire that so rare a treasure should neither be lost to our country nor desecrated by irreverant hands.'

Bodiam Castle lies in East Sussex not far from the Kent border, and had, when built, access by river to the sea. It was the romance of the place which captured Curzon.

> At Bodiam not only does the watery cincture remain, but no trace of the modern world appears to invade the ancient and solitary beauty of the scene; ... (it) transports us at a bound to the days when the third Edward was fighting his foreign wars or the hunchback Richard was casting his nefarious die for the throne. The magic of the scene is enhanced by the rural peacefulness of the surroundings. ... It is environed by parkland and is embowered in trees, and scarcely are any traces of modern agency or of human occupation visible from the margin of its tranquil waters.

That was before he had heard about Tattershall, but the owner, Lord Ashcombe, felt much as he did and would not part with it. Not until 1917 was he able to buy it from Lord Ashcombe's son after his father's death, and not until 1919, when the Great War had ended, could he start on the work of excavation and restoration, for which he again employed William Weir. It is extraordinary how the romantic at once gives way to the scrupulous care of scholarly research and restrained practicality. Harold Nicolson who, in 1925, after Curzon had died, edited the monograph which he had written on Bodiam, writes in a forenote of 'the Castle that he loved with so boyish a passion'. To be able to combine that with respect for accuracy and with restraint in practice forms an ideal for everyone engaged in the care of ancient places.

Curzon's career had proceeded majestically, and he held the office of Foreign Secretary under three Prime Ministers from 1919 to 1924. It was, however, a great blow to him that the third was Stanley Baldwin when he had felt sure that it would be himself. A year later he died, leaving to the National Trust his two restored castles. His will read: 'Convinced that ancient buildings which recall the life and customs of the past are not only an historical document of supreme value, but are a part of the spiritual and aesthetic heritage of a nation, imbuing it with reverence and educating its taste, I bequeath for the benefit of the Nation certain properties which

I have acquired for the express purpose of preserving the historic buildings upon them.'

Curzon's career, eminence and brilliance tend to obscure his deep felt concern for people. The Second Lord Esher said of him, 'His heart was sound enough, but his temper was hasty. What of that? A minor fault.' Rosemary Meynell, writing in the 1970s, recorded the warmth with which country people remembered his kindness and friendship. In a way which is now difficult to appreciate, his benefaction to the Trust, which demonstrated his faith in it as custodian of his work, was a form of accolade which was to raise the Trust both in general esteem and in the regard of other potential benefactors.

More than sixty years after Curzon's death, his lovely Robert Adam house, Kedleston, was passed to the Trust by the present Lord Scarsdale, who had fought long and hard for just such an outcome.

Another benefactor carried the Trust a lot further along the path of preserving buildings with two gifts during the 1930s. Ernest Cook was a grandson of Thomas Cook, the great nineteenth-century travel operator. The Wagon-Lits International had been sold shortly before the Great War – wisely as it turned out – and Ernest Cook had a considerable private fortune and was no longer engaged in business, although he retained a financial interest. He had a London house in Bryanston Square and another in Sion Place, Bath. Although I am concerned here with two particular gifts, Mr Cook continued a relationship with the Trust, and made further benefactions, up to the time of his death on 14 March 1955 at the age of eighty-nine. The complex negotiations of later years to which we must come later must be considered against these first gifts.

There seems to be no record of the reasons which brought Ernest Cook in touch with the SPAB but it is quite clear that the then Secretary, A.R. Powys, had a close and businesslike understanding with him, and interested him in the preservation of Montacute House in Somerset. This exceptionally fine Elizabethan house belonged to the Phelips family. Curiously enough Curzon had once rented it and, despite the claims of his own home at Kedleston, declared it to be the most beautiful house in England. Despite their long tenure – going back beyond the building of the house – Gerard Phelips advertised the house for auction on 3 July 1929. It did not sell, but the event alerted Powys and by April 1931 he had found a donor who would supply the money.

Powys thought that the Society would become the owner but Benny Horne, now advising the SPAB as well as the Trust, held that the Society, not being incorporated, did not have power to hold property. There was in the process of formation an Ancient Buildings Trust which could do so, if and when incorporated, but might not be a permanently secure owner. That was no doubt true, but there is some slight feeling that Horne was working to steer the property to his first love.

The Trust was not immediately receptive. Ronnie Norman wrote to Powys on 10 September 1931:

> It is so important a matter that I think Trevelyan Peel [Finance Committee Chairman] and I should have an opportunity of considering his [Horne's] report beforehand ... I don't think it is necessary to circulate it to other members of the Com'tee ... the National Trust – receiving no money –

should have no responsibility for maintaining – that is clear. But beyond that we should be satisfied that the Ancient Buildings Trust are likely to maintain the buildings properly. If the ABT came to grief and the NT was left with the property we could not let such buildings go into decay without grave discredit.'

Here again the Trust is being regarded as useful mainly because of the guarantee of permanent protection. However, Powys had not waited to hear the Trust's decision. On 3 September Mr Cook wrote him:

> Following on the conversation we had with reference to the suggested purchase of Montacute I now send herewith a banker's draft for £30,000 payable to the order of Midland Bank Ltd. 449 Strand W.C. which please pay in to the credit of the Society for the purchase of Montacute. If, however, you are unable to purchase that property my gift of this amount is to be applied to the general purposes of the Society. Although up to the present time you have not secured Montacute I hope that you may be able to do so.

This very straightforward, generous and entirely unfussy letter was written in Ernest Cook's own sloping regular hand. The next day Powys replied with an equally straightforward and businesslike acknowledgement, adding that if the Society could buy '... the property will be at once handed to the National Trust in the way Mr Horne and I have discussed with you.'

Montacute was indeed secured and conveyed to the Trust in the same year, with a ceremony falling on 11 June 1932 when Lord Esher, on behalf of the SPAB, handed the deeds to the Princess Royal to pass them into the keeping of the Marquis of Zetland for the National Trust.

While conducting this exciting transaction Powys and Cook were engaged on something far more adventurous. Cook, through the SPAB, bought the Assembly Rooms at Bath. Built in the heyday of the spa's popularity in 1791, the Bath stone building contained a splendid suite of rooms, and its fame was passed down to history in the literature of Jane Austen and others. It was sadly decayed though when, on 9 October 1931, Bennie Horne wrote a formal report to the Trust, asking that it take over for the SPAB the premises which had been bought for £30,000.

> At present the main portion of the building including the Great Assembly Room and the Octagon Room are let to a Cinema Company, the filled-in arcade is let as a public house, the card room as a lecture hall, and there are two conservatories let to florists. All these degrading uses of the building are to be done away with but in the meanwhile they produce an income of £2,000, and none of the tenancies can be determined before March 25th 1933.
>
> We have been acting for the SPAB in this matter and have inspected the property. There cannot we think be any question of the great importance of preserving this beautiful building and restoring it to its original condition as far as is possible.'

The SPAB were to manage and maintain the Rooms: 'It has been specially stated by the benefactor who has provided the money that in taking over the property the

Trust are not to be liable for the expense of upkeep ....' Things were not to be as simple as all that. The SPAB could not produce the necessary funds for restoration and subsequent management but secured the interest of Bath City Council who agreed to take a lease at a rent of £500 and to restore and manage the property. There was a difference of opinion over the length of the lease, the Society offering forty-two years and the City wanting ninety-nine. A compromise of seventy-five years was proposed and the Trust's Chairman, Lord Zetland, and Ronnie Norman gave their consent. At that point the donor turned against the lease to Bath and offered to take a lease himself, and when the SPAB began negotiating on his offer he withdrew it, while still maintaining his objection to the lease to the City Council.

That was in 1933 when the leases of the property ended and vacant possession was obtained, but the matter was not settled the following year when Powys tried to get a formal decision, and reported that Lord Esher, Chairman of the SPAB, 'is definitely of the opinion that in the public interest the Society should now ...' agree to a seventy-five year term. Negotiations went forward again but the Donor again intervened and in March 1935 wrote to Powys about the City's plans for the building '... their use as a library would be the greatest possible mistake ... I approved of the idea but since then I have changed my view of the matter. Personally I should regard it as a disaster if those grand rooms are not to be available for concerts or entertainments.'

Ernest Cook goes on to voice a suspicion that Bath are trying to downgrade the future use of the building and to renew his offer to take it over but – 'I cannot make any arrangement with the SPAB after the way your Committee treated my offer ...'. He would, however, be prepared to deal with the Trust. The National Trust took this sufficiently seriously to agree to ask the Bath City Council to withdraw but nothing came of Mr Cook's second offer and on 22 April 1936 *The Times* was able to announce that Bath had taken a lease – this time for just £1 a year – for seventy-five years, and would spend £20,000 on restoration. A year later the Town Clerk told Benny Horne that they had already entered into contracts for over £28,000 and there were still a number of other things to do, so that seemed satisfactory.

The Donor was still restless, and by 1937 was dealing through an agent, Captain Hill, whom we shall meet again, soon. There were more complaints from Mr Cook about the lease to the City and Powys has suggested that it was because of pressure from people who were serving as members of committees of both organisations – (Lord Esher perhaps?). The Trust's Secretary wrote firmly to Captain Hill, 'I can only say that our Committee *knew absolutely nothing* of it ...' Captain Hill replied in a manner which was to recur often over the next twenty years, '... the matter is rather difficult to discuss with the donor but when I see him next I will reopen the subject.'

Despite so much prevarication and so many second thoughts the building was restored and on 18 October 1938 it was formally opened at a Ball attended by the beautiful young Duchess of Kent. The Rooms were a palace of sparkling beauty, and the decision to save and restore to something of its original use was fully justified.

Four years passed and in the Baedecker air-raid of 1942 the Rooms were completely gutted by fire. In 1934 Powys had written to the Trust about the value of the building for insurance, 'I think it unlikely that a greater amount of damage would be done by any fire there.' He could not have known the effect of a shower of incendiaries. The Rooms did rise again from their own ashes, amid further dissensions and problems over money, and they have now become a settled part of the life of the city. But problems still beset the Assembly Rooms. In 1988 they have been closed for urgent repair following the loss of pieces of plaster from the ceiling and walls.

However, Mr Cook, for his part, had placed squarely in the hands of the Trust responsibility for great buildings, the burden of which was to grow year by year and which continues.

CHAPTER VIII

The Nineteen Thirties:
A Decade of Expansion

The decade of the 1930s saw a complete change in the personalities involved in the National Trust. There was a new Chairman, a new Secretary and later new members of staff. New benefactors made their appearance, and new ideas were initiated.

It was in 1927 that Oliver Brett first made his appearance on the Trust's Committees. The elder son of the second Viscount Esher, he was to succeed to the title soon after he joined the Trust. His father had been at the centre of national political life from the latter part of the previous century; adviser to Edward VII and to George V, and his views carried weight with the Governments of the day as well. He was one of Curzon's contemporaries, and his friend. He married an American lady with enough money to enable his son to choose his way of life.

Although he did stand for Parliament as a Liberal before the Great War, Oliver Brett did not really want a political career. His father's aesthetic interests had provided him with an early background in which his own tastes were formed. As a young man he became deeply involved with the theatre, maintaining that interest throughout his life – campaigning particularly for the establishment of a National Theatre – but his real love was architecture. He chose to pursue that through the medium of two organisations – the Society for the Preservation of Ancient Buildings, and the National Trust – while living his life in the agreeable medium of London Society.

His son Lionel, who became a professional architect and a President of the Royal Institute of British Architects (and to whom I owe the foregoing assessment of his father) has pointed out that Oliver Brett's generation had moved from the nineteenth-century obsession with the mediaeval to concern itself almost exclusively with the taste of the eighteenth century and to eschew the Victorian. In consequence, because the period was undeniably one rich in fine buildings, he and his contemporaries looked principally towards the preservation of such works. Perhaps the Assembly Rooms at Bath may be taken as an example of this predisposition.

Chorley first noticed Oliver Brett when he joined the newly formed Publicity Committee of the Trust in 1928, but only a year later he was appointed to the Executive. It was a gift by him of £1,000 which Chorley particularly remembers, since at that time of extreme financial stringency it was an extremely handsome gesture. It was that benefaction, coinciding as it did with his appointment to the

Committee, that gave rise to the story that he had done a deal with Hamer to gain his place. This was certainly quite untrue, but equally the Trust was only too willing to accept the services of a man whose position and means were likely to be of value.

By 1935, when Ronnie Norman wished to retire from the Chairmanship of the influential Finance and General Purposes Committee, Lord Esher, as he had become, was the automatic choice to succeed him. He had been a member of Council since 1931 and in 1936 became Chairman of the newly formed Country Houses Committee in which his influence was to be of paramount importance. He had already been Chairman of the SPAB for several years.

In his son's opinion, Lord Esher was a tough character, intolerant of bores, and hating pomposity. He was rough on those whom he did not like and enjoyed taking the self-important down a peg. Chorley, Christopher Gibbs and others remember him for his wit and puckish humour, but also for his ability to wound. Chorley noticed this particularly with regard to some members of staff, but fellow Committee members were not immune. Carew Wallace, the earliest post-Second War recruit to the staff, remembers him saying to the ageing Sir Edgar Bonham-Carter whose views he found tiresome, 'You really are very old, Sir Edgar!' To a land agent proposing further acquisitions in the old rotten Borough of Newtown Esher was dismissive on the grounds that 'Newtown was such a dreary and boring place.' Simon Buxton, another land agent, saw Esher's quirky conduct as an opportunity. 'If you can make Lord Esher laugh your problems are over.' To be remembered in so personal a way is the mark of Oliver Esher's lively and, in so many ways, delightful personality.

Ronnie Norman was held to be the obvious choice to succeed John Bailey as Chairman. He was much grieved by his friend's long illness, during which he acted as Chairman, but he refused the office. 'I had no objection to doing the work, but I thought they wanted a different sort of person as Chairman of the National Trust. Those were the days when estates did not come pouring in on us in the profusion they do now. We depended largely on the goodwill and favour of the great Landlords. I thought therefore that it was very important that our Chairman should be one of their sort whose words they would heed accordingly and whose example they would follow.' His choice in the end fell upon the Marquess of Zetland. Zetland had at one time been Curzon's secretary, and shared his interest in India, becoming Governor General of Bengal; finally he became Curzon's official biographer. If Curzon, whom he so admired, had entrusted his two great salvage projects to the Trust then surely the chairmanship of the organisation must be acceptable – and it was. He was to hold the position from 1932 to 1945 and during that time the Trust not only firmly established itself in the life of the nation but began to take new and important initiatives.

Zetland was restricted in the time he could devote to the Trust because soon after he took over the India Office. This distancing from the affairs of the Trust has resulted in there being very little personal recollection of him in that role, but two incidents explain both that and his contrasting success. Fedden records how the Secretary, Donald Macleod Matheson, was required to go round to the India Office before every meeting and go through each item on the agenda in detail. Christopher Gibbs, as a young Assistant Secretary, thought like others on the staff that the Chairman had no knowledge of the properties of the Trust and had no interest in natural beauty, but standing in one day for the Secretary on presenting the agenda for discussion, was amazed at the clear grasp that Zetland showed of all the problems. This sort of experience was shared by the Royal Geographic Society of which he was President (as Curzon had been before him!). In that active office he was generally accepted as being a man of outstanding quality.

Chorley has left us a detailed appreciation in which he says that:

> As chairman of a committee, *tout pure* Zetland can have had few equals in his time; certainly he was the best I ever served under .... It was not until one had seen him at work that one realised his true worth. He was a slightly dandified figure who looked as if he wore a corset; his voice was rather unattractive and his delivery somewhat pompous. Indeed as a speaker he had little ability either to make his subject attractive or to hold ... his audience, all of which disadvantages were underlined by an irritating gesture he made by a jerking movement of the head repeated continually .... But he not only knew his agenda, he also had all the material aspects of the subject ... at his finger ends, could evaluate their importance and the weight of the interventions by the different speakers .... Somehow he would cut the long-winded short without wounding them and at the moment that he judged that all the relevant points had been made ... he would sum up in a few masterly sentences ... I cannot remember any occasion when I felt he had made a mistake over this or when his evaluation of the situation was challenged.

These opinions are borne out by the selection of correspondence which has survived in what was his file. It cannot possibly be a complete record but it covers all sorts of subjects over the greater part of the period of his chairmanship and the documents are marked in his own rounded and flowing hand, designating the subject. He seems to have been quite ready to tackle his fellow Ministers in the interests of the Trust and there is correspondence with Lord Swinton (Air), Leslie Hore Belisha (War) and Walter Elliot (Health). Members of the Executive Committee felt free to approach him on their pet subjects, and the Secretary could consult him freely and with confidence. The late 1930s saw the Trust promoting legislation to improve its ability to extend its work and in that Zetland was closely involved as well as trying to help with other amenity legislation in the House of Lords. Taking into account the circumstances of the times – almost equally divided between the slump and the Second War – Zetland's chairmanship can fairly be judged by the record of the Trust's achievements.

The change of Secretary which took place on Hamer's retirement at the end of 1934 was an important one, for Donald Macleod Matheson held the office, also until 1945. A scholar of Balliol, he had risen to be an Assistant Secretary in the Gas Light and Coke Company, a semi-public corporation which was a well-organised and highly efficient concern. Chorley was present when Matheson was interviewed and says that he was quizzed over the drop in salary which would be involved. He replied frankly that this had been a matter for consideration but that he had talked it over with his wife and they were agreed that his health would better stand up to working for the Trust than under the stress he experienced with the Company. In the event it did not, either because he had underestimated the increasing pressure of work in an expanding National Trust or because he was really not strong. Christopher Gibbs remembers him as 'often ill' and indeed letters written on his behalf testify to that while, in 1944, he had almost a full year off work, during which time James Lees-Milne deputised for him.

However, he turned out to be a good Secretary. Chorley regarded him as the ablest of those in his time other than John Winnifrith, the first Director General, and describes him as a man of complete integrity, who never spared himself. Others support this view and say also that he was sensitive and somewhat shy, and that his interests lay mainly with the side of the Trust concerned with the open country. Absence of self-interest is exemplified by his readiness to remain at his own salary level – £1,000 per annum – when in 1942 a Chief Agent, who was to be his subordinate, was recruited at £200 a year more.

Victoria Spencer-Wilkinson had not been surprised when 'the appointment of a bright young man' as Assistant Secretary put an end to any prospect of promotion and so she left and went on a trip to South-East Asia. Bruce Logan Thompson was the bright young man. He had been at Cambridge and he read for the Bar before joining the National Trust. He worked first with Hamer and then with Macleod Matheson at Head Office for some years. Both Christopher Gibbs and James Lees-Milne recall him with affection and describe him as an extremely modest and self-effacing man, whom people were too inclined to take at his own valuation and therefore often underestimated him.

In 1932 Bruce Thompson left London to look after the Trust's affairs in the Lake District with the title of Northern Area Representative. His book on the Trust's properties in the Lake District, published in 1930, has already been referred to. It shows very clearly his knowledge both of the country and of its history. He established himself at High Cross Lodge, Troutbeck, and acted as the first full-time representative of the Trust's Headquarters staff anywhere in the country. He continued in this role after the Trust had appointed a land agent to manage its Lake District properties, and although he retired officially in 1952 he continued to help with the Trust's work long after.

He did serve on the Estates Committee for a while but this was probably neither suitable nor congenial for him. At one meeting in which the discussion developed more on the lines of a business venture than on those of a charitable crusade he made only one intervention: 'Gentlemen, I do beg of you that you have some regard to zeal for the Cause!' His record is best summed up by James Lees-Milne who wrote, in December 1977, after hearing of his death:

> You have no idea what he did for the Lake District where he lived and worked …. He knew everyone in the Lake District, rich and poor, exalted and humble. Not a farmer, not a shepherd did not know and love him. For thirty years or more he literally devoted his life to promoting the Trust's interests up there …. But truly I would put Bruce Thompson top of the list of devoted servants of the Trust, whose work for the Trust was inestimable.

By the mid-1930s the Trust's financial position had improved, possibly due to the activities of the Publicity Committee which produced an increase in membership and in donations and bequests. This, together with the new brooms of Zetland and Matheson, was responsible for the beginnings of a policy of more adequate staffing at Headquarters. Another Assistant Secretary was engaged in 1935. Christopher Gibbs came from the sort of family in which nearly everyone was somebody's cousin. The family lived at Goddards near Abinger in Surrey; the house was by Edwin Lutyens and the garden by Gertrude Jekyll. After Winchester and University College, Oxford, he trained as a land agent and was employed for a while by the then prominent firm of Lofts and Warner. After he left them he was unemployed for a while and he occupied himself in two ways which attracted the notice of the Vaughan-Williams family. He organised a highly successful pageant and fair at Abinger, written by E.M. Forster with music by Ralph Vaughan-Williams, and also became secretary of a committee of landowners in the area of Leith Hill in Surrey. This was chaired by Roland Vaughan-Williams of Leith Hill Place and it successfully concluded an agreement to stop all development in the area, which was subsequently formalised by the Planning Authority. It was an achievement which could not have been managed by the Authority itself, legislation at that time being entirely ineffective without the active co-operation of landowners. So it was that when Mrs Vaughan-Williams mentioned Christopher Gibbs to Macleod Matheson it transpired that the Trust was looking for a land agent. He went for interview before Ronnie Norman, the bushy-browed Nigel Bond and Esher, and he got the job.

Christopher Gibbs had coxed his boat and rode point-to-pointers. He was – and remains – the sort of person who liked to deal immediately with any task, and paper was never allowed to stay long on his desk. Because of the small size of the executive staff he was immediately immersed in National Trust matters, large and small, and in the four years before the Second War he picked up a good working knowledge of much of the Trust's properties, except in the Lake District where Bruce Thompson did all the work. As a Territorial gunner he went off to war in 1939, but Matheson found him in hospital three years later and arranged for his release from the Army to help with the large amount of land which by then had come to the Trust. He was to serve for some sixteen years as Deputy Chief Agent and then a further six as Chief Agent until he retired at Christmas 1966.

In 1936, the year after Gibbs joined, the Trust had found for itself a new mission, the preservation of country houses, and needed someone to deal with that. The job was to go to James Lees-Milne. Alone of all the members of the Trust's staff he has published an autobiography covering the years up to 1941, and subsequently his diaries from 1942 to 1947. He became a key figure in the evolution of the Trust and much will emerge about him as the story unfolds. In the meantime some of his antecedents are particularly relevant to his future work. His home was on the Worcestershire side of the Cotswolds. He went to Eton – to which he attributes special friends, and through those friends to the awakening of 'a love of literature, the arts and above all civilised living'. He did not go then, as many of his contemporaries, to university but through the eccentricity of his father to a secretarial college to learn shorthand and typing. Thereafter his mother took a hand and he went up to Magdalen, Oxford. The experience there of a chance visit to the beautiful house at Rousham implanted in him a desire that the treasury of English country houses should be preserved. At the same time his reaction against the fashionable left-wing policies of the 'intellectual elite' of the University at that time, led to the formation of his own ultra-conservative views.

He came down with a degree in 1931 but without prospect of lucrative employment until his secretarial training got him a job with Lord Lloyd who engaged him 'almost as a joke', and with whom he stayed for three and a half years! 'He was an exacting taskmaster and disciplinarian, for which I am immensely beholden to him. From the start I feared and liked him. In the end I was devoted to him.' There is no doubt that in those years Lees-Milne, who presented himself as woolly and absent-minded, acquired an efficiency and ability to work without which his career with the Trust could never have been effective. It was in order to get him a job with 'prospects' that Lord Lloyd got him into Reuters, which he hated. He was heading for the sack when at a weekend house-party Stanley Baldwin, Prime Minister for the third time, was present. Lees-Milne's grandparents and the Baldwins had been Worcestershire friends and the great man invited him for a pre-breakfast walk to talk about old times. When the conversation turned to Reuters, Lees-Milne suddenly poured out all his troubles. ' "What you must do", he was told with emphasis, "is this. You must get your notice in first. Immediately, without delay. Tomorrow morning … Having done so you must not repine. Friends will come to your rescue".'

So they did. The Trust was launching its Country Houses scheme and needed a secretary; Vita Sackville-West recommended him and he was appointed. Mr Baldwin was a good friend always to the National Trust but in his advice to Jim Lees-Milne he probably did it more good than at any other time.

At Head Office Miss Patterson was by the mid 1930s running the office and, as Christopher Gibbs found, mothering everybody. She had been joined by Winifred Ballachey who was responsible for keeping records and for the correspondence filing. Perhaps her most important duty was the keeping of the muniment book in which all legal documents were listed. Since the Trust's landed estate was already quite big, and much fragmented, both the deeds by which a property had been conveyed to the Trust and the tenancy and similar documents which regulated its various uses were very numerous indeed and vitally important to management. Winifred Ballachey's scrupulous care not only ensured that every document could be traced and found, but enabled her to acquire an amazingly comprehensive knowledge of properties, few of which she would ever herself see. Both ladies were in very different ways warmhearted and friendly and maintained in a growing organisation the necessary thread of continuity and stability which became extra important during the Second War and its aftermath.

It is too easy to give the impression that the Committees of the Trust were not productive of significant personalities other than a few dominants. Nothing could be further from the truth and to restore the balance I shall look at a few who may in some measure be both representative and at the same time made their own individual contributions.

One such personality was Colonel Edward North Buxton, an East Anglian of the same family as the E.N. Buxton who had been prominent in the Epping Forest case in the 1860s. A brewer by trade, he was a keen amateur of natural history, and had been on the Executive for some ten years – (from 1924) – without making much of a mark when his interest seems to have been caught by the National Parks movement. The Addison Committee sat in 1929 to take evidence and with Chorley and the Council for the Preservation of Rural England Buxton became very active in its promotion. In appearance he was large, with slightly protuberant eyes, wore a heavy, drooping moustache and hairy tweed suits. His speech tended to come in barking staccato sentences. At first sight he might have been the archetypal Colonel Blimp. That was by no means the case: he was endowed with an innate courtesy, had a well-informed mind and a great deal of common sense, allied to very strong principles. He was affectionately known as 'the Boomer', or 'the Reverberator'. Chorley claims that Buxton once showed him a bittern's nest and was tickled to death by the coincidence. This combination of qualities which he put to the service of the Trust – on the Council, the Estates Committee (of which he was Vice-Chairman for fourteen years), the Executive and numerous sub-committees until 1957 – may be regarded as characteristic of the qualities which have given ballast to the central policies of the National Trust.

There is always room for the eccentric, at least in small quantities, and this in the 1930s was supplied by a rising civil servant, Herbert Gatliff, an Assistant Secretary at the Treasury. His devotion to the preservation of the countryside led him to work for the Youth Hostels Association and the Trust. He was a great rambler and it was said that first thing on a Monday morning he might be seen mounting the stairs to his Whitehall office in khaki shorts with a rucksack on his back after a weekend's hiking. He was brimful of ideas which he communicated to the staff by writing at length, in pencil, on something which appeared to be very like lavatory paper. If this could be deciphered it often contained a great deal of sense and his suggestions were offered without any touch of arrogance. At a time when many of the Trust's policy-makers thought largely in terms of open space preservation he was among the first to urge the importance of preserving farmlands too.

Major H.M. Heyder was the opposite of Gatliff. Tall, reserved and gentle he had retired from the Indian Forestry Service and from the 1920s until the early 1950s acted as Honorary Adviser on Forestry. He treated this task very seriously, and visited every newly-acquired property which had any degree of need for the management of trees. His reports were full and detailed, admirably clear, and contained sensible and practical prescriptions for management. It is to the credit of Hamer and Matheson that they did not hesitate to make full use of him; in a country and at a time when the practice of forestry, in the sense of properly caring for trees and woodlands, had fallen into abeyance, the Trust consciously did its best to take a positive and constructive attitude to that part of its responsibilities. To Major Heyder the Trust also owes the first atlas of its properties, for the production of which he paid.

The Trust's growing land holding and its lack of resources both of knowledge and of staff to deal with management were responsible, so Christopher Gibbs says, for the appointment to the Estates Committee of Captain John Birrow Hill, a land agent. West Wycombe village which had been acquired from the Royal Society of Arts in 1934 was under John Hill's management and it was this contact that led to his joining the Committee. He had a bluff, direct manner. He had little interest in the side of the Trust which aimed at the preservation of the countryside and especially of open spaces for the enjoyment of the, mainly, urban population. He did, on the other hand, care deeply for the traditional rural estate, its proper management and the welfare of its tenants. Because he came to act for Ernest Cook and negotiated for him with the Trust over benefactions intended and effected, he will appear again. In the meantime, with his short figure and bluff, direct manner, he added a John Bull image to the Trust and, Christopher Gibbs says, dictated to the Estates Committee on management matters.

From many benefactors of the Trust it is difficult to select examples, but three stand out, all of very different characters. Most of us know of Beatrix Potter as the author and illustrator of classic children's books. To the National Trust, however, she was Mrs Heelis and her long life spans the period from the Trust's origins to its achievements in the first third of the twentieth century.

Although Beatrix Potter was born in 1866 to wealthy middle-class parents, living a formal and restricted life in London, her antecedents were firmly in the north-west. On her mother's side she was a Crompton from Chorley Hall, her great-grandfather Abraham being described as a crusty, eccentric radical. Among other land he owned a farm at Tilberthwaite in the Lakes, which he had bought 'for pleasure'. Her paternal grandfather, Edmund Potter, had been born of poor parents in Manchester, prospered in textiles and became Member of Parliament for Carlisle. He was a radical, a friend of Cobden and of Bright, and a dissenter in the Unitarian Church, through which he became a friend of the Gaskells. This tough independent and commercial background was not apparent in the circumstances of Beatrix's early life. Rupert Potter, her father, though qualified as a barrister, followed a leisured life in which he devoted himself to draughtsmanship and photography and the routine of spending a month away at Easter and three months in the summer every year with his household.

Beatrix had an isolated childhood, spending the greater part of her time painting and studying natural history. A scientific interest in the subject is illustrated by the stories of her capture of small animals, her skinning, dissecting and the boiling down to the skeletons of mice and frogs. Over a period of fifteen years from the age of fifteen she kept a journal in code which was not discovered until nine years after her death, in the attic of Castle Cottage, Sawrey, bequeathed to the National Trust under her will. It was not until 1958 that it was deciphered by Leslie Linder and it was published in 1966. The journal shows from the very beginning a girl with an acute and observant mind, wide interests and a talent for trenchant comment, no respecter of persons or reputations. If Octavia Hill's aesthetic taste was formed by Ruskin, Beatrix was exposed to that of Sir John Millais, her father's friend whose studio she frequented. '10th June 1882. Went to the Academy. Think it rather bad. Few striking pictures many simply shocking.'

In July that year the Potters rented Wray Castle on Windermere for their long summer holiday and her father's photographs of Beatrix show a smallish, not unattractive girl, with a confident, almost bold look. Hardwicke Rawnsley was incumbent at Wray at the time and they met for the first time. Hardwicke's tenderness towards young females may or may not have been extended towards Beatrix but they became and remained close friends. Her biographer, Margaret Lane, says, 'To Beatrix he was even more appealing, for in the warmth of his mental and physical vigour, which was prodigious, her shyness melted and she made the stimulating discovery that it was possible for grown up people to have enthusiasms.' Hardwicke's grandson, Conrad, goes a lot further:

> We know that from early in their friendship there was ardent hero-worship on her side for Hardwicke. It is a compelling thought that there might have been something deeper than this …. Would Hardwicke have sought to take Beatrix instead of Eleanor as his second wife had she not already been married to William Heelis three years before Edith's death? My father (Noel Rawnsley) always believed that he would and that Beatrix would surely have accepted him.

During her journal years Beatrix was often in the English Lakes and, in 1896, was staying with her parents in a house at Sawrey (then called Lakefield, now changed to Ees Wyke). Although socially still tied either to her mother's apron strings or her father's coat-tails, she did enjoy considerable freedom on these holidays. When riding her pony up to Troutbeck she saw 'an aged shepherd … much bent and gesticulating with a stick. … This aged Wordsworthian worthy, awoke the echoes with a flood of the most singularly bad language' [directed at his dog].

Some review of Beatrix's early years has been necessary in order to see in perspective the next two phases. With her own money she was able in 1905 to buy a tiny farm called Hill Top, in the village of Sawrey. This was her first effort to gain some independence from her parents. She had already written and illustrated a children's book about a rabbit called Peter and on Rawnsley's advice had submitted it to Frederick Warne's. They turned it down so she eventually published it herself and upon sending a copy to Warne's was rewarded with acceptance, provided that she produced coloured illustrations. Thus began her writing period: in the succeeding eight years she published thirteen stories, which provided an income which was to grow into a small fortune. Her contact with Warne's also brought an open romance into her life for the first time. Norman Warne proposed marriage in the same year that she bought Hill Top, but her parents objected strongly (their daughter was only thirty-nine!). Before matters were put right Norman Warne was dead.

Beatrix had achieved a degree of emancipation and in 1909 with her increasing income bought Castle Farm, adjoining Hill Top, and there she made her home, marrying in 1913 her solicitor, William Heelis. This seems to have completed the emergence from the chrysalis of the individual that the journal reveals had always been within it. Beatrix gradually cut down on her writing activities and, in her own words, became 'almost sick to death of Peter Rabbit'. Instead she turned her attention over the remaining thirty years of her life to farming, the promotion of the Herdwick breed of sheep, and the preservation of the Lake District.

Until 1920 she had Hardwicke Rawnsley to inspire her and to be her point of close contact with the National Trust, and from the time of her marriage she began to subscribe towards National Trust projects. She was, however, mainly engaged in learning and practising the special sort of farming needed in the Lakeland fells and, as her means accumulated, extending her own holding. Her major stroke was to buy in 1923 the 2,000-acre Troutbeck Park, and its herd of 'hefted' Herdwick sheep. (Hefted stock are those bred year by year on the same fells and which, within limits, will stay there without being fenced in.) She believed in hill farms of a proper size.

104

As she wrote to Eleanor Rawnsley, 'Smallholders are hopeless; first they sell off all sheep stocks, and then they cut all timber, and then they concentrate on hens.' She was quite clear in her view that the beauty of the Lakes and the system of farming were indissolubly linked. Her vigorous commonsense, business aptitude and grasp of Westmorland sheep farming received its accolade when she was elected Chairman of the Herdwick Sheep Breeders Association, and from that eminence she was in a position to direct and lecture the National Trust on its policies.

In the mid-1920s Mrs Heelis was sixty and from subsequent correspondence with Hamer it is clear that she already intended to leave her land to the Trust, but it was not until the autumn of 1929 that she became involved directly in the acquisition of property for the Trust. James Marshall of Monk Coniston wanted to sell the rest of his estate (Monk Coniston Hall and the low grounds had already gone) and in a stream of letters to Hamer she plotted to secure it. There had been some muddle between them over a joint project at Wray, on Windermere, when the Trust failed to buy at auction a parcel which could have given a lake frontage and the chance to recoup by re-selling back land. She was not going to let Coniston be a muddle: she would buy the whole and re-sell a large part to the Trust.

The vendor was a problem: 'He is so erratic it may mean anything or nothing.' That was when he first told Mrs Heelis he wished to sell. Then there was a tremendous hiccup: 'There may be a disaster. Mr. J. Marshall is afraid that his London solicitor Mr Owen has sold the whole to the Forestry Commissioners. He has telegraphed to stop it .... J.M. is like a child. Provided he was allowed to fish for the trout with which he stocked his tarns, he apparently would not be difficult to deal with.' In a postscript to the same letter: 'Mr J.M. does not know it is the Trust he is swayed by the hope of money paid down; and the fishing. Let him fish for life! it is but a poor one, he is a reckless driver. If he is still free I think we had better close with anything reasonable.

Close she did, though not without making it very clear to Hamer that she would require the Trust to take much of the estate off her hands. 'I will say at once I cannot afford to present anything to the Trust, much as it would please me to do so – because this speculation means selling out what is the mainstay of my income, and replacing it by rents. And if the Trust has friends who would buy and present Tilberthwaite and Tarn Hows [parts of the estate] it would need to be taken into consideration that these were the plans. I could not be expected to sell them on the mean average per acre and find myself saddled with the rubbish.' One of her problems was that she was especially fond of Troutbeck and wanted to keep money in hand to add to it. 'Apart from a sentimental interest in Holme Ground – and a strong desire to help save a most picturesque region – I have no feeling of affection for Coniston at all.'

She was also hampered by the presence in the district of her widowed mother. 'My mother is known to be so rich that no one would subscribe to help *me*! She is hopeless. I tried in vain to *borrow* money at the time of the Wray sale.'

In the end it all went as planned, although slowly. Sir Samuel Haslam Scott subscribed to pay for Tarn Hows, Lord Esher gave for Holme Fell and it was Beatrix Heelis herself who paid, under promise of anonymity, for her great-grandfather's former farm, Holme Ground in Tilberthwaite. In all more than 2,500 acres came to the Trust, which slowly repaid the balance of its debt to Mrs Heelis. A year later she had secured to add to her part of the property the smaller estate of the Thwaite, and was writing to Hamer to know whether when the next rents came in, 'do you anticipate being able to pay off a little more?'

This was a magnificent and strategically important addition to the Trust's estate, equal in area to a quarter of what had been accumulated over thirty-five years. It was part of the deal that Mrs Heelis should manage the property for the Trust. She had indeed already been worried about how the Trust, acting as it did through a series of Local Committees scattered throughout the district, would be able to cope properly with an increasingly large estate. Hamer had, in 1929, called a conference of the Lakeland Committees and told them plainly that the time was coming when the Trust would have to employ an agent. Mrs Heelis was seriously alarmed.

> The speech you made ... was momentous as regards the Trust. You ranged definitely and publicly with the landlords. I think it was inevitable sooner or later but I did not realise you might have to 'go the whole hog'; an *absentee landlord with a typical land agent*. I think that is the system which has made what socialism exists in the countryside. I thought you would have to have an agent sooner or later – but oh dear – oh dear; – Mr Hamer, I *did hope* he would be a gentleman. I said something joking to Bruce Thompson – if he didn't like London – some day he must retire into one of our houses and manage our estates in the north.

Bruce Thompson did, as we know, go to be the Trust's representative in the north and the success of that move must be credited at least in part to Mrs Heelis. Not that one would think so from letters in 1938 and 1939 to Matheson, full of complaints about Bruce, 'I regret heartily that I ever presented Holme Ground to the Trust ... he [BLT] seems to have no understanding about anything; and he is not learning either.' Then again: 'A man cannot help being born dull. Thompson is supercilious as well.' When Matheson took issue with her – 'I did *not say* Mr Thompson to be unsatisfactory as the Trust's representative in the Lake District. What I said was that he shows no judgement in dealing with trees and woods at Coniston.' Poor Bruce!

By this time Beatrix was seventy-three, and the farming years had taken their toll in arthritis and rheumatism. She had always been sharp, even when its only expression was in her journal. She had long before acquired a reputation for being 'formidable'. So Benny Horne told his god-daughter Bunty and her sister Ruth when he took them to tea with her while on some Trust business in about 1928. 'On no account talk to her about her books, she doesn't like it.' However, she turned out to be very friendly, taking a liking especially to Ruth who at twelve was already a forthright sort of person, which may have appealed to one who was herself outspoken. She took them upstairs at Hill Top and showed them some of her original illustrations, especially Tom Kitten all rolled up in pastry for the rats to cook and eat him. 'I thought then she looked like Mrs. Tiggywinkle. She was fairly short, greyish, with twinkly eyes. She was delightful to us.'

In a letter to Samuel Cunningham in 1936 she made clear both her policy and her eventual intentions:

> For years I have gradually been picking up land, chance bargains, and specialising on road frontages and valley heads. I have a long way towards

3000 acres .... It is an open secret that it will go to the Trust eventually ....
I own two or three strikingly beautiful spots. The rest is peaceful country,
the foreground of the hills, I think more liable to be spoiled than the high
fells themselves.

'Eventually' was to be 1943 when she died peacefully at Castle Cottage, Sawrey.
From her and William Heelis, who outlived her some three years, the Trust
inherited about 4,000 acres in all and a substantial sum with which to buy more land.
Hill Top, Castle Farm and half the hamlet of Sawrey came too, and now forms such
a place of pilgrimages that its popularity threatens to destroy it. In July 1988 William
Heelis' solicitors office in Hawkshead was opened as a gallery to display Beatrix
Potter's artwork and provide information on her life and work in the Lake District.

Few can really understand the importance to the Trust and to the nation of what
Beatrix Potter did. It was she who brought the Trust into the full comprehension
that the English Lake District is made and maintained by its farming and, as she
lectured the Trust in her lifetime on the proper conduct of its management so in her
will she took care to enjoin similar standards. 'My house property shall continue to
be let at moderate rents to the same class of tenants as heretofore, and my farms
shall be let at moderate rents to good tenants.'

The Herdwick sheep, so dear to her, were to be retained by the Trust for there was
a danger that changing fashions in breeds might tend to oust them. 'Hunting by
other hounds or harriers shall be prohibited over my Troutbeck property.' (Not
foxhounds, of course, because hill foxes are a menace to lambs, and only at Troutbeck
where the area was sufficiently large to make the enforcement of the ban
practicable). Beatrix Potter's real memorial is, and should remain, the standard of
management of the Trust's now immense Lakeland farm property.

Rosalie Chichester was a very different sort of person, but another who loved plants,
animals and the beauties of nature. She was an almost exact contemporary of Beatrix
Potter, born one year earlier, 1865, and dying six years after Beatrix, in 1949. There
had been Chichesters at Arlington in North Devon since the fourteenth century and
they continued prominent and influential in the county. Rosalie's grandfather had
served in the Navy and then sat as Member for Barnstaple from 1831 through the
three subsequent elections. He was honoured with a Baronetcy in 1840, dying in
1851, to be succeeded by his son Bruce, who was still a minor.

Sir Bruce Chichester married in the year his daughter Rosalie was born. His wife
was a daughter to Thomas Chamberlayne of Cranbury Park in Hampshire and the
connection is of importance because Chamberlayne was a noted yachtsman whose
cutter, the *Arrow*, was the only British yacht to beat the *America*, after which the
America's Cup is named. Sir Bruce followed the mid-Victorian pattern of expensive
entertaining which involved among other things substantial additions to his father's
charming but relatively small house, Arlington Court and the purchase and
maintenance of a schooner of 276 tons, the *Erminia*. Rosalie at the tender age of
three went with her parents on a long Mediterranean cruise and as a girl of twelve
enjoyed a similar adventure. She became and remained fascinated by the sea and
ships.

She was only fifteen when her father died, leaving her his sole heir and she continued living at Arlington with her mother, who outlived her husband by twenty-seven years. She never married, although she was an attractive young woman. Her father's high living had left the estate deeply in debt and mother and daughter changed their lifestyle accordingly. Not only was Rosalie less of a catch for an aspiring husband than she might have been, but their retired mode of living brought her less into society.

There is no record of the way in which Miss Chichester's attention was drawn to the work of the National Trust but, in 1909, the year after her mother died, she made a gift of Morte Point to the Trust as a memorial to both her parents. This triangular headland, thrusting out into the Bristol Channel, guards the immense expanse of Woolacombe Sands from the north. Dropping from over 500 feet at its landward end, in sweeping undulations to low, rocky cliffs and clothed in sheep-grazed turf, with wild flowers and bracken and furze brakes, the views from it are breathtaking. Beyond the point extends a reef of razor sharp rocks to the Morte Stone and the tides surging up and down the funnel of the Bristol Channel turn this sea into a race of tumbling white water, where on one night alone in 1852 no less than five ships foundered.

Rosalie Chichester continued to add to her gift until 1920, in the course of which she must have come into contact with Hamer (Nigel Bond had been Secretary of the Trust when her first gift was made). At all events she was writing to him in terms of acquaintanceship on 12 May 1921, 'I am anxious to leave the National Trust a large piece of land, chiefly woods, as a Nature Reserve and also as a "beauty spot". This will include two farms and will bring in an income of about £400 a year.'

Miss Chichester was by then fifty-five and had devoted much of her energies to paying off the encumbrances on her properties, which she eventually did in 1928. She must have succeeded sufficiently by the time she wrote her proposition to Hamer to be reasonably sure that she could leave at least that part free from mortgage.

The proposal was enlarged three years later when, almost to the day, she wrote again, by this time presumably having made more progress with her retrenchment. Her economies had not stopped her indulgence in travelling, which had been one of her main occupations over the years. The letter was written in pencil because 'I had a severe illness in New Zealand in January 1923 and am still an invalid and can only write lying down.' This was sixteen months later. It had not stopped her from thinking things out very carefully. She had

> added by two codicils some more land and a sum of money (£25,000) the interest to be spent on the estate .... May I suggest that the estate be kept separate from the house ... so that it may be used as a National Park, such as one sees in Australia and N.Z. though of course on a smaller scale, where the native plants and birds are not interfered with – unless the Trust should find it necessary in the interests of the Estate – and at the same time a place where the public can enjoy the scenery etc.

'I should like to feel that Arlington Estate which has been in the family for considerably more than 500 years remains much as it is at present.' She wound up with some sensible points – the house was close to the road and there would be no need to use the very long drive, by which in carriage days the Chichesters had reached the Barnstaple turnpike: she would prefer the house to be used as a Home of Rest or convalescent home, with its furniture: but – 'these are *only suggestions*, the Trust may have other views.'

By 1933 her plans had matured and in a letter to Hamer (undated but to which he replied on 24 November) she sums up the position with clear foresight and judgement:

> My affairs have all been settled and my Trustees instructed if the National Trust does not accept my terms, they [the Trustees] are to make other arrangements, so nothing can now be changed.
>
> It is not at all likely there will be any surplus as there is much to be done during the next 50 years or so, when there is sufficient money in hand – For instance the farms and cottages will have to be rebuilt or modernised. I was trying to do something towards this when the War came and heavy taxation put a stop to this. No one in future will be content to live in the present style of house and rightly so. The houses will probably have to be rebuilt or greatly altered. Then again wages will certainly rise and you will not get a staff of suitable *trustworthy* men unless they are well paid. It will be necessary to have 2 Parkkeepers in addition to the usual staff, as one cannot always be on duty. These men *must* be well paid and of a superior class as one should act as overseer and be able to shoot to keep down vermin ....
>
> A large place open to the public must have 'parkkeepers' about. At present our staff manage as best they can and we live here and see to things but in the future there must be responsible men about who are interested in their work.
>
> Then the fence will have to be kept in order and part if not all renewed from time to time, perhaps a more substantial fence will be found needful, this may cost some thousands.
>
> The big pond [The Lake] should someday be cleaned so that the island where the herons build is surrounded by water .... The Lake adds to the attraction of the place but during the last 50 years or more has been filling up with mud carried down by the stream. When I was a child I used to go out rowing with my father who had a boat and we rowed where now there is dry land, shrubs and small trees! Besides the usual upkeep of a place, wages, replanting, the above expenses must occur from time to time. It would be well to keep something in hand in case of an expected rise in taxes and such like.
>
> This house would have to be let at a nominal rent unless very great improvements are carried out for no one but ourselves would live in such an old fashioned place.
>
> Excuse such a long letter but I wanted to explain matters and to show you you need have no fear of a surplus, rather the reverse.

Miss Chichester had been developing her idea of her nature reserve and the fence to which she refers was an extraordinary affair: some eight miles long round the lake and woodlands of the valley of the River Yeo, it was built with iron posts and angle iron palings about eight feet high, pointed at the top where they sloped outwards.

109

It was expressly designed to keep intruders out, especially hounds, for both the Devon and Somerset Staghounds and fox and other hounds hunted the district.

In 1926 Jan Newman was engaged as Houseparlourman at Arlington Court, where he joined a staff which consisted of a lady's maid, two housemaids, a cook-kitchenmaid, an 'odd man', two daily women and a laundrymaid. He was sent to sleep in Kennel Cottage for no males were allowed to sleep in the Court. His main duties, laid down for him by Miss Chichester's companion Miss Peters, were to be the Hall and the Dining Room. 'The Hall enthralled me,' he wrote fifty years later, 'with its great cases of stuffed birds, butterflies and albatross, a kangaroo and a large bear; while on the tops of the cases were sets of Famille Rose china, great dishes and vases decorated with animals and insects. One morning, dusting these, I had my first glimpse of Miss Chichester. I dropped the top of a vase. "What has the boy done?" I heard her exclaim. From then on I was the Boy.'

The house with its staff and the estate with its fourteen men – keeper, woodman, driver, gardener and builders – continued in its accustomed way until the Second War. In 1939 Miss Peters died, Jan went off to the RAF and Miss Chichester never left the house again. She had kept in close touch with the Trust and in 1936 gave Potters Hill, a great 30-acre lump behind the sands of Morte Bay – writing that she had 'made some paths the hill being too steep for elderly people ... I should much like to give the hill now to commemorate the King's [George V] Silver Jubilee.' There was also long correspondence about the incidence of Estate Duty on her death and in March 1946 she conveyed the Arlington Estate of 2,780 acres to the Trust, subject to her own life interest, a move which eliminated the problem of taxation. She retained the ownership of her other properties including that around Woolacombe.

At Miss Chichester's death, in 1949, the Trust became fully possessed of beautiful country and a charming house, and collections of such variety and originality that they, as well as the woods and park, give intense pleasure to over 70,000 people who see them year by year. The business of taking up the reins of management was difficult and exciting. That story comes later.

Different again and delightfully unique were the benefactions of Ferguson's Gang. Anonymous in their own time, it is possible now to trace at least some of their identities through their secret contacts with the Trust. What this latterday 'Robin Hood' organisation achieved for the National Trust is known and recorded: the preservation, restoration and endowment of Shalford Mill, near Guildford and the Old Town Hall at Newtown in the Isle of Wight, and the Priory Cottages at Steventon in Oxfordshire, the acquisition of Mayon Cliffs and Trevescan Cliffs at Sennen in Cornwall: a total cost of £3,500 – contributions to fourteen separate appeals.

The Gang was formed in 1927 and held an official banquet; it recruited more members over the next few years before starting its nefarious work for the Trust in September 1931. The Gang members were at the time clearly disturbed by the furore over the sale of Stonehenge Down. Their meeting passed a resolution 'That England is Stonehenge, and not Whitehall', which was passed and 'universally carried'. Then toasts were drunk to, among others, 'England', 'The National Trust, England's preserver' and 'Ferguson and his Gang'. A constitution was drawn up whose main aim was the preservation of England and the frustration of 'the Octopus' (creeping urbanisation?).

Ferguson's Gang and its colourful members (the Bloody Bishop, or Beershop, Red Biddy, Sister Agatha, Bill Stickers and the rest) were extremely active over the next few years in raising donations and saving properties for the Trust. Many of their exploits were chronicled in the popular press of the day and, in February 1932, the *Evening News* revealed something of their identities to its readers: 'The 'gang' was formed by a young Society woman who, after a brilliant career at Cambridge University came to King's College and banded her friends together under the name of the "Ferguson's Gang". She is the grand-daughter of an Earl whose name is one of the best known in the land. It is nothing like Ferguson!

'Her husband is a well-known author, and they live in one of the prettiest spots in Devonshire .... There are now five young Society women in the "gang" .... Each is devoted to the preservation of British beauty spots, and they use some of their money to this end ... Their wish, one of them told me yesterday, is to do whatever good in this way they can, and to remain completely anonymous.'

One of the properties rescued by the Gang was the eighteenth-century water mill at Shalford which they purchased and provided with an endowment for its upkeep. The first instalment of the endowment was delivered in characteristic fashion: 'A few days ago one of the "gang" visited the offices of the National Trust in Buckingham Palace Gardens, S.W.

'She was masked and announcing herself as "Red Biddy", deposited with the secretary £100 in silver and hastily left in a taxicab.' (*Daily Mail*, 1 February 1933).

It would be wrong to leave the people of the 1930s without special reference to Stanley Baldwin (later Lord Baldwin of Bewdley). His family had been yeoman farmers in Shropshire, moving from there at the start of the mechanical age to Stourport in Worcestershire, where they entered the iron and steel trade. They prospered and in that trade Baldwin worked, not entering politics until he was over forty. In the works he was directly accessible to any employee and the firm never experienced a strike or stoppage. Sometimes his co-operation with his workers was unconventional, to say the least, such as the occasion when one of them wanted his broken iron bedstead mended – for which permission was given – and had to be smuggled into Baldwin's house through the back door and out through the front so that its owner might not be teased by his mates as to the cause of the breakage!

His daughter, Lady Lorna Howard, from whom that story comes, knew her father as a man with a deep love of the country and of country things. His recreation was walking, often in the Forest of Wyre, and he indulged in a passion for pigs.

From October 1922, Baldwin became Chancellor of the Exchequer and was long remembered with affection for reducing excise duty on beer by a penny a pint. Then, in 1923, he succeeded Bonar Law as Prime Minister for nine months of office and took office twice more – from 1924 to 1929 and for a National Government from 1935 to 1937. In 1925, Baldwin published a small book *On England*. In one passage he wrote:

> To me, England is the country, and the country is England. ... the sounds of
> England, the tinkle of the hammer on the anvil in the country smithy, the

corncrake on a dewy morning ... the sight of a plough team coming over the hill ... The wild anemones in the woods in April, the last load of hay being drawn down a lane as twilight comes on ... the smell of woodsmoke coming up in an autumn evening.

These are the things that make England, and I grieve for it that they are not the childish inheritance of the majority of people in our country today.

Little wonder that Stanley Baldwin was so ready and willing to lend his name to the Trust's appeals – Stonehenge, Ashridge, Avebury, the Farne Islands – and in each case was joined by the other party leaders. No Prime Minister before or since has more often or more publicly given support to the Trust. The value of this support at that point in the growth of the Trust was of exceptional importance. In his own time – with his bowler hat, his pipe and his phlegmatic manner – he was regarded as the typical Englishman. We can also say that with his love of the country and his care for his fellow men he represents too the moving spirit of those who worked for the National Trust.

CHAPTER IX

Land Use
and
Country Houses

In 1928 the Publicity Committee of the Trust was formed and it continued in being until 1969. Lord Chorley remembered this as one of the first matters in which he was involved, because he was lobbied on the subject by Rupert Thompson, a member of the Trust who had not previously taken any active part. The idea, once formulated, seemed as do so many new ideas, long overdue and Chorley needed little persuasion to put it forward. Mr Thompson, 'a businessman, of a quiet rather refined personality who lived in one of the terraces in Regent's Park', needed equally little persuasion to become Chairman. So the Committee came into being, with one of the big guns of the advertising world on it, Sir Stuart Campbell. Despite his role as midwife, Chorley showed some distaste for the work of the Committee – which he left in 1932 – and only gave a grudging acknowledgement of its achievements. It was, however, probably much more successful in those early days than it has appeared to those who have looked back after the Second War.

One indicator of its success is the rise in membership. In 1928 this stood at 1,550 and in five years rose to 2,750, at a time when the effects of the Depression were at their worst. This figure rose again to 7,250 in 1938 and was 15,800 ten years later. For this rise the pre-war Committee must take a lot of credit.

In particular the Committee enjoyed very good relations with the Press and the radio. The former can be judged by the coverage given to Ferguson's Gang, and to the friendly nature of the reporting in all the papers. The links with *The Times*, in particular, had been very close from the start and there was an unwritten rule that new acquisitions should be first announced in its columns. Appeal letters no longer had to have the Prime Minister's signature to gain publication and follow up letters reporting progress seem to have been welcome. The BBC gave air space to broadcast appeals and to features on preservation.

The Committee's realistic approach is best demonstrated by its use of the cinema, a suggestion which, Chorley claims, originated with him. This was as forward looking as using television in the 1960s. It certainly took the Trust into every part of England. Even F.A. Holmes saw one of the films and was reluctantly impressed by Mr Hamer's recorded commentary. Credit for one series of films goes to the Council for the Preservation of Rural England where John Arkell, with Chorley's support (in his CPRE role) made a series of films which tended to use National Trust properties and consequently benefited both organisations.

Annual members' dinners were arranged, splendid affairs in venue, menu and speakers. Chorley on one occasion suggested that George Winthrop Young should be asked to speak and he did do so, possibly persuaded by his friend George Trevelyan. The famous mountaineer must have appealed very strongly to the outdoor, rambling and climbing fraternity which constituted an important section of the Trust's supporters.

After the Second War the Trust was to be served by quite a string of paid staff who included publicity in their duties. Indeed for three years from 1946 Gwynne Ramsey had a full-time appointment, but he went on to great success in the commercial world and subsequent Assistant Secretaries took on the work as part of their responsibilities. The appointment of Peter Ryan in 1958 helped the Trust through the difficult period of the 1960s but the Publicity Committee itself never seemed to recover the authority and purpose of its early years and with the appointment of a Director of Public Relations in 1969, its existence ended.

One particular enterprise, undertaken in 1935, was in the end a great success and remains today the one thing by which the majority of people, members or not, recognise the National Trust. That is the creation of the Omega symbol. As the Trust reported in its February 1936 *Bulletin* there were something like three hundred properties, nearly all of which needed some form of notice. A standard form was needed, 'which would be easily recognisable by the general public but would not offend when placed on mountainsides, in woods, in meadows or on ancient buildings.' So a competition was organised with a panel of distinguished judges: William Ormsby-Gore, Kenneth Clark, Lord Crawford, Guy Dawber, Charles Holden, Sir Charles Peers, Frank Pick, Sir William Rothenstein. The panel received 109 entries, none of which was considered suitable! The judges then held a restricted competition, inviting only six proven designers to submit drawings incorporating either a lion, a rose or an oak. They selected the one submitted by Joseph Armitage, whose studio was in Lambeth and who had worked on the King's Beasts outside St George's Chapel, Windsor. He had chosen the omega shape to be different from the ordinary run of notice boards, and felt the oak leaves were less often used in heraldry and easier to reproduce than a lion or a rose.

Christopher Gibbs as a new Assistant Secretary had to go to Lambeth to organise the production of the symbols. A standard plate was made onto the back of which were fixed the bye-laws, printed on metal, and telling the visitor 'IT IS FORBIDDEN'! This was later changed to 'PLEASE AVOID' but a diligent search may reveal genuine originals still lurking here and there. Fifty years further on the National Trust, feeling the need to make its open space preservation work more apparent to the general public, is relying to a considerable extent on the better and more widespread use of the Omega symbol. A house style manual, advising on how the Omega symbol should be used on concepts as diverse as signposts, printed material and information boards, is being prepared by the Trust's Production and Design Manager, Marjorie Norman.

In 1930 the Pilgrim Trust was founded by Edward Harkness as a grant-making charity with an initial fund of 2 million pounds. Its first Chairman was Stanley

Baldwin, then out of office. Dr Tom Jones, was appointed Secretary. No doubt the appearance of so rich a benevolent institution started a buzz among hopefuls throughout the country; if so, the National Trust was no exception. In October that year John Bailey reported to Ronnie Norman that Hamer had been in Wales 'staying with a man who is an intimate friend of Jones' and would find out how best to approach him. This was done with such effect that, by early 1931, Hamer was on close terms with the Secretary whom he addressed as 'Dr Tom'.

The Pilgrim Trust was to become a regular and significant benefactor of the Trust, but more important by far than the money was the spring of an idea which it released in George Trevelyan's mind. On 8 January 1931, Trevelyan wrote a confidential letter to Hamer in which he recounted a long discussion he had had with Dr Jones about the formation of a new, and secret, relationship between the Pilgrim Trust and the National Trust. The idea was that the Pilgrim Trust should provide a 'large sum' (£100,000 was mentioned) to the National Trust for the purchase of land in advance of any threat of development. Trevelyan was particularly concerned with the preservation of the coastline. He felt that such an arrangement would allow the National Trust to have 'a forward policy, and go out to find out places of beauty to buy beforehand, instead of waiting till they were already attacked by the estate breaker and bungalow builder.'

Jones was sympathetic to the idea and promised to sound out some of his trustees, also in confidence. Hamer responded promptly to a part of Trevelyan's letter which cast the Pilgrim Trust in the role of tidier-up of unfinished appeals, suggesting that it should 'finish off Longshaw, provide the Haresfield endowment and finish off Coniston, Polperro and Bolt Head. £5,000 should do this.' He also sent to the Pilgrim Trust in February a statement on the National Trust and its work, a draft of which had accompanied Trevelyan's letter. John Bailey was active too, going to see the Pilgrim Trust Chairman and lobbying John Buchan, MP, who was one of the Trustees. 'No one knows better than you or Mr Baldwin that present developments are, not slowly but very rapidly, destroying the face and beauty of Britain.' Bailey may well have felt that his status as a literary critic of high repute gave him an especial leverage with Buchan, and he went on to press the exceptional urgency of the needs of the National Trust.

The first grants were made on 18 February 1931. £5,000 for the Trust's administrative costs; £1,000 for preliminary investigations for forward planning. Hamer recruited three investigators for Welsh projects, two to look at Snowdonia and one for Pembrokeshire. Trevelyan had earlier mentioned the latter, saying of Tom Jones, 'the idea of Pembrokeshire touched him on the Welsh nerve.' Others became active, Ronnie Norman and Lord Northbourne reconnoitring the Dover Cliffs and Sir James Berry, who lived at Dunsmore near Wendover, putting forward a plan for securing part of the Chilterns. All this activity resulted in a long report to the Pilgrim Trust in July 1931 which suggested purchases in nine different areas: the Chilterns, the Lakes, Dovedale, the Malverns, the cliffs of Dover, Snowdonia, the Pembrokeshire coast, the Devon coast, the Seven Sisters in Sussex. The report wound up with an 'order of precedence':

'1. Snowdonia *or* the Pembrokeshire Coast
2. Malvern Hills

3. Dover Cliffs or Seven Sisters

'Smaller schemes to which we would call your attention are Gatesgarth and Glencoin (which would add to existing properties) and the Devon coast (which would assist a further acquisition).

We have instructed our investigators in each case to survey their areas from the point of view of camping and the reports are nearly all favourable.'

The last sentence is of interest since it indicates a special interest on the part of the Pilgrim Trust in the positive enjoyment by people of the land to be preserved.

This submission took some while for the Pilgrim Trust to digest and in January 1932 it finally turned down the Seven Sisters proposal on the ground that 'it should not be impossible in such an area so near the large urban populations to raise the remainder of the fund required.' What had really happened was that the Depression had hit the Pilgrim Trust's investments. Even in 1934 Tom Jones was obliged to write that, 'owing to the American situation the amount of income available for this year for grants is severely restricted.' The immediate result of that was that of three appeals – Wembury on the South Devon coast, Watersmeet on its north coast and Dovedale – only the last received a grant.

There was a small problem the same year which illustrates how right the Trust was, and is, to avoid being involved in anything which might smack of expropriation by the State. There was a joint attempt by the Trust and the Pembrokeshire County Council by which the Trust, using Pilgrim Trust money but keeping its provenance secret, would supply the Planning Authority with the funds needed to pay compensation. The County sent a memorandum to all coastal landowners to explain the scheme and mentioning the involvement of the National Trust. One recipient was the Earl of Cawdor, whose Stackpole Estate lay for ten miles or more along the south coast of Pembrokeshire. He was furious and wrote very sharply to the Trust to say so. He was particularly resentful of clumsy phrases which implied the possibility of compulsory purchase. Matheson seems to have laid his fears to rest but the incident was a disagreeable warning.

There were repeated efforts to mount operations which would make use of Pilgrim Trust funds, such as setting up a revolving fund to help a scheme to preserve country houses and another to buy property through the Trust's company, Countryside Trust Limited (which had been set up to handle matters which were outside the Trust's powers), and to hold it until a big appeal could be launched. The only venture which really got off the ground was the Pembrokeshire Coast Appeal, launched inauspiciously on 5 April 1939. Based on Pilgrim Trust money and with purchases actually in the bag before it started, it achieved in the few months left before the Second War a modest success, which features later in the chapter on coastal preservation.

In September 1939 the Pilgrim Trust closed its office at 10 York Buildings, which in 1940 was blown up by enemy action. Its money had been a help, but what was really vital to the National Trust was the Pilgrim Trust's part in arousing it to the necessity and practicality of having a 'forward policy'.

In the 1920s a benefaction had been made which set a precedent for a whole new range of activity by the Trust twenty years later. Aside from its intrinsic importance, it introduces another set of benefactors in the Cadbury family. Edward and George Junior were grandsons of the Quaker John Cadbury who founded the Birmingham chocolate business, the former becoming Chairman until his retirement in 1939. They both had houses on the Lickey Hills south of the city and in effect created a green belt by buying considerable areas of land there which they then gave to the City Council, the Bourneville Trust or to the National Trust.

The first gift to the Trust was made in 1925, although the idea had been conceived eighteen months earlier, George Junior writing to Hamer that:

> We have already given a considerable area to the Birmingham Corporation, but have not been entirely satisfied with the management of the land under their care. At the same time they or the County seem the proper persons who should ultimately hold it. We do not anticipate that the land would be required immediately for the public. The probability is that we should wish to go on with our tenancy for some years. At the same time we are anxious to safeguard it from ever being spoilt.

When the gift of the seventeenth-century Chadwich Manor and 414 acres of farmland and woods had been made, John Bailey wrote to *The Times*:

> The point I wish to emphasise is that it marks a new departure. It is a gift of a new kind. What Mr Cadbury and his brother are giving us is not a large open space to be handed over to the public as a recreation ground. We have many of these and hope we shall receive many more. But there is a limit to the amount of land that can be so sterilised. Yet land not sterilised at all but still devoted to the ordinary purposes of agriculture add immensely to the amenities and the beauty of the neighbourhood of towns. That is the purpose of this gift, the first of its kind. The object of it is to preserve an agricultural and pastoral oasis in the midst of what may become a merely urban or suburban district. Access will be given where possible by paths up to the hills. But the farms will remain farms and will not become parks or playgrounds.

The precedent thus established by the Cadbury gift was recalled in 1934 when negotiations were in hand for the gift by prospective devise of the immense Wallington Estate in Northumberland by Sir Charles Trevelyan, George's elder brother. Benny Horne, in commenting on a draft of the will, asked whether the acceptance of a devise 'of an estate of this magnitude' was one that could safely be promised. He saw that the house, garden and park clearly came within the objects of the Trust, but did that great extent of farmland? The only other case he could quote where the Trust held land like that was at Chadwich Manor, 'but this is only 430 acres and will shortly be surrounded with built up land.' He thought it probable that the Charity Commission might not intervene to prevent it but he feared that the Treasury, contemplating the loss of revenue from Estate Duty, would persuade the Government to do so.

The Cadbury family were to make several more benefactions but none more important than the gift of Chadwich Manor.

A new form of land use came into being in 1919 with the formation by the

117

Government of a Forestry Commission. Lack of timber had plagued the country since the seventeenth century. The Secretary to the Navy, Samuel Pepys, was driven to distraction by the scarcity in the royal forests of good oak suitable for ship building and the cost and difficulty in time of war of importing Baltic fir for decking planks. The rural revolution of the next century reversed this in some measure, the now wealthy landowners using the planting of timber trees as an investment for the future. However, their successors in the second half of the nineteenth century were to find their market eroded by cheap timber from the New World and British forestry went into a long decline.

During the first of the two World Wars the rate of shipping losses from enemy action and the shortage of home-grown supplies prompted the Government to set up a Commission with the Secretary to the Board of Agriculture, Francis Acland, as Chairman. It was on the basis of his report that it was decided to set up a Government agency, not only to re-establish crops of timber in previously existing woodland, but to establish wholly new forests. The second task was one which had enormous potential for changing the face of the hill country in Britain. In the first place, it was only practicable to afforest really big areas where land was cheap and agriculturally relatively unproductive. In the second place, the greatest need was for coniferous timber and conifers, particularly those from North-West America which grow very well indeed in the generally wet climate of British uplands.

It was in the Lake District that concern was first expressed about the effect which large-scale afforestation would have. This is not surprising, because the comparatively small area of the district and its intensive use for recreation make it more sensitive to change than are the Pennines or the mountains of Wales or Scotland. The Forestry Commission bought land early on in Ennerdale, which provoked no opposition – the Patron Saint must have been snoozing – until planting began. Then Chorley's friends in the Fell and Rock Climbing Club found that the rough tracks by which they had been accustomed to reach their climbs were planted out and their movement over the fells much restricted and obstructed. This the Club first tackled as a local difficulty, and the resulting discussions brought Chorley into contact with local foresters and with the details of their work on the ground.

The National Trust became involved possibly because the Commission's Chairman, Sir John Stirling Maxwell, had been since 1905 an elected member of the Council and since 1906 on the Trust's Executive Committee, (and so remained until 1945). Chorley considered him 'very sensitive to natural beauty'. Representations were made to the Commission and an account sent to *The Times*, the upshot being that a lease for five hundred years from 1927 of 3,624 acres was granted to the Trust. This was largely land which was not economically plantable and it may be asked what the gain was. In landscape terms perhaps little, but it demonstrated an apparent willingness on the part of the Commission to consider 'amenity' and showed the Trust making a public stand against afforestation in the wrong place.

In 1932 there was a change of Chairman in the Forestry Commission, Stirling Maxwell being succeeded by Sir Roy Robinson (later Lord Robinson of Kielder, his title being taken from the vast forest he created on the moors of Northumberland). This former Rhodes scholar was ambitious and energetic and ruthless in the prosecution of his task, which he saw primarily as the establishment of great new forests. In the uplands the Commission's choice for its main plantings was the Sitka Spruce. Unfortunately it is the least attractive of coniferous trees, its branches rigid and angular, its outline spiky and its foliage an uncompromising bluish green. Not until it approaches maturity does its great size give it a certain splendour. This was the tree with which Robinson was rapidly clothing huge areas of the hills of Britain when, in 1935, it was announced that the Commission had bought 7,000 acres for afforestation in Upper Eskdale and Dunnerdale.

This time there was a real uproar. The forces of preservation had been strenghtened by the formation of the CPRE. Locally the Friends of the Lake District were strongly entrenched and represented by two vocal and lively characters, Kenneth Spence and the Rev. H.H. Symonds. Within the National Trust, Trevelyan and Chorley with their very strong local connections were deeply concerned.

According to Chorley, Trevelyan made an independent move, entering into discussion direct with Robinson to achieve a concordat by which the Commission would agree not to afforest land in the centre of the Lakes in return for a reasonably free hand on the fringes. Certainly Trevelyan, as Chairman of the Estates Committee, reported to the Executive on 11 February 1935 to that effect. Chorley says that the exclusion zone was to be limited to Borrowdale and the adjacent valley heads, and that Trevelyan strongly recommended agreement. The Trust was only prevented from selling the pass by his, Chorley's, request, as the Trust's representative on the CPRE, that no final decision should be taken without consultation. He then went off to see Herbert Griffin, now Secretary of the CPRE. The upshot was the creation of a Joint Informal Committee of the Forestry Commission and the CPRE, which was to deal with all matters of amenity where afforestation was concerned.

Their first consideration was the Lake District. By July 1936 a report was issued recording an agreement that the Commission would voluntarily respect an exclusion zone of some 300 square miles, taking in virtually all the Lakes except Ennerdale, which had already gone, and the valleys to the south. The parties differed on the latter and the CPRE would not accept that the Commission should have a free hand there.

Nevertheless the agreement was a tremendous achievement and has served to keep the heart of the Lake District free from endless disputes and from the actual damage that afforestation in that place would have caused. Was Trevelyan prepared to settle for a lot less? He was certainly a pragmatist and recognised that half a loaf was better than no bread. Likewise Robinson was shrewd and tough. It may well be that Trevelyan thought that it was the best deal likely to be achieved and Chorley in his concern may have overestimated Trevelyan's commitment to it. Among the signatories to the 1936 Report were Robinson and Francis Acland, Trevelyan and Edwy Buxton. John Dower (who had married George Trevelyan's niece, Pauline) did all the groundwork. But it was far from all over, although Baldwin may have thought that it would be settled when he made a statement to the House in February 1936, in reply to a question by Geoffrey Mander. 'The Commissioners have now decided on a scheme for planting only 1,600 acres out of the total area of 7,240 [Eskdale and Dunnerdale].'

The subsequent history of that particular area illustrates only too well the need for persistence in the battle for preservation, because a quarter of a century was to pass

119

before the Forestry Commission finally parted with its land. The Commission, in restricting its planting, had agreed to enter into a covenant with the Trust that public access would be permitted to the 5,580 acres of fell that would not be planted. This had not been completed by 1941 and, when pressed, Sir Roy Robinson said, 'It might be the duty of the Forestry Commission to make a new set of terms, and throw over all the agreements made.' That is hardly an attitude which invites confidence, and indeed it was not until 13 August 1943 that a press statement recorded the completion of the undertaking.

The disagreement within the Joint Committee was still unsettled in 1950. By this time the National Trust's land agent in the north was Cuthbert Acland, youngest son of Francis, and he supplied to the Secretary a draft memorandum covering the whole range of the Trust's objections to further planting – both amenity and agriculture – which was sent on to the Commission. It provoked a somewhat dismissive response from Owen Sangar, the Commission's Director: Acland described it as 'snooty'! The whole question was becoming one of particular urgency for the Trust, not only because of the general threat to the landscape, but because their own property would be gravely affected. In the complex and almost unalterable conditions of hill sheep farming the separation of fell land from farmsteads in the dales creates insoluble problems. The Trust had owned Cockley Beck and Dale Head farms since 1929, and in 1943 had paid compensation to the Commission for an undertaking that Butterilket should not be planted. The Commission's continuing itch to plant up Blackhall Farm would have produced just such a problem.

Acland began secret negotiations with the Land Commissioner of the Ministry of Agriculture. He not only had responsibility for agricultural interests but would act for the Forestry Commission if there were to be a sale. Acland's worries increased because he had news that the Forestry Commission was making a positive effort to enlist the support of the Ministry of Agriculture and the National Farmers' Union. There were to-ings and fro-ings in the ranks of the Trust and the CPRE and continuing prevarication by the Commission at both local and national level. An effort was made in 1956 by Lord de la Warr, as Chairman of the Estates Committee, to get the Minister of Agriculture, Derrick Heathcoat-Amory to settle the business. It was not until 1958 that John Hare, his successor (who later as Viscount Blakenham was to give great service to the Trust) finally recorded in a letter to Lord Esher, 'we must be very careful not to spoil such a beautiful part of the country' and agreed to a sale.

So, in 1961, Blackhall Farm of 2,700 acres and Butterilket of 3,300 acres were conveyed to the Trust, the money being found from a bequest by Miss A.M. Goodwin, whose family had enthusiastically approved that use for the money back in 1955. H.H. Symonds's part in this is enshrined in his gifts of four small farms, and by the gift of a fifth by the Trustees of his memorial fund in 1963.

Only the Lake District could have provided a battleground on which the forces of amenity had a chance of winning on such a scale. For the Lakes that was a good thing. But there was a much wider result: the pros and cons of large-scale afforestation were publicly examined and the Commission forced to realise that some care would have to be exercised in future afforestation proposals in sensitive areas. The Trust learned that the only way to be sure of securing land against damaging afforestation was to own it, and it has often acted on that lesson since.

Events at the Annual General Meeting of the Trust on 19 July, 1934, radically changed the character of the National Trust's policies towards country houses. The crux of the matter was outlined in a speech by the Philip Kerr, Marquis of Lothian. He argued that:

> ... the country houses of Britian with their gardens, their parks, their pictures, their furniture and their peculiar architectural charm, represent a treasure of quiet beauty which is not only specially characteristic but quite unrivalled in any other land ... Yet most of these are under sentence of death, and the axe which is destroying them is taxation, and especially that form of taxation known as death duties.

He went on to review the increase in rates: 8% in 1904, 15% in 1914, then 40% and from 1930 50%. He was not attacking the system, 'there is indeed much to be said for them as an instrument of social justice ... But let no one mistake that they spell the end of the old rural order.' He went on to quote Winston Churchill ('with whom I do not always agree') – 'the world tides which are flowing will remorselessly wash away all that is left.'

With the help of *Country Life*, he estimated that there were about sixty large (over twenty bedrooms and a suite of state rooms) and six hundred smaller houses. Not so numerous, he thought, to be an impossible task for preservation. He postulated one very important condition: '... preserve includes use as a dwelling house. Nothing is more melancholy than to visit these ancient houses after they have been turned into public museums ... If they are to be preserved, they must be maintained, save perhaps for a few great palaces, for the uses for which they were designed, ...'

One measure of protection would be achieved if the Treasury would exempt them from death duty and allow the cost of their maintenance against tax, provided that the organism was kept intact and public access given 'from time to time'. He saw this as 'part of that new order of planned private enterprise which is coming to replace both the unrestricted individualism of the early capitalistic era, and the universal socialisation of early Socialist thinkers.' This would, however, only be palliative and unless something more was done '... the big houses, at least, will be stripped of their contents, the roofs will be taken off to escape rates, the gardens will run down to weeds, and the parks will become the prey of the speculative builder who sees site value in proximity to an historic ruin.' It was specifically for these larger houses that Lord Lothian saw a role for the Trust. He drew attention to the effect of the 1931 Finance Act which exempted from Estate Duty – and from aggregation of its value for the taxation of other property – any land given to the Trust to be held inalienably.

The Trust's correspondence file, opened in 1932 to deal with the legal problems which were eventually dealt with in the National Trust Act 1937, has much material on it which relates to the preservation of country houses. For example, a report in 1932 from Horne and Birkett shows dissatisfaction with the powers available under the 1907 and 1919 Acts, because the splendidly entitled Mortmain and Charitable Uses Acts prevented donors from retaining a life interest if they gave property to the Trust. Leases back to donors were also subject to doubt as to their legality. The Trust knew that wider powers were needed if Lord Lothian's ideas were to be put into practice.

Whether the intentions of Sir Charles Trevelyan with regard to the future of his 13,000 acre estate of Wallington in Northumberland were independently formed it is not possible to say, but within two months of Lord Lothian's speech Benny Horne was considering a 'Draft Scheme of Proposed Testamentary Gift' by Sir Charles.

> Sir Charles proposes to devise the Estate ... to the National Trust. He feels that the National Trust would be the most suitable owners of a house of such historic interest, and containing collections of such beauty and value as Wallington, and of an estate so attractive to the public for its wildness, its extensive views, and the beauty of its woodlands. He has the fullest confidence that the National Trust will be able to develop both of them for the use and recreation of the people and that they will observe his wishes as expressed hereunder.

The document provided that, 'The house is to continue to be the home of the Trevelyan family as long as the Testator's wife or any of his children are alive ...'. Failing his own family the Trust was to be free to choose, but to give consideration to his descendants or those of his brother George. 'In any case in selecting a tenant Sir Charles would express the hope that they would consider the suitability of such a tenant's social outlook rather than the length of his purse.'

Benny Horne saw two problems; the first to which reference has earlier been made in connection with the Trust's holding of enclosed farmland, was whether the Treasury would regard it as being eligible for exemption from Estate Duty. The other was that the reservation of a right for the family to live in the house would render the devise invalid. There was no progress on Sir Charles's idea for some years, but the existence of a proposal in so definite a form made virtually at the same time as the Lothian speech suggests that Sir Charles had been developing his intentions for some time.

In June 1935, Zetland and Norman went to see the Chancellor of the Exchequer, Neville Chamberlain, and put before him the points on which legislation would be needed as set out by Horne three years before. Their presentation was unwise, if truthful, because they admitted that their proposals would not go far to saving country houses and the Chancellor batted the ball smartly back into their court, 'I quite agree, and think that some more comprehensive effort is needed to deal effectively with the problem.'

Nothing is clearer evidence of Lord Zetland's close concern with the business of the Trust than his involvement in its Country Houses Scheme. By the end of 1935 he had settled in his own mind how things should go in the long term. He wrote out a note which Matheson was to put to the next meeting of the Finance and General Purposes Committee. This proposed the formation of 'a Country Houses Association as a Branch of the National Trust.' He set out in detail the composition of its Management Committee, giving Trust nominees a majority, asked whether it should be under the ultimate control of the Executive and, if not, how was control to be preserved. 'I am anxious to avoid the risk of the proposed Association starting off as an independent body,' he wrote. 'The organic link between the Association and the National Trust should be I think, the proposed Committee of Management.' Looking to the future, he said, 'the new Association will become before long something more than an organisation for promoting the throwing open of country houses to the public and advertising them. I believe that the only effective way of preserving the country houses permanently will be getting them transferred to the National Trust.'

By January 1936 Matheson had had discussions with country house owners and particularly with Lord Methuen of Corsham Court near Bath. He and Lady Methuen had made a study of the state-sponsored French scheme, *La Demeure Historique*, which had branches in Belgium and Spain. They were on the point of starting an English branch, but agreed to hold their hand and give the Trust a chance. Matheson, who had been continuing the informal talks with the Treasury, had now been asked to deal with the Office of Works so that the proposals could be formalised. He had drafted a memorandum which could be sent out to owners – perhaps some thirty or forty – so that they could attend a meeting at which the proposals would be discussed and a committee formed.

The established position of *La Demeure Historique* made it at the very least a starting point from which the Trust's new and very different campaign could start. Accordingly, on 25 February 1936, there was a reception attended by many of the owners of important houses – Lord Salisbury and Lord Londonderry among them – at which the Duc de Nouailles explained the French system. Lord Zetland already had in mind a person to take the chair – Lord Kennet who had been at the Treasury and a Minister of Health. However, when approached Lord Kennet pleaded pressure of other obligations and declined, and so did Ronnie Norman, the second choice. In the end Lord Zetland himself took the chair with a Committee of eleven others, five of whom were National Trust Committee members. Among the others were the Marquises of Lothian and Salisbury, Lord Methuen and his friend Sir Alexander Lawrence, formerly Treasury Solicitor. It was in March 1936 that the Trust recruited Jim Lees-Milne to be Secretary to the Committee, at a salary of £483.12s.0d a year. It is possible that this appointment was, in the long run, the biggest single reason for the eventual success of the scheme.

This Historic Country Houses Committee issued a memorandum which was circulated to 250 owners in July 1936. It began with the premise that little could be achieved without Government help and that the Government 'have intimated that if the National Trust can submit for their approval a list of important houses, whose owners are desirous of co-operating in the scheme, they may be prepared to consider granting concessions, including possibly a measure of relief from taxation, upon conditions which would assure to the nation at large some corresponding benefit.'

There were two proposed courses for owners to take. Scheme 1 envisaged a gift of a house to the Trust, with an endowment to maintain it, and with right to reserve to himself, his son or daughter to be a tenant. The Government's part would be to exempt the whole transaction for death duties and the endowment from income tax and to arrange that the reservation should not be in breach of the law of property. In return the owner was to open the house and garden to the public at a reasonable charge for a minimum number of days – probably about thirty. He would keep all except ten per cent of the takings which would go to the Trust as an advertising levy.

Scheme 2 was very different. In this case the owner would retain the freehold of his property but make a capital contribution to a fund to be held by the National Trust as trustee for all owners participating in the scheme. From this fund the Trust would make grants to any participating owner as and when it became necessary to

123

do work to maintain the house. The fund once in being would not attract death duties and the Government would exempt it – and grants made from it – from income tax.

By October Matheson was ready to report to the Committee. Either he or Lees-Milne had seen forty-two owners and would have seen more had the timing been better, but too many were away in August and September either on the grouse moors of Scotland or abroad! Jim Lees-Milne produced a long report listing responses:

No. circulated	250
Replies	83
Seen	42
Definite refusals	10
Scheme 1. possible acceptances	9
Scheme 2. possible acceptances	6
Favourable to either scheme	41
Ready to collaborate at a more advanced stage	24

The more detailed responses were predictable – few really wanted to part with their houses – Scheme 1 – unless they had no heirs and had a strong wish that their estates should remain intact after their deaths. Others could afford to make the gift but not to endow it. Others again had their only capital in house and land and could not part with it at all.

The main objections turned on the fact that the Government had not agreed to give relief from death duties to reservations in favour of a widow or children if property were left to the Trust. In response to that the report says:

> ... it has been explained they would be invited to put their faith in the unbroken record of the National Trust always carrying out the wishes of testators and in their declared policy always to let houses to the families of the previous owner. Many owners have been impressed by this assurance especially when told what irreparable harm would be done to the reputation of the Trust, if in any one instance the National Trust disregarded their pledge.

This is the first record of the device which has come to be known as the Memorandum of Wishes, a document not legally binding upon the Trust – and therefore not attracting the penalties of legally binding reservations – but one which by formal resolution of the Executive Committee the Trust promises to honour to the best of its ability. It has become a cornerstone of the preservation policies of the Trust.

As to Scheme 2, 'Nearly every owner who has replied to the memorandum or who has been interviewed has shown undisguised and bitter disappointment over this Scheme.' One can scarcely wonder at that, nor that owners 'would not be prepared to contribute money which might well be expended on someone else's house.' Curiously enough the Earl of Harewood found the idea attractive, but the Marquis of Salisbury sensibly pointed out that the fund would have to be enormous if it were to be of any appreciable assistance to impoverished members of the scheme.

There was an interesting division of opinion as to whether opening of houses was profitable. Lord Harewood complained that he was put to great expense by char-a-bancs using his drives at Harewood House, and Mrs Roper at Forde Abbey pointed out that the public require constant supervision in the gardens as well as the house and that the mess made involves much labour for her staff. On the other hand Mrs Whitmore Jones of Chastleton advertised extensively and was believed to maintain her property on admission fees. Today there is still a division of opinion on this matter.

The report wound up with the recommendation to concentrate on Scheme 1. As to Scheme 2, it was thought that there was scope for some loose organisation like a country house owners' co-operative, assisted in some small measure by Government in terms of minor tax reliefs, but otherwise free from Government interference. Forty years later indeed something very similar did emerge in the Historic Houses Association. The report was accepted and the Scheme 1 policy adopted. Lord Esher took on the chairmanship of what became a wholly National Trust committee and the Country Houses Scheme as generally recognisable in its final form emerged. Lord Zetland and Macleod Matheson must be given their due share of the credit. Indeed the latter continued to be an important mover in the advance of the scheme. There is no doubt, however, that Jim Lees-Milne's report was the basis on which the scheme was built.

The Trust was far from being out of the wood, but the next three years were busy ones in which Jim Lees-Milne conducted a wide correspondence with enquiring owners such as Admiral Meade-Featherstonhaugh of Uppark in Sussex and Squire Ketton-Cremer of Felbrigg in Norfolk, the second of whom had discussed the matter with him. Every enquirer received a copy of the booklet which explained the scheme.

One of the legal obstacles to an owner co-operating with the Trust arose from the practice of entail, whereby property was in effect placed in trust and the successive 'owners' were only tenants for life. Their heirs had a right to succeed to the property which could not be alienated from them. This was modified, adversely from the Trust's point of view, where a tenant-for-life had power of sale. The value realised remained in trust for the successor but the property as such was gone. In order to get over this the Trust embarked upon further legislation which eventually emerged as the National Trust Act, 1939, which gave power to vest settled lands in the Trust. These had to be declared inalienable and a lease had to be granted to the tenant for life and his successors. There was a provision that should any beneficiary of the settlement object then the Trustees of the settlement would have no power to proceed.

This is dry stuff, but it is necessary to understand that power in England had for centuries been based on landed property: the English country house had become the citadel and treasury of the power base. The campaign to remove it from its exposed position on the battlefield, obliged its would-be rescuers to penetrate and dismantle all the defences which had been erected to protect it. They had almost – but not quite – succeeded.

It is a relief to turn to some positive progress: in 1937 Sir Geoffrey Mander, the

MP who had intervened to save Harts Head and had raised in the House the problem of forestry in the Lake District, gave his house of Wightwick Manor in the West Midlands to the Trust. In 1936 he had been staying with Sir Charles Trevelyan, who had told him of his negotiations with the Trust, and he wondered whether something of the kind might not be done with Wightwick. This really was a poser: the house was only fifty years old, built by the Liverpool architect Edward Ould for Theodore Mander, paint and varnish manufacturer. Its furnishings had been heavily influenced by John Ruskin and the Pre-Raphaelites: William Morris wallpaper, tapestries and tiles, Kempe glass and de Morgan tiles. The charming, secluded garden with its terraces had been designed by Alfred Parsons, RA. 'The house is furnished in appropriate manner and contains the original bed in which Charles II slept for two nights after the Battle of Worcester in 1651 at a house two or three miles away.' That was the best Sir Geoffrey could do. 'The place is not, of course, of historic interest but it is a singularly attractive example of modern half-timber work in Elizabethan and Jacobean style, and the inside is as good as the outside.'

Poor Matheson, how could he recommend acceptance, and how could an offer with an endowment be refused? He tried to explain how it was different from Wallington, without much success. He was saved by a favourable report by Clifford Smith of the Victoria & Albert Museum, and by Lady Trevelyan who, as a member of the Executive Committee harbouring a Pre-Raphaelite hall at Wallington, bullied the Trust into acceptance. On Sir Geoffrey's part the transaction stands out as a model of its kind: there were no quibbles, no second thoughts, no prevarications. That this house, a celebration of Pre-Raphaelite taste and of the teaching and practice of William Morris, should have so early found its way into the care of the Trust has been a stroke of quite remarkable good fortune.

There was no other advance to encourage the Trust. Lees-Milne went off to the war and the most Matheson could do, in March 1941, was to record that Lord Lothian had confirmed that he would leave his house and estate at Blickling in Norfolk to the Trust; that Hatchlands in Surrey, with its Adam decoration and Repton park had been offered – the first settled property to be considered – and accepted. Stourhead in Wiltshire had been accepted as a devise, but seven other proposals had gone wrong for various reasons, including Canons Ashby in Northamptonshire, where the owner had died and his successor was not favourable.

In February 1942, Lord Esher addressed a memorandum to Lord Zetland and the Committee. 'I am disturbed by the failure of the Trust to obtain any considerable number of country houses, and by the apparent difficulty of reaching agreement between the Trust and those owners who have shown an inclination to take advantage of our services.' One problem was a blemish in the 1939 Act which left endowment funds liable to death duties, but the main one was the endowment itself. 'I hear on all sides that we ask too much, that our standards are absurdly high, that we do not understand or try to appreciate the owner's point of view ...'. The Trust, he said, sought to cover itself and 'In pursuit of this ideal we look askance at water derived from wells, old fashioned central heating, at inadequate bathrooms, at ill-paved roads and unscientific farm buildings, handicaps to which the owner has long been accustomed .... Making it clear that in our eyes his house is little better than a pig-sty, we allocate money in the endowment to improve all this, on the plea that, although his affection for his ancestral home may make him blind to the squalor in which he lives, we have to think of days when his family may die out or not wish to live there any more. We conclude by capitalising our dreams at 3%, thereby producing a figure fantastic in this owner's eyes.'

Disregarding for a moment the technicalities around which the Trust's policies were formulated, it is necessary to remind ourselves of the condition of the times. Despite the extraordinary generation of wealth in the nineteenth century and the widespread provision of such things as supplies of mains water, electricity and sewerage in towns, such things were still far from universal in the country, where the seventy-year-long depression of agriculture had applied a brake to progress. The Trust was operating at a time when, although the scale was soon to tip the other way, few could envisage that there would be any change or need for change. Zetland responded sympathetically, agreeing that the endowment was a problem but also reminding himself that it was necessary to protect the Trust 'from contingencies which are quite likely to arise'.

Lord Lothian's death in 1942, whilst working as Ambassador to the United States, fulfilled his démarche of 1934 by bringing to the Trust his exceptionally lovely house of Blickling in Norfolk and, as an endowment, 4,767 acres of farmland and woods, with estate houses, little villages and, as an uncovenanted bonus, a number of minor buildings beautiful and valuable in their own right. This must be regarded as the event which marked the end of the beginning, even if the Wallington negotiations and the gift of Wightwick antedated it.

Another house, West Wycombe Park in Buckinghamshire was even then in the process of transfer. The Trust's tiny headquarters staff, evacuated from central London because of the danger of bombing, was miserably ensconced in one of the even tinier Lutyens pavilions on Runnymede where they were discovered by Captain John Hill, agent for Sir John Dashwood, who was engaged in transferring his house and park to the Trust. John Hill coerced both his principal and Matheson into a move which established the Trust's Head Office at West Wycombe until 1943, even though the formal conveyance of the property was scarcely completed. This act of autocratic kindness was typical of Hill. It was to this new location that Lees-Milne, blown up by a near-miss in London in 1940 and subsequently invalided out of his regiment, rejoined the Trust. The country house story is very much his until, in 1951, he withdrew from his work as Secretary to the Committee, becoming Adviser to the Trust on Historic Buildings.

While the consultations had been going on in the 1930s there had seemed to be little progress but the publicity and the discussion which Lees-Milne had been engaged in with numerous owners created a climate of opinion in which the Trust's final scheme was seen as a possible option. As early as 1938, the little Devonshire manor house of Bradley outside Newton Abbott was given to the Trust. Great care had been taken to retain all the features of its many periods, even the Gothick Victorian barge boards which Lees-Milne referred to as its 'frilly underwear'. In later years this modest, but architecturally fascinating house, with its equally modest and sometimes shabby furniture, was to suffer in the Trust's regard in comparison with the grand mansions with their elaborate furnishings and rich treasures.

It was on 11 May 1942 that Lees-Milne went to see Miss Davy, who was Lord Astor's private secretary. The cause of this encounter was Lord Astor's intention to give Cliveden, with its gardens and woods above the Thames, to the Trust, with as little delay as possible. There was to be an endowment of £200,000 and the Canadian Hospital, established for the Canadian Red Cross in the Great War, would bring in the enormously high rent of £3,000 per annum. Lees-Milne established a wholly proper nephew-aunt relationship with Miss Davy, which enabled him to deal with Lord Astor's insistence on an immediate answer. The hospital rental, if secure, would have at least reduced if not obviated any need for an endowment. Miss Davy explained that it did not really matter so much to Lord Astor since the incidence of taxation was such that it would reduce his income by only £150 a year.

Cliveden had been so grand a house, and Lord and Lady Astor's political entertainment had brought it such publicity between the wars, that there could scarcely have been a more newsworthy boost to the Trust's scheme. Concurrently, another Buckinghamshire owner, Lord Courtauld-Thomson, offered his house Dorneywood near Burnham Beeches, subject to his own and his sister's life interest (they were each approaching eighty). With it went £30,000 endowment at once and a further £170,000 on his death. The idea was that, like the much grander Chequers Estate, it should be used as a residence for a Cabinet Minister. The details were modified later, but the Trust seems to have had little hesitation about accepting the gift, despite the fact that architecturally the house was not of great importance.

In September 1943 Lees-Milne got news of another house which was to come to the Trust. Mrs Ronnie Greville had left Polesden Lacey near Dorking with something approaching 1,000 acres, together with the residue of her estate. On a lovely site, in a garden with eighteenth-century features, the house itself was in essence a simple neo-Grecian villa. After Mrs Greville bought it in 1906 she had 'Edwardianised' it, regardless of expense. Mrs Greville had been a Society hostess: Edward VII had been a close friend and visited Polesdon Lacey; George VI and Queen Elizabeth, as Duke and Duchess of York, had spent part of their honeymoon there; the famous, the rich, the aspiring had resorted to her house parties over more than three decades. It was these associations and its park, woods and fields as much as the house and its treasures that found acceptance in the sight of the Trust, together with the munificence with which it was endowed. There was, and still is, an intellectual and emotional difficulty which faces the National Trust when called upon to decide on the acceptability of places such as Cliveden, Polesden and Wightwick. The fairly recent past is seldom much valued, yet because of that it is more likely to be dissipated than the relics of the distant past. Today the taste and the money of pre-Great War Society can be glimpsed in the survival of Polesden Lacey.

Mrs Greville's will in favour of the Trust had first been drawn up in 1938 and was re-drawn several times over the next few years. One provision in an early draft could could hardly have been opposed by the Trust and Matheson wrote to her solicitors, Dawsons, that 'the Trust would be very glad to have the advantage of the advice of H.M. the King in carrying out Mrs Greville's wishes …' In the event George VI expressed himself content to leave matters to the discretion of the Trust. In 1977 Queen Elizabeth the Queen Mother attended with evident pleasure a garden party for long serving members of the Trust's staff. It was also a celebration of her daughter's twenty-five years as Queen, and her own Presidency of the National Trust, as well as a return to the house of her honeymoon days.

The problem of the way in which houses were to be used after they came to the

Trust continued to present itself in different ways. Blickling was occupied by the Royal Air Force and no immediate decision was needed. Lord Astor remained at Cliveden but had expressed the wish that after his family left, the house should be used for purposes connected with the Trade Union Movement or an American university. Dorneywood was to be used as a ministerial country house. There was no prospect of family or special use at Polesden Lacey. Lord Zetland had written to *The Times* in February 1943 specifically suggesting that an owner giving his house to the Trust should allow it to be used as a centre of residential adult education. In this he was strongly supported by Lord Methuen, who hoped that his own house, Corsham Court, would be similarly used. Others were not so keen, because the idea conflicted with that of rural employment generated and guided by the landowner.

In September 1943 Lees-Milne produced an encouraging report for his Committee. There had been a large number of enquiries from all over the country from County Councils and other bodies seeking premises for youth and adult education colleges, girls'schools, horticultural institutions, fellowship houses for the aged poor, Boys' Clubs, hostels for industrial workers and an out-of-town centre for Greenwich Observatory. He noted that not all houses would be suitable but that compromise was often possible. Above all, this prospect of rent-producing use would diminish the need for endowment. This early anxiety over the soundness of the main plank in the Trust's scheme – continued use of houses as family homes – should have been a clear warning of problems to come.

That year saw an exceptional gift which incorporated a country house of particular interest and charm. Miss Matilda Talbot gave Lacock Abbey, and the village of Lacock in Wiltshire with park and farmland, in all about three hundred acres. The Abbey, with its medieval monastic remains, Tudor conversion and mid-eighteenth century Gothick hall is fascinating in its own right but the village, with a range of dates, styles and constructional designs ranging back over seven hundred years is a rare survival. How much the gift was prompted by the Country House Scheme is uncertain but the gift was of priceless value. One way and another the family has continued its occupation of the house and has positively assisted in its preservation and presentation ever since.

Sir Charles Trevelyan, having been the first country-house owner on the scene, was among the earliest to push his intentions through to completion, even if in so doing he caused some headaches for the Trust. Nothing much was practicable until after the 1939 Act had been passed. That out of the way, there were only two hurdles: the first was Sir Charles's wish to make a legal reservation of rights for his family and the second was that Benny Horne was quite sure that 'the rich farmlands' could not properly be declared inalienable and would attract estate duty.

George Trevelyan had a difficult time being loyal both to the interests of the Trust and his brother, but he was always prepared to advise the Trust to the best of his ability. On the first objection he wrote to Matheson, in October 1940, that, 'If he altered his will so as to remove the legal claims of his family he could surely trust the National Trust to fulfil his *wishes* ... or he might effect a change in his lifetime and become the first tenant.' Matheson replied, '...if the National Trust does not carry out the wishes of benefactors of this kind, the whole of the country houses scheme will inevitably be hopelessly wrecked.' The following year Sir Charles did decide to make the gift in his lifetime, reserving a life tenancy to himself. By April 1941,

Horne was considering a draft of a deed of gift and of a memorandum which expressed the donor's wishes. On 9 June, the Executive Committee resolved that they 'will as far as they are able but without being under any legal obligation whatever carry out the wishes as expressed in a memorandum ...'. So the device of the use of a Memorandum of Wishes came into being and it has served its purpose for now more than forty years and has been the keystone of many transactions of the greatest importance.

In a draft press release prepared by Sir Charles for publication on 1 November 1941, there is a clear statement of his reasons. 'Sir Charles Trevelyan has had a double motive for his action. He is a Socialist and believes it would be better if the community owned such houses and great estates. He was also influenced by Lord Lothian with whom he discussed the whole question some years ago.' It will be understood that as tenant for life Sir Charles retained the occupation and full management of the property. On this 13,000-acre expanse the elegant and restrained, essentially mid-eighteenth century house, with its contents assembled over two hundred years, and its gardens and parkland, was the least problem in terms of what might go wrong. It was in the village of Cambo and on the farms that the liabilities to tenants constituted inescapable obligations. It was also the very time when an agricultural revolution was to bring changing needs which were impossible to foresee and difficult to assimilate when they came.

Since the responsibility would fall wholly upon the Trust when Sir Charles died it was reasonable that the Trust should keep in touch with things through its staff. By 1950 Cuthbert Acland, who had been the Trust's agent in the north for the previous two years, began to send alarm signals to Head Office, but not until December 1951 did a member of the Estates Committee, Willie Vane, go with the Chief Agent and Acland to meet Sir Charles and his elder daughter, Pauline Dower.

Things were such that the County Agricultural Executive Committee were threatening to put Sir Charles 'under supervision' – a statutory power under the Agriculture Act 1947 – for bad estate management. The Trust's worries may be summed up as revenue being too low and repairs and improvements to houses, cottages and farms being badly neglected. The meeting brought no reassurance to the Trust and the Chief Agent wrote to poor George Trevelyan, warning him that things were serious. It seemed advisable to employ the Trust's heaviest artillery in the shape of its Chairman, Lord Crawford, but his letter expressing somewhat vague concern was met by a bland response from Sir Charles.

The Trust became an owner of very large areas of agricultural land just at a time when the industry was about to emerge from a full seventy years of hopeless depression. Sir Charles cannot be blamed for the fact that in old age he conducted his management in a way that had been forced upon him since he succeeded his father. But by January 1958 things were becoming really very serious. His two daughters, Mrs Dower and Mrs Jennings, met Acland and his assistant Ben Proud (who was to become responsible for England east of the Pennines and down to the Humber). Sir Charles was already ill and on the 24 January he died. Among those who spoke in his honour at a memorial gathering was Arthur Blenkinsop, a young Labour MP for Newcastle East, who was to be a supporter of the Trust and of all conservation and outdoor interests. He wrote of the curious nature of the event 'in a wholly non-religious ceremony in a consecrated building'. The Trust's stewardship of Walling-

130

ton will be examined later. At this point what matters is to note that, in spite of the problems of estate management it pointed up, Sir Charles Trevelyan's benefaction was in its conception, its negotiation and its completion a pioneering exploit whose example was to be followed often in the years ahead.

Right at the end of 1935 Lord Sackville invited Donald Macleod Matheson 'to talk over the question of the preservation of country houses', and by February 1936 he was able to write that he is 'in principle … very willing to come into the second category' of the two schemes put forward by the Trust. Lord Sackville's house, Knole, in Kent is of supreme historic and architectural importance but also it is probably about the most difficult and expensive 'house' in the country to maintain. The inverted commas are used because it is really not a house but a mediaeval village. The buildings occupy about four acres and many date from nearly five hundred years ago when Archbishops of Canterbury used Knole as their country palace. It is a huddle of courtyards great and small, crenellated towers and parapets, halls, galleries, ballroom, brewery, barns and garrets. Later on, in 1943, Jim Lees-Milne was to record in his diary that Lord Sackville had a butler and one housemaid to look after two hundred and fifty bedrooms, and added, 'Most large houses upon acquaintance look smaller than at first they appeared. Not so Knole. It is a veritable rabbit warren. It turned out today that … we had all three overlooked the north wing which consists of fifteen bedrooms as well as reception rooms.' In addition to all this, the pictures and furnishings of the state apartments include seventeenth-century state beds and silver-mounted sconces, tables and mirrors.

In view of the character of the place and its contents it is not surprising that, despite the early and promising start to the negotiations, it was to be twelve years before the transaction was completed. Late in 1936 a very promising and sensible draft scheme was put to Lord Sackville: there were four main points.

(i)   The whole of the park was to be bought by the Local Authorities who would give the freehold to the Trust and themselves find the money to maintain it.
(ii) Lord Sackville would give the house and gardens to the Trust which would subsequently maintain it, he reserving the right for himself and his heirs to live in the 'occupied' part.
(iii) The Trust was to raise whatever capital was needed for an endowment.
(iv) The Trust to pay the costs of a private Act of Parliament which would be needed (with the law as it was) to break the entail.

There is a 'modern' feel about the first three parts of this proposal and it would not now seem to be so very far reaching. It foundered at the time partly because of the legal difficulties and partly because of the Trust's failure to raise capital. Among wealthy benefactors approached by Matheson was Viscount Bearsted of Upton in Warwickshire (a house which, with its splendid picture collection, he gave eleven years later to the Trust). He got a dusty answer: '… the fact that an endowment fund would not be for the public but for a particular family robs the appeal of much of its sentimental value.'

In fact Lord Sackville was not by Lord Bearsted's standards a rich man. His income was derived from a settled fund of about £200,000 which yielded about £7,000 a year, of which he spent £5,000 on maintaining the property leaving £2,000 for himself and his family. The fact that the contents of Knole were even then valued at roughly £2 million was neither here nor there if they were to be given to the nation.

Although some of the legal obstacles were resolved by the National Trust Acts of 1937 and 1939 there remained a problem in that the 'heirlooms' were subject to entail and the 1939 Act did not cover chattels. Negotiations dragged on intermittently. By 1942 Lees-Milne was writing that '... Lord Sackville is as tired as we are over rather nebulous and general correspondence and conversations over the last five or six years which have proved fruitless.' The following year the Executive Committee of the Trust took the step of resolving to accept the property, incurring a deficit of £2,000 a year, emboldened by the receipt of Mrs Greville's legacy, part of which they earmarked for the purpose. But the year dragged by with further setbacks, including a new obligation to find £4,000 for initial capital expenditure and with Frank Mason, the Sackville's resident sub-agent, constantly making new difficulties or reviving old ones. In the end the Country Houses Committee minuted that '... the concessions made to the Sackvilles about Knole could not be further extended .... The finances of the Trust would not permit of the acceptance of any other house without enough endowment.'

Eventually the Sackville Trustees did apply to the Court for a direction on a proposed gift to the National Trust and, on 8 July 1946, Mr Justice Vaisey made an order for vesting the property in the Trust and, indeed, making two useful modifications of the scheme in its favour. Completion took place in 1947. Predictably, in 1949, the Trust's new land agent Ivan Hills, was worrying about money, the endowment income of £2,963 and the £4,000 from visitors fees only just exceeding in total the £6,500 annual expenditure, which was rising rapidly as wages increased.

The gift of Knole can only be regarded as a first step in its preservation. There was no conception at the time of the extent to which money would have to be found for the building and for its contents and no foreknowledge of the various changes which would help to supply it. What was crystal clear in everyone's mind, and perhaps especially Lees-Milne's, was that Knole was in peril and that Knole must be saved. It had been.

1943 to 1950 brought a steady stream of benefactions. The charming early nineteenth-century house at Dinton in Wiltshire by Jeffry Wyatt (later Sir Jeffry Wyatville) was given by Bertram Philipps in 1943; Hatchlands near Guildford, which featured as a prospective devise in Matheson's first meagre list, was given by Harry Goodhart-Rendel, the architectural historian in 1945; and the Gunpowder Plot house, Coughton, in Warwickshire, was given by Sir Robert Throckmorton in 1946. Saddest and finest of all, the Stourhead Estate, came by the will of Sir Henry Hoare who died on Lady Day, 1947, his wife following him six hours later. It was a very splendid gift. The house, with its fine furniture, sits in level parkland looking east towards the low ridge of chalk downland that marks the western edge of Salisbury Plain, across some of the most fertile farmland in the country. Then to the west lie the rides and woods, temples, grottoes, follies and lakes.

The sadness comes from the underlying cause: Sir Henry's only son was killed in the Great War and from that time on he had difficulty in taking any active measures in the care of his property beyond ensuring its eventual care by the Trust. In a survey made three years after his death there was scarcely a house, cottage or barn in which

132

every window and door was not rotten, no ornament or folly which was not in dire need of repair. The care and exertions of the Trust have helped to revive this superb place.

As these benefactions were gradually being realised, action by the Government was beginning to introduce new factors into the Trust's preservation plans and these will be looked at separately. After its long and at first discouraging history the Country Houses Scheme was at last in being and had shown enough positive results to call itself a success. It was to grow and grow but the initiators, and the Country Houses Committee they set up, with Lord Esher in the chair and Jim Lees-Milne at his right hand, had achieved what they set out to do.

CHAPTER X

The
Post-War Period

Chorley believed that Zetland and Matheson had intended to re-organise the Trust with a fully professional staff when they first came together as Chairman and Secretary in the mid-1930s, but that re-organisation was delayed, first by shortage of funds, and then by the outbreak of war. By the time the first uncertainties and disasters of the war were over the National Trust began to plan for the years ahead.

The first outward sign of this was in 1942 when a Chief Agent was appointed with the specific task of building up a pattern of management centres throughout England and Wales. They were to be staffed by land agents directly employed by the Trust. Later that year Matheson, through the offices of a member of the Executive Committee, Lord Conesford, secured the recall from the army of Christopher Gibbs – at that time sick and in hospital – and appointed him Deputy Chief Agent. It was not so easy, however, to get supporting staff and all that could be done was the recruitment, in 1943, of Eardley Knollys as an Assistant Agent. Although he had no formal qualifications the appointment, like most made by Matheson, was a great success.

Knollys at the outbreak of war was thirty-seven, and two years over the age limit then for service in the armed forces. He had been private secretary to Viscount Hambleden and then set up as an art dealer, but the business folded with the war. He was brought up as a countryman, his father having been a founder member of the Land Agents' Society and was agent to Lord Ashcombe at the Grange, in Hampshire. It was a natural decision to go as a farm worker in Dorset as his contribution to the war effort. It was an advertisement in *The Times* which drew his attention to the National Trust and he went for an interview with Matheson and Lord Esher. He got the job as agent on the strength of his rural background. Sensible and sensitive, practical but with a highly developed aesthetic appreciation, Eardley did such work as was possible in the circumstances and later, when more professionals became available, moved over to become the Trust's representative in the south and west until his retirement in 1958.

Matheson's next move was to prepare the way for bringing the legal work of the Trust into Head Office. Benny Horne was by this time elderly and Matheson had been impatient of some of his ways of doing business. It was the oft-repeated story of organisations outgrowing the people that have built them up. The informal and wholly personal way in which Horne had been accustomed to initiate new moves, and negotiate with potential benefactors without prior consultation, was no longer acceptable. Quite apart from that, and despite the fact that the advice given by Horne and Birkett seems to have been quite sound, the new stresses imposed by the legal complexities of the Country Houses Scheme may have made Matheson feel that he needed advice which was readily at hand.

It is interesting that all the principals involved came into the Trust's employ on Matheson's initiative. When Lord Astor first began to negotiate with the Trust about his proposed gift of Cliveden, Macleod Matheson had a ready-made link with the agent. Hubert John Forster Smith had been born in 1899, the ninth and last child of Arthur Smith, a friend of Rawnsley who became Master of Balliol. It was at Balliol that he and Matheson met and got to know each other well after the First World War. It was natural that Matheson should discuss Cliveden management problems with Smith, and that led on to broader discussions about management of the Trust's properties. They corresponded on the subject through the first part of 1941, Matheson saying that he had persuaded his Committee that they should depart from their practice of employing local agents and that the Trust intended to appoint a Chief Agent: could Smith suggest possible candidates? Then in August came a letter from Matheson inviting him to apply for the job. There was a formal interview with Lord Zetland, Norman and Lubbock, but there seems little doubt that Matheson intended that Smith should be appointed. It was, of course, convenient too, because by that time the gift of Cliveden had been virtually settled, and this gave rise to a myth among the staff of the Trust that the appointment was part of the deal with Lord Astor: wholly untrue but still persisting forty years on!

The man selected to be at the head of this important change in management methods was not a trained land agent. Like many others in the early 1920s Hubert Smith had put his very small capital into land and had begun to farm in Sussex. Within twelve months the short lived prosperity of agriculture burst like a bubble. Not only land values, but worse still stock values dropped catastrophically. For Hubert Smith it was a disaster and he was fortunate to find a job as a farm manager with £4 a week to support his wife and baby son. An offer to go to Cliveden as agent on £500 a year seemed like a miracle.

The estate was not large but for the next seventeen years he had the sole management of White Place Farm which he ran, except for one season, at a realistic profit including interest on capital, which was no mean feat in those days. Farming was regarded as an important activity at Cliveden and they were pioneers in the newly developing techniques of dairy farming. Smith's experience was widened by becoming responsible for the agricultural aspects of the Astor stud at Newmarket and the brood mares' pastures in Wiltshire, and there was an asparagus farm in Kent to deal with too. Later a major occupation was an investment, designed for the benefit of the Astor sons, in farmland on the Borders.

Matheson's choice of Anthony Martineau to become Solicitor to the Trust was no less sound, although his pre-knowledge of the man was by no means as deep. He had just arranged a worthwhile job in the Ministry of Food when Matheson got in touch. Martineau had been a member of the Trust for some time before the war – which marks him as exceptional, in the sense that there were only about 7,000 members then. If Martineau cared for anything he cared about it passionately and he did very much care for the preservation of the countryside. In 1942, Sir Richard Acland had decided to give his huge Somerset and Devon estates (see pp. 341–3) – Holnicote and Killerton – to the Trust.

This was an action far from universally approved of. Martineau keenly followed the debate and *The Times* published a letter from him in support of Acland and the Trust.

He had written, after his discharge from the army, asking the Trust whether they had a job for him and Matheson must have marked him down then. With considerable heart searchings as to whether it was right to let the Ministry of Food down by leaving, but assured by all his friends that he should go to the Trust, Anthony Martineau became an Assistant Secretary towards the end of 1943.

The creation of the job was clearly a device for placing a lawyer on the staff before Horne and Birkett were officially relieved of their appointment, and initially Martineau was required to do no legal work but to get to know the business of the Trust. However, by the end of 1944 the business of parting with Horne and Birkett was dealt with and Martineau became Solicitor to the Trust at a salary of £600 a year. Two years later he was restyled 'Legal Adviser' by which title he and his successor were known until 1967. To assist him he had that now vanished species, a solicitor's clerk. H.E. Knope was the perfect foil and the pair made the legal department of the National Trust a highly efficient and extremely economical unit at a time when the number of transactions requiring documentation was about to increase very rapidly. Knope was small, bright, friendly and quiet, with an infinite capacity for taking pains and allowing nothing to escape him.

Anthony Martineau was a good and thorough lawyer and his work was dominated by his devotion to principle and to what he conceived to be the proper interests of the charity he served. A fluent letter writer, and indeed a fluent speaker in conversation, he made a reputation for himself as one who would never compromise. He described himself as being regarded as 'the most cantankerous man in London' and was not prepared to dispute the truth of that. It was, of course, quite untrue, but it was in some ways a useful reputation to have with the outside world.

1945 was to be a year of major change, Zetland giving up the chairmanship and Matheson retiring. It again fell to Ronnie Norman to find a new Chairman. Throughout the war Oliver Esher had been the mainstay of the Trust's committee work and it would not have been surprising if he had been selected to succeed Zetland. Since he had made preservation – especially the preservation of buildings – a large part of his life, it was equally unsurprising that he should have been disappointed when he was not chosen. Norman was not obliged positively to reject Esher, because he himself had again been offered the chairmanship and had again refused it, but undertook at the same time, 'to find,' in his own words, 'a better man. This I certainly did in the person of Lord Crawford ...'

David Crawford was to be Chairman for twenty years and it is hard to write about him without exaggerating his good qualities, although he was in himself simple and unassuming. Handsome, with charming manners and a very good brain, he was interested in and observant of everything that came his way. To travel in his company was to feel as though one's sight had suddenly been restored after a lifetime's blindness. Pictures were his greatest love, but after that buildings, gardens and countryside were all matters in which his knowledge matched his enjoyment.

In administration he was competent and clear-headed and his directions to the Secretary from distant Balcarres in Fife (from which he commuted when necessary) were brief, positive and very much to the point. In the business of handling committees he may not have come up to the standard which Chorley ascribed to Zetland, perhaps because in his kindness he was reluctant to cut short even the most tiresome member. He nevertheless always succeeded in producing a consensus, generally in line with his own views and without leaving anyone feeling dissatisfied or frustrated. The staff had the very highest regard for him and perhaps one of his greatest contributions to the welfare of the Trust was to imbue its employees with ideals and standards of conduct which spread throughout the already fast-growing organisation.

Cecil Lubbock, Honorary Treasurer from 1932, also retired in 1945 and was succeeded by Edward Holland-Martin. This relatively young man was on the face of it an unlikely person to be committed to preservation societies. He had been an Executive Director of the Bank of England before the war, passionately interested in horses and racing and a member of the Jockey Club. Nevertheless, Holland-Martin had been involved with preservation since the mid-1930s and had been a member of the Trust's Finance and General Purposes Committee since 1944. His home at Overbury, below Bredon Hill lay in very beautiful country, to which he was deeply attached. He was assiduous in his work for the Trust, visiting new properties, calling at the office to discuss problems with the staff and presiding at interviews to select new recruits. He was always respected, particularly for his courage when, after a very bad hunting fall had injured his back, he refused to resign himself to being an invalid. He never became close to their hearts, however, as some other prominent committee members did. His neighbour Lees-Milne described him on one occasion being 'as friendly as I am sure a swordfish can be'.

It was in the appointment of a new Secretary that the Trust had problems. There are many mysteries about Matheson: Christopher Gibbs noted that before the war he used to disappear abroad, being very secretive and saying only that it was Government work. His six months' leave of absence in 1944 on health grounds, when not apparently ill, was also odd. Finally, why did he retire in 1945? Carew Wallace has said that he believed that Lord Esher, supported by Lees-Milne, engineered his departure. Certainly the latter recorded that when a successor was being chosen he lobbied against inviting Matheson to return. He also says that there was some idea of making the Chief Agent, Hubert Smith, Secretary and he lobbied against that too. Quite rightly, in all probability, because Hubert's value lay in other directions. Lees-Milne also reported Harold Nicolson as having been canvassed for the job, but saying that he would not take it if it were offered because he intended to go back into politics.

In the event they chose George Mallaby, a senior civil servant in the Cabinet Office. Almost everyone speaks well of him. Officially he held the position from June 1945 until May the next year but Lees-Milne still regarded him as 'Secretary-Elect' in September and he must have been combining two jobs, for he was present at some of the Cabinet meetings of the new Labour Government. His months in office coincided with a period when everyone expected Government to project into peacetime the multifarious activities it had assumed in war – and to an extent it did. Civil servants in particular felt the way in which the wind blew and were inclined to trim their sails accordingly. This put the Trust on the defensive. However, Mallaby was soon plucked back by his service to a distinguished future in forming the new Ministry of Defence.

The choice of Admiral Oliver Bevir to take the Secretaryship is in retrospect surprising. The Executive Committee no doubt wished to have a figure of some stature. On the other hand, according to Chorley, the Admiral looked on the job as an interesting and not too demanding occupation in his retirement. There is little evidence that he had much knowledge of or enthusiasm for the now very widespread interests of the Trust. Jim Lees-Milne's diary is positively spiteful in some of its comments but it reflects the impression that Oliver Bevir made. Jim in his cups described him to Esher as 'a nice Philistine' and quotes Fedden as saying after meeting the Admiral and his wife that they were 'King and Queen Low Brow'.

The Admiral worked hard, travelling the country, often with Lees-Milne, and taking a constructive and well-thought out part in the continuing negotiations with Government over country house preservation. Whether real or assumed there was something of the Jolly-Jack Tar in his manner, – a young typist recalls his singing sea-shanties as he climbed the office stairs and the Committees could not resist teasing him. In a wholly competent review of the Trust's finances he predicted that all would be well 'provided that legacies remain buoyant', causing an uproar of such hilarity that business came to a halt. One of the accusations made against Oliver Bevir has been, simply, that he was stupid. That he most emphatically was not. He had, however, committed himself to a milieu in which he had no experience. Within three years he decided to go, wisely both for himself and for the Trust, but that meant a third change in four years which was bad for a growing organisation at a time of rapid change.

Third time was lucky. J.F.W. Rathbone became Secretary in place of Bevir in 1949, enduring with difficulty six months' tutelage on the opposite side of the Admiral's desk. It was at that time the custom for the half dozen senior staff to take afternoon tea in the Secretary's office, to exchange opinions and to gossip. Immediately upon the Admiral's departure the venue was changed and tea served in the Boardroom. The new Secretary's first decisive administrative act must have alerted Anthony Martineau to a serious problem for it was at about that time that he raised doubts as to the propriety of the staff consuming tea and biscuits paid for out of charitable funds.

Jack Rathbone had been brought up in Liverpool, for which the Lake District serves as a playground and it was there, on walking holidays from his uncle's house below Skiddaw near Keswick, that he first became aware of the National Trust. His family name was well known both locally and nationally and had a reputation for radical philanthropy. He became a solicitor and worked principally as a conveyancer until the war, during which he was taken into the Judge Advocate General's department and finished with the rank of Brigadier. His friend Desmond Shaw-Taylor introduced him in post-war London to Eardley Knollys and Edward Sackville-West and they in turn introduced him to the Trust. Eardley took him to picnic at Stourhead before it was open to the public and the impact of the experience was such that he longed to work for the Trust. He credits Lord Esher's support for the fact that he was appointed and it is certain that Esher in turn was influenced by Rathbone's friends. Rathbone took office at a time when the six years of war had been followed by four years of partial stagnation in the direction of the Trust. He was to be Secretary until 1968, nearly nineteen years, and the period was marked by great events for which much credit is due to him. Yet in the first ten years it was much in the provinces that progress was initiated, and the central administration of the Trust remained a somewhat piecemeal, after-thought affair, resting on the framework planned by Matheson.

As the war ended and men and women returned from the services, new staff began to appear in what seemed very considerable numbers. After the Trust's wartime sojourn in West Wycombe, the head office returned first to Buckingham Palace Gardens and then to two charming seventeenth-century houses in Queen Anne's Gate, providentially left to the Trust by Mrs Murray Smith. They, with the next door house bought later, served the Trust until 1982, successive waves of employees treading the ancient stairs of the five storeys from semi-basement to attic. Christopher Gibbs and Matheson had to rush to occupy the property to prevent requisition, despite the damage done by the blast from a flying bomb. They worked in great discomfort and cold – wearing balaclava helmets, discarded flying boots and any available warm clothing until the repairs were done.

Margaret Sach started work there in 1946. She was just twenty, and was interviewed for the job by Winifred Ballachey who was in charge while Miss Patterson was on holiday.

> In the front room of No. 42 there were about five filing cabinets and five girls in the same room. I sat at a large dining table with three others, all working hard on manual typewriters at the speed of light. Mrs Randall worked for the Admiral, Miss Tansley for Christopher Gibbs, and Leila Bedford (about my age) for Cubby Acland. She had worked for Gordon Wordsworth, grandson of the poet, who had given her a silver compact which she treasured ... In that terrible winter we had no heat or light, and we had to wear blankets in the office ... I remember the Council well: to me they seemed like something out of the Bible – a stream of very elderly men creeping up the stairs....
>
> Mr and Mrs Lovell were caretakers, with their bedroom in the attic and their living room and kitchen in the basement. The front door was kept locked and Lovell had to climb the stairs every time the bell rang. On Committee days he wore a black coat and pin stripe trousers and had to wait in the hall to take the coats. The basement was liable to flooding and there were ghastly smells due to the outside drains. He was very much under Miss P's thumb and she kept him on the run and he used to grouse and grumble.
>
> Miss P. was terribly frugal and every pencil and rubber had to be accounted for. But we did have beautiful cream cakes for tea – "Fullers" they were – and Lovell used to produce this at 4 o'clock.

Miss Patterson was, unbelievably, the 'Snooks' who had worked with Victoria Spencer-Wilkinson in the 1920s, and the Trust had been her only job, through the vicissitudes of the war and the moves to Runnymede, West Wycombe, back to Buckingham Palace Gardens and then to Queen Anne's Gate. She had shared a house in Cheyne Walk with Jim Lees-Milne from 1943, sitting out air raids on the stairs or sharing the comfort of glasses of neat whisky.

While Miss P. ruled the office, Winifred Ballachey ran the membership. 'When this was in No. 40 the girls worked in the attic and the little green books were all lined up against the window wall. Miss B. sat in the same room. She knew practically all the members' names by heart and so did the girls because they used to say, "Oh! Good old so-and-so has paid her sub. again!"'

It was in that atmosphere that the post-war staff assembled. Among the first back from the wars was Colin Jones, who had been engaged by the Trust as a Land Agent just before the war, during which he had been sent to join the staff of the War Department Land Agents' Department. He elected under the new system of regional management to take responsibility for the Midlands. For that purpose he based himself near home at Ross-on Wye, from where his bailiwick reached up the Welsh Marches to the Mersey across to the Humber and down to the Wash!

In the West Country the Acland gift of Holnicote in West Somerset – about 12,400 acres – and Killerton near Exeter – another 6,400 acres – required special measures. Hubert Smith found George Senior in 1944 to take on the management of the southern half of Devon and all of Cornwall. Born in 1894, George had served as a gunner in the Great War, and afterwards graduated in agriculture. He was a bluff Yorkshireman with no frills and a pretty quick temper, but had an excellent and well-informed brain and an engaging sense of humour. He took to the job like a duck to water, seeming instinctively to know what was required of him, and displaying an unshakeable loyalty to the cause. With West Country folk his direct and sometimes uncommunicative character did not always go down well, but he served the interests of the Trust admirably until his retirement in 1956.

Freddie Reeks had become Steward for the Aclands at Killerton in 1929. This title signified a sort of resident sub-agent, the overall management being in the hands of an Exeter solicitor. It was an agreeable life, the perquisites including the provision of a horse and the full-time services of an 'outside man'. Gradually he was given more responsibility, including, in the 1930s, supervision of the Holnicote Estate fifty miles to the north. As a Territorial soldier in the Royal Corps of Signals he went off, like others in 1939 and was transferred to the War Department Land Agent's Department, finishing the war with the rank of Lieutenant Colonel.

It was a condition of Acland's gift to the Trust that Reeks should be offered employment on his return, but the pattern of regional management – and the prior employment of Senior – constituted a problem. In the event Freddie Reeks himself elected to go to Holnicote, for which he had formed an affection, and for the next twenty years he became responsible for North Devon and West Somerset.

An early recruit to work from Queen Anne's Gate was Carew Wallace. He was a graduate of the Oxford School of Forestry, spending four years at Wadham College before joining the Sierra Leone Forestry Service in which he spent the next four years to 1936. On his return he trained at the College of Estate Management and became a Chartered Surveyor, and worked in an architectural practice. After his release from the Service at the end of the war he found that because of the restriction of the building licence system there was not much work. Having been for a long time interested in both old buildings and the country he applied to the Trust for a job, was taken on and fitted into the new regional system. He became responsible for the Home Counties north of the Thames and for a while for East Anglia too. His background is of particular interest because one of the Trust's problems in

140

recruitment was to find people with sufficiently broad interests. Forestry has long been recognised as one of the disciplines which embraces science and practical experience, and Wallace's interest and experience in buildings provided a base for the Trust's other major interest.

Cuthbert H.D. Acland had a more secure entrée. As mentioned earlier he was the youngest son of Sir Francis Acland, brother of Richard who had made the gift of his estates to the Trust in 1942. Cubby – the nickname by which he was known everywhere – wrote to George Trevelyan from India before he was demobilised, enquiring about the prospect of working for the Trust. Cubby, like many younger sons of propertied families, had trained as a land agent and before the war was employed by the well-established firm of Cook and Arkwright.

The immediate vacancy was in the three south-eastern counties, where Cubby became Area Agent in 1946, working from Head Office, but he always had his eye on the Lake District. His mother came from there, the middle brother Geoffrey lived there, and his Cropper cousins were also strongly established. When Gordon Wordsworth retired in 1949 from there, Cubby left the south-east to work in the north until his retirement in 1973.

There is so much to say later about his work there that it must be left for the time being, but we can record now that in Hubert Smith's view Cubby was the best Land Agent working for the Trust in his time. His mind was as incisive as his manner, but it was also capable of taking very long views. He was good with subordinate staff and the traditional type of tenant, whether of a farm or cottage, and with his colleagues. He was not at all good with those whom he regarded as pretentious or obstructive, and into that group might come local authority officers, academics advising on their specialities, his seniors on the staff and the Trust's committees. He was a great gardener, keen sailor, a fast driver of fast cars and an irrepressible teller of Cumbrian tales, told in the vernacular and with appropriate gestures. That he made enemies goes without saying, but they were greatly out-numbered by friends and in that most important part of the country he left the Trust more widely and soundly based than ever before.

His place in the south-east was filled by Ivan Hills, from an Essex family, whose first job was as a factor (as the Scots call their agents) in Sutherland. He served with the Seaforth Highlanders in the war in Africa, Sicily and Germany before returning to take a temporary post with the District Valuer in Tunbridge Wells. No finer refresher course in estate management exists than a spell in the DV's office. When the Trust advertised for an agent in the south east he was preferred to another candidate, Nicolas Corbin largely because he was already living there.

Nicolas de Bazille Corbin, a Guernsey man, was not disappointed because he was offered, and took, the job of Area Agent in East Anglia, relieving Carew Wallace of part of an impossibly extensive area. Corbin was a survivor of an appalling accident. Son of a country parson in Essex, he had intended to become a professional soldier, entering the county regiment by way of the Supplementary Reserve. In France in December 1939 he was one of a group of young officers undergoing a course of training. A sapper officer instructing them intended to demonstrate that the German anti-tank Tellermine would not explode except with the application of heavy pressure, but when he stood on the mine it did explode. There were few survivors: Corbin, only a few yards away, was one. He spent the next two years in hospital, bits of metal embedded all over his body. The lasting damage was to his eyes. His sight was maintained through the use of the then revolutionary contact lense. His ankles required the support of high ankle boots. He went up to Queens' College, Cambridge and then had the good fortune to train in estate management with an exceptional Land Agent, J.J. Morgan of Ilminster.

To complete the pattern of regional management as it formed by 1950 mention must be made of three others. Simon Fowell Buxton formed an Area Office for the counties of Wiltshire, Hampshire, Dorset and the eastern half of Somerset, basing it at Stourhead. He was a tall, mild-mannered, intellectual man. It was a considerable loss to the Trust when in 1957 he decided to leave and practise on his own, one of the very few who, once recruited, subsequently left. His reason for going was that if he stayed he would become bankrupt. It is true that against the steady inflation experienced from 1949, the level of salaries paid by the Trust had fallen disastrously. It was not until the early 1960s that a more realistic pay policy was pursued.

Two sub-agents were recruited, one Ben Proud to help Acland in the north and the other John Trayner to take on the newly acquired Clumber Park in the vast Midland area. Later Proud was to relieve Acland of the eastern half of the north, and Trayner was to do the same in the Midlands. Acland was fortunate in the selection of Proud. He had had one of the best of basic trainings having studied agriculture at Armstrong College, Durham University, which then had a great reputation for science. He served articles with Newcastle land agents and qualified in 1935. A Territorial soldier with the Green Howards, he commanded a company as captain in 1939 but the next year was taken prisoner at Arras and spent the rest of the war as a POW.

On demobilisation he took office as a War Department Land Agent and being relatively senior he might have had a very successful career there, but he applied for the job of assistant to Cubby, and got it. This was a vocational move. 'I joined the N.T.,' he says, 'because I thought it fulfilled all those ideals I held concerning good land agency, the preservation of good buildings and the maintenance of farm buildings and cottages.' For ten important years they worked together, Acland supplying the leadership and policy, dealing with public relations and his speciality of forestry, while Proud dealt with the repair and improvement of the scores of farms and hundreds of cottages in their care. Although new people were to come along as the years went by, these were the men who put their stamp on the conduct of the Trust's work throughout the country, and most of them continued in their posts for between twenty and thirty years.

Insofar as it was possible Hubert Smith chose cohesive districts for the new areas which would continue to function as sensible units of management regardless of what new properties might come to the Trust. At the same time he had to try to locate the offices close to the centre of the workload, and if possible at a place where there was accommodation for both offices and staff. With regard to the latter, it was still the custom to provide houses for employees in the country and in any event the post-war shortage of houses was severe.

It was these considerations which prompted the selection of Polesden Lacey, Stourhead, Killerton, Holnicote, Blickling and Clumber, all of which – except Holnicote – continue to serve their purpose nearly forty years on. Had it not been for these two reasons, Smith would probably have selected centres on purely 'strategic principles – communications and staff availability. It was impossible to predict where the weight of new work would fall. He planned for, and actually recruited, an agent for Wallington, in 1948, but that expectation was deferred until Sir Charles Trevelyan's death ten years later. In the East Midlands, with its office at Clumber, there was very little work in Northamptonshire and if there had been it would have been very difficult to reach it in reasonable time. It was providential for that Area that, thirty years later, when there was an immense increase of work in the south, the M1 motorway had been built.

New people were also beginning to appear whose contribution was to be principally to the aesthetic sphere of the Trust. The most dynamic of these was probably Robin Romilly Fedden who combined Representative in the South East with the curatorship of Polesden Lacey, in 1946. He was to succeed Jim Lees-Milne as Secretary to the Historic Buildings Committee in 1951, a post which he kept until his retirement in 1973, by which time he was also Deputy Director General. Robin Fedden blended scholarship with activity. Physically he was spare of frame and capable of considerable endurance. He had great charm and a positively delightful stammer in private conversation, which miraculously disappeared when he spoke in public. He had the sort of temper which, although it could be quite violent, was never out of control. It was principally provoked by bad service either from people or machines. Fedden was a great traveller who specialised in unusual places and modes of transport. Canoeing down the rivers of north-east Turkey was one of his expeditions. Before the war he had written books on subjects as diverse as the Crusader Castles and a study of suicide. With a fluent but economical English style, his books, articles and office memoranda make pleasant reading. When, in 1968, he produced *The Continuing Purpose*, a combined short history of the National Trust and a text book account of its current legal, financial and administrative position, he made even that readable.

Another country house curator was to make his mark on the Trust in a different way. Joshua Rowley had returned from the war which he spent with the Brigade of Guards in North Africa and Italy. Sitting one day in Boodles and wondering what he should do for a job, he overheard two people talking. One had been offered a job with the National Trust by a man called Lees-Milne but he was not going to accept. The job was to be custodian of a house in Warwickshire called Packwood. Rowley determined to apply. Become Keeper he did although no one quite knows why. Neither can Rowley really explain except to say that it was just what he wanted to do at that time. Lees-Milne, though he found Joshua congenial and helpful was mystified. 'Why on earth should he want to bury himself in Packwood ...?' Later on: 'Joshua still mystifies me. Why does he want to be isolated in this lonely place.'

Packwood had been given to the Trust in 1941 when country houses were only just beginning to be offered and when the exigencies of the war curtailed opportunities for critical examination. It is a house of Tudor origin, with much mid-seventeenth century work. Internally it was so much altered by the donor, Baron Ash and his father before him, as to be almost entirely twentieth century, although such things as flooring and panelling were brought in from other old houses in the neighbourhood. Had the offer been made ten years later it is probable that it would have been refused. Indeed, in 1946, the Trust could hardly bring itself to accept another and more famous Warwickshire house, Charlecote, because of the very extensive alterations made to it in the middle of the nineteenth century.

At all events aesthetic opinion in the Trust had begun to look with disdain upon the house and this was exacerbated by the character and conduct of the donor. Baron Ash – 'a pernickety man; not a rational man' according to Rowley – constantly tried to interfere in the smallest matters. Amongst other things he demanded the spending of capital which he had given as an endowment, declining to see that if that were gone there would be no income. His attitude caused him to bump up against the stubborn streak in the otherwise gentle Colin Jones whose Area included Warwickshire. Getting no satisfaction there, Mr Ash turned his attention to those at Head Office. Rowley was in the middle of all this and his calm commonsense contributed largely to the fact that the potentially explosive situation was never detonated.

After five years at Packwood, Rowley was brought to Head Office in the post of Assistant Secretary with responsibility for the Trust's publicity. Both there and in his later role as a committee member he devoted himself to forming a bridge over the gap which had already developed between 'management' and 'aesthetics'. He was promoted to Deputy Secretary in 1953 and it is a pity that he could not stay on in that capacity for more than a year.

It was with this framework of administration and management that the Trust entered the first decade of its second half century and an increase – almost an explosion – in its responsibilities.

CHAPTER XI

New Views on Historic Houses

The advent of a Labour Government with a large majority in 1945 brought new influences to bear on the Trust. Governments had never been hostile to the Trust, some had been positively helpful and we have seen how Baldwin felt about it. Nevertheless, now for the first time there was a Government not only prepared but anxious to advance the Trust's interests. In part this was due simply to the feeling that the Trust was a Good Thing; its work had been very much in line with the attitude of middle-class Fabians whose influence was strong in the Labour Party. There was also a feeling that the old order really was at an end, that there were some pieces which needed to be picked up. It was thought that the organisation would be a useful instrument to do that and might later be taken over by Government when convenient.

How much this informed the views of the new Chancellor of the Exchequer, Hugh Dalton, is not possible to say but he at once began to help the National Trust with money. There was a Jubilee Appeal in 1945 and Dr Dalton promised a pound for every pound raised by the appeal. Not surprisingly at that time public response was very poor and had the appeal rested on public subscription it would have been a wash out. With the Government's contribution of £60,000, a total of £120,000 was raised.

The Trust decided to spend the money on the acquisition of a property which would be nationally noticed, popular and well-used as a public open space. One of the properties considered was Clumber Park, some twenty-five miles south-east of Sheffield, in Nottinghamshire. The Duke of Newcastle was in the process of selling up his entire estate there. One of the lots was the park, an area approaching 4,000 acres, with the River Poulter running through it, dammed to form two lakes covering about 100 acres in all. The idea was at first discarded, partly because the Duke had pulled his house down in 1938 and the great stable block and the nearby chapel by S.F. Bodley stood oddly in abandoned pleasure grounds, while ammunition dumps and Nissen huts spread throughout the devastated woodlands. However, the Trust drew a blank elsewhere and returned to the idea. It had much to commend it: situated halfway between the two great cities of Sheffield and Nottingham, and on the edge of the Derbyshire and Nottinghamshire coalfield, it was surrounded by the villages which had been built to serve the pits. Moreover, although Sheffield had the

Peak District for its back garden, Nottinghamshire, Lincolnshire and the southern part of Yorkshire had no open spaces of any extent.

There was one drawback: money. There was simply none to maintain the property. In a scheme based on its traditional custom of finding local funds, but on a scale never before attempted, the Trust recruited a consortium of no less than eight local authorities to form, with the Trust's nominees, a management committee to supply the necessary funds. In his inimitable way Captain Hill conducted negotiations with the Duke's Trustees, and the property was successfully secured. The arrangement was to last more than thirty years and in the end it was a Conservative Nottinghamshire County Council which, by withdrawing from the consortium, brought it to a close. The years of co-operation had brought great credit to all concerned. The concept of the great open space, a 'lung' for the industrial populations around, proved to be precisely what had been hoped for. Since the 1950s a million and a half visitors have been to the Park each year.

Hugh Dalton's next step was to create the National Land Fund. A very large sum of £50 million was to be used to acquire property for preservation as a memorial to those who had died in the war. The property when acquired might either be held by the Government or passed to an approved organisation, of which the Trust was one. The Finance Act of 1910 had contained a provision whereby property could be given to the Inland Revenue in lieu of tax, but only twice in thirty-six years had the facility been used, to a total value of only £7,300. The Chancellor in his Budget statement said, 'I propose that, from now on, much more use should be made of this power to accept land in payment of death duties.'

This was a remarkably far-sighted provision which, in various ways, has borne good fruit, though Dalton would perhaps have been disappointed that it did not work better. In the first place, it immediately aroused suspicions that it was designed to be a back door method of the nationalisation of property. To the extent that it was probably necessary to carry with him the more extreme members of his party, Dalton may have allowed this to be tacitly assumed. Secondly, the prospect of having so large a sum available created immediately ambitions and jealousies among Government departments, museums and galleries and other eligible organisations. Thirdly, the Fund was under the immediate control of the Treasury, and was dispensed initially with a bad grace and in such niggardly amounts that after some six years of its existence it stood, with accumulated interest, at a higher figure than when it was created.

In the event, comparatively little property passed to the Government through the Fund. Museums and galleries benefitted but the principal beneficiary was the National Trust. It is hard to know why this was so. Probably it was simply that as far as property other than works of art *per se* were concerned, the Trust had more straightforward and proven qualifications to be a custodian and above all was the cheapest choice. The Conservative government did, in the 1953 Finance Act, extend the operation of the Fund to works of art, but in 1957 the Chancellor, Peter Thorneycroft, in his Budget speech, announced the intention to reduce the Fund from the £60 million to which it had grown through lack of use, to £10 million, which as he rightly said, 'will suffice to meet all demands on the Fund under present policies, which we mean to continue.'

Arthur Blenkinsop, a long-time champion of the Trust, attacked this proposal for which there was no financial advantage to the nation.

> He [the Chancellor] was fair enough to admit that its abolition will do nothing to help the Budget. It makes no contribution to budgetary financing of any kind. Again we may ask why he bothered to abolish it. Presumably he did so because as long as the Fund remained at its present size there was always bound to be some pressure – in my view rightful pressure – upon the Government of the day to make use of it for the purposes for which it was established.

Whether more constructive use of the Fund would have developed if it had not been reduced is impossible to say. However, it continued with that very low base and with its various defects until 1980 when the whole system was remodelled in the form of the National Heritage Memorial Fund, with its own trustees and secretariat and freed from the dead hand of immediate Treasury control, though still dependent on Government funding (see pp. 173–4).

However, the effect of the new Government policy introduced in 1947 on the Country Houses Scheme was immediate. It offered owners a new way of ensuring the future of their property and meeting their estate duty liabilities at the same time. The major drawback was that the Treasury would not begin to consider giving any form of endowment which was not in land. The ball began rolling when the 5th Earl Mount Edgcumbe died and his successor offered his property at Cotehele, on the Cornish side of the upper reaches of the Tamar estuary, to the Commissioners of Inland Revenue in lieu of estate duty, with the intention that the house should be given to the National Trust. There was no question as to the merits of the fine medieval house. Jim Lees-Milne on his first visit likened it to a West Country Knole, which was high praise indeed. The offer included the estate of about 1,000 acres, composed of no less than eighty farm holdings, some of them very small but many of remarkably high rental value because the early flower and vegetable market of the West Country was still flourishing, the produce sent up to Covent Garden daily by train, and the steep sheltered little fields were ideal for the purpose.

This being the first offer under the new scheme, the Treasury called a meeting to which Hubert Smith and Christopher Gibbs were summoned, to find officials from various Ministries assembled, discussing which should have the estate and making it quite clear that it should not go to the Trust. This was duly reported through family channels to Lord Mount Edgcumbe who was furious and went direct to the Minister, with the predictable result that the gift was made to the Trust.

That this particular property should have been the first, and that it came as early as 1947, was providential. First, there was the question of quality: no one could begin to argue against the merits of the house or its romantic and beautiful setting. Second, it illustrated the problems of financing such a venture. The estate was supposed to be self-supporting, as indeed it was at that time. No one could foresee how rapidly its agricultural prosperity would decline, and no one realised that domestic and agricultural conditions which had been satisfactory for a hundred years would almost immediately be regarded as intolerable. The endowment in the form of inalienable land prohibited any manipulation which would provide a hedge against a change of circumstance or inflation, which was to begin in earnest two years later.

The Mount Edgcumbes must have found it an awful wrench to part with a home that had housed the family for so many centuries, but they gave no sign of regrets and were helpful and friendly in the extreme. When the 6th Earl died the contents, which as heirlooms had been retained in his possession but left in the house, were given to the Trust by his successor through a similar Land Fund transaction.

Government must have recognised quite soon the financial risks attendant upon the maintenance of such properties; although there was stiff opposition for several years from the Treasury to transfers to the Trust, it was eventually regarded as a cheap way out, and the Trust for its part began in the early 1950s adding up the deficits which had been incurred by its General Fund on maintaining gifts from the Government. Meanwhile a different devise was tried out for two great houses within the London fringe.

Ham House on the bank of the Thames, across the river from Twickenham, was one of the best survivals of early seventeenth-century houses and contained a marvellous collection of Stuart furniture. It had been in the hands of the Tollemache family for nearly the whole of its existence and, had there been enough money to endow it, it would have passed lock stock and barrel into the care of the Trust. The Director of the Victoria and Albert Museum at the time was Arthur Leigh Ashton, a most determined and abrasive character. It was his idea that the property should be bought by the Government and put into the care of the Victoria and Albert, but Sir Lyonel Tollemache was adamant that he would not trust the Government with unrestricted ownership. A compromise was evolved whereby the house and grounds were given to the Trust, which then granted a lease to the Ministry of Works. The Government bought the contents and the Victoria and Albert became the managers. It may have been the only way out but there were immediate regrets. Esher returned from an inspection with Ashton lamenting that the house was being stripped of all the accretions since 1700 and turned into a museum.

Very soon the Earl of Jersey found himself in a similar position and the same device was adopted for Osterley Park in Middlesex just north of the Great West Road. This time, forewarned by experience, Lees-Milne insisted on a provision in the lease that none of the furnishings should be removed without the Trust's consent. The Trust had to accept from the start that there was no way in which these houses would fit into Lothian's original concept of continuing family homes. They became museums pure and simple. They did, however, further demonstrate to Government that, as against National Trust ownership, this was a very expensive option. The Trust's estimate of the income which would be needed was little over a quarter of that required by the Victoria and Albert, largely due to the latter's high rate of staffing at much higher wages.

It is true that the houses and their most important contents have been preserved and also that as landlord the Trust has been able to exert some beneficial influence. Nevertheless the extraordinary structure of management has sometimes affected the presentation of the properties as a whole. Unbelievable as it may seem, the V & A are only responsible directly for the museum aspect. Repairs are done by the Property Services Agency and the gardens and parks are looked after by the Royal Parks. With such a division there has hitherto been little prospect of new initiative. Only after thirty years has the Trust, using largely its own resources, been able to restore the garden at Ham and the park at Osterley.

Concurrently with the two foregoing transactions, the Government decided to buy Lord Ashburnham's house at Audley End in North Essex. The house had long before been offered to the Trust and had been the subject of protracted but fruitless negotiation; the Trust's lack of means being the stumbling block. Then towards the end of 1947 the Princess Royal, whose husband Lord Harewood had died, turned to the Trust for advice about Harewood House and its estate near Harrogate. Although technically and legally her position was no different from that of other owners, both the Trust and the Treasury felt somewhat tentative in considering the application of the Land Fund to the home of the King's sister.

The result was a series of meetings between the Trust and the Treasury which provoked alarm and anger at the official attitude. Lees-Milne, in particular, felt that both the Treasury and the Ministry of Works officials 'were ignorant and contemptuous of the functions of the National Trust ... they seemed to welcome the prospect that the National Trust would very soon be financially on the rocks ... obliged to go cap in hand to the Government.' Esher sensibly pointed out that 'the important people have not been approached' and suggested an interview between Lord Crawford and the Chancellor of the Exchequer, Sir Stafford Cripps.

There was some reassurance when the meeting took place, Cripps intimating that in his opinion the Trust was the proper body to hold historic houses. He suggested that, in order to identify the scale of the problem, a schedule of the most important houses and their collections should be drawn up. Incidentally the delicate problem of Harewood gradually receded, other measures, mercifully, enabling the family to keep the property in their own possession.

However, in early June Lees-Milne was still deeply despondent. He noted a great falling off in the number of houses being offered and put this down to the new options open to owners, such as transfer in lieu of estate duty or outright Government purchase, as at Audley End. In contrast the Trust's total lack of money for preserving country houses prevented it from taking any that were not in first class order and handsomely endowed. He thought it unlikely that the Trust would be offered any more gifts of houses or land and that the Government would take over more and more houses and their collections.

At about the same time, Sir Edward Bridges wrote to Lord Crawford on behalf of the Chancellor, who 'feels that the time has come when we ought to have an organised plan for dealing with such houses, but he also feels it is a subject of some difficulty in several respects and before he attempts to lay any particular plan before his colleagues he has in mind to appoint a small committee so that the different views on the subject can be ventilated.' He went on to point out that whatever the outcome the issue would raise problems of policy for the Trust both difficult and important. Bridges was one of the most powerful men in the Civil Service, of which he became the head. At the time he was at the Treasury, and he later went to the Cabinet Office. He was in touch with the Trust as a member and later Chairman of the quasi-autonomous Box Hill Committee. It is probable that, once the position had been discussed between his Minister and the Trust's Chairman, Bridges saw to it that the Trust was at least given a fair hearing.

Whatever Bridges' part in the matter, a committee was very quickly set up under Sir Ernest Gowers and by January 1949 the Trust was busy preparing a memorandum of evidence. It is an interesting sidelight on the use of the Trust's committee structure that the Finance and General Purposes Committee had become a ruling caucus and all matters of importance went through its hands before reaching the Executive. In this case Jim Lees-Milne's draft memorandum was, on Esher's explicit instructions, circulated to his Committee and their comments invited on it before their next meeting. One of the jobs that Bevir did well was the review of opinions and courses of action. Harold Nicolson was given the task of re-writing the draft.

However, Nicolson said firmly that he disagreed with the policy of the statement and so in part did most of the Committee. Bevir's excellent and scrupulously fair summary demonstrated that on the most important issue – money – there were three definite views:

- that the Trust would be best off with an annual grant which it could spend as it wished on country house preservation. Uppermost in many minds had been the success of the new Arts Council funded annually with an Exchequer Grant.
- that specific grants only should be accepted lest an overall grant might lead to overall supervision by Government.
- no grant whatsoever should be accepted. This was Nicolson's strongly held view: '...if we once allow ourselves to be under this financial obligation to the Treasury we shall find that the Ministry of Works becomes the expert department for looking after houses and that we are gradually squeezed out as a group of amiable, aristocratic amateurs.'

Lord Esher reflected that the number of houses likely to require the Trust's protection over the next fifteen years would strain its resources. He was aware of the power of the Ministry of Works, and the strength of its case where museums, schools or institutions were involved. However, he felt that, 'It is when the family remains that our custody is superior to the Ministry of Works, and as many families should be retained as possible, as it is only they who can maintain the "country house" atmosphere and who also make the best custodians ....' As to money, he came down on the side of the Arts Council precedent, thinking in terms of £$\frac{1}{2}$ million annually, but seeing as a snag the inevitable advent of a Treasury assessor on the Finance Committee!

The memorandum that went in the end was excellent and its recommendations practical and to the point, with the annual grant being the financial solution put forward. The Gowers Committee was prompt and efficient and it reported only eighteen months after first having been constituted.

Gowers reported on 23 June 1950. Jack Rathbone had a 'black market', private advance copy, and there were feverish consultations with Crawford, Esher, Rosse, Martineau and Lees-Milne which enabled the Trust to get a letter printed in *The Times* on the day the report was published. It gave the report a warm welcome but with two major regrets: that the Trust's Country Houses Scheme, to be supported by Government money, had not been accepted and that there was no recommendation to include chattels with the in lieu procedure.

The essence of the report was that the country houses and other historic buildings of Britain justified some measure to secure their survival. The best way to achieve this would be an allocation of money to the Minister of Works, from which grants would be made towards the cost of repairs, on which the Minister would be advised by a new non-Government body. The Land Fund would remain available for the acquisition of such houses as owners decided to part with.

The questions of endowment and chattels were still unresolved and Lord Crawford went in the autumn to see the new Chancellor, Hugh Gaitskell – another Dalton protegé. However, in 1951 the Government, with a too slender majority, resigned and the Trust had to pursue the matter with a new administration, which to its credit took the matter up quite quickly, pricked along by such questions as that asked by Kenneth Robinson, (then a young Labour MP on the Executive Committee of the Trust) of David Eccles, the Minister of Works, 'whether he will introduce legislation to implement the Gowers Report?'

A draft bill was produced which provoked a deliciously acid and aggressive memorandum by Martineau, justifiably, because it was muddled and unworkable. The whole of 1952 and the early part of 1953, was taken up by the Trust trying to make up its own mind about the form of the Bill and what it should say about it to Government. By this time Jim Lees-Milne had given up the Secretaryship of the Historic Buildings Committee to become 'Adviser' and his work was taken on by Robin Fedden who conducted most of the negotiations with the Ministry of Works official.

In February 1953 Harold Nicolson went to see the current Chancellor, Rab Butler, to secure his help about the provision of endowments. The Trust, to Butler's relief, had abandoned the idea of capital sums from the Land Fund, but what about an allocation from the annual grant provision for capital investment, which would build up into an endowment fund? 'Butler professed himself in entire agreement with this view,' Nicolson wrote to Rathbone, but added, '... my experience is that Ministers are very apt to agree with one's requests and that after consultation with their officials this agreement is diluted into other forms ... I think we had better continue in unctuous pessimism.' How right he was! Within four days Butler wrote to Nicolson and Lord Wemyss (who had accompanied him on behalf of the National Trust for Scotland) to say that – no, grants would only be made for specific repairs! The National Trust for Scotland (NTS) had been formed in 1931, with much the same powers as the National Trust, but this is the first sign of the two acting in concert. Jamie Stormonth Darling, Director of the NTS, wrote gratefully to Rathbone thanking him for keeping him closely informed with the progress of negotiations. The pressures involved in the run up to this particular legislation forged more than anything else a close collaboration which still exists.

Suddenly all the problems seemed to fade away – not necessarily solved but no longer forming obstacles. The Bill had its first reading in June and on 31 July 1953 received the Royal Assent. Robinson and Edward Keeling (Conservative MP for Twickenham and on the Executive) were both given full credit for their work by Rathbone, and he in his turn got a warm letter from Mr Root of the Ministry of Works. It was a great relief to see the Bill reach haven smoothly, helped by Lord Esher's magnificent speech, and the work on the stage and behind it of the other National Trust representatives.

'We quite understood your point of view on endowments (on which the Trust had caused an amendment to be moved) and we were grateful to you for limiting your amendments to the points on which you feel strongly.'

On the top of this letter Rathbone wrote, 'Mr Fedden. All thanks (or most of them) are due to you.' Fedden's endorsement was 'Nonsense!' but whether that applied to the whole comment or the qualifying words in the bracket is hard to say.

It was left to Sir Alan Lascelles in a thoughtful, scholarly and lively address to the AGM of the Trust in 1954 to explain just what the Historic Buildings and Ancient Monuments Act 1953 meant in terms of country house preservation. It has set up three separate Historic Buildings Councils – one each for England, Wales and Scotland – Sir Alan being Chairman for England. Clause 1 of the Act defined the Council's duty as 'to advise the Minister of Works in the exercise of his powers under Part I of the Act.' These powers boiled down to the making of grants for the repair of historic buildings – any buildings, not just houses.

To illustrate the question of how to assess merit, he quoted from an address by Osbert Lancaster to the Royal Institute of British Architects '... there are three grounds, and only three, on which we are logically entitled to press for the preservation of any building – the ground of its own intrinsic aesthetic merit; of *pietas*; and of its scenic usefulness.' Sir Alan's own definition of 'pietas' was a combination of 'good' and 'old'. 'Anything to which an Englishman wishes no positive harm is good, old.' He suggested that this would apply to the Tower of London, the Albert Memorial and the gasometers at the Kennington Oval.

He was cautious in dealing with the amount of grant that might be made. Dealing with continued occupation by families he took the sting of envy out very neatly. 'To us, remember, the house is the thing ... (whether it be a castle or a cottage) ... Our aim is to help a house keep an occupier – not to help an occupier keep his house.'

To remind his audience of the wide scope of the Historic Buildings Council he referred to buildings other than houses. He regarded that position as being fairly satisfactory. 'But as regards *houses*, the future seems to me to be heavy with clouds.' That is how the Historic Buildings Council's first Chairman saw his task and it was with this system that the National Trust had to pursue its Country Houses Scheme.

It is probably fair to say that from the point of view of keeping the Trust's houses in repair the system has worked very well. By 1960 the Trust had acquired a number of country houses either by gifts made privately or from the Government through the Land Fund. The vexed question of the inclusion of contents in the 'in lieu' procedures had been satisfactorily settled in the Finance Act 1953. The acceptance of houses was made easier with the prospect of the Historic Buildings Council's help in meeting the costs. What still remained was the Treasury's obstinate refusal to permit the giving of endowments in cash.

In part-payment of estate duty the Government had, between 1947 and 1960, accepted and given to the Trust ten properties of which six were country houses – Cotehele, Ickworth, Petworth, Saltram, Berrington and Hardwick Hall – and all except the first named with their important contents. In the same period Croft Castle and Dyrham had been acquired with help from the Ministry of Works, on Historic Buildings Council advice, and through the same channel almost £304,000 had been given in grants for repairs. At a time when the Trust was struggling unaided to do its work of preservation, this help was munificent in the extreme.

In order to overcome the endowment problem a device was adopted by the

Government, and reluctantly accepted by the Trust. It arose in the case of houses which seemed to all the parties concerned – and that included the owners – to be of over-riding importance, and where the means of ensuring their future was not otherwise to be found. Then special measures were warranted. In simple terms the Government took the houses and their important contents in part payment of estate duty, transferred them to the Trust and gave an undertaking, in varying forms, to meet the annual deficit through a maintenance grant given by the Historic Buildings Council. There were five of these houses: Saltram, near Plymouth (1957); Beningborough, near York (1958); Hardwick Hall, Derbyshire (1958); Dyrham, Avon (1961); Sudbury Hall, near Derby (1967).

It would be unfair to over-stress the unsatisfactory nature of the arrangement. For the Trust it meant just what so many people had been afraid of when contemplating the effects of Government financial help. It meant that they could not manage the property in accordance with their own standards and priorities. For the Government and the Historic Buildings Council it meant an annually recurring liability which, even if placed under the strictest of limitation, curtailed their ability to look after other properties. The relationship between the officers of the Trust and the Historic Buildings Council was excellent and both did their best to work within the money available. Nevertheless, there were always conflicts over priorities. Things were aggravated by the coincidence that, during the 1960s, the Trust's standards of presentation and its provisions for visitors were being very much improved and the number of visitors was rapidly increasing. Such things as car parks, lavatories and tea rooms either had to be provided or enlarged, and garden paths, floor coverings, security alarms, fire warning systems and a host of requirements, quite apart from the ordinary maintenance of a house, made increasing calls for more money.

To thresh out the amount of money needed and the jobs which must be done or which must be deferred took both organisations an inordinate amount of time and trouble, for they were both under-staffed. There were some special features which were adopted to overcome certain problems. At Dyrham, in order to get round the difficulty of supplying capital, the Ministry of Works undertook a programme of major repairs and the work of converting part of the house into flats, which would help to produce income towards the maintenance of the house, before conveyance to the Trust. At Hardwick Hall a separate annual provision of money was made from which the repair of the entire structure of the great house was to be undertaken. This has been continued at an agreed and practicable rate over the succeeding twenty-five years. At Sudbury a third party, the Derbyshire County Council, was drawn in to meet a part of the deficit.

Another device adopted was to try to find a tenant of substance who would undertake the whole responsibility for maintaining the house as lessee. This was simply an enlargement of a much earlier system which had been widely applied to smaller houses and generally with the Trust as landlord keeping responsibility for the structure. The mediaeval Speke Hall on the edge of the Mersey (and now also on the edge of an airport) had in 1944 been let to the Corporation of the City of Liverpool. In 1947, the Trust made a similar arrangement with the Stockport Corporation for Lyme Park on the moorland edge of the Peak. Later, in 1960, it made an arrangement with the Cheshire County Council for Tatton Park and, in 1966, with the Staffordshire County Council for Shugborough. This method again produced a qualified success. These houses were preserved, but the changing financial position of the tenants and the growing understanding of the needs of both conservation and presentation led to a growing dissatisfaction with the arrangements. Indeed Stockport was only saved, financially, by the local government reorganisation in 1974, when the Greater Manchester Country Council became responsible.

The Government even tried out the system which had so much worried Rathbone in 1952 – the employment of the Trust as an agent to manage a house in the ownership of the Government. In 1969 the owner of Heveningham House in Suffolk mounted a campaign to oblige the Government to buy the property, to prevent what was represented as an inescapable alternative: sale of the property and its contents. The campaign succeeded and the Government found themselves with a house capable of being lived in and with no ready-to-hand method of looking after it. The property was offered to the Trust, which agreed to take it if it were endowed. The endowment was denied, as usual; the Government decided to re-sell to a private owner, and asked whether the Trust would look after it until a buyer was found. So dual control began and continued in the hands of Nicolas Corbin as Area Agent. He found all the problems that Rathbone had foreseen, and more besides, such as the division of responsibility between different sections of the Ministry and the difficulty of getting authoritative decisions. Corbin's character was such that he rather enjoyed carving his own way through the obstacles of officialdom and he feels that he succeeded in exercising management at a sufficiently efficient level, although he continued loud in his complaints of the tiresomeness of the Ministry. At intervals the property was offered again to the Trust but with no endowment.

By 1978 the Trust felt that the arrangement had gone on long enough and gave notice of its intention to withdraw and eventually in 1980 did so. Both Corbin and the Duke of Grafton, a member of the Historic Buildings Council and Chairman of the SPAB, feel that the Trust's decision was a mistake and that there would have been a better outcome if it had endured patiently for a few more years the irksome role of agent for the Government. This view depends on how one looks at the problems involved for the Ministry and the Historic Buildings Council in co-operating with the private owner as opposed to the Trust. Whatever one may feel about the outcome, the incident proved conclusively how unsuitable the agency solution is, and again how vital it was that endowment in some form should be available to the Trust.

The essence of the whole problem was that the Trust needed to be directly in control of its more important properties. In order to be in a position to impose its own standards and methods on the management of a property the Trust had to be in possession of the money to do so, and so the issue of the provision of an endowment by the Government remained crucial and unresolved.

It was in 1977 that a case arose in which the National Trust was in no way concerned, but which finally pushed Parliament and then the Government towards some sensible action. The Rothschild family had in the nineteenth century established themselves in five houses in the Vale of Aylesbury. Halton House was bought in the 1920s by Hugh Trenchard to establish the Royal Air Force apprentices' training school and the RAF Hospital. Tring Park has become a school. Waddesdon was given to the Trust in 1957 and Ascott at Wing in 1950. The fifth,

Mentmore Towers, had passed by marriage to the Rosebery family. In 1974 after his father's death, Lord Rosebery decided that he must sell, and offered the property direct to Government. The house – the only surviving example of a country house by Joseph Paxton – he offered for £2 million, with its contents. The Government, which in this case by inference means the Treasury, after two and a half years of prevarication refused, saying that insufficient funds were available, (despite there being £18 million in the Land Fund!). There was little dispute as to merit or money value, the latter being said to be substantially below the true price. Neither owner nor Government involved the National Trust, though numerous others tried to, and eventually obliged the Trust to write to *The Times* saying that it had had no part in the negotiations but if asked would certainly consider playing a part. It was not asked. Lord Rosebery gave the Government a closing date for his offer, it passed and the house sold for £3 million and the contents for £6 million. This fiasco, and the public outcry that followed resulted in the Public Expenditure Committee of the House of Commons calling for evidence, through its Environment Sub-Committee, on the operation of the Land Fund.

The Trust's evidence had two main points: first that country houses, their contents and gardens will usually be cared for most economically and appropriately if they remain in private hands. Therefore owners should be helped as much as possible to continue in possession, subject to provisions for public access and the proper maintenance of the property. The second point was that the Land Fund should continue to operate and that it should be specifically empowered to provide capital for endowments.

The Trust was at the same time careful to emphasise that it was not acquisitive of houses unless their survival was at risk and that it only positively sought to acquire coastal land and beautiful country. This was a period of quite intensive debate among Government departments and agencies, amenity groups and the public as a whole, and the task of presenting the dilemma was no easier than it had ever been – the Trust does not seek to acquire what is not in danger, but when it is in danger it may be too late!

At this time the Trust's senior executive had become known as Director General and the man in that office was J.D. Boles, of whom there is more to say later. To him goes very much of the credit for co-ordinating, especially with the National Trust for Scotland, the evidence for the select committee and for feeding MPs and others with the information on which they could press the Government for action. The Labour Government of 1974 was in its last months before going out of office when a White Paper was published, but the new Conservative Government moved surprisingly quickly. By the Spring of 1980 a new Act reached the statute book setting up an entirely new body, the National Heritage Memorial Fund, with independent Trustees appointed by the Prime Minister. It was given an initial £12.4 million to serve as its own endowment and was thereafter to receive an annual grant of an unspecified amount. It has the power to assist with grants the preservation, acquisition and maintenance of any property of outstanding interest which is also important to the national heritage. Above all, it is free to use its resources without reference to the Treasury.

The Conservative Government improved on the White Paper in one respect, and retained the old procedure whereby property could be accepted by the Inland

Revenue instead of money in satisfaction of capital transfer tax (which had replaced estate duty in 1975). The cost was to be defrayed from the NHMF, which was a problem, but it did at least remove the financial decision from the Treasury. Added to this, the 1972 Finance Act had given to the Trust exemption from capital gains tax, both on gifts and on its own transactions and also complete exemption from estate duty (subsequently capital transfer tax) on gifts of money or property. This favourable treatment by the Chancellor may well have originated with the influence of Frederick Bishop, the Trust's then Director General, whose standing with members of the Government was high.

The transformation for the Trust was instant. It was also demanding in the extreme. The Fund's Trustees were fortunate in having from the start a Chairman, Lord Charteris, and a Secretary, Brian Lang, intelligent, practical and sympathetic to the wide range of their responsibilities. (In 1987 Brian Lang left the Fund to become the Trust's Director of Public Relations.) It was their policy from the start to help others to help themselves, expecting always that there should be major financial contributions from other sources towards any particular scheme which they intended to help. The Trust's annual reports from 1982 record the result.

In 1981 the Dryden family, descendants of the poet, were at last persuaded to part with their sixteenth-century Northamptonshire house, Canons Ashby, which was in such bad repair that it was on the point of collapse. They did not have the means to restore it, nor were they in a position to do so, living thousands of miles away in Zimbabwe. The Trust on this occasion did literally 'save' the house, but it could not have done so without the helpful and flexible attitude of the Trustees of the Fund. Not only did they contribute a large slice of the money needed for repair, but four-fifths of the £1,254,000 needed for the endowment. There had been absolutely no reason, moral or legal, why the Treasury should not have provided endowments from the original Land Fund and yet despite having the power, time and again they declined to do so.

In 1982 the Trust was able to buy 3,100 acres of the Derbyshire Peak, comprising its most dramatic and well known features – Kinder Edge and the Downfall – receiving its first major grant from the Fund, but being obliged to raise on its own a further £200,000 (which it did successfully by public appeal). Having begun with a property that was archetypal 'open space', there followed, in 1983, the acquisition of Belton House, near Grantham (the very house, ironically that Lord Brownlow had hoped to save when he sold Ashridge in the 1920s).

This late seventeenth-century house, which is of exceptional beauty and immensely important architecturally, was a very different proposition. With its park and estate, it was for sale on the open market and the likelihood of it surviving intact with its accumulated contents was negligible. Lord Brownlow was eventually persuaded to give the house and gardens to the Trust, but the park and contents had to be paid for – and they were, by a grant of £4 million from the Fund, which supplied another £4 million for capital repairs and endowment. That the Trustees should have been prepared to make such an immense provision shows both the ability to recognise exceptional circumstances and the courage to commit the necessary resources to deal with them.

In the same year the Trust and the Fund were engaged in tackling another problem of equal financial dimensions. Calke Abbey lies, curiously secluded in its

156

magnificent park, just on the Derbyshire side of the county boundary with Leicestershire. The Harpur Crewe family which owned it appear to be among those who not only throw nothing away but continue to look after what accumulates. At first it seemed that even if the house, park and contents came to the Trust through the 'in lieu' procedure there could be no chance of raising £7½ million which was needed for capital repairs and improvements. The Trustees of the Fund took the initiative in calling a conference of everyone concerned and miraculously there was a solution! The Trust found two benefactors and also scraped together its own funds to produce £1 million. The family and the Fund promised another £1 million each and more revenue-producing land was promised, the gap being reduced to £3 million, which it seemed could only be found from Government. For this the Fund applied, and actually got it by special provision in the 1984 Budget.

When one considers the goodwill, flexibility and generosity displayed by all parties concerned with this sort of transaction, it is difficult to realise that it is the same subject as that which caused the frustration and ill-feeling among those trying to promote the preservation of country houses over half a century before. It in no way detracts from the part played by successive Governments and their officials, and by the grant-making bodies, to remind ourselves that, from the very beginning, it has been the National Trust which has seen the dangers and has led the campaign.

There is no reason to suppose that the development of the means of preservation is finished. In 1983 the National Heritage Act re-organised the somewhat higgledy-piggledy arrangements within the Department of the Environment for the care of Ancient Monuments and Historic Buildings by creating the Historic Buildings and Monuments Commission as a semi-independent agency and it is likely that from there new ideas will originate.

Moreover, another plank in the Trust's platform has been progressively strengthened – the assistance to private owners to continue to maintain their own property by means of tax concessions, as well as grants – especially the setting up of their own endowment funds – in return for a reasonable degree of public access. Furthermore, a new realism on the part of the National Trust, born of hard experience, has led it to adopt a formula for calculating the amount needed for an endowment. This, the 'Chorley formula', so-called after its deviser, Lord Chorley's son Roger, is designed to enable the Trust to withstand the erosion of inflation over a long period. It goes some way to explain the huge sums involved: sometimes people regard the Trust as an expensive option. This is because an endowment appears expensive at the outset because of the initially large capital outlay. In the long run, the option is almost certainly cheaper than funding an annual deficit out of public funds year by year. For a private person there is always the option to take a different course of action – sell an old master; sell the whole property – if events make it impossible to continue. The expense of financing the perpetual responsibility of the Trust means that it will always be what it was originally intended to be – a safety net only.

CHAPTER XII

Houses with Special Connections

Among the pioneers of the National Trust, Hardwicke Rawnsley was acutely conscious of the historical connections between places and people. It is surprising that in the first forty years of the Trust's existence only two properties were acquired specifically because of their association with famous people. The first, in 1909, was the cottage at Nether Stowey where Coleridge lived and did much of his best work. *The Ancient Mariner* and the first part of *Christabel* were written at Nether Stowey and it was there, too, that 'a person from Porlock' interrupted the laudanum-induced flow of *Kubla Khan*. Perhaps for Rawnsley and others it was of equal importance that Wordsworth and his sister stayed there and forged the links which later bound the Lake Poets together.

Nine years later Quebec House at Westerham was accepted. It had been left by the will of Joseph Bowles Learmont of Montreal to the British Government but was declined and the Executors selected the Trust as the best non-Government organisation to become the permanent owner. From his widow's letters it seems that Mr Learmont intended that the house, because of its connections with General Wolfe, should become 'a shrine for Canadians'. This was at a time when Canada had contributed her full share to the Allied cause, with the great victory at Vimy Ridge her finest memorial. The house is an agreeable building of Tudor origin and a pleasant early eighteenth-century appearance, set in what is still a decent, small Kentish town.

It was not until 1936 that the Trust really embarked upon the preservation of houses with personal connections and then it began to collect them at an average rate of one a year until 1950.

Number 24, Cheyne Row, Chelsea is an elegant house in an elegant street, with a pedigree which goes back to the reign of Queen Anne. But really it is because Thomas Carlyle lived there from 1834 until his death in 1881 that it is preserved by the Trust. Indeed it was bought by public subscription for that purpose as long ago as 1895; and handed on to the Trust in 1936. It fell to Carew Wallace to open the house to the public after the War, when the contents, which had been stored away for safety, were returned. Lord Crawford took a detailed interest in what was being done and Wallace was greatly impressed by the knowledge he displayed of Thomas Carlyle's life and work. Lees-Milne actually met a man, Reginald Blunt, son of the Rector of Chelsea, who remembered both Carlyle and his wife Jane, recalling that on taking milk from the rectory cow, and garden produce in season, he was rewarded by the gift of a china apple on a plate, which he still possessed.

A very different kind of property came in 1937 when Dr Lawrence offered to the Trust Clouds Hill Cottage near Wareham, Dorset where his brother, Colonel T.E. Lawrence – Lawrence of Arabia – had spent the last years of his life and near to which he had died when he crashed his motorcycle in 1935. The ugly, jerry-built cottage, set in dreary heathland and hedged with rhododendrons so as to be invisible from the road, speaks more clearly than anything else could of a character that set little store by any except the simplest of physical comforts, and wanted most of all seclusion and the company of books and music.

Across the road in another small house lived Pat Knowles and his wife Joyce, who acted as friends and caretakers and who, after Lawrence died, transferred to the Trust their loyalty to his memory and the care of his few possessions. Clouds Hill is perhaps of all places most truly the one in which the memory of the man is the thing that really counts. That the Trust should have had the percipience to see that, and to agree to look after it, is in some ways one of the most creditable of all its acts.

What would have most appealed to Hardwicke Rawnsley was the salvation of the house in Cockermouth where William Wordsworth, on 7 April 1770, was born. Dr Ellis, the owner, put the house up for sale when he was leaving the practice. Bruce Thompson backed the idea of an appeal for £2,000 which would be enough, he thought, to buy the place and endow it. There was a move to form a Wordsworth museum there, but he was against that, and against having to raise an additional £4,000 which its sponsors thought necessary. Thompson, writing to the Secretary, displayed the undisguised double motive which often affected the Trust's actions, '... by emphasising the birthplace (which, oddly enough, does appeal) we could save a very nice eighteenth-century house.' That was in 1937. A year later the appeal was not making much progress, despite active support from Eleanor Rawnsley, and in August *The Times* reported that the house had been sold to provide a site for a 'bus station'. This was a sharp spur to effort and in London Christopher Gibbs found Lucy Robinson from Horsham, whose £500, together with £750 from a legacy from Sir Alfred Wyons, would bridge the gap. Bruce Thompson tackled the Directors of the Omnibus Company, who agreed to resell for the £1,550 they had paid, plus the architect's fee of £50 that had been incurred.

The Kent hamlet of Smallhythe has some beautiful and ancient half-timbered buildings, and in 1913 local people unsuccessfully tried to involve the Trust in the preservation of a cottage, said to be of the fifteenth century, which they feared was likely to be demolished. At that time a well-known and nationally much-loved actress was living just across the road in a house of similar antiquity. Ellen Terry had bought Smallhythe Place in 1899 and she lived there until her death in 1928.

Ellen Terry's daughter, Edith Craig, deliberately kept the house as a memorial to her mother, assembling a collection of her belongings, some of her stage costumes and mementoes of her long partnership with Henry Irving. In 1938 she offered Smallhythe Place to the Trust. In such an ephemeral subject as that of the theatre, the idea of preservation in perpetuity must have seemed to the Executive Committee of the Trust as something they could not guarantee. They had received Lees-Milne's report: 'Certainly a most attractive property. Of its kind, I think it is the best museum I have seen. Apart from the Ellen Terry connections, the house is very good and has been admirably conditioned [sic]. The same may be said of Miss Craig's cottage, the priest's house, also half-timbered of the same date.' The Committee agreed acceptance, but with the condition that they should be free to remove the museum to another place. This does seem strange, but it may simply have been the Trust's constant fear of incurring expenses without new resources. The condition was withdrawn when Miss Craig, who was then 71, undertook to leave her 'small fortune', which produced £300 per annum, to the Trust.

Rudyard Kipling's widow had approached the Trust in 1937 intending to leave to it the property in Sussex – Bateman's at Burwash – which her husband had bought in 1902, and where he had done much of his writing. There was no hesitation on the part of the Committee. On Mrs Kipling's death in 1940, the attractive house, built by a Wealden ironmaster in the seventeenth century, with its good if modest garden and 300 acres of pasture land came into the Trust's care. Kipling's *Rewards and Fairies* and *Puck of Pook's Hill* are rich with descriptions of the neighbourhood. Much of the imprint of Kipling's ownership remains, not just in the intimacy of his study, which still contains his books and paraphernalia, but in the furnishings, the garden and the water-driven turbine at the nearby mill, which once generated electricity for the house.

The Kiplings and the Baldwins were first cousins, and Stanley Baldwin's daughter, Lady Lorna Howard remembers 'Uncle Ruddy' with warmth and affection, and also of course, the Kiplings' surviving daughter, Elsie Bambridge. Mrs Kipling had wished to make it a condition that the house should not be occupied, but the Trust demurred, mainly on financial grounds. She gave way, taking care, however, to set out in a very sensible memorandum attached to her will on what terms the house might be let. One provision was that Stanley Baldwin would give his consent to any letting, but when Matheson wrote to him on the subject, he courteously declined to be involved. Two properties acquired in 1943 are quite different but share one characteristic – they are exceptionally agreeable places in themselves. Woolsthorpe Manor, on the limestone that runs up through Lincolnshire, was built in about 1620 of the same stone on which it stands: here Isaac Newton was born in 1642. The Suffolk-Essex boundary of the River Bure as it runs through Dedham Vale is of great beauty. Here are to be found Flatford Mill and Willy Lott's Cottage, both of which have close connections with the landscape painter, John Constable. The throngs of summer visitors to the tiny hamlet go there for the river, the rowing boats, the cream teas, and share in their own way Constable's pleasure in that pleasant place.

Two Dorset Hardys are commemorated by the Trust: the poet and novelist Thomas, who was born in a tiny thatched cottage at Higher Bockhampton, three miles east of Dorchester on the fringe of 'Egdon' Heath; and 'Kiss-me Hardy', Admiral Sir Thomas Masterman, whose monument stands on a hill top ten miles to the west. Thomas the novelist is well commemorated in his birthplace. Its isolation at the end of a long unmade-up track and its rustic antiquity both correspond with the pictures of rural life which Hardy drew in his writings.

The Trust can be proud of its treatment of an approach by George Bernard Shaw. 'Dear Sir,' he wrote on 5 October 1943:

I am the owner of a 10 roomed house in the village of Ayot St Lawrence in

Herts. where I have lived for the last 35 years – longer than in any other of my residences. I am in my 87th year and about to make my last will … Has such a trifle any use or interest for the National Trust?

Hubert Smith went to see the great man and there followed a perfectly sensible and business-like exchange of correspondence on the subject of his intentions. With very little hesitation his offer to leave it in his will was accepted in the following month, to be converted in May 1944 to a gift, subject to his life interest. Lees-Milne had been to visit Shaw in February and kept a very full account, starting with a description of the house, 'a very ugly dark red brick villa'. Indeed it is just that, having been built in 1902 as the New Rectory and bought by Shaw four years later and re-named 'Shaw's Corner'.

Their talk ranged over a multitude of subjects, including the preservation of the house. Shaw said that he did not want it to be a dead museum, so much as a living shrine, though what that might be and how it could be achieved is not recorded. He approved of the Trust owning Clouds Hill. He knew Lawrence very well and had, with his wife, corrected the *Seven Pillars of Wisdom*, cutting out, he said, much which was occasioned by Lawrence's guilt complex.

Bernard Shaw lived on until 1950, when in his will the important contents of the house were left to the Trust, but no money at all, despite the fact that his estate amounted to £360,000 on probate. Jack Rathbone was rightly very fussed and consulted Matheson who confirmed that the Trust had promised to hold the house as a permanent memorial. There were problems about the suitability of the Shaw Society as tenants – and no wonder, when G.B.S. had forecast in a postscript to a letter in 1944 that 'the Shaw Society will die of old age in four years at the most.'

However, the Trust stuck to its obligation to open the house to the public and in 1951 the village was overrun with an influx of visitors. There was an enraged outcry and complaints that the Trust had been discourteous in not consulting local interests and, worse still, that it was in breach of the planning laws. The Planning Authority refused to be drawn in, maintaining that planning permission was not needed. Hugh Dalton, at the time Minister of Town and Country Planning, first told Rathbone the same thing, but later wrote to Carew Wallace giving a contrary judgement: '… to turn a house into a museum is to make a material change.'

In order to finance the maintenance of Shaw's Corner the Trust launched one of its few hopelessly ineffective appeals. By 1952 only £342 had been raised towards a target of £¼ million. In view of the publicity given to Shaw's will and his legacy to found a new alphabet it is not surprising that the British public were unenthusiastic. The village need not have been so concered. Visitors dropped from over 18,000 in 1951 to under 10,000 in 1953. Now, thirty-five years later the annual number is around 11,000.

To stay alive in popular memory some sort of romantic element is needed. Benjamin Disraeli's life, his political career, his literary output, all seem to radiate that glow which Queen Victoria clearly appreciated in her Prime Minister. His choice of country estate, Hughenden Manor, near High Wycombe, likewise has that sense of warmth despite its modest extent, unattractively Victorianised house and dullish gardens. Inside there is enough of Disraeli still left to give the same feeling of strongly personal connection.

It is, however, the house of another Prime Minister which, perhaps for similar reasons, is the memorial par excellence. Chartwell had been in the ownership of Winston Churchill since 1922 when, somewhat against his wife's better judgement, he bought it for £5,000. What is hard to appreciate is that Churchill, despite the standing of his family, his brilliant career in politics and enormous output of writing, was almost always short of money. It is true that he and his family lived comfortably in the style and manner of their friends but this was sustained almost entirely by his earnings from books and articles, especially during the long years of the 1930s when he was out of office.

It was the position of the place that appealed to the Churchills; the deep secluded valley running out of the chart (or rough heathlands) of north-west Kent into the Weald, not the house, which is described as 'a grey Victorian mansion, built round, and on the site of a much older house, hemmed in by ugly laurels, it was damp, dreary and ugly.' Mrs Churchill realised what would be entailed in re-building it to make it habitable. Mr Churchill did not. In the event Philip Tilden was chosen as architect and after a struggle – in which recurrent outbreaks of dry rot plagued the progress of the work and added to the costs – the present house emerged, but at an expense which they could ill-afford. From 1924 on Winston Churchill and his family made their principal home there and it grew to be an integral part of his life and theirs, even though Mrs Churchill was never quite reconciled to the unending worries it brought in terms of finding money for the proper care of the house and garden and the little farm. This worry surfaced from time to time in Churchill's mind and he recurrently faced the prospect that he would have to sell. In 1938 he wrote to his wife that 'no good offer should be refused, having regard to the fact that our children are almost all flown, and my life is in the closing decade'.

With the following year came the outbreak of the Second World War, and Churchill's great role as Britain's wartime Prime Minister. Yet, despite his supreme achievement, money worries resurfaced with the post-war general election and his rejection by an apparently ungrateful country. It was at this time that a group of friends – anonymous then as now – hatched a plan by which they would buy Chartwell from Churchill for £50,000 and give it to the National Trust, with an endowment, subject to the absolute right for him and his wife to occupy it for their lifetimes. It was a stroke of genius, for it left Mr and Mrs Churchill in full enjoyment of their home while securing for the country a permanent and personal memorial.

Despite his gloomy prediction in 1938, Churchill lived on to serve another term as Prime Minister, to receive the Order of the Garter, and into old age. After his death in January 1965, Lady Churchill could, had she wished, have remained in possession of Chartwell for the rest of her life, but she decided to hand it over straightaway to the Trust. Mary Soames's account of the meeting between her mother and the representatives of the Trust illuminates the significance of the decision.

> Neither my mother nor I have been to Chartwell since she and my father had left there for the last time. The sensitive understanding of Robin Fedden and Ivan Hills of the National Trust helped her, but she was calmly fixed in her mind about her intentions, and she at once addressed herself to the main theme of her thoughts concerning Chartwell's future. By the terms

of the original sale of Chartwell in 1946, only the house and grounds were designated for the National Trust. There was no commitment about the furnishings; the house could have been handed over an empty shell. But from the beginning both Clementine and Winston felt that the house should be 'so garnished and furnished as to be of interest to the public'. This intention Clementine now affirmed to Mr Fedden and Mr Hills, telling them at the same time she wished the house to be seen as it was in its heyday during the 'twenties and 'thirties, rather than in its later day practical, but rather topsy-turvey, arrangement. My mother delegated to Grace Hamblin and to me the task of working closely with the National Trust in carrying out all the details which the takeover and readaptation of the house would involve.

Grace Hamblin, a local girl, had 'helped out' in the office at Chartwell during a holiday period in 1932, and had become the full-time secretary the following year. Already in February 1965 Rathbone noted that 'Lady Churchill has suggested that we take on Grace Hamblin as curator ... [she is] a great ally of Ivan Hills'. He also thought that Lady Churchill was 'absolutely right' about returning the house to its 1930s condition and that the Trust must rely a lot on Mary Soames.

At that first meeting a great deal was settled, which is an indicator of the close spirit of agreement amongst everyone there. In particular, and most wisely, it was agreed that Victor Vincent should continue as Head Gardener. By May it had been arranged with the Treasury that the principal contents should be taken in lieu of estate duty, but Lady Churchill added much besides, including a large number of pictures by Sir Winston, many of which she later left to the Trust. The business of getting the house ready for opening was hectic; the interior had to be returned to its arrangement of nearly forty years before and decorations and fabrics renewed to repeat that style. A car park had to be made, paths laid out, a restaurant, which Hills found Mrs Soames very keen to provide, and lavatories made for the visitors.

In the garden Lanning Roper was engaged by the Trust to act as consultant and adviser. From this delicate position, in which he could very easily have upset Lady Churchill, he succeeded in winning her approval and the confidence of Mr Vincent, though he was to say later that by the time the house was opened he felt as though he had been run over by a steam roller. Lady Churchill was thrilled by the opening of the house in June 1966 and with the immense popularity it achieved with the visiting public, which it still maintains.

It would be idle to pretend that there were no pressures and problems. The huge flow of visitors at one time threatened to trample the garden into a sea of mud, and admissions to the house had to be made by timed tickets so as to preserve an even and not overcrowded flow. In all this the key to efficient and happy working lay in the person of Grace Hamblin whose calm commonsense, straightforward and friendly charm, humour and unpretentious efficiency not only carried through the work of that hectic first year but saw the thing through for seven years more. In Jean Broome, who succeeded her when she retired in 1973, the Trust was fortunate in finding another person in the same mould.

Throughout the succeeding twenty years Mary – now Lady – Soames has continued to play the same role. 'It is my concern,' she has said, 'not to let the picture slip.' Standing in the place of a donor she believes she has no rights but does have great influence. In the nature of things her first National Trust collaborators have gone on to other things, retired, or in the case of Robin Fedden, died. That relations are as good with their successors must be as much her doing as theirs. Are there no regrets? Yes, just one. The kitchen garden with its grass paths was one of her mother's favourite places and the Trust, fearful of the costs involved in vegetable gardening, decided that it could not afford to maintain it. That decision was rooted deep in the folk-memory of everyone faced with the task of maintaining the immensely costly nineteenth-century regime of the kitchen garden and it will take a great act of piety to reverse an almost superstitious belief in the impossibility of reviving it. Yet in so nearly perfect a conclusion, it surely should be done.

Houses with personal connections continued to come into the Trust's guardianship. In 1950 the Trust had accepted Lamb House, in Rye, from the widow of the nephew of Henry James, the American novelist, 'as an enduring symbol of the ties that unite the British and American peoples'. James had lived there much of the time from 1899 to his death in 1916, and some of his writing was done there. The Trust had no difficulty in accepting the house, a charming example of early eighteenth-century domestic building; James and the post-war 'special relationship' with the States was a bonus.

This literary link was brought a generation closer when the Trust agreed to accept Monks House at Rodmell, also in East Sussex, notched into the north face of the South Downs. Here Leonard and Virginia Woolf had come in 1919 and it remained Leonard's home until his death in 1969. Curiously enough a cottage not many miles away, Charleston, which had been the home of the Woolfs' friend Duncan Grant was offered for preservation at the same time. The house was plain mid-Georgian, jammed up against a busy farmyard and dignified only by wall paintings by Virginia's sister, Vanessa Bell, which seemed unlikely to survive for many years on the damp and crumbling plaster. But were the associations shrineworthy?

The Trust's decisions were carefully balanced: Monks House was, with help, a safe proposition financially, and regardless of the shrine factor could be held without incurring any serious problem or breach of principle. Duncan Grant's house presented very serious financial and management problems and the National Trust resolved that unless these were overcome it would not be able to accept, leaving matters to a preservation trust to see whether it could handle the issue.

The question of whether it is right for the Trust to take on buildings on the basis of their association with someone famous still continues to be raised. Until some wise counsel can devise a reliable yardstick, the National Trust will continue to have a somewhat erratic record in this respect.

CHAPTER XIII

Gardens

On 25 November 1947, Jim Lees-Milne attended a meeting in the Trust's Head Office in Queen Anne's Gate which had been convened at the instance of the Chairman of the Royal Horticultural Society, Lord Aberconway. Major David Bowes-Lyon, a brother of the Queen, and Dr H.V. Taylor also attended on behalf of the Society. The proposal made by Lord Aberconway was that a joint committee should be formed to raise money and administer a select few of the very best gardens in England. Only gardens of great beauty or gardens of historic interest could be considered. A Gardens Fund and a Gardens Committee (half the members from the Trust and half the members from the Royal Horticultural Society) would be set up.

The first reaction from the staff was of warm approval. Hubert Smith, who was already involved in negotiations with Major Lawrence Johnston over the garden at Hidcote Bartim, near Chipping Camden, thought that the idea might help in such cases. However, when Admiral Bevir drafted a recommendation to the Trust's committees a couple of months later, they had changed their minds and, encouraged by the Solicitor, they fired off a memorandum to the Secretary in which they stated their complete disagreement.

This had its effect and the Admiral noted that '... most members of the staff feel that it [the joint scheme] is dangerous' and went on to add his own very sensible comments: 'In the past the policy of the Trust has been to try and get a capital endowment for every property and I suggest the Committee should consider very carefully any departure from this practice.

'Gardens are different from any other property in that, if they are let down for only a short time, a long time and a great deal of money is essential to restore them.

'The second difficulty is management ... Difficult situations might well arise if the estates staff were to be even partly under the control of a Gardens Committee.' He thought a successful scheme required a separate organisation, and he toyed with the idea that the RHS should hold leases of gardens acquired under the scheme.

Lord Aberconway, successful industrialist, was a formidable man. His grandfather had created a great garden above the Conway valley at Bodnant. He himself had not only developed it, but was a very considerable plantsman, and under his direction the garden had acquired an immense range of plants of exceptional quality. He was also a genial and courteous person, and very hospitable. Hubert Smith liked him and got on very well with him, possibly in some measure because of Hubert's own competence as a gardener. It was Lord Aberconway's initiative which partly led and partly drove the National Trust into the preservation of gardens.

From the beginning, Aberconway committed the Trust to matters far outside its statutory terms of reference when, in addressing the Annual General Meeting of the Society in March 1948 he said, 'Only gardens of great beauty, gardens of outstanding design or historic interest would be considered, and those having collections of plants or trees of value to the nation either botanically, horticulturally or scientifically.'

The joint appeal went forward with a leaflet which first mentioned that 'everyone deplores the fact that conditions render it difficult for owners adequately to maintain these national assets' and went on to commend a 'scheme which has been started to save certain of the more important gardens, so that they may be preserved for the Nation for all time; monuments, as it were, of English gardening.' Vita Sackville-West made a broadcast appeal in October and, at David Bowes-Lyon's instance, the Queen promised to open Sandringham gardens twice the next summer.

The first result was that the Trust was able to accept from Lawrence Johnston the exceptionally beautiful and endlessly interesting garden at Hidcote that he had created on the flattish fields of the northern Cotswolds over the previous forty years. It is no criticism of that splendid creation to ask whether it could at that time be regarded as a 'place of historic interest or natural beauty'.

The Trust, however, refused to split hairs or to confine itself within the stricture of words. Stated positively, this was not simply a bending to Lord Aberconway's will, but a deliberate action. The annual report for 1948 says: 'Perhaps one of the secrets of the National Trust's strength has been its willingness to increase the range of its responsibilities, and this year a start has been made with an extension of its protection to yet another of our national heritages, the English garden.'

In June 1948, Vita Sackville-West started rolling a ball which was to become a very important part of the scheme. The Queen's Institute for District Nurses, which over sixty years had become one of the most admired and effective of charities in the field of medical care, was being wound up and incorporated in the new National Health Service. One of their money-raising efforts had been the collection of entry fees to gardens which private people opened to the public specially for that purpose. Since the Institute no longer needed money the fund-raising arrangements would no longer be needed.

Miss Sackville-West's overtures to the Institute's Gardens Committee chairman, Mrs Fleischman, were moderately received. A month later Lord Rosse had been able to talk to her and things were changing for the better, although there were apparently 'rivals in the field'. Negotiations designed to make the National Trust/ Royal Horticultural Society Joint Gardens Scheme a beneficiary of the Institutes's system, first providing what was needed for the nurses and then increasingly for the Gardens Fund, went slowly and were beset by minor problems.

In October Admiral Bevir wrote to Rosse: 'To be quite candid I have been trying to put the brake on Aberconway a little bit, because I feel that we shall get the best result by agreement and not by trying to bully the District Nurses' Committee.' In December the Trust's Finance Committee, sitting on the sidelines, displayed its quiet commonsense and, first emphasising that agreement with the Queen's

Institute was vital, went on to recommend that Mrs Fleischman should be co-opted on to the Gardens Committee and Lord Aberconway on to the Executive, thus at one blow harnessing their loyalties to the Trust.

By January 1949 agreement was reached. That year was devoted – on the part of the Trust – to trying to help the Institute build up the efficiency of what was now termed the National Gardens Scheme, finding more people who would act as county organisers and approaching owners who had not previously participated to get them to open for the Scheme. This, helped by the appeal publicity, was immediately successful in reviving the organisation, eight more counties participating in 1949 and a further six intending to rejoin in 1950. The 1949 gross receipts were some £12,000 which was the highest figure since the end of the war.

However, it must be remembered that the first call on the money was for the Queen's Institute and the NT/RHS Gardens Fund only received a small percentage on a sliding scale, and the appeal as a whole was not a success. The balance at the end of the year 1951 was only £7,612. Even if the money were to be patiently accumulated it could not possibly, on its own, be sufficient to achieve what Lord Aberconway had had in mind. Quite separately, however, the National Gardens Scheme has justified the intentions of those who worked so hard to set it up. For a long time the Gardens Fund share, although welcome, was small in comparison with the needs of the Trust's gardens. In 1979 it came to £12,727, a figure doubled a year later and by 1987 it had risen to nearly £77,500. Even recognising the effect of inflation over this period, this was a splendid contribution.

Meanwhile, in 1949, Lord Aberconway entrusted nearly 100 acres of his garden at Bodnant to the Trust. This was not a gift within the terms of the NT/RHS scheme, because he handsomely endowed the property and retained the management in his own hands. It was nevertheless very important for its own sake. The garden is on an immense scale with a spread of design in its various parts and with the most superb specimens of different plants. Important too was the effect on public opinion, which obviously thought 'if the Trust is good enough to look after Bodnant, then it is good enough to hold any garden.' That, of course, was a mistaken view. The Trust certainly became the owner but the care of the garden remained entirely in the hands of Lord Aberconway and of Charles Puddle, then the Head Gardener. After Lord Aberconway's death in 1952 his son Charles succeeded both to the barony and to the management of the garden and continued his father's personal and highly competent involvement in all aspects; in recent years Mr Puddle on his retirement has been succeeded by *his* son. The very fact that this great garden is included in the list of what the Trust owns has inevitably enhanced its reputation as a garden owner.

1949 also brought an enquiry from Lady Londonderry about the garden at Mount Stewart, on the shore of Strangford Lough in County Down. This gift to the Trust did not mature until 1955 and again was not made under the aegis of the joint scheme, being financed quite separately, but again it is an early example of the effect of what amounted to a declaration by the Trust that it was in the business of preserving gardens.

Similarly Michael Rosse had the previous year mentioned to Admiral Bevir the idea that his father-in-law's garden at Nymans, in Sussex, might come to the Trust with its 1,500 acre estate as an endowment. That again did not come about at once, nor was it within the terms of the joint scheme, but Colonel Messel left it to the Trust by will on his death in 1953. Another genuine step forward came with the gift of the Arboretum at Winkworth, near Godalming in Surrey, from Dr Wilfred Fox, supported by maintenance grants from the County and District Councils.

The proceedings of the Gardens Committee were not especially productive. They were reluctant – to the new Secretary's shock and surprise – to concern themselves with advising the Trust generally and joint-scheme gardens were slow to materialise. Their agenda in October 1950 included the problem of whether the Cathedral Amenities Fund should pay for a hedge, or a two-foot high stone wall around the Cathedral Green at Exeter or, as Mr Cochrane, son of the donor of the fund, wanted for the sake of economy, a one-foot high wall. They also considered what to do about Sir Stephen Tallents' collection of plants with historical connections at St John's Jerusalem in Kent, about which he had been badgering his old friend Hubert Smith. These included Napoleon's willow, from a cutting taken from the one by his grave on St Helena, the Wellington cypress which had been struck from a branch which fell from his funeral car and – perhaps the only genuinely poignant plant in the list – a box which was grown from a plant brought from Hougomont within two weeks of Waterloo. If only one could credit the reality of its provenance one might also award a high place to the Omar Khayam Rose from Edward Fitzgerald's grave, given to Sir Stephen by Philip Guedalla! The Committee also received a report on Bodnant, to which there had been 34,372 visitors and where it had been necessary to build a charabanc park.

It was not until 1954 that the joint scheme produced its great coup. Inexplicably Captain Arthur Soames had decided to sell his Sheffield Park Estate in Sussex, doing so without consultation with his son Christopher, Winston Churchill's son-in-law. There was a deal with the Ashdale Land and Property Company, one of the dealers in land which were thriving in the post-war period, buying large areas cheaply for cash and re-selling at the much higher break-up value.

The house was interesting, having been rebuilt to designs in the Gothick style by James Wyatt around the turn of the eighteenth century and it was the focal point of the most superb gardens, laid out by Lancelot Brown in 1777 and refined later by Repton. In the late nineteenth century, Captain Soames's uncle had filled them with the trees and shrubs brought in from all over the world. These had grown into some of the most beautiful specimens especially of conifers, rhododendrons, and the autumn colouring plants – maples, mespillus and tupelo trees.

There was this time no doubt whatsoever as to the likely fate of the garden. The estate was breaking up around it and the great oak wood on its northern edge was sold to a timber merchant and clear felled. There was no hope of the Gardens Fund supplying enough money to buy the garden and, as for the house, the Trust decided that it could not afford to maintain it. In these circumstances the Trust showed the strength and superior effectiveness of its organisation, as opposed to the impotence of a Gardens Committee acting within the joint scheme. It had at its disposal a variety of funds which had been given or left to it for acquisition and from one of these, the Penfold Fund, it set aside £17,000 to acquire the garden, stables and four cottages, and restrictive covenants over the house. Jack Rathbone, in his eagerness, took negotiations largely into his own hands. He made an offer in January 1954, securing an option to give time for an appeal to be made for money with which to

TOP A farmhouse on the Holnicote estate, Somerset. In 1944 Sir Richard Acland gave the Trust his 12,000-acre estate at Holnicote, along with Killerton in Devon.

ABOVE The Old Post Office at Tintagel, originally a 14th-century stone house, and one of the first buildings to come to the Trust on the recommendation of the Society for the Preservation of Ancient Buildings

ABOVE Thomas Carlyle outside his London home. 24 Cheyne Row, Chelsea, where he lived from 1834 to 1881. The house was bought by public subscription in 1895 and handed over to the Trust in 1931.

TOP Florence Court in County Fermanagh. One of the most important houses in Ulster, it was built in the mid-18th century and belonged to the Enniskillen family.

ABOVE Hardwick Hall in Derbyshire, the great Elizabethan house built in the 1590s by Elizabeth Shrewsbury, 'Bess of Hardwick'.

ABOVE The magnificent ruins of the medieval Cistercian abbey of Fountains in York-shire provide a stunning backdrop to an early 18th-century garden, Studley Royal. This jewel in the Trust's crown was declared a World Heritage Site in 1988.

OPPOSITE The Long Gallery at Blickling Hall, Norfolk, showing the fine Jacobean plaster ceiling and some of the house's great collection of books. When Lord Lothian, the instigator of the Country Houses Scheme, died in 1942 he left Blickling and its estate to the Trust.

TOP Bodiam Castle in Sussex, which captured the imagination of the Marquis of Curzon, who bequeathed it to the Trust.

ABOVE The old kitchen at Compton Castle, Devon. The medieval fortified manor house, once the home of Sir Humphrey Gilbert, the coloniser of Newfoundland, is still occupied by the Gilbert family.

TOP Greys Court in Oxfordshire, home of the de Greys from the 11th century. The great medieval tower can be seen to the right of the photograph.

ABOVE A box mangle and other laundry items at Erddig, near Wrexham. The Trust decided to admit visitors through the domestic offices rather than the front door.

ABOVE The great landscape garden of Claremont in Surrey, worked on by four masters: Sir John Vanburgh, Charles Bridgeman, William Kent and Capability Brown. The impressive turf amphitheatre is ideal for concerts.

form an endowment. The appeal leaflet was signed on behalf of the Joint Gardens Committee of the Trust and the RHS by David Bowes-Lyon, now its Chairman. It was largely aimed at RHS members, who were promised the same free access as they already enjoyed at Bodnant and Hidcote. £1,000 a year was thought to be needed.

The appeal would have been a complete failure had not Rathbone and Ivan Hills, the Area Agent, between them visited every local authority in the county, down to parishes, and from this they secured promises of £670 a year for up to twenty-one years. The RHS was able only to produce £93 a year. Incidental expenses were unavoidable and for those the Trust turned to another fund which was kept by the Finance Committee as a sort of contingency reserve, the Gordon Daviot Fund. The author (Josephine Tey in real life) had left to the Trust the royalties on some of her work and this regularly replenished the fund established under her pen name.

In this way these quite exceptionally splendid gardens passed into the care, ostensibly of the Gardens Committee, but in actuality of the Trust. There were mistakes due to haste and an excess of zeal. The whole approach to the gardens, which previously had been from the house, was lost and replaced by ownership of a long drive without any control of the land through which it passed. The house, which could have been bought for £9,000 or less, although the key to the design of the gardens, was only subject to the limited and negative control precariously provided by restrictive covenants. A more experienced and venturesome operator would have obtained the freehold of the house and its immediate surroundings, hedging the prospective cost by means of a long lease in which the Trust, as landlord, would have had direct control of the things that mattered.

That does not detract from the principal element of success which has been the preservation of a garden under virtual sentence of destruction. It is, perhaps, an opportunity here to pay tribute to the role of the Head Gardener. Mr Setford had been working for the Soameses for over fifty years and agreed to see the Trust in. Much of the planting done in the early years of the century had been his work, involving enormous planting pits from which the Wealden clay was dug and removed to be replaced with dung, compost and loam. No wonder that many of his trees had reached a height in feet greater than Setford's seventy years. Fred Dench took over from him when he finally retired. He came from the great garden of Borde Hill not far away and was a man of easy good humour and iron determination.

Sheffield Park, in common with so many gardens, had come to a halt with the outbreak of war fifteen years earlier and though in no way derelict, it needed new thinking and new initiative to revive it, and this Fred Dench provided. His early death was sad, but his successor Archie Skinner was able to use the increasing resources of the Trust to build on what had been achieved and to extend the garden in its same style into parts which previously were under-used. As for money, Rathbone need not have worried! Before long the popularity of the garden with its long, long season stretching regularly into mid-November attracted enough visitors to allow it to run at a profit; the only garden to be contributing its surplus to the Gardens Fund. Tragically, Sheffield Park Garden was one of the most severely hit of the Trust's gardens in the storm of October 1987. Eighty per cent of the mature trees were destroyed in some areas of the garden.

It has been said earlier that the most important consequence of Lord Aberconway's idea was to bring the whole activity of gardening into the consciousness of the Trust, and one of the first necessities was to have some expertise on the staff. Eardley Knollys had suggested in 1949 to the Secretary that the Trust needed, and could well afford, a full time Gardens Adviser, and this was taken up again by Hubert Smith in 1951. The Secretary put this to the Gardens Committee who said, first, that they could not provide the advice and second that there must either be a paid official or, alternatively, a locally based volunteer to supervise each garden. The Secretary favoured the latter because the stipendiary would have cost at least £1,000 a year 'which we just cannot afford'.

It was another two years before the Chief Agent was asked to find a Horticultural Adviser and not until 1954 was Miss Ellen Field appointed. Intelligent, energetic, quiet and sensitive she was very well received by gardeners and land agents alike. She produced a short but comprehensive report on the pleasure grounds at Stourhead, which showed every indication of her grasp of essentials and the good working relationship which she enjoyed with the agent, Simon Buxton. Then one wet night in November, driving back to Exeter from Cotehele her car was in collision with a lorry and she received injuries from which she later died. She did not have time to leave a mark upon any garden of the Trust but she did establish that the appointment was a necessary one, and as a pioneer she is to be remembered. The Trust advertised in the journal of the RHS and in *Country Life* and appointed as a result Graham Stuart Thomas.

Graham Stuart Thomas affirms that he decided at the tender age of eight that he would be a horticulturalist when he grew up. In those distant days that meant a nurseryman. His formal training was two years at the Cambridge Botanic Gardens, where the system was that the student gave his services to the garden and in return was taught gardening and was allowed to attend – free of charge – any lectures in the University on botany. From there he went for a year to Six Hills Nurseries in Hertfordshire to indulge his interest in alpines, in which they specialised. An attack of scarlet fever made him so ill that it was a further year before he could resume work and when he did he chose to go to the lime-free sands of Surrey as alpine and herbaceous foreman in a firm of wholesale nurserymen. There he stayed for twenty-five years, using his meagre holidays – one week a year, later doubled to two weeks – to visit gardens elsewhere in the country. He looked on his appointment as Horticultural Adviser not so much as a job but as a marvellous opportunity. Indeed to begin with the job itself was so modest – and the salary only £400 a year – that he hoped to do it in his spare time. The Chief Agent, to whom he was directly responsible, made special arrangements to take him at the weekend to see the garden at Blickling and, since at that time almost everyone still worked on Saturday mornings, there was no problem about the gardeners not being available.

Moreover he was to advise on only seven gardens – Blickling, Glendurgan, Sheffield Park, Hidcote, Cotehele, Killerton and Stourhead. This curious restriction reflected the limitation of the direct responsibility of the Gardens Committee to gardens acquired under the joint scheme (in some mysterious way, although there were only two such gardens, they assumed responsibility for another five). The Gardens Committee was to continue in being until 1968, when the committee structure of the Trust was reorganised with a Properties Committee having overall responsibility and being advised on specialist matters by panels, one of which dealt with gardens.

Thomas is forthright about his view of the Gardens Committee: 'They were a dictatorial and opinionated body!' He also uses the word 'bigoted'! He found the Panel much better, although being a group of people making a brief and occasional visit to a garden, likely to create difficulties if they sought to do more than advise on policy and standards. Garden management has certainly been the least tractable of all the management problems of the Trust, and although it is possible to identify many of the causes it is not easy – perhaps it is impossible – to prescribe a remedy.

To start with, efficiency on the part of the staff is not enough; they must be responsible to the government of the National Trust and carry out the policies and practices which the Trust may prescribe. It is in the failure of the governing committees of the Trust to devise a satisfactory way of exercising its overall control that the chief difficulty seems to lie. But why? It has been able to do so in architecture, fine arts and estate management, in all its wide field and the dozen other specialist matters which concern it. Perhaps it is in part rooted in the original idea that the Gardens Committee should actually and directly manage gardens (which it never could and never did). In turn that idea may have been mistakenly conceived because most members were themselves managing a garden. This involvement breeds an unconscious attitude of mind which is unwilling to accept in any garden an element of which it does not approve, and which also prompts a desire to make specific and detailed prescriptions for what shall or shall not be done.

The whole business is complicated further by the inevitable involvement of the full-time property managers, which was already worrying the Chief Agent and others in 1948, and donors or their successors who might legitimately hold strong views. The idea of the competent, locally-based volunteer to replace the missing garden owner would also have added another complication in the exercise of central responsibility. Even so it has regularly been revived, Lord Gibson for example, when Chairman, searching for a method by which 'the seeing eye' could be recovered.

None of this seems to have prevented Graham Thomas from becoming an effective adviser. He served in that capacity for nearly twenty years, never more than part-time and with no help until 1971 when John Sales, who had been lecturing in horticulture at Writtle, was appointed full time Horticulturalist and succeeded to the position of Adviser, full-time. In his turn a horticulturalist, Paul Miles from Notentt's Suffolk nurseries, came to help. All these worked from their homes. Thomas used to keep a carbon duplicate book in which at the end of each day he wrote up a detailed report, the top copy of which would go at once to the land agent managing the garden and which at his next visit would form the basis on which he reviewed progress – or lack of it!

There are now over a hundred gardens tabled in the Trust's *List of Properties* and on at least three-quarters of these Graham Stuart Thomas was singlehandedly responsible for the advice which brought them to a high standard of care. Not all are either especially important or extensive, but his work has included, in addition to the original seven, many which are exceptionally so: Mount Stewart and Rowallane in County Down, Knightshayes in Devon, Powis Castle in the Welsh marches, to name a few. He has been showered with honours by the RHS and for his work for the Trust received the OBE in 1975.

It would be idle to pretend that there were never any difficulties, faults, failings or mistakes. The Gardens Committee repeatedly found fault with him and

Rathbone felt that despite his skill and knowledge his taste was suspect. Horticulturally he had some minor weaknesses, mainly of prejudice, for example hating trees that tend to grow into difficult shapes such as the variety of cryptomeria, the leaves of which glow with a glorious bronze in winter. With useful plants he tended to fall into a trap of which he was very well aware, that of repeating them in garden after garden. One such was the grey-leaved senecio which spread so far and wide that his colleagues renamed it *senecio Thomasii.*

Thomas himself has said that, regardless of his existing horticultural experience, he had from the start a great deal to learn and that each garden that he dealt with added to his store of knowledge. When he started, garden history, which was of paramount importance to the Trust, was studied only partially and sporadically. Much indeed was known, but that knowledge had not been brought together to form the minor discipline that it now does. Within the Trust gardens had been regarded mainly as aspects of country house management, which required the sort of automatic and relatively unthinking care that housekeeping then did. It fell to Thomas to create, very gradually, a new attitude towards standards which rose as his own understanding grew.

Gardens are nothing without gardeners, and in this the Trust was, and is, remarkably well served. At first this was a question generally of inheritance, the Trust acquiring property already looked after by men – or women – trained in the service of the previous owner and in a tradition of intensive hand labour which had reached very high standards. At Chartwell there was Victor Vincent; Jack Lilley at Trelissick; at Nymans Cecil Nice, who had been trained by the great Harold Comber; and of course, the Puddle family of Bodnant. At Killerton Arthur Godfrey, whose father was a thatcher, had started as a garden boy in 1933, doing all the odd jobs such as picking sprouts, washing vegetables and fetching milk from the home farm. Apart from two years in another garden and the six years of war (five of which he spent as a prisoner of war, captured with others of the Devonshires in Belgium) he spent his whole working life at Killerton, retiring in 1983, fifty years in all.

It is a tribute to Graham Stuart Thomas that he was able to earn the respect and trust of men such as these, and the younger ones who were to follow.

The pattern of management was in some cases quite different and where the donor or donor's successor could either manage or make a continuing contribution to the style of the garden there have been outstanding successes. Mention has already been made of Lord Aberconway's position at Bodnant and Lady Soames at Chartwell. At Nymans Colonel Messel's daughter and son-in-law, Lady Rosse and Lord Rosse, took on the management, she trained, like Cecil Nice, by her father's head gardener and he an extraordinarily knowledgeable plantsman.

As experience and knowledge have increased, so has another factor, the supply of money. This has given the Trust's garden management a freedom which was undreamed of in the 1950s, and has encouraged it to tackle problems on a scale and of a complexity which would have been – and indeed were – once ignored as impossible. An example is the rescue in 1978–80 from a rhododendron jungle of the eighteenth-century pleasure grounds at Claremont, near Esher, where features conceived by four of the great landscapists had been completely obliterated. One of the most courageous acts was the felling of three Lebanon cedars about a hundred years old which had been planted where they almost wholly obscured the turf-banked amphitheatre which lay beneath the bushes.

In North Wales the garden at Erddig was even more derelict than the house and, while the restoration of the house would always have been in the Trust's mind, it would not, twenty years earlier, have expected to be able to do much more than make some tidy lawns. By 1980, however, this too had been reconstructed and replanted in its eighteenth-century form. Another bold effort was to persuade the tenants of Ham House to accept a restoration of the formal gardens in the seventeenth-century style. Not only did this require the agreement of the Victoria and Albert Museum and its gardeners, the Royal Parks, but it also had to overcome the hot resentment of local residents who had become accustomed to a large park known for years as 'the Wilderness' having the appearance of natural woodland, which it very nearly was.

All this activity and increasing responsibility has driven the Trust to enter the extra-statutory field to which Lord Aberconway committed it in 1948. '... having collections of plants or trees of value to the nation either botanically, horticulturally or scientifically'. It has found itself engaged in taking the national lead in producing a Catalogue of Woody Plants. This involves accurate identification, plotting on maps and recording on the computer of the Royal Botanic Gardens currently carried out by Michael Lear. Year by year births and deaths, of course, require regular updating. This should be regarded perhaps as little more than one of the penalties of success for, from its uncertain beginnings, the Trust's involvement with garden preservation has most emphatically been a success.

CHAPTER XIV

Managing and Modernising:
The Large Estates

Probably the major pre-occupation of the Trust during the 1950s, certainly of its staff and of its Estates Committee, was the management of the larger estates. By the start of the decade the Trust already owned Blickling with 4,700 acres, Holnicote 12,400, Killerton 6,400, Arlington 2,800, Slindon 3,500, Cotehele 1,300, Attingham 3,800, Brockhampton 1,700, Stourhead 2,600, while in the Lakes an extensive estate had been assembled and continued to grow. To these were added, in 1951, Ysbyty Ifan in North Wales of 26,000 acres, in 1956, the adjacent properties of Buscot and Coleshill, nearly 7,500 acres, and, in 1958, Wallington with its 13,000 acres came under the Trust's management. This acretion of 85,800 acres in sixteen years would under any circumstances have been a large lump to assimilate, but in the circumstances of the time it was exceptionally so. In the first place, all these properties were thoroughly rural in character, and they and their inhabitants depended overwhelmingly upon agriculture for survival. It had been hard to make a living and the results were pretty meagre.

The Second World War had given a boost to agricultural productivity but this had been achieved with largely nineteenth-century tools, buildings and techniques. Horsepower was only just on the way out and the tractor only just on the way in. On the Killerton estate, in 1945, the blacksmith's shop had nearly 150 workhorses on its books for regular shoeing, and five years later the farm stables on a number of the Blickling holdings were still fully stocked. The buildings used for farming were almost all at least fifty years old and many were a great deal older. In the mid-nineteenth century a lot of ingenuity had been applied to labour-saving devices such as the use of descending levels for storage so that gravity took the produce through the mill or to the stock. The seventy-year-long depression, however, had stopped further development and most 'model' farmsteads had fallen into disuse. Housing for people was not in any different case. The piped mains water systems which had been universal in towns for over half a century seldom reached country hamlets. Many of the estates operated their own private supplies but these were seldom available to all the properties and many were dependent on wells, pumped by hand, or on water collected from springs on higher ground and piped down to the house below. Electricity was far from universally available and dairy farms used generators, or the flywheel of a tractor, to work their milking machines. As for sewerage, it was generally non-existent and houses relied either on cesspits or septic tanks, or simply an earth bucket.

This was the state of affairs when the Trust succeeded to the ownership of these great properties. Perhaps it would not have mattered so much had it not been that, at the same time, there was a general desire for improvement. In common with other rural landowners, the Trust found itself morally and practically committed to an immense programme of modernisation. There appeared a number of Government carrots and sticks. Grants were made available for the repair and improvement of houses, and also for the provision of new farm buildings, water supplies and land drainage, and a rural electricity scheme was promoted. At the same time housing authorities became stricter about the application of minimum legal standards and readier to apply closing or demolition orders for those houses unfit for habitation. In agriculture the Minister had powers to apply supervision orders to both landowners and farmers and, as we have seen, was in 1958 on the verge of doing so in respect of Sir Charles Trevelyan at Wallington.

This pressure was in tune with national opinion. The country remained rationed and hungry long after the war had ended. 'Dig for Victory' remained the battle cry for years.

In the woods, the situation was similar, or in many ways worse. No large-scale tree planting in privately-owned woods had been carried out for nearly a century, and the maturing plantations from before that time had almost all gone in the two wars. The need to restock the nation's woods with virtually any sort of tree that would grow seemed urgent and there was an official policy aimed at building up a 'strategic reserve' of timber against the next emergency.

There were some dissenting voices, particularly early on. More than 100 acres of Berkhamsted Common on the Ashridge estate – that very place where the victorious battle against enclosure had first been won – had, by direction of the War Agricultural Executive Committee for Hertfordshire (colloquially known as the 'War Ag'), been cleared of trees, bushes and gorse, ploughed and cropped for corn since 1942 (much to George Trevelyan's annoyance). A similar fate had overtaken an even larger area of Maidenhead Thicket. Also, as we have seen, Stonehenge Down had been fenced and ploughed.

In 1946 there was a blazing row over Crowlink on the Sussex coast west of Eastbourne. This farm of 600 acres had been bought in the early 1920s as a building speculation, just like Peacehaven further along the coast towards Brighton. It had been secured for the Trust by public appeal between 1928 and 1931, with particularly strong financial support from a London businessman, William Campbell, who was a member and Vice-President of the Society of Sussex Downsmen. Inevitably during the Second World War much of this land was brought under the plough. Afterwards the Society wished to see it revert to natural growth, while the 'War Ag' and the tenant wished to re-organise it for practical farming. The Society opposed all fencing and cultivations. The land '… open and free to the public, grazing by sheep in charge of a shepherd is naturally not objected to.' Their view was put very clearly: 'As it was acquired by the public as a stretch of open downland, it matters not whether it is growing wild with gorse etc., it is the property of the public.'

There was a meeting of all the parties in May 1946 when the Society agreed to some fencing, with provision for access with gates and stiles. A time limit of four years was set, after which the position would be reviewed. The Trust had fielded a strong team from the Estates Committee headed by Sir William Gavin, at that time Chairman of the Agricultural Mortgage Corporation. Herbert Gatliff and John Cadbury completed the Trust's team and they may well have been equally effective, because Gatliff's rambler background would have gone down well with the Downsmen, while John Cadbury had remarkable powers of quiet persuasion. Whether the Society considered its deputation had shown weakness is not clear, but there was an immediate reaction against the agreement. The Commons Society was approached, and offered sympathy but advised that the Trust was within its rights. A campaign was launched in the *Eastbourne Chronicle* against the Trust, and sustained not only by correspondence and reports but by lengthy editorial comment.

By October the row had reached *The Times* which published a photograph purporting to show offensive fencing. In fact, as the tenant Captain Davies said in a letter to the press, the fence in the photograph had been in existence for over twelve years. That puts its date at about 1933–4 and illustrates only too clearly the state of the farm at that time. Anthony Martineau had cause to refer to this when he received a letter from the Treasury Solicitor, written on 24 October and opening with the somewhat ominous words, 'I act for the Attorney General in matters referring to charities …'. The Society had initiated a process known as 'moving the Attorney General' who had the power to direct charities, if necessary, to oblige them to conform with their charitable trusts. Martineau was able to reply that, as long ago as 1927, the Trust had approved a report which showed that the state of the land was so bad that all except a strip along the cliff edge must be enclosed for better control of grazing. Edward Keeling, one of the MPs on the Executive Committee was prompted to ask in the House what the Attorney General intended to do and received the gratifyingly firm answer that 'no action on my part is called for.'

Though in 1949 Sir William Gavin and Christopher Gibbs meeting the Society again could report 'a very successful meeting' this should not be looked upon as a victory for the Trust. It was in fact a part of the process of learning that, in the management of open spaces, concessions have to be made to the needs of farming, while at the same time the essential purpose of the open space must be preserved and respected. Crowlink is now what may be regarded as a model for this kind of approach. The farm is productive to at least seventy per cent of its maximum potential. The landscape as a whole retains the charm of space and variety. There are areas in which the natural flora – and in consequence the fauna also – is uninhibited by any cultivations and is controlled by grazing only. The whole area is easily accessible by footpaths, while the cliffs, in a wide band stretching back several hundred yards from the edge, are open and unrestricted. The Trust is proud of this, but it should acknowledge the part played by its critics in establishing this standard of management.

It was in 1949 that the Trust held the last of its Local Committee Conferences, under the chairmanship of Sir George Trevelyan. There were then over a hundred local committees and the Royal Horticultural Society Hall in Vincent Square was packed. Captain John Hill had been put up to speak for the Estates Committee on farming. Red of face, dewlapped, or to use the West Country word, 'chollery', and in fair round belly, he preached the national need to dig for victory. He wound up '… and so I say to you plough your commons, improve your heathlands, drain your marshes ....' When he sat down Dr Abercrombie of the Longshaw Committee in the front row was on his feet, thin, small, yellowish, almost gnome-like. Facing the hall he said with warmth and feeling, 'No one can for a moment doubt the sincerity of the last speaker. His words came straight from – his stomach!' To rounds of applause he went on to urge consideration for 'the toilers in the great cities'. Both men were in some measure right, but the process of adjusting to accommodate both views was not quick or easy.

Willie Vane (later Lord Inglewood), a young Conservative MP on the Estates Committee, was put up to explain the Trust's forestry policy. Handsome, polished and fluent, he spoke with smooth confidence of the national need to replant its woodlands and how, since good forestry produced beautiful trees, it was the Trust's intention to do that. He recognised that there was likely to be some doubt among his hearers that timber production was acceptable, and incautiously tried to brush it aside. 'As for the controversy about conifers,' he said, 'it is just too childish.' At that George Trevelyan sat bolt upright behind his chairman's table. 'Just what do you mean by that young man?' he rapped out, in professor-to-student tones. 'You must know that the National Trust has played a great part in preventing the planting of conifers in the Lake District.' Poor Vane was then allowed to explain that what he had meant was that it was childish to confuse such obviously unacceptable use of conifers with a general indictment of their use in forestry.

The Trust's involvement in forestry forms an important and early element of its management history. There are references in correspondence to the importance of trees and their care well before the First World War. In 1930, with Trevelyan as chairman of the Estates Committee, the Trust accepted the services of an Honorary Adviser for Forestry. Major Heyder was ex-Indian Forest Service, which was one of the few fields of professional forestry open to Englishmen before the formation of the Forestry Commission in 1919. George Trevelyan had strong views, as we have seen, against the mass planting of conifers in the uplands, but was very conscious of the value of trees and woods in the landscape, and also of the cash value of timber trees to the ever-impoverished Trust. It is probable that he brought in Heyder to help. Heyder made his first report on the woods at Ashridge, fourteen years later formulating suggestions for a working plan. His method was a model of meticulous recording, and his recommendations were sensible and economical. He brought to the Trust a degree of professionalism which it had not acquired previously in any department. Very tall and slim, with a small moustache and the long-sighted eyes of the outdoor man, he was quietly spoken, courteous and kind. He cared deeply about what the Trust was trying to do and gave the fullest possible attention to what he did for it. Both Hamer and Matheson seem to have recognised his value. Time after time when there were practical problems it was he who was asked to go to inspect and report. He became a member of the Estates Committee in 1933 and served on it for twenty years.

The special feature of forestry, as opposed to other rural activities, was then – and in some measure is still – that it had to be carried out directly by the landowner. There were timber and underwood merchants who would buy, cut and cart woodland produce but very few contractors who would do the work needed to plant and grow the trees. In contrast to farming, in which the Trust played no direct part whatsoever, its committees and staff were perforce engaged on the day to day work in the woods. This bred an interest and an expertise in woodland management within the Trust far greater than in other departments. From 1945 Major Heyder was joined as Honorary Adviser by Lord Bolton, a West Riding landowner and a keen and expert forester, who headed the Government Timber Control Commission during the war. Although his task then had been to secure the maximum amount of timber for the war effort, he exercised his authority to protect exceptional stands and was responsible for saving the extraordinarily perfect crop of beech trees in the park at Slindon in Sussex. It is to him the Trust owes the recruitment of one of its most influential and colourful members of staff, John Workman.

Workman's family were sawmillers in Stroud, below the Cotswold Edge. In the 1930s, and indeed later as well, the price of land was so low that it was possible for a timber merchant to buy an estate or a wood for the value of the timber, which he would then fell and convert in his mill. Workman's father did just that, buying property on the lip of the hills at Kingscote and Ebworth, with a number of farms and woods containing stocks of superb beech. In the ordinary course of events the trees would have been cut down and the woods left derelict, but Mr Workman fell in love with his trees and instituted a system of management to secure their survival. His son John, having first studied electronics at Clare College, Cambridge, and then worked on farms for two years, read forestry at Oxford, taking his degree in 1949. He spent six months widening his experience in Sweden and then returned to Gloucestershire to work with his father. That was a mistake: not only were father and son too much alike in temperament to work well together, but there was not enough scope allowed for an original mind and a radical character.

That was the situation, when, in 1950, Lord Bolton, as President of the Royal Forestry Society and judging its woodlands competition, visited Ebworth to present to Mr Workman the Society's Gold Medal for the magnificent Pope's Wood. They already knew each other well and had worked together both in the Society and on the consequences of the Forestry Act 1948. Lord Bolton soon discovered that young Workman wanted more to do and suggested that he should help as a volunteer with the surveys of woods belonging to the National Trust which were then under way.

Interviewed by Hubert Smith, who knew Bolton well and shared the general regard for him, Workman began as a volunteer making visits on his motor cycle to such distant and disparate properties as Arlington Court in Devon and Hatfield Forest in Essex. He very soon made himself sufficiently useful to be asked to work, for a modest remuneration, every other week. The Honorary Advisers began to take a far less active part and by 1953 Workman became a full-time Forestry Adviser and the Forestry Sub-Committee was wound up. It is not at first easy to understand why Workman made such a mark on the National Trust. Certainly he brought to the job a good brain and education, and a background very deeply rooted in the real countryside. (The word 'real' is needed because so much of today's countryside, although still composed of fields and woods, has lost the society which it once fostered. To know John Workman's background read the book by his friend and neighbour Laurie Lee, *Cider with Rosie*.) Friendly, extrovert up to a point, good looking, lively, John Workman was and is easy to get along with, having a sharp wit and a delight in teasing without hurting. These qualities have combined to make him acceptable to the hundreds of very different people with whom he has had to work.

The essential point, however, of his influence is that, while balanced in judgement, he cares immensely, and there is in him an authoritative core and an inexorable persistence in pursuit of what he believes to matter. He describes himself as intensely political with a very small 'P', radical and, in general terms, left of centre. He is now astonished at how tolerant are people whom he considers conventionally well-placed. 'They know I don't ride, shoot, gamble, dance, have grandchildren, and am difficult and argumentative and always in the thick of things' and yet 'I am still amazed how generous they are!' His political philosophy is a belief in a similar tolerance and fair shares for all, and his own way of life – even though, since his father's death, possessed of a very substantial property – has been simple and modest. It was this man who for more than a quarter of a century travelled continually throughout the country, meeting the area agents and their office staffs and foresters, woodmen and wardens, donors, benefactors, tenants, local committees, Head Office committees, Government agencies and officers, and organisations of all sorts concerned with the countryside.

Success in forestry is dependent on continuity of purpose over a long period. The very shortest period in which a woodland product can be harvested is found in the system of coppicing. In this a young tree is cut back to the ground and allowed to regrow, which it does with a number of stems which are, in their turn, cut after ten, twenty or thirty years, depending on the size and character of the material required. At the other end of the scale, trees such as oak and beech need a hundred years or more. It can only be by chance that this degree of continuity is achieved without a written plan, scrupulously respected and regularly revised. In England such plans were rare and even the finest woodlands are as much happy survivals as deliberately cultivated crops. After the Second War the Government decided that it would give grants to encourage owners to re-stock their woods and at the same time ask the owner to dedicate his land in perpetuity to forestry use and agree to manage it in accordance with a plan of operations. These were the main elements in the Forestry Act of 1948.

The nationalising policy of the post-war Labour Government aroused a defensive and suspicious attitude among all sorts of otherwise liberal-minded people, including the committees of the National Trust. It was with extreme reluctance that they agreed to consider dedication of the Trust's woods, urgently though the money was needed. The Government's agency for the process was the Trust's old adversary, the Forestry Commission, which did not help in building confidence. Fortunately the Commission appointed one of their senior men as Private Woodlands Officer. George Ryle, later to become Director for England, was a wise, sensitive man, flexible in his approach to problems and free from the prejudices which too often accompany professional expertise. To him the country owes in large measure the acceptance of sensible forestry practices.

Ryle, off his own bat, produced in 1952 a plan of operations for Box Hill. He chose the place because he lived nearby and was fond of it, and because 'while it *must* be maintained pre-eminently for its public amenities, it was becoming urgent that bold and positive action should be taken if the woods were to be saved from further gradual decrepitude.' He also wanted to demonstrate to the Commission that a simpler form of plan than the one originally prescribed could be applied to an area of mixed woodland without an excessive amount of work. He did the whole job in five days. Finally he saw the task as a way of embodying the ideals which he was preaching: 'As it is the mutual desire of the Forestry Commission and the National Trust that all the woods belonging to the Trust should be brought under the best sylvicultural management, it was hoped that a plan of this nature would help. It seems that on Box Hill amenities and forest management for full timber production are completely compatible. Under systematic management these woods could one day become a source of very substantial revenue to their owners while retaining their character as irregular chalk-hill beechwoods.'

He was well aware of the problems when he sent his plan to the Chief Agent. 'I believe this area is managed by a local committee whose wrath will no doubt descend on my head ... I shall be quite ready to don a tin hat for the occasion and to face the Committee!' Yes indeed; the Committee Chairman was the formidable Edward Bridges, and as Christopher Gibbs noted on the letter which the Chief Agent showed him, 'I don't think this is going to be easy to put over without giving offence.' The plan was eventually presented to the Local Committee with a discursive and wide ranging covering report. Bridges was not wholly displeased although he found a number of things to query, not necessarily as being incorrect but 'more a point of emphasis'. The real problem was that Major Heyder had reported on the woods in 1948 and Ryle's proposals ran contrary to Heyder's advice on several important matters. The fact is that English forestry had advanced a lot and had become less dependent on European patterns on which it had been modelled earlier. The new ideas and greater flexibility were more suited to the Trust's needs and the tacit acceptance of this almost certainly contributed to the winding up of the Forestry Sub-Committee.

John Workman picked up Ryle's initiative. A special Deed of Dedication was agreed in which the most important variation from the standard was to allow the Trust to terminate the dedication on grounds of amenity. He also produced a plan of operations for Box Hill which followed Ryle's in most ways, but with some important alterations in emphasis – just as Bridges wanted. The woods were eventually dedicated in 1957.

The Executive Committee remained cautious and made it a rule that every new proposal to dedicate must have the 'Objects of Management' approved by them. This usually fell to the lot of John Workman who, as the years went by, took an increasingly large part in the detailed preparation of the plans. The Trust's agents were mostly keen and well informed foresters and what they did not know they were able to learn from the activity of the Royal Forestry Society and the Commission. The latter, through the good offices of George Ryle, instituted a special course for the Trust's agents, based in the New Forest. This was attended by their Chairman, Lord Radnor, who had been a member of the Estates Committee of the Trust, and by their Director, Owen Sangar, who had been Sir Francis Acland's adviser in his avant garde re-planting at Killerton. The rapprochement between the Commission and the Trust was a remarkable achievement by both parties, due in large measure on the part of the former to the highly intelligent and sensitive character of Ryle, and for the Trust, to the good sense of Hubert Smith and the especial aptitude of Workman for the reconciliation of differing viewpoints. Not that there was an instant conversion. In the Lakes the battle to prevent the planting of Black Hall Farm was still on and not to be settled until 1958. Cubby Acland resolutely declined to arrange for the dedication of any of the Trust's extensive woodlands in the Lakes until a full ten years after the Executive had approved the principle!

However, the restocking of the Trust's woods went on apace from 1950, or before, and for the next thirty years. The orthodox system usually involved fairly complete clearance of all bushes and scrub, fencing against rabbits and the planting in lines of trees of about three or four years growth bought from commercial nurseries. Since the intention was often to end up with a wood of broadleaved trees these constituted an element of between twenty-five and fifty per cent of those planted, the others being conifer. This system had been in use for at least 200 years, the conifers then used being larch and pine. The introduction in the nineteenth century of a number of other conifers offered a wider choice. The conifers were thought to protect and encourage the broadleaved trees and to produce a straighter and more rapid growth. Also, since the broadleaved trees were not useable for fifty years or more but conifers began to be useful in as little as ten years, they could produce early returns to offset a little the great expense of planting. The lines of tiny trees had to be kept open by hand weeding with a hook for several years. There was then a danger that fast growing conifers would overwhelm single broadleaved trees and plantations had to be watched and a thinning of the conifers begun.

It was Workman who devised a system resistant to the ill effects of neglect. By planting the trees in a series of groups like the squares on a chequerboard, each species had enough of its own sort round it to enable it to grow without excessive competition. This type of tree growing was the inevitable consequence of the complete clearance of all trees over a very large area, which produces a totally different condition from that in the natural woodland where trees of all ages are found in the same area and only a few are ready to harvest at one time. The skill of producing and managing woodland of uneven age was hardly known in England and practised on only a few privately owned estates; in any event the wartime fellings had left no question of it in many cases. Workman encouraged where he could the introduction of planting in groups within woods, either where spaces existed, or where they could be made by felling. Even where timber still stood it was often two hundred years old and might be expected, in the case of beech especially, to live for another fifty at the most. The sooner, therefore, that young trees could be introduced even at the cost of cutting fine old trees down, the less would be the gap in time while the wood was re-established.

At Wallington, John Workman and Ben Proud undertook just such a felling and group replanting in 1960, in a wood of fine but very old beech not far from the house. A group of agents on tour observed this and Rathbone was appalled by what seemed to him an act of vandalism, although the consensus of opinion was that the action was right and necessary. Happily by 1980 the wood looked quite beautiful again, the patches of young trees well up among the remaining ancients and the new variation of height, density, light and shade presenting a livelier pattern than that of a uniform wood.

The complexity and intensity of the Trust's woodland work, the application both in energy and money needed to pursue it, and often the moral courage needed to act rather than leave problems to accumulate for the future, bred a common bond among the Trust's staff.

The complexities and exigencies of estate management with which the Trust was confronted after the War were formidable. Nicolas Corbin has summarised how things were at Blickling, when he took over the management in 1948.

> There were 134 cottages, mostly picturesque red brick with pantile roofs. Some had not been painted since the end of the Great War. Only two had piped water and W.C.s. None had bathrooms. Less than half had electricity laid on. Water was from wells, many of which were under twenty feet deep and contained surface water. Cooking was done on open fires and in splendid wall ovens from which came marvellous bread and delicacies such as 'pork cheese'. Each cottage had a cast iron boiler for washing clothes and for heating water for the Friday night bath. Providing 'amenities' under the Housing Act was not plain sailing, one District Council being very difficult over the non-existent damp courses, bedrooms also used as passages, low ceilings and so on. Tenants did not always like the inconvenience of being modernised, and having electricity (said to be bad for the eyes) and many hated the 'flat' tap water.

It was to be many years before it was possible to bring even modest improvements to housing in some of the Blickling villages. North Norfolk is extremely short of good natural water supplies and private improvement had to wait on the arrival of mains water, while sewerage problems were even worse. Many cottages were far too small to accommodate bathroom, lavatory and kitchen of adequate size, and waiting for a semi-detached house to fall vacant so that two could be joined into one was a further cause of delay.

What constituted better conditions was not always agreed between agent and tenant. At Brockhampton, in Herefordshire, Colin Jones sought to improve the lot of one farmer, dependent on an earth closet, by providing an Elsan Chemical toilet, which worked on a similar but theoretically more hygienic principle, using a chemical fluid instead of a shovelful of earth to put in the bucket after use. Jones was somewhat put out on his next visit to see the bright green Elsan lying on its side in the yard and enquired why it was not yet in use. 'What use is that thing,' asked the farmer scathingly, 'for me, my wife and our three children? We goes on using the old three-holer.'

Farming problems were as numerous and as urgent. In theory, the farms should have generated enough income not only to keep them in repair but to provide a surplus for other estate needs. In practice, rents were so low that they did not suffice even for repairs, let alone for new investment. At Blickling Corbin found the rents only 10 per cent above pre-war levels, and when he re-let his first farm at a rent of 36 shillings an acre the Marquis of Lothian's former agent, Christopher Birkbeck, thought this on the high side. In Devon, Harold Salter was the third generation to have been tenant of Newlands, on the Killerton Estate, his grandfather having taken the tenancy in 1847. He had a passion for local history and had studied his grandfather's diaries, and was delighted to discover that when in 1959 his rent was increased it at last reached the level which it had been 112 years before. Perhaps worse than the very low level of rents was the attitude of tenant farmers – why should rents which had stayed the same for so long suddenly increase, and what would happen if there were to be a farming slump, just as before? How could they meet their obligations? This produced a degree of resistance which for twenty years after the war inhibited agreement on reasonable rents. The slow rise in income reduced the Trust's capacity to re-invest while the sheer drag of the negotiations occupied much of their agents' energies.

Even so, farm tenants were as anxious as anyone to become more efficient and one of the keys to that was to reduce labour costs. Whether on the arable farms of the eastern counties, the mixed farms of the Midlands and south, or the grass farms of the west, a large number of people were engaged on farm work. On most farms, large and small, each member of the family took a share of some sort, and on quite modest sized farms half a dozen hired hands were employed. In 1939 the wage bill would have been about £12 a week; in 1950 nearly £40. Any measures which could enable more work to be done by fewer hands were welcome.

Quite separately, and not before time, the authorities made a determined effort to secure clean, tuberculin tested, milk. This meant that the place where the cow was milked and the dairy in which the milk was cooled and stored had to be of a high standard of cleanliness. Since the mid-1930s, when the Milk Marketing Board was formed with a virtual monopoly, dairying had been the one dependable department of the industry, and virtually the only one which provided a regular monthly income. It was no wonder that a very large number of farmers kept some dairy cows, perhaps a dozen or a score. To keep a herd much larger than that meant that you were a big dairy-man. The effect of the clean milk campaign was that, in order to keep its tenants in business, the Trust was faced with finding sufficient space in the farmsteads, replacing cobbles with concrete and wood with steel. Light and ventilation were required, clean water both for the dairy and cattle to drink, and accommodation for the new milking machines.

At Blickling, Corbin had to deal with twenty-three separate farms. At Wallington there were a similar number, at Killerton more than thirty, while at Ysbyty well over sixty. At Holnicote, lying in the Porlock Vale and reaching up the hills on either side, Freddie Reeks had another score or more of farms. This last case was complicated by a complex distribution of land. For the farm tenants themselves there was a two-fold strain: that of adjusting their business to the new demands and opportunities, and at the same time coming to terms with their new landlord whose character, status and motives they found hard to understand. In the Porlock Vale the tenants on the Holnicote Estate banded together, all signing a round-robin of protest against a proposal to raise the rents. This reaction was more a result of geography and history than anything else. As to the latter, although the Acland family loved Holnicote and lived there at intervals, Killerton had been their principal home for a century and a half. Holnicote never had the continuity of personal care and, in Freddie Reeks's words, 'was alternately spoiled and neglected'. Geographically, set in a basin between hills and the sea, the inhabitants lived as though at the bottom of a bag, and the community was enclosed and inward-looking, feeling itself shut off from the outside world. It was an uncomfortable time for Reeks, living as he did in the midst of it all. Indeed for all the Trust's agents the relationship with the large number of farm and cottage tenants at a time of change and uncertainty inevitably absorbed a very large part of their energies.

In 1958 the Trust inherited three large properties on the death of Ernest Cook, whose gifts of Montacute and the Assembly Rooms at Bath have already been described. Since about 1937 he had employed John Burrow Hill as his agent. Even at that early date two characteristics of their negotiations emerged: Mr Cook showed signs of becoming unpredictable and easily offended if he did not get his own way, and Captain Hill's function as an intermediary was to obscure relations with his client.

Soon after 1937 Mr Cook began to buy agricultural estates. At that time they enjoyed a fifty per cent remission of estate duty on the death of the owner. Very much later, after Ernest Cook had died, Captain Hill asserted that, 'His policy was that his estate should be preserved for all time and managed in accordance with the best traditions of the old Landlord and Tenant system.' One of his purchases was the Boarstall Estate on the heavy clay of the Vale of Aylesbury and from it Mr Cook gave to the Trust, in 1943, the part-moated fourteenth-century gatehouse of Boarstall Tower.

Most of the properties were of a similar character, perhaps because at that time farms on heavy clay land were difficult to work and correspondingly cheap. For example, in 1940 Mr Cook bought the West Grinstead Estate in the Sussex Weald at £104,000 for over 3,000 acres. (In 1984 it was on offer with a smaller acreage for £4 million!) Natural beauty did not seem to feature in Mr Cook's criteria for purchase, nor did he seem particularly interested in historic houses on the properties. From 1946 onwards there are signs that his particular object had become the protection of his fortune from falling into the hands of the Government. The Trust's Jubilee Appeal alarmed him because he saw in Dalton's pound-for-pound offer 'the first step towards nationalisation'.

From then on his relationship with the Trust seems to have been overshadowed by this suspicion. In three cases he did buy property at concessionary rates, convenanting with the vendor that he would leave the estate to the Trust. One was Coleshill, south-west of Oxford, with its exceptionally fine seventeenth-century house by Sir Roger Pratt. Another was Buscot, which lies between Coleshill and the Thames. Part of the deal with the vendor, Lord Faringdon, was that there should be a lease-back of the house and grounds, with an immediate gift of it to the Trust. The terms of the lease and the obligations which the Trust incurred, without equivalent means to meet them, led Lord Esher to comment that 'the sinister combination of Lord Faringdon and Captain Hill were too much for Admiral Bevir'. That transaction was made in 1949. The third property was Bradenham on the Chilterns, and, in terms of natural beauty of the land and importance for its preservation, the only one which came within the Trust's normal requirements.

Otherwise the next few years were occupied with constant pressure by John Hill to get the Trust to accept all the other estates and endless and often acrimonious correspondence accompanied it.

In order to try to clear matters up Lord Crawford did try to by pass Hill and wrote to Ernest Cook directly – who replied in the warmest and most understanding way. The breach was sufficiently healed for the Trust to be prepared in October 1951 to review its decision but, even before the Committee met, Hill wrote saying in effect – 'it's all off'. A month later the reason emerged. An Ernest Cook Trust had been formed as an educational charity, endowed with all the estates other than the three which were the subject of covenant with the vendors that they should go to the National Trust. Even after that Hill tried to get the Trust to release Mr Cook from his obligations, but Lord Crawford declined, wisely writing direct to Mr Cook explaining that Buscot House had been accepted because the estate was to come later, and in any event Hill had made a public statement on the future of the three properties. On 14 March 1955 Ernest Cook died and by the terms of his will the Trust became possessed of Bradenham, 1,111 acres, Buscot 3,800 acres and Coleshill 3,600 acres. A sad twist to the story is given by the complete destruction by fire a year earlier of Coleshill House, due it was thought to overheating tinder-dry woodwork with a blowlamp.

Ernest Cook's record as a benefactor of the Trust cannot be diminished by the undoubted fact that his benefactions could have been even greater. What blame attaches to John Hill in this? Certainly he interposed himself completely between Cook and the Trust. Certainly too, his judgement as to what the Trust could or should accept for preservation was bad. His insistence on virtually complete acceptance was self-defeating. All this time Hill had also been a member of the Trust's Estates Committee which makes his position even more invidious. The Trust agreed to retain John Hill as agent but in view of his conduct it resolved to introduce a resident sub-agent on the Buscot and Coleshill property, a step entirely warranted by the size and complexity. John Hill was furious, refused to meet the man appointed or to pass on to him any information or to accept him in that position. The Trust then took the course of dismissing John Hill, having the concurrence of Ernest Cook's executors, Major and Mrs Steward.

It was into this miserable atmosphere that Sir Dawson Bates was pitched by the Trust. Luckily he was technically one of the most competent of the agents employed by the Trust and it was in fact fortunate that he was not obliged to act as a subordinate to Hill. He was able to give to the property a quarter of a century of careful, methodical and thoughtful management which brought it through the social and agricultural revolution with far less stress than might have been supposed. He was burdened with an area the shape of which must go down as Hubert Smith's one major mistake. It ran in a narrow belt from the Birmingham end of Warwickshire in the north, through Oxford, Berkshire and Hampshire and later to the Isle of Wight.

The National Trust's direction of management lay in the hands of the Estates Committee, which had been accustomed to take a direct interest in the detail of what was done on its properties, and to give instructions to its staff. Right up to 1948 all agents were expected to attend its monthly meetings in London, whether they had business on the agenda or not. In that year Trevelyan retired from the Chairmanship of the Estates Committee and was succeeded by Earl De La Warr. 'Buck' De La Warr had succeeded very young to his family estates in Kent, which had been very seriously encumbered with debt, and he devoted himself to restoring them to solvency. In doing so he had become a competent agriculturalist and estate manager. He also entered politics and served in the National Government of the 1930s under the label of National Labour. He held eight offices in Government between 1929 and 1940, amongst them two stints as Parliamentary Under-Secretary to the Ministry of Agriculture. He then saw war service as a sailor and did not serve again in Government until he became Postmaster General, this time as a Conservative, from 1951 to 1955.

De La Warr was very much involved with the Country Landowners' Association which struggled to establish for its members a voice in public affairs which had been drowned by the clamour of the urban majority. There he found a young man, John St Aubyn, whose family owned estates in Cornwall and Devon. He was working in London as a solicitor specialising in property law. De La Warr brought St Aubyn on to the Trust's Estates Committee, recognising in him someone with a like-minded attitude to a landowner's responsibilities.

The whole-hearted and liberal response of the Trust to the financial demands of its new estates was due entirely to De La Warr. It was he who for some fifteen years persuaded the Finance and General Purposes Committee to disburse very large sums of money for cottage and farm improvements. He was fortunate in that, as Honorary Treasurer, 'Ruby' Holland-Martin entirely understood the practicalities of rural estate management and recognised the Trust's responsibility. Lord Esher, Chairman of that Committee, did not, and at Head Office the staff was divided, Smith and Gibbs fully supporting De La Warr, Robin Fedden opposing, and Jack Rathbone wavering. In his book on the Trust, Fedden expresses his serious doubts about the spending of money on these things. Writing in 1968, he records that the cost had amounted since the war to some £1,700,000, the greater part being drawn from legacies and donations, the only source of freely usable reserves.

He concluded: 'Enough has been said to indicate the great drain over more than twenty years on the Trust's free funds … A time is perhaps almost in sight when the burden will be eased. A greater proportion of free reserves can then be devoted to other purposes.'

He was certainly mistaken. The Trust had undertaken to look after its new properties 'in the manner as far as possible of the best private owners' (to quote an often-used phrase) and had it not done so it would have broken its promise to donors, and would have betrayed the tenants who depended on it. The Trust's response to need bred a recognition among donors, tenants and that section of Government and the public concerned, both of its goodwill and its competence. Within the Trust it fostered that spirit of trusteeship which motivated people such as De La Warr and St Aubyn.

This division seriously increased a rupture within the staff which had been started in the 1940s by Lord Esher's mischievous wit. He had not liked the new estate management structure which was being built up, nor was he sympathetic to the land management side of the Trust's work, even though his appreciation of landscape was almost as strong as that of the fine arts. He loved to tease and found Hubert Smith a splendid target. When the agents were tiresome he dismissed them as 'mangold wurzels'.

None of this would have endured for long had the administrative structure of the Trust been properly devised. The machinery depended entirely on the system of areas controlled by land agents, who received their instructions from Head Office committees and heads of department. Into this were inserted a number of regional representatives, some full-time, like Eardley Knollys in the south-west, some part time like Richard Stewart-Jones and the Earl of Euston, some honorary like Colonel Charles Brocklehurst in Cheshire and Sir Giles Isham in Northamptonshire. They were responsible to the Historic Buildings Secretary, James Lees-Milne, in London and to the Historic Buildings Committee. The contact between them and the area agents was at best intermittent and erratic. They had no desk in the Area Office, nor any working routine. There was a general tendency for the agent to carry on with what he regarded as his work and to be too busy or forgetful to consult his representative. For example, in the course of the repair of the fourteenth century moated manor house of Lower Brockhampton in Herefordshire, Colin Jones allowed the architect to install replica carved barge boards on the gables. This in SPAB doctrine was a heinous crime; Ruskin would have been outraged, and so was Richard Stewart-Jones when he discovered them. Richard was right, but what other than some sort of error could be expected with a representative living at Inkpen in Berkshire and work in Herefordshire being directed from Ross on Wye with no formal or regular contact between the two?

Members both of the committees and of the staff were aware of the schism which threatened and, in January 1956, Sir Philip Nichols put a memorandum to the Executive Committee suggesting the need for administrative reform. As a result, a committee was set up 'to investigate and report … with a view to the possibility and extent of further decentralisation.' Originally it was chaired by Sir Norman Kinnear, but he was disabled in an accident and Sir Philip, career diplomat and one-time Ambassador to the Soviet Union, took over. His colleagues were well chosen – De La Warr, McLeod Matheson, Lees-Milne, young John Smith and Adrian Hadden-Paton. The last named was on the Estates Committee and Chairman of the Ashridge Local Management Committee and held the most conservative and orthodox views on management.

The Committee (which the disrespectful among the staff renamed 'the Disorganisation Committee') reported in January 1958 and produced a competent and brief review of the Trust's history, growth and present organisation. The Trust's primary objective was that '… sound finance and efficient estate management are essential means. But above all the Trust must be guided by considerations of taste and amenity.' They found that the system worked 'reasonably well' but that 'the machine has shown a tendency to become clogged at the centre.' The report continues: 'The management of properties is the responsibility of Area Agents who are the only full-time executive officers of the Trust in the field. They are generally responsible for all aspects of the Trust's work except for questions of taste in relation to historic houses and their contents which are dealt with in some areas by part-time representatives and in others by Head Office. This present system entails some delay, confusion and overlapping.'

The solution proposed was the appointment of five Regional Secretaries who would represent the Secretary of the Trust. At Head Office committees would be streamlined and reduced in number from eleven to seven. This was a sensitive and sensible report but the direction of the Trust at that time was not ready to impose a drastic re-organisation. Ten years later, in very different circumstances, the Trust was to be re-organised and there are marked similarities between the Nichols' suggestions and what in the end was done. Only two Regional Secretaries were appointed – Michael Trinick who was agent and Representative in Cornwall, took on Devon and Cornwall, and Carew Wallace the northern Home Counties and East Anglia. The arrangement worked quite well to start with, but, with the rapid growth from the early 1960s onwards, it became unwieldy, and the extra layer of administration extraordinarily expensive. It did, however, last for some twenty years although it varied in form.

Sir Philip Nichols and his colleagues were right: changes were needed but they did not begin for ten years and another ten were to pass before a complete solution was produced. This was made possible not only by a better framework but also by the continued growth in both property and financial resources.

It may be here that we should look more closely at some of the new people of the time, starting with Hugh Fitzroy, Earl of Euston, heir to the Duke of Grafton. It was Lord Esher who engaged his interest initially on behalf of the Society for the Preservation of Ancient Buildings. Esher had been Chairman of the Society for more than twenty years. He was looking for help and a possible successor and persuaded Hugh Euston to become his Deputy. He already had one particular friend on the Committee of the Society in Richard Stewart-Jones, whose lively energies had spearheaded a number of crusades during and after the war.

Euston was prepared to devote time to the Society. However, he also needed a job and told Lord Esher so. As a result, he became, part-time, the Regional Representative in the South-East when Fedden went to Head Office. He had no formal training either in architecture or the fine arts, having read history for his degree. What he knew had simply rubbed off from his background and those with whom he had been in contact. As far as the Trust's work was concerned he learned a great deal from Lees-Milne, with whom he went on numerous expeditions, and from Fedden. He became Chairman of the SPAB in 1960 and remained in that office for more than twenty-five years. He was appointed to the Historic Buildings Council when that was formed in 1954, chaired their Churches Committee from 1967, and is still with the reconstituted successor body. For the National Trust he formed the new East Anglian Regional Committee in 1965 and was Chairman until he retired under the fifteen year rule in 1980. He may be regarded as a first rate advertisement for the non-professional approach.

Richard Stewart-Jones's name has been mentioned already several times. In 1934, when just twenty, an inheritance from his grandmother enabled him to leave the Merchant Navy, and he devoted his independence and his time to old buildings, securing for himself as mentor the knowledgeable and committed Secretary of the Society for the Protection of Ancient Buildings, A.R. Powys. He became a member of its Committee, quite the youngest in a group generally middle-aged and elderly. His energies were by no means wholly absorbed and he developed and consummated a love of Chelsea, particularly those houses in Cheyne Walk into which old Lindsey House had been divided. He bought Number 97 from Bryan Guinness, simply saying how much he could afford to pay (and his means were quite modest) and outlining a scheme whereby his mother and sisters would have part and he would take lodgers to make ends meet. This direct approach to a problem was typical of his attitude to anything which seemed important to him. By 1952 this first plunge had resulted in nearly the whole of that beautiful 1674 building being entrusted to the care of the National Trust.

After the war, through which he had cheerfully soldiered in the ranks, the conformity required for the King's Commission not being in his line, he became first the Trust's London Honorary Representative and then in 1954 Representative for Berkshire and the counties to the south and north west. He blew through the organisation like a brisk, refreshing breeze until in 1957 he died from one of a series of heart attacks which he had done his best to ignore. He was only 43. Lord Esher wrote of him, 'It is not easy to find ... the intelligent, instructed and sensitive men that we require to carry out our urgent and complicated tasks. Stewart-Jones was the perfect example of a temperament and character dedicated to the preservation of beautiful things.'

Against the comet that was Richard Stewart-Jones one would not at first notice Christopher Wall as any sort of star in the firmament. He was intended for the Army, went through Sandhurst and in 1949 was commissioned into the Grenadier Guards. In 1956, he assumed a new career with the Trust as Assistant Secretary with special responsibility for Public Relations. Like others on the staff, he thought very highly indeed of Lord Crawford and was 'impressed by his high standards which sometimes surprised one, because until it was explained one hadn't appreciated the complexities. That is wisdom and percipience. Authority gave him the power to impress, and to secure from other people what he knew to be right.' Indeed from attendance at Committee meetings he also learned from others: Oliver Esher, Harold Nicolson, Michael Rosse and John Smith among them. Nicolson he admired for his balance and his commitment to the Trust. Smith, who was still relatively new, 'was obviously going to be a leading light, full of ideas, a lot of which were quite impracticable, but some quite brilliant. The best education was the discussion of ideas: everything was treated independently and the answer was intended to be what was best for the subject, and not policy generalities. Flexibility and adaptability were the hallmarks.'

The organisation of the Attingham Summer School was partly Wall's responsibility and it gave him the chance of attending the courses, hearing lectures from distinguished scholars such as Nikolaus Pevsner, John Summerson and Alec Clifton-Taylor on buildings, Helena Heywood the furniture expert, and Mark Girouard and John Harris. He also leaned heavily on Jim Lees-Milne, by that time no longer tied to a routine job and ready as ever to guide the interested on the path of his own enthusiasms.

Articulate enough in private and with those whom he knew well, Wall was quiet in casual company to the point of seeming withdrawn. When listening to another's argument he gave it the thoughtful consideration that he did to anything he considered of importance but he was very slow to respond. That, added to his style of work which is thoughtful, methodical and endlessly patient, has obscured the exceptionally high standard and continuity of his work.

From Head Office he was to go, in 1961, to the newly formed North West Midland Area, based in Attingham, during which time five major historic houses were added to those already in the Trust's care there. He was responsible for Derbyshire, where Hardwick Hall was but newly acquired and where he later had the extremely difficult task involved in taking on Sudbury Hall. He shared with Fedden the responsibility for North Wales, which included the ancient Marcher castle of Powis and the neo-Norman Penrhyn. In 1971 he moved to the Home Counties area, based at Hughenden in Buckinghamshire, retaining for several more years his responsibilities for Hardwick and Sudbury. Among his new duties there was that of trying to regulate applications from the owners of property on what had been the Greenlands Estate of over 3,900 acres which the then Viscount Hambledon had given restrictive covenants. Christopher Wall brought to this the same careful and painstaking application which had characterised the far more rewarding work of looking after the Trust's own properties. Wall's long career with the Trust has been followed right through because, apart from the early appointment of Fedden and Knollys, he was the first of a new line of full-time Representatives. His quiet success in the role has formed the pattern for future Representatives.

By 1971 there were still only five full-time Representatives. One of them was Michael Trinick whose career and place in the development of the Trust is of considerable interest. Like so many of the post-war staff he had served in the forces – the Bombay Sappers and Miners. On demobilisation he trained as a land agent at the Royal Agricultural College, going to London as an assistant to the Chief Agent in 1950. He spent three years at the Trust's Head Office and, in addition to his principal job of helping Hubert Smith and Christopher Gibbs, was taken up by Jack Rathbone, acting as his ADC on a number of tours of the properties. This long spell under the influence of the centre provided him with the same excellent grounding, as it did later for Wall. In his case it was especially valuable because, in 1953, he went to Cotehele to act as George Senior's sub-agent in Cornwall and, save for an extension of his responsibilities into Devon and West Somerset, remained there, out of reach of any direct central influence, until he retired in 1984. In 1956, upon Senior's retirement, he took over the job of Area Agent in Cornwall and the Plymouth corner of Devon. Eardley Knollys found him interested in the interiors of houses and apt in the business of historic buildings and encouraged him to take an active part in the work. Trinick was not satisfied for long with what he thought was the rather limited role of a land agent, and Knollys and Lees-Milne encouraged him to change to being a Representative. The opportunity came in 1955 when Saltram House near Plymouth was being considered by the Trust and there was no one nearer than Knollys who could deal with it. Michael Trinick was duly appointed but retained his job as Area Agent. He turned himself into a local historian, researching the history of houses and their owner's family and writing guide books, or revising them, for properties in his care.

Although the Trust's agents were single-handed, in the provinces, they had the help of a number of remarkable people, some inherited with the properties and some newly recruited. At Stourhead, in Wiltshire, Simon Buxton, when he came to set up an Area Office for the countries of Hampshire, Wiltshire, Dorset and East Somerset, found Ewart Epton, who had started work there in 1925 as Estate Clerk. Sir Henry Hoare was then sixty, and Lady Hoare sixty-three, and they retained the same habits – and in the case of Lady Hoare the same dresses – as before the Great War. Epton had a struggle to modernise any of his responsibilities. For example the indoor staff, ten of them, received their wages quarterly by cheque and it was more than ten years before he was allowed to pay them monthly in cash. Right until the last he was obliged to quote for new servants, even fifteen-year olds, 'Wages £x per year, all found save beer.'

The loyalty Epton had given to Sir Henry and Lady Hoare he gave in equal measure to the Trust. His knowledge of the estate and the district was encyclopaedic and Buxton could rely on records and accounts being methodically maintained. Likewise at Killerton, George Senior was well served by two very different people. His area consisted of the southern half of the large county of Devon and all of Cornwall. For this his office staff consisted of Betty Davey, a bright modest girl whose parents were tenants on the estate. She was responsible for all the correspondence and other typing, for the rent demands and collection, for accounts and for wages. Senior's right hand man was Arthur Floyd, whose father had been gamekeeper on the Holnicote Estate. He himself had been employed by the Aclands since 1912, except for service in the Great War. He was Head Forester and, having served under that forestry pioneer Sir Francis Acland, had a knowledge and experience which many men in similar positions elsewhere seldom acquired. It was not, however, his long service and skills which were so important, but the fact that he was known and trusted by everyone. In the immediate post-war years he was obliged to double his work with that of Estate Clerk of Works. In this role he was of even greater value to the newish owner, the National Trust, acting conscientiously as a bridge between the strange landlord and the tenants.

The Area Offices themselves were not, of course, ready made. They are now known as 'Regional' and some have moved location. All have expanded enormously, both in accommodation, equipment and people. When Rosemary Bray went to be secretary to Simon Buxton in the Wessex Area in 1955 the office had been established for eight years, occupying the old estate office in Stourton village, next door to Mr Epton's house. There were fifty-three properties in the area with a total acreage of 8,423. To manage this the Area Agent had the assistance of Epton and Rosemary Bray! This contrasts with the present position in which the former Area Agent, re-styled Regional Director, has four land agents, nine others performing various executive functions, and fifteen supporting staff – and Rosemary Bray! Boundary changes and new properties have increased the number of properties to one hundred with an area of 45,558 acres.

In 1958 there were changes in the north. Sir Charles Trevelyan had died and Ben Proud, who had been Cubby Acland's assistant when that area covered all England north of the Mersey and the Humber, moved to open an Area Office at Wallington. The eastern half of the former area was to be run from there. Anne Kennedy came as his secretary.

> The Wallington office was unbelievably primitive. It was upstairs in the Long Gallery [now the Clock Tower Café]. We used two rooms, B.J.S.P. [Proud] and I worked in one and the only other member of the office staff, Jack Prior the Clerk, had the use of the large room. My desk was a trestle table and I sat on a long bench as used by the visiting public when served with cups of tea in the Long Gallery in those days.

By October, despite the arrival of the paraffin stove, they felt the cold badly but in November moved to 'better' quarters in the estate village of Cambo. There was no telephone and incoming calls were taken by Mrs Prior next door. She would go to the bottom of the outside stone staircase and whistle, and her husband would run down to take the call. It became home for nineteen years.

Ben Proud and Anne ran the Trust's affairs from the Scottish border to the Humber; from Lindisfarne Castle in the north, to East Riddlesden Hall in the West Riding, to Beningbrough near York. They were joined in 1964 by Arthur Sobers to keep the accounts. Between them they had to do everything. Ben Proud not only designed the improvement work to houses and cottages: he also drew all the plans himself. Public relations, opening of properties and advertising all fell to them. The typewriter was the only machine, and anything to be copied was done on that. The remittance advice notes – 150 to 200 in a batch – were churned out by Anne on the typewriter.

In 1968 Yorkshire was detached from the area and Ben Proud went down to manage there. Despite that, the work of the area continued to increase and, in 1977, the office was moved from Cambo to a former temperance hotel on the estate at Scots Gap. The transformation over a short twenty years seems incredible to Anne Kennedy, now taking charge of her third National Trust agent, and with a staff of nearly twenty. Oil-fired central heating (with a generator to fall back on in Northumbrian winters), carpeting, copying machines, a computer, and the first ever British Telecom Herald telephone system to be installed in the Newcastle area.

The growth of the Trust can be emphasised in a hundred different ways, but it is in these provincial offices that the changes are most clearly seen. One day in the autumn of 1949 George Senior excused himself from attendance on a visitor. 'I shall be busy for a couple of hours this afternoon. Betty and I have to do the estimates for next year.' Sure enough in that time the income and expenditure for south Devon and Cornwall for 1950 was worked out in some detail. In 1984, the turnover in Cornwall alone was £5 million and the office staff which handled this huge sum numbered forty.

CHAPTER XV

From Canals to Coastlines

The Trust emerged curiously strengthened from the problems of the 1950s. The new structure had become established and tested and the new staff had absorbed its traditions and ethos. At no stage since the Great War had its work stood still, but the 1960s were to see a surge of effort and a burgeoning of new ideas.

In 1960 Oliver Esher retired from the Executive and from the General Purposes Committee, of which he was Chairman. He had served the Trust for thirty-one years, and had marked the work of the Trust with his own enthusiasms and prejudices. It is probably fair to say that, in the work he did for the Society for the Preservation of Ancient Buildings and the Trust, it was the preservation of beauty for its own sake that activated him. He was concerned to keep the control of the Trust in the hands of those whose priorities were similar to his, and was emphatically against any positive steps to enlarge the membership. This chimed very much with the natural inclination of Jim Lees-Milne and, to some extent, with Robin Fedden's, while for Jack Rathbone admiration and fondness for Lord Esher made it hard for him to take an opposite view.

The people who came to fill the gap were by no means new to the Trust. Michael Parsons, sixth Earl of Rosse, had been active in the field of architectural preservation since the mid-1930s, when he had been instrumental, with three others, including Lees-Milne, in founding the Georgian Group, of which he became Chairman. One of the events which prompted them to create this Group was the callous demolition of the Adelphi Terraces. He came on to the Trust's Historic Buildings Committee in 1944, the Executive in 1945, General Purposes Committee in 1946, Gardens Committee in 1948. He was tall and handsome, with immense charm. The Trust quickly learned to make use of him over a wide range of subjects. His home was Birr Castle in the Irish Republic, where he and his wife Anne kept considerable state. In England he divided his time between a house in Yorkshire and a Victorian London house in Stafford Terrace.

Rosse was an enthusiastic gardener from early on. As a twenty-first birthday present, in 1927, he had been given a great collection of trees for planting at Birr. He was a tireless and informed traveller, his honeymoon in 1935 having taken him and his bride to Ceylon, Bali and Japan, returning home by train through China and the Soviet Union on the Trans-Siberian Railway. In the matter of plants his acute powers of observation were matched by a very considerably botanical knowledge and this pattern was repeated in all the things in which he was interested – architecture, landscape, and the arts. He was also able to get on easy terms with all sorts of people, while retaining an unobtrusive authority. For example, in 1946, when the Trust formed the consortium of local authorities to manage and help to finance Clumber Park, Rosse was nominated as one of the Trust's representatives, and the local authority representatives elected him as their Chairman. For four years Rosse held the committee amicably together, gently guiding them towards the sort of management at which the Trust aimed. There was also an emotional dimension to the problem: Clumber Park had been the home of Lord Rosse's mother and had it not been for his cousin's, the Duke of Newcastle's, curious conduct in first destroying the house (because, it is said, he did not like it) and then breaking up the estate, Rosse might have been enjoying a very different relationship with the place.

Another founder member of the Trust, representing the City of Sheffield, was Hartley Marshall. An Alderman and one-time Lord Mayor, he was a pattern-maker by trade, a life-long Socialist and had been a Trades Unionist of importance since the time of the Great War. He was elected Chairman of the Clumber Committee in 1958. Following the example first established under Lord Rosse, Hartley continued as a successful Chairman until, in 1967, he ceased to be eligible to represent Sheffield, whereupon he was nominated by the Trust as one of its representatives, was re-elected to the chair and held it until 1974.

Another Irish peer had been active on behalf of the Trust for a long time. Randal John Somerled, Earl of Antrim, had his home in Northern Ireland, at Glenarm in the county from which he took his title. He came from a family whose reputation was as romantic as their castle of Dunluce, perched on an unassailable, craggy cliff above the sea. Antrim had taken on the chairmanship of the Trust's Northern Ireland Committee in 1947. At that time the Trust's possessions in Ulster were few and, with the exception of the fine stretch of Whitepark Bay, somewhat insignificant. Antrim, catching the tide of the times, gave an impetus to the Trust's work there which has placed it in the front rank of all conservation work in the Province; the details are reviewed in a later chapter.

In 1948 he joined the Executive and was elected to the Council in 1956. When the 1960s opened he was mainly noticed for the way in which he had promoted Northern Ireland interests within the Trust, and for an exceptionally agreeable personality. He was on the short side and somewhat round, already very bald, while his immediately and permanently memorable features were the wise, direct eyes, slightly hooded, which took in everything around him. He had a tremendous sense of, and relish for, fun and loved to tease, with kindness. He is perhaps best described by Mark Norman – 'a roly-poly Puck with a permanent twinkle in his eye and gusts of laughter! He was shrewd, and not fooled by attempts to take advantage of his good humour.'

John Smith (he was knighted in the 1988 New Year's Honours List) came straight on to the Executive without previous experience of the Trust at the tender age of twenty-nine. He had been to Eton and New College, Oxford, and had spent five years in the Fleet Air Arm. He was in Coutts Bank and it was 'Ruby' Holland-Martin who introduced him. That was in 1952. Smith was not just a clever young man, though he was indeed that. He was a visionary, capable of great feats of imagination, and imbued with a great enthusiasm for everything and everybody and an innate understanding of the nature of buildings and landscapes. Lord Chorley has left a record of how he appeared to an elder statesman. '... a young and unconventional Conservative who had made a most favourable impression on us all. He was very enterprising and full of original ideas in connection with any job he undertook; at first sight these did not always seem very convincing, or perhaps one should say feasible. Difficulties which one might have considered insuperable had a habit of withering away before his attack, ...' His impact on the Trust was such that it was to him that the Chairmanship of the General Purposes Committee was entrusted on Lord Esher's retirement.

One might have expected that Ronnie Norman's son Mark would have come automatically into the government of the Trust in his father's wake, but it was in fact his partner in Lazards, David Bowes-Lyon, who engineered his appointment. Bowes-Lyon had formed the opinion – through his Gardens Committee experience – that the Trust was hopelessly unbusinesslike, and he thought that the young Norman would help to improve matters. Norman first joined the Finance Committee in 1953 but very soon the General Purposes Committee as well and so found himself a member of what he rightly recognised as the ruling caucus. Thus began a thirty-year-long involvement with the Trust. From the very first he took the view that the Trust's finances were badly run. 'Ruby' Holland-Martin, the Treasurer, was a cousin, but Norman thought that he either had no idea of how to run a business or, alternatively, that he did not recognise that the Trust *was* a business and needed to be run as such.

Ronnie Norman had passed on to his son the direct manner in speech and action which were his own characteristics. Mark, well-built and energetic, had begun the war as a gunner with the Yeomanry of his native Hertfordshire. In late 1940, he was extracted by his friend Peter Fleming to participate in a scheme in which a specially selected group was sent to the Middle East to recruit from Wavell's Italian prisoners a volunteer corps which would be used to topple Mussolini. Strange to say, not one was found who would volunteer. Fleming appealed to Wavell for another and more attainable objective and so they went off to lend their support to the Regent of Yugoslavia whose neutrality was being threatened by the Germans. Their route lay through Greece, but when they arrived at the Monastir Gap they found that a German airborne division had also arrived. Wisely they retraced their steps and in due course, were evacuated from Greece. In the course of the evacuation Norman was badly wounded and returned to England. On recovery he went to the Cabinet Office as an Assistant Military Secretary to 'Pug' Ismay.

That he had been involved in two of the more ludicrous episodes of the war may have served to suppress in Norman any predeliction for hare-brained schemes and contributed to making him the wise person who was later to help in guiding the Trust. When he returned to civilian life, he re-entered the business world that he had left, and he was almost wholly taken up with a most demanding life which led to the chairmanships of major companies. He could spare for the Trust no more time than was needed to read papers and attend meetings, and it was not until he had retired from much of his business commitment that the Trust had the full benefit of his irrepressible high spirits and abundant good humour.

There were, of course, later recruits to the Trust's work and one of these also came from the business world. R.T.P Gibson was some six years younger than Norman and had followed him at that remove through Eton and Magdalen College, Oxford. Like Norman he went to war with the Yeomanry, but of the neighbouring county Middlesex, and with many others was taken prisoner in the Western Desert in 1941, escaping two years later when Italy went out of the war. After that he spent three years with the Special Operations Executive. He then had a year in Political Intelligence in the Foreign Office.

He re-entered civilian life working in the family business, becoming a director of S. Pearson & Son Ltd in 1960. He had previously been on the board of the *Financial Times*, as was John Smith, and in 1961 he also joined Royal Exchange Assurance of which Smith was Deputy Governor. He and John Smith clicked at once when they first met and remained close friends thereafter. Gibson also knew Jack Rathbone well because of their shared love of music, and Hugh Euston too. It was on holiday together that Euston discovered in Gibson a deep interest in old buildings, and that led to his becoming Honorary Treasurer of the Historic Buildings Trust. It was Jack Rathbone who invited Gibson to meet Lord Crawford, but it seems likely that, while all these connections influenced events, it was John Smith who suggested roping him in to the Trust. Gibson joined the General Purposes Committee in 1961 and within the next two years he had joined, first, the Publicity Committee and then the Executive. Despite his business commitments he found time to become very actively involved with the work of the Trust, and the Trust at once took up for its own advantage this willing and competent help.

The General Purposes Committee, with John Smith in the chair and Mark Norman and Pat Gibson as members, after Lord Esher's departure had been given a wholly new direction. The philosophy of the business world was brought to bear on the more traditional approach of Chorley, Rosse and Antrim. The effect was not immediately noticeable, but it was to grow.

The Trust took up with equal decisiveness the services of someone outwardly very different from Gibson. Len Clark was born later in the same year as Gibson. A Londoner, he took his recreation in walking and early became involved with the Youth Hostels Association. Hiking in the Chilterns or the North Downs, Len Clark encountered those open spaces which were the great features of the Trust's possessions in the 1930s, such as Box Hill and Ashridge. His working life was as a Local Government officer in London. His politics were firmly Socialist. He was also a Quaker and a vegetarian. From all this it might be supposed that Clark would have fitted badly into an organisation liberally sprinkled with peers and plutocrats, but in fact the opposite has been the case. In the first place, while no one could be firmer in adherence to his principles, equally no one could be less stuffy or obtrusive about them. Secondly, Clark found himself impressed by and in sympathy with what the Trust was doing when he first came as the YHA's nominee to Council in 1962. This recognition of the Trust's value led him to wish to contribute to what was being done. He felt that it 'spread right across the board and produced a shared culture across the nation'. He particularly liked the mix of its activities and history and saw it as forming a bridge between different elements throughout the country in the cause of conservation. In response, his new colleagues in the organisation liked his quiet, thoughtful and positive style, the shrewd cool but deeply felt commitment, and by the end of the decade Len Clark was firmly estabished in the centre of the Trust's councils.

In 1960 Hubert Smith retired and was succeeded as Chief Agent by Christopher Gibbs. His eighteen-year tenure had successfully established the new professional management cadre, and his own expertise in farming, forestry and nature conservation had set standards for the whole organisation. He had also taken pains to ensure that the rapidly growing staff, scattered as they were across the country, should find and keep a sense of family, of belonging. He instituted an annual event in which he gathered all his land agents and their wives for a few days to meet each other and to study problems of professional interest. Initially the venue was decided by the whereabouts of the annual show of the Royal Agricultural Society. A day was spent at the showground, prodding cattle, pricing machinery and meeting friends, and two or three days looking at problems on National Trust estates in the neighbourhood and, if possible, on privately owned property too. The latter enabled the agents to see such places as Geoffrey Woolrych-Whitmore's woodlands at Dudmaston in Shropshire. These were a model of intelligent management and, nearly thirty years later, were to be given to the Trust by his successors, the Laboucheres. As Chairman of the Estates Committee, Lord De La Warr was responsible for standards of management, and he was courageous enough to add example to precept by showing the land agents round his estate in Kent. It has the distinction amongst other things of having on it Christopher Robin's 100 acre wood, though the only visible characters on that day were Rabbit's Relations.

As the years went by, these annual meetings were widened to include other members of the staff besides the agents, and when the Royal Show settled down to a permanent site in Warwickshire, the Trust devised its own itinerary. In the early days, Anthony Martineau's conscience had been seriously disturbed at what he feared might be a grave misuse of charitable funds, and it was with difficulty that he was reassured by his colleagues who themselves had no doubt that the gain to the Trust in improved efficiency far outweighed the expense.

Not that the events were dull – far from it. In the Lake District, Cubby Acland arranged an imaginative mix with inspections of the new sheep handling equipment at Glencoyne Farm on Ullswater, and demonstrations of Ben Proud's technique in vernacular building – for example a bicycle wheel adapted as a template to guide masons when building the round rough-stone pillars. Supper round a bonfire on the Claife shore of Windermere had to be earned by rowing races in the Trust's heavy clinker-built skiffs, normally hired out to holidaymakers. Also, on the principle that an agent should be familiar with all the ground under his management, there was a nine-mile walk over the fells, including the 3,000 foot Great Gable.

That inspired John Tetley, agent in North Wales, to parody 'Tom Pearse':

> And when shall I see you in Langdale once more?
> Puff along, wheeze along, give at the knees.

It was for such occasions that he composed 'The Song of the N.T. Agent' sung to the tune used also for 'The Church's One Foundation' or – for the older generation – 'We are Fred Karno's Army'. It began:

The Agent: 'I am an N.T. Agent, I live an N.T. life,
        'And roughly every third weekend I spend with my dear wife.
        'I care for stately houses, a most historic lot,
        'Entirely built of Portland Stone, and virulent dry rot!
        'I am an N.T. agent my taste is very raw –'

The Representative:
        'But I'm the Representative who deals with the décor.
        'On colour, period, design I have the surest touch'

The Agent: 'I hardly like to mention that it costs just twice as much.'
        'I am an N.T. agent, I live on my Domain,
        'They sometimes tell me what to do … it's always QUITE INANE!
        'And when Head Office writes to me with this or that idea,
        'I write and say "That's quite first class! – but it
           wouldn't work up here!"

Throughout the country this was a time when the relief from the tensions of war and the restrictions of its aftermath first began to be felt. Harold Macmillan had formed his first Administration in 1957, and was soon to tell the country that it 'had never had it so good'. Professor Galbraith's phrase 'the affluent society', began to be taken up by journalists and politicians. It was of Africa that Macmillan spoke of 'a wind of change', but he might well have applied it to the National Trust, and the personification of that change was John Smith.

On 19 March 1958, John Smith wrote a letter to Lord Crawford in which he initiated what was to be a new area of responsibility for the Trust: 'Here is the letter about canals with which I have been threatening you. I think the National Trust ought to approach the Transport Commission to *discuss* the preservation (providing it costs the Trust no money or trouble) of those canals which the Transport Commission wishes to abandon.' There followed four full pages of explanation and advocacy. At that time the Bowes Committee was sitting on the question of what should be done with the now mostly obsolete canals. Since the canal companies had been set up by various Acts of Parliament, abandonment also required legislation. This was in preparation. Smith wished to get in before it was too late. He argued that the Trust should take an interest in the canals because they represented a huge area of amenities (tow paths, fishing, scenery, boating, peace and quiet) and contained a wealth of historical remains – monuments of industrial archaeology 'like the original non-rotative parallel-motion beam pumping engine designed and built by Watt (no less) …' on the Kennet and Avon, as well as many buildings from lock-keepers' cottages to bridges and warehouses.

As a result, this question did go before the Executive in April and approved an approach to the Transport Executive provided it involved no financial liability. An Inland Waterways Association had been formed (under the presidency of that most engaging and many-sided man, A.P. Herbert) as a pressure group and to represent canal users. Throughout the summer there was considerable public discussion. *The Times* ran a long article on the problem. John Smith spent the summer lobbying his colleagues as to the value of preserving canals. In early September he persuaded Jack Rathbone to take a boat trip from Cropredy. There was another, two weeks later, with De La Warr and Kenneth Robinson. The latter wrote about it to Rathbone. 'It was a pleasant day and I do agree about the desirability of keeping canals open. I still see the financial obstacles as well nigh insuperable, however.'

In his original plan to Crawford, Smith had mentioned that the Transport Commission might be using an old act to close by warrant the Stratford-on-Avon Canal and so avoid the necessity for new legislation. A Stratford Canal Preservation Society had been formed to prevent that. On their behalf Mr Clifford, their Chairman, appealed to the Trust for help. Smith addressed a comprehensive memorandum on the subject to the Executive Committee, the Trust having received a tentative offer from the Transport Commission of the fourteen-mile southern section. He described its features – thirty five locks, three aqueducts, twenty-eight bridges and seven barrel-vaulted cottages; its linking of the Avon with the Grand Union Canal; its cast-iron split bridges (split to permit the passage of a tow-rope).

To accept the offer, he urged, would be to perform the true function of the Trust: to act as a longstop. Moreover, 'I believe it will bring about a spectacular increase in our membership. Everybody is sickened by the decay of the canal. … If we accept there will be a surge of enthusiasm; and most of these people will join the Trust.' He was confident that the Canal Society was well able and very willing to undertake the management, and that the finances although complicated were less intractable than would be supposed.

> Finally, let me appeal to the Committee's adaptability and enterprise. When the Trust was formed there was no thought of our owning large numbers of country houses, or gardens: but when the need arose we met it: let us now take another step forward, and come to the rescue of a third new sort of property which, like the other two, is at once a source of pleasure and a manifestation of the English genius.

This very personal document was addressed to the Executive by John Smith in his capacity as Assistant Honorary Treasurer, thus associating his office with the proposal. He continued to handle the matter personally, sending the Secretary a draft scheme to cope with procedure and to satisfy the objections which had been raised by local authorities. A financial summary was included which estimated a capital cost of £81,000, to be met by a grant from the Transport Commission of £66,000 and the balance to be raised by appeal. Before completion of restoration there would be a surplus of nearly £3,000 per annum and afterwards slightly better than break-even. This encouraged the Executive to go on with negotiations and, in February 1959, they were told that the Commission had agreed to transfer to the Trust 'certain selected canals' on leasehold, with an option to purchase. On this basis they agreed to take the Stratford Canal, subject to finance being satisfactory. In April, having received another memorandum from John Smith full of technical details, the Executive finally took the plunge (in this case a particularly appropriate word): 'Taking account of the fact that the estimates were not in respect of inalienable property'. In other words they could dispose of the canal if it became a burden.

The work of seeing the legal side of things through fell to Martineau's new young assistant, solicitor Robert Latham. His route to the Trust had led via Repton, National Service in the Army and Trinity College, Oxford, to serving articles to a firm of solicitors in the Lake District. It was there that he became aware of the

National Trust. He did leave the Lakes to join the distinguished firm of Farrers in Lincolns Inn Fields but he always intended to return to work in the Lakes. That he did not do so was, he says, because he believed he could do more for the Lakes by working for the National Trust.

So it was a fairly raw, and undoubtedly enthusiastic, young man who went to work with John Smith on the business of securing the canal. He simply loved the job. 'John was marvellous, and a wonderful chap to work with. I respected him enormously, and I still retain that respect.' It was quite a tricky operation, tied up with Parliamentary precedents and procedures. These were circumvented by the device of a Petition to Parliament which was accepted in March 1960, and that cleared the way for the proposed lease and option to purchase. In September that year, Smith and Rathbone set up what was for the Trust a most unusual arrangement. The Stratford Canal Society was to be treated as a local committee of the Trust, and Smith and Latham were to become members. An architect and canal enthusiast, David Hutchings, whom Smith had met in the course of his preparatory work, was appointed as Organiser at the modest salary of £1,050 per annum, and given the status of a representative for the purpose of the annual report. Rathbone was to take direct charge of the project and the Committee and the Organiser were to be responsible directly to him.

Meanwhile costs were rising and Government money falling. The balance to be found by the Trust steadily increased until Rathbone was obliged, in October 1960, to get authority to appeal for £22,000. This was, for the Trust at that time, a large sum and the first major appeal to be undertaken since the joint RHS/NT gardens appeal had fizzled out ten years earlier. John Smith got off to a good start and it was reported in the papers that, at the annual dinner of the Inland Waterways Association, 'a director of Rolls Royce and Coutts Bank made a surprise appeal ... Immediately the 65 diners promised £8,000.'

David Hutchings went to work with great energy and the story of the restoration is one of high endeavour and ingenuity. There was a great response by voluntary workers from the Inland Waterways Association, the Scouts, the Civic Trust and other organisations. They were backed by help from the Royal Engineers, the Royal Air Force and, notably, men from HM Prisons. Hutchings conducted a voluminous correspondence with the Secretary and every two or three months came to meetings with him and Smith (by now in the chair of the General Purposes Committee).

By the time it was all done, David Hutchings had supervised the removal of 300,000 cubic yards of mud, built 70 new lock gates and rebuilt many of the 36 lock chambers. The cost had been £61,000, with the appeal bringing in £53,000, of which the Pilgrim Trust gave £10,000 and the Government, in the end, only £20,000. The balance came from a free fund of the National Trust. A ceremonial opening by the Queen Mother, President of the Trust, went off in sunshine and fine style on 11 July 1964.

The National Trust found it had won golden opinions from all sorts of people. The whole enterprise did precisely as John Smith had predicted in raising morale within the Trust and it surely contributed to the rapidly increasing membership. However, from that time on the story of the canal is one of continuously worsening finances. A new appeal was launched in 1965, which, perhaps wisely, had no advertised target and it was kept going with new leaflets in the two following years.

Even at that early date the haste and shoestring resources of the restoration began to be evident. The growing popularity of the canal and its increased use by amateur bargees brought more erosion to the banks and damage to lock gates. As time went on, the new lock gates themselves began to deteriorate long before their proper expectation of life had expired. Culverts under the canal in those places where it ran on an embankment had not been rebuilt. They were an integral part of the drainage system of adjoining land and some threatened to collapse. It was becoming all too apparent that a large injection of funds was essential and urgent to prevent the situation getting even worse.

The Trust had never declared the canal inalienable and had always imagined that at some stage it would be passed on in good order to some sort of successor body. However, as time passed and the deficit mounted, the prospect of finding such an inheritor became increasingly remote. By the early 1980s the general funds of the Trust were meeting a yearly bill of £40,000 and over, while the cost of complete repair was thought to be over £1 million. Efforts to form a new body, the Stratford Canal Trust, foundered on the insistence of its members that the National Trust should agree to allow them, in the course of extending navigation to Warwick, to make a canal through the park at Charlecote, which had to be refused.

What the outcome will be is wholly unpredictable. Perhaps the Trust will become rich enough to continue to carry the burden. Perhaps some benefactor will wave his wand over the financial problems. Perhaps Government will resume the obligations it formerly shed. Whatever the outcome, Latham is in no doubt that it was the right thing to do at the time. 'It was a holding operation and if the Trust had not undertaken it, the canal would have gone forever. We should have restored it, as we did, but then have handed it over to a successor body.*

By contrast an account of the Trust's concurrent acquisition of the Wey and Godalming Navigations is simple and undramatic. The difference between the two cases generally reflects the planning and resources which have been devoted to the project. In September 1963, Ivan Hills, Area Agent in the South East, reported to the Finance Committee on the finances of fifteen miles of river, navigable from Guildford to the Thames. This had been accepted in July by the Executive as a gift from Harry Stevens, subject to finance, and to the condition that it would not be held inalienably. The offer was almost certainly inspired by the Trust's restoration of the Stratford Canal. In addition Mr Stevens and his partner brother were elderly and wished to ensure the preservation of the navigation which dated back to 1683. Hills's review of the position was detailed and cautious and he wisely took the advice of Philip Henman, a benefactor of the Trust with direct experience of operating barges and lighters in the Port of London.

The picture which emerged showed that generous estimates of expenditure would be covered by a conservative estimate of income, and that wharfage and other property in Guildford not essential to the navigation would constitute a big reserve of capital. Since this was still a working navigation, no question of restoration arose. In any event, navigable rivers enjoy enormous advantages over canals. The water

---

*In April 1988 the southern section of the Canal passed from the Trust to British Waterways. The Trust agreed to contribute £1.5 million over five years towards the cost of essential repairs and maintenance.

comes naturally from the catchment, the river follows a natural fall and there are no embankments or aqueducts, nor interference with the drainage of adjoining land. Hills summed up the value of Mr Stevens' offer: 'In my view an opportunity is offered of combining the preservation of an attractive and historically interesting feature with successful operation of its ancillary business.'

The Committee did agree and, moreover, decided to face reality and hold all except the disposable part inalienably. Hills relied upon the wise guidance of Philip Henman, whose backing was wholehearted, and who, as an additional safeguard for the Trust, guaranteed to underwrite any loss for up to £3,000 a year for three years, and later made an outright gift of £2,000. So successful was the operation that, four years later, the Guildford Corporation gave the short extension to Godalming to the Trust, and the property has run smoothly for twenty years, yielding all those benefits which John Smith had listed for Lord Crawford.

There was great excitement both in the Trust and in Dorset when, in 1961, Mrs Bonham-Christie died. She had bought the island of Brownsea in Poole Harbour in 1930 and had lived there in increasing isolation until a few days before she died. The island is a curiosity because of its position, lying as it does within the huge expanse of the harbour but distant only by about a quarter of a mile from the intensively developed north shore. The nearest part of the mainland, the peninsula of Sandbanks, had been little more than sand dunes at the turn of the century but over the next sixty years had become completely covered with hotels, houses and boat yards, with property prices sky high.

The island had had a chequered history. Henry VIII's gunfort covering the harbour mouth had evolved into the castle a Victorian mansion with the usual accretions of pleasure grounds, kitchen garden, vineries and a home farm with a model dairy. The clay of the south shore had sprouted a large brick and tile works, while the north had been worked as a pyrites mine. These industries had long gone when, in 1907, Baden-Powell was invited to bring his new Boy Scouts organisation to hold its first camp close by the claypits. A new owner, Charles Van Raalte, tried to revive the economy of the island by starting a bulb growing enterprise, but that was not a success although, when Mary Bonham-Christie bought the property, there were still some thirty families there.

Under her rule the island acquired its mysterious reputation. Her first step was to evict the remaining population and to assert her right of privacy by forbidding the general public from setting foot upon the island. The papers had a field day with stories of a strong-arm lady of Swedish nationality forcibly ejecting trespassers. Then, when the island took fire and burned for three weeks until the trees over three-quarters of it were destroyed, there was talk of arson and an act of vengeance.

Be that as it may, Mrs Bonham-Christie won, and except for occupation by the services during the Second War, the whole island remained secluded and untouched for nearly thirty years. In the mild climate of the coast nature took over, covering almost every evidence of the pattern imposed by man. Upon the news of Mrs Bonham-Christie's death there was a sudden uprush of speculation and two main groups quickly evolved – one which saw 500 acres of highly profitable development land on which they might get their hands, and another which aimed to frustrate just that.

It was Christopher Gibbs who alerted the Trust to the possibility of preservation but, curiously enough, it was Jack Rathbone who pursued the idea. He and Christopher at once began negotiations with the Treasury, in the hope that they would agree to use the Land Fund. With the executors, they tried to get the Treasury to take the property in lieu of estate duty. Rathbone went down to Poole to see the magic island for himself. Mrs Bonham-Christie's heir was her grandson John who was camping in one of the remaining habitable cottages on the quay, and he sent the launch to ferry the Secretary of the Trust across. It so happened that a westerly gale against an ebbing spring tide raised waves so steep that the short journey took a long time, with the seas breaking from time to time right over the wheel house.

Rathbone, having made this exciting crossing, was then placed in an ancient, open bull-nosed Morris for a tour of such of the island that could be reached. Only a quarter of the mile-long central road was passable, then arching rhododendrons barred the way. A track was still passable to the south shore with its view across the harbour to the Isle of Purbeck and Corfe Castle. All that could be seen of the island was heath, pine wood, brambles and gorse. The two lakes were hidden in rhododendrons; the vineries stood derelict, trees thirty feet high rearing up through the glassless roof. The grazing marsh enclosed by a sea wall lay half flooded through defective sluices. The Castle, shuttered, cold and damp, showed dry rot in a dozen places. Rathbone was enchanted, and was utterly convinced that it must be the National Trust which should awake this Sleeping Beauty with its kiss.

John Bonham-Christie was a key figure who needed to be carefully handled and made to understand how much the Trust would wish look after his property and show an interest in matters which concerned the family. It was in the church – desecrated by trespassing vandals – that Jack Rathbone almost put a foot wrong. Noticing an inscription on a tomb, 'IN BONAM MEMORIAM' he turned to his host to enquire – 'One of your relatives?'

This was only a slight hiccup, and Rathbone went ashore to put all his energies into achieving success. The first problem was that property developers were talking to the executors in terms of very high value, and when this sort of price was put to the Treasury it was very properly turned down. The Dorset County Council then took a hand and indicated that no planning permission would be given for development on the island. This dropped the price but the turning point was John Bonham-Christie's decision to accept a valuation which the Treasury could agree so that the island which his grandmother had protected in her own way should receive the permanent protection of the National Trust. Even so it was a nail-biting time for Jack Rathbone and Christopher Gibbs as they sat in the office late into the evening waiting for a 'phone call from the Treasury. When the call came the message was 'Yes'!

The hard work was to come. If the island came to the Trust as a gift there was still the problem of money to manage it. The island had to be staffed, and the staff had to be equipped. The public had to be admitted and, once on the island, they had to be provided for. The Castle had to be repaired – or demolished. There was no mains electricity, no mains water and the sewage was discharged, raw, into the harbour. Above all there was the unalterable fact that everything – visitors, staff, material and workers – had to be brought across that water which had received the Secretary so roughly on his first visit.

The figure pitched upon for all these problems was £100,000 and that could only be raised by public appeal, but never was an appeal taken up more passionately and effectively than this one. Helen Brotherton lived in what was locally known as the Diamond Ring on Canford Cliffs. Her father had made Hercules bicycles with tremendous success. She had worked for the Government during the war, looking after the interests of women workers, to such good effect that she had earned an OBE. In leisure she divided her time between sailing and running the Dorset Naturalists Trust. She had inherited all her father's business acumen, and had a passionate and informed interest in natural history and landscape. Among all the local people over whom the mystic island of Brownsea had cast its spell it was she who decided that its protection should be her crusade.

Once in touch with Jack Rathbone, the two worked with intensity to raise the money needed. By telephone and by letter they united their efforts. One source of support was obvious – the Scout Movement. It was less than forty years since the first camp had been held and in the interim the movement had encircled the world. The Appeal Committee cashed in on the connection and secured £25,000 from two Trusts, specifically on behalf of the Scout and Guide movements, and issued a special leaflet with a photograph of the camp of 1907 on the front. This was backed up by an undertaking by the Trust to arrange annual camping facilities for both movements in the same part of the island.

The main appeal leaflet had featured a picture on the front page of the beach along the south shore, and inside a view over the flooded marshes to an isolated house below a high bluff, crowned with even higher pine trees, which had escaped the holocaust of 1932. The leaflet promised that the Trust would give access to the beaches and the heathland, and that there would be a sanctuary for birds and rare plants. Helen Brotherton, as the Honorary Secretary of the Dorset Naturalists Trust, felt that the 'sanctuary' should be entrusted to their management. The flooded marshes had become a splendid feeding ground for duck and waders and there was a flourishing heronry in the pine trees. The house would be home to a warden and form a headquarters. This proposition was accepted by the National Trust and a lease promised.

The Castle was a great problem: it occupied a marvellous site opposite the harbour mouth with its own landing place, the Family Pier, but it required an immense amount of money to put it into repair and to maintain it afterwards. Empty of its contents, with its Tudor origins encased in later building, and with no special distinction of interior decoration, it was not suitable for public access. There were numerous contenders for its occupation but the Trust needed an occupier who was financially sound and whose use would not impinge excessively on the island. When the John Lewis Partnership was accepted – the intended use being as a holiday home for the Partners (in fact all the staff in that interesting 'workers co-operative') there was an instant murmur of jealousy and frustration, justified on the grounds that the public was to be excluded from a choice spot.

John Smith was sensitive to the possibility that the Trust might be being taken for a ride by the various organisations and personalities who were eager to get a foothold on the island. He decided to see for himself and with Pat Gibson came down to spend a day on the island. They had a very complete inspection and Smith's worst fears were laid to rest. On their departure John Smith asked if the launch would take them round the island so that they could see it all from the harbour. It was an ebbing spring tide and Barry Guest, the boatman, was doubtful whether there would be enough water on the south side but agreed to go as far as he could. Gibson was in conversation with the agent in the stern and by the time he noticed the screw churning up mud it was too late. Smith had persuaded the boatman to see if he couldn't get through – and he couldn't. From this predicament they were rescued by an elderly bait digger in a tiny dinghy in which the party was rowed gingerly round to the island quay, with no more than two inches of freeboard and the wavelets slapping the backs of the two passengers in the bow. The upshot of the visit was that the two main proposals went ahead.

It has often been a feature of the Trust's work that help has freely been given by all sorts of people and organisations. At Brownsea Island the Royal Marines ferried heavy loads in their landing craft; the Harbour Engineer, Sandy Chapman, gave free – and economical – professional help on repairs to the quay, the sea wall and the construction of a pier; the Royal Army Medical Corps undertook research into the problem of the mosquitoes which infested the overgrown island; the Post Office lent machinery to bury the field telephone wires used for communication across the island; the Electricity Board gave and erected a pylon in the centre of the island.

Helen Brotherton's Appeal Committee attracted a young reporter on the local paper. Warren Davis became the Honorary Publicity Officer, and himself contributed reports to his paper on plans and progress. It was from this first contact with the Trust that he became one of the two first appointed Regional Public Relations Officers, in 1966, when he went to work in Devon and Cornwall. Miss Brotherton's best single contribution, however, was her recommendation to the Trust of Alan Brombey as Head Warden. He was of a Harbour family, of the sort that occupies itself with boats, fishing and wild fowling. He had worked on Furzey Island for the Iliffe family and was then employed to look after Round Island, where he lived with his wife and two daughters. One of his proudest possessions was his canoe and punt gun – an extraordinary weapon which if discharged into a surprised flight of duck might bring down a couple of dozen with one discharge.

Life on an island – even one as close to civilisation as Brownsea – calls for special qualities, and these were proven. He was subsequently to display every other quality necessary for the job – versatility, tact, intelligence and a high degree of success in personal relationships. Already knowledgeable about birds, he rapidly became expert, and the punt gun was exchanged for binoculars. He turned to a general interest in plants and insects, in particular in moths, with a collection of well over two hundred different species all found on the island. With his wife he ran a shop, set up in the old island post office, designed and produced a special National Trust flag, and from the first opening of the island to the public he has played host to visitors who have come in numbers starting at 51,000 in 1963 and rising to 110,000 in 1987.

Jack Rathbone's Sleeping Beauty has certainly been awakened, and in the process much of that cobwebbed charm inevitably has gone. It constitutes a very clear lesson as to what can and what cannot be 'preserved'. In this case and in very many others there is in the Trust's work as much of creation as of preservation.

The major event of the 1960s – indeed one of the two or three greatest initiatives in the Trust's history – was a campaign on a national scale, mounted with the boldest of objectives. It was back in 1936 that Christopher Gibbs had taken the train down to South Wales to be shown round the Pembrokeshire coast, preliminary to the appeal for its preservation which had been rendered pointless by the outbreak of war. He had also been involved at that time with coastal preservation in Cornwall, where there was an active group of supporters including Peggy Pollard (who had ties with the underworld of Ferguson's Gang). The acquisition in 1936 of Pentire Point and the Rumps had involved a major appeal, and was intended as a first step in a planned preservation of the whole peninsula.

The general interest in coastal preservation which had shown itself in the pre-war joint Coastal Preservation Committee was still alive. Max Nicholson, Director of the still young Nature Conservancy Council, latched on to this with the intention of promoting the Conservancy's status. He called together a big committee with representatives from Government departments and planning authorities and, somewhat belatedly, the CPRE and the National Trust.

Christopher Gibbs went as the Trust's representative:

> I soon got fed up with them all. They seemed only to think of putting high rise flats in coastal towns! I felt therefore that it was up to the Trust to show what could be done by private enterprise. I got the Executive Committee to approve an Appeal. This was not before I had a personal row with John Smith and dear Jack [Rathbone] – when I really lost my temper. Ran Antrim, however, was a strong supporter, and had the vision to think it a good idea.

Christopher Gibbs wrote this account in October 1984, more than twenty years later, but there is no doubt of its accuracy. Even when not really cross he was able to appear so, going red in the face and emitting great growling clouds of smoke from his pipe. In a very rare genuine loss of temper he must have been formidable.

The minutes of the Executive Committee for 21 March 1962 say, 'The Chief Agent sought the views of the Committee about the launching in due course of a general appeal, in conjunction with the CPRE, for money to buy land or covenants for the protection of the English and Welsh coast.' The Committee agreed, despite some continued opposition from the Chairman of the General Purposes Committee and the Secretary.

The preliminaries took a long time. Later in that year the Trust's agents were asked to identify the parts of the coast in their areas which warranted preservation. Their responses produced an aggregate of about 900 miles, or about one third of the total. Northern Ireland, omitted from the original minute but implicitly included, produced 275 miles, a reflection of its unspoiled character. Since no guide-lines were issued, the assessment by the agents was entirely individual and consequently uneven, and a detailed comparison of that with subsequent acquisitions shows a number of disparities. However, it was sufficiently accurate to provide some indication of the scale of the enterprise.

The purposes and policies of the campaign were carefully devised and although refined by the senior staff and the Committee were essentially those originally put forward by Gibbs. They were:

206

- To focus public attention upon the problem of coastal preservation.
- To acquire control over coastal land deemed most worthy of preservation either by gift or purchase of the freehold, or of restrictive covenants.
- To improve and maintain the Trust's existing coastal properties and any later acquired.

The amount of money to be raised for the purpose was initially set at £1 million. Privately Christopher Gibbs also hoped that the acquisition of land through the appeal would bring with it revenue from rents which could then be applied to the general purposes of the Trust, though he wisely refrained from adding that to the formally expressed objectives.

With a campaign of so far-reaching a nature it was essential to carry with it the goodwill of central and local Government, and negotiations with departments and planning authorities occupied most of the year. These brought not only the promise of sympathetic co-operation but also some tangible benefits. The Ministry of Housing and Local Government gave special dispensation to local authorities to enable them to contribute. The Ministry of Defence offered to give first refusal to the Trust of any coastal land it was releasing (unless the 'Crichel Down' policy of offering it back to the original owner supervened). The Crown and the Duchy of Cornwall, owners of by far the greater part of the foreshore (the area between high and low water-mark of tides), agreed to negotiate long leaseholds to the Trust, thus enabling it to exercise control.

The process of consultation was carried much further in the coastal counties. There the Trust set up small committees which were usually chaired by someone of special standing in the county, often a coastal landowner, and generally included the County Planning Officer. Through these committees the Trust intended to keep in direct touch with local interests and to eliminate the aura of suspicion which programmes of acquisition often engender. The committees were asked to review priorities and proposals, to help with information as to ownership and to act where appropriate as a contact between owners and the Trust. This did in general work very well. The idea had been tried out successfully in Cornwall where the Cornish Coast Advisory Committee had been formed in 1956.

It had been decided to launch the appeal in the Spring of 1963 but it was not until November 1962 that John Smith reported to the Executive on the intention to appoint an Appeals Director. It was February 1963 before the job was offered to Conrad Rawnsley, grandson of one of the original founders of the Trust – Canon Rawnsley. 'Young' Rawnsley had entered the Royal Navy through Osborne, retired with the rank of Commander, and lived at Petworth in Sussex. It was his wife who saw the advertisement in *The Times* and suggested to him that he might like the job. He has described his grandfather Hardwicke Rawnsley as 'a human dynamo' and a large part of that energy was certainly transmitted to the grandson. Once his interest in the idea was engaged he prepared himself very thoroughly for the interview.

Although Rathbone and Gibbs were not too favourably impressed by Conrad, John Smith was. On 1 February he wrote to say:

You will have heard from Jack Rathbone, but I thought I would also write to say how much I hope you will now be joining us. I hope you did not feel I was ungracious when we met, but I felt I could not reveal my enthusiasm before seeing the other people and discussing it with my colleagues. I agreed vigorously with all – so far as I remember – of what you said: I could hardly believe my ears – and the notes you left behind are much the most imaginative I have seen.

In mid-March Rawnsley accepted the job, although there seems to have been some doubt as to precisely what his duties were and to whom he should be responsible. In April the Executive Committee decided that, while his main function should be the coastal appeal, 'all other fund-raising activities of the Trust should also come under his control.' The Publicity Committee, whose Chairman was Donald McCullough, (brother of the well loved BBC Children's Hour 'Uncle Mac'), clearly supposed that they would be in charge.

Conrad Rawnsley's plan of campaign was based on the creation of a 'Field Force' under his control. This was formed with six regional directors for the North, Midlands and the South of England, for London, Wales and Northern Ireland, to whom some thirty county commissioners were responsible. These 'counties' were not entirely in conformity with local government units, some cities being treated as 'counties' and some counties being grouped under one commissioner. Then there were to be one hundred district supervisors, five hundred wardens to recruit new members (the first year's £2 subscription to go to the appeal) and twenty-nine action committees formed *ad hoc* by commissioners as they deemed expedient. All except the directors were volunteers, just receiving their out-of-pocket expenses.

As may be imagined, all this took time and the Field Force was not in being until 1964 was well advanced. Meanwhile there had developed some difference of opinion with the Publicity Committee, particularly over a new element which Rawnsley introduced into the appeal. He felt very strongly that with preservation must go enjoyment, and that it was not only expedient but morally essential to promise that the Trust would make provision for 'amenities' – car parks, lavatories, refreshments, camping and caravan sites. McCullough was at odds with the Campaign Director over this, insisting that there should be no concessions to caravans. On the other hand two of the Director's ideas were approved: the campaign was to be called 'Enterprise Neptune of the National Trust', and it was to be heralded by the lighting of bonfires on the sites of the Armada beacons. The bonfire idea Rawnsley had already put to the Trust at his first interview!

By the end of 1963 the General Purposes Committee began to feel that a more direct management of the appeal was needed. They invited Lord Antrim to supervise it, which he did at first on his own. By mid-1964 he had formed an Enterprise Neptune Committee consisting of Holland-Martin (as Honorary Treasurer), Pat Gibson, Mark Norman and Maurice Lush, and the minutes of its first meeting recorded that it had been 'vested by the Executive Committee with absolute authority over the administration of Enterprise Neptune'.

It was high time to have the appeal put into the hands of a small executive group. Conrad Rawnsley had previously been obliged to bring virtually all his proposals before the Executive Committee which was a cumbersome and time-wasting process. Moreover the Executive found itself asked to consider matters on which it had neither the expertise nor inclination to decide. Despite Rawnsley's energy and application the preparations began to resemble those for the Armada, and it became clear that the appeal could not be launched until 1965. However, the groundwork went forward with Antrim giving a small dinner at the Fishmongers' Hall in November 1964 with the object of bringing the appeal 'to the notice of the leaders of industry and commerce'. The Trust's members were told about it at the meeting in the Royal Festival Hall the following March. These meetings, which were in the nature of a 'jolly' and at which no formal business was transacted, had been introduced in 1962 as a public relations and recruitment measure.

One of the main causes of delay had been the time taken to secure Royal patronage, but by early 1965 the Trust received the agreement of Prince Philip, Duke of Edinburgh, to stand as patron. Conrad Rawnsley's Armada beacons, timed for St George's Day, 23 April, became the peg on which was hung the general publicity for the appeal, and it was very well done indeed, getting the widest possible coverage, even the BBC's *The Archers* programme featuring one being arranged near Ambridge.

There was a grand luncheon in the Mansion House on 11 May when Prince Philip spoke to 250 guests. That, too, was well reported, raising directly in contributions some £64,000. Immediately after that event the Government announced that it would provide £250,000. For some reason, no doubt a fear of precedent, the money was not to be given to the appeal fund but would be paid at the discretion of the Treasury to be used towards specific acquisitions. It is largely to the credit of the two members on the Executive Committee, Arthur Blenkinsop and Nicholas Ridley, and the high standing of Lord Crawford, that this handsome sum was forthcoming.

The money was needed. The Trust's agents with coastal land in their area had had nearly three years in which to prepare their offensive. The Trust already owned 125 miles of coastal land which, in many instances, served to form a nucleus for expansion. The first purchase was in South Wales, not in Pembrokeshire which would have been appropriate, but at Whitford Burrows in Glamorgan. This 670 acre peninsula, with its sand hills, birds and fairly rare plants, is probably not the sort of place which in popular imagination was the prime target of Neptune, but in fact it is very vulnerable not simply to development but to insensitive management.

Purchases were dependent on willing sellers, and along the Pembrokeshire coast the now prosperous owner-occupiers were disinclined to sell. This applied, too, along that most famous of coasts, the White Cliffs of Dover. The reverse was the case in West Dorset where the small coastal farms did not lend themselves to the intensive farming which had brought prosperity to so much of the county's farms. In 1961, Eileen Morland had succeeded in securing a memorial to her late husband. Frustrated in an attempt to buy the great hill of Pilsdon Pen for the Trust, she was determined to succeed and bought, at great expense, the 270-acre farm of Westhay and Stonebarrow Hill which runs into Lyme Bay just west of Charmouth. Three years later this splendid gift to the Trust was to form one flank of a planned campaign of acquisition which was put to the Executive Committee on 2 September 1965.

A mile to the east of Westhay rises the spectacular flat-topped hill called Golden Cap. It takes its name from the deep layer of yellow sand which is exposed on the seaward side where the hill has slipped over the blue lias clay into the sea. As a young man succeeding to the Chideock estate in 1936, Humphrey Weld had to sell much of the land, and he gave the National Trust restrictive covenants over the top of the hill. That formed a second fingerhold on the coast. Then four miles further east, where the high cliffs drop down towards the estuary of the River Brit, the Trust had been promised by R.C. Sherriff (the author of *Journey's End*) the devise of Downhouse Farm, 167 acres running up to the height of Thorncombe Beacon. This would secure the eastern flank. The plan was to acquire as much as possible of the coast between. Arland Kingston, who was Assistant Land Agent in the Area, had worked in Dorset before and he was able to put together information, not only on the ownership of most of the property, but also the likelihood of the Trust being able to buy. The Executive Committee gave overall approval to the plan, and it caught the imagination of Lord Antrim who gave it very strong support.

It was in direct response to the Neptune appeal that Mr Sherriff did not hold on to his property, but made a gift of it in 1966 and, in a whole series of transactions, the plan matured quite rapidly. By 1970 the greater part of those six miles of coast were secured. There remained much more to do and further acquisitions have been made until by now it constitutes a cohesive estate of about 2,000 acres. Fittingly, the freehold of Golden Cap was bought as a memorial to Lord Antrim, and a memorial stone placed there in 1978. The property fulfils Conrad Rawnsley's concept of what the Trust should provide: there is access by car to the Stonebarrow and Chardown ridge, there are holiday cottages and camping places at St Gabriels, and there are fifteen miles of paths.

In Cornwall, where the Trust had been consistently active in coastal preservation ever since the purchase by appeal of Barras Head near Tintagel in 1897, conditions for acquisition were also generally favourable. Michael Trinick, the Area Agent, had as Assistant Agent Alastair Finlinson, who became much involved with the prosecution of Neptune in that county. The idea of progressive aggregation was by no means new. For example on the north coast just west of Newquay a 600-acre ownership had been assembled in five separate transactions between 1951 and 1961. That particular estate was to be rounded off in 1972 when Neptune supplied money to buy eleven acres at the southern end of Holywell Beach.

Similarly, on the south coast between Polruan and Polperro the Trust had been building up its protection since 1936 when 57 acres of cliff, running east from the Combe below the village of Lansallos, was bought by subscription. By the time Neptune was launched, 542 acres had been acquired in the course of seven separate transactions. Some were gifts, some used money subscribed locally, and some used the special purpose funds which since the war had been given, generally as legacies, to the Trust.

There was an immediate call on Neptune in its very first year to buy Lansallos Barton, the farm which backs the cliff land owned since 1936. At the same time Alastair Finlinson, armed with maps and photographs of the 148-acre Frogmore Farm, a mile to the westward, went to call upon a prospective benefactor, Mrs F.E.N. St Barbe. She had a mews flat behind Harrods, and Finlinson was not confident of immediate success. However, on his presentation she agreed to buy the farm, 'sight unseen', reserving for herself a life interest, with remainder to the Trust. When Mrs St Barbe died in 1975 she left money to the Trust which was used to buy Highertown Farm, 125 acres standing high above Lantivet Bay. This, preceded by three other

210

acquisitions, completed the long-term preservation plan begun forty years before, with an aggregate of 1,129 acres. Would it have been achieved without Enterprise Neptune? Perhaps, but there can be no question but that the scheme was given tremendous impetus by the appeal.

Similar activity was going on up and down the country, the weight of the work falling almost completely on the Trust's land agents, in addition to their other responsibilities. Finlinson, for example, was involved in fourteen coastal acquisitions between 1965 and 1968. Purchases often involved the least work, especially if the sale was by auction, but gifts often involved repeated visits and patient negotiation, while the very business of keeping informed as to what might be available, and where, was a constant preoccupation. After acquisition there was the consequential business of deciding management policy and putting it into effect. The Trust's committees required briefing on proposed acquisitions and, as the flow increased, members began to ask for fuller information so as to be better able to judge both merit and priority. This meant the preparation of maps and the production of photographs. Eventually in Cornwall and Devon oblique aerial surveys of the greater part of the elegible coastline were commissioned.

The position at the end of 1970 showed really substantial progress and even if the appeal had then closed it would have justified itself. Over £1.7 million had been raised from the following groups of donors:

Companies	£304,000
Local Authorities	£377,000
Charitable Trusts	£277,000
Other sources	£818,000

1969 had produced one of those curious events which catches the imagination of the public to a point far and away beyond its importance. Lundy (the name means Puffin Island and the addition of the latter word to its name is tautological) – in the western mouth of the Bristol Channel, was put up for sale. It had been owned by the Harman family and had enjoyed, or at least claimed, extra-territorial rights such as its own postage and freedom from the rates of the Devon County Council within whose boundaries it was. Lundy is just over three miles long, north to south, and not much more than a quarter of a mile wide. The western side is precipitous and takes the full force of the Atlantic swell. The east is steep, but less so and, at its southern end, offers a landing place on a shingle bank unless the wind is easterly. The roof of the island is flattish and bare. Such a place is bound to have a romantic history and it is scarcely possible to distinguish fact from myth until at the very outset of Victoria's reign it was acquired by the Rev. Hudson Heaven, who set about civilising the place. Such features as Milicombe House, the home farm, the church and the inn are largely due to him and his family.

The Harmans, having succeeded to 'the Kingdom of Heaven', ran the island quietly and competently, holding on to such of its liberties as were challenged from time to time by the mainland. They catered in a modest way for visitors, but the only way that tourists in any numbers could reach the island was by the round trip made from Swansea via Ilfracombe by Campbell paddle-steamers. These had to land their passengers by boat and at the least prospect of bad weather blowing up landings were curtailed or abandoned.

Despite its remote and element-protected position there was, when the sale was announced, a national panic. No-one could say for sure what dreadful thing would happen to Lundy, but something certainly would. The most consistent bogey was the possibility that some arcane religious body would buy for itself a remote security in which to practise its awful and wholly un-British rites. The Trust must do something.

It was in that atmosphere that Major-General Sir Julian Gascoigne, Chairman of the National Trust's Regional Committee for Devon and Cornwall, accompanied by his Regional Secretary and Area Agent, took ship – if the open deck of a trawler can be so described – from Ilfracombe to visit the vendors and to see the island. He was pursued by the Press in another craft while a television crew bribed its way onto the foredeck of the trawler. The owners of the island allowed none of the representatives of the news media to go futher than the landing place, save only the man from *The Times* who was later permitted to interview the General.

The Trust's representatives could see no good reason why the island needed preservation by the Trust, and on Julian Gascoigne's advice the Executive Committee decided not to proceed. The nation, however, would not take that 'no' for an answer. Jeremy Thorpe, the Liberal MP for North Devon, headed an independent campaign to raise the money, both to buy the island and to give it with an endowment to the Trust. It is hard to refuse such a proposition and so the Trust agreed to accept, feeling secure in the knowledge that the money – about a quarter of a million pounds – would not be forthcoming: but it was. Jack Hayward, an extremely wealthy and patriotic businessman who lived in the West Indies – his patriotism earned him the soubriquet of 'Union Jack' – came forward with the whole of the purchase price. Jeremy Thorpe's appeal raised some £70,000 beside and to cap everything, John Smith's private charitable trust, the Landmark Trust, offered to take a lease of the island, finance all repairs and improvements and open it to the public.

So it was that, on a grey and blustery day in 1969, the Campbell paddle-boat plunged with a queasy load of subscribing supporters down the Bristol Channel to Lundy where the seas miraculously calmed sufficiently for them to disembark. Jeremy Thorpe and his wife gave notabilities – including John and Christian Smith and 'Union Jack' Hayward and the Harman family – a celebratory lunch, at which Thorpe declared, 'I have saved Lundy *despite* the National Trust!' The Bishop of Crediton descended in an RAF helicopter and there was a service of thanksgiving in the Church with the youngest Harman daughter adding her violin to the scratch accompaniment.

As a vehicle for Neptune publicity the whole affair was splendid. As an essay in coastal preservation it was almost certainly needless. The Landmark Trust has with great pertinacity re-organised the management of the island to give the maximum public benefit, with holiday cottages and a renovated inn offering excellent facilities for holidaymakers. The expense has been great and to honour its obligations, which the Landmark Trust has consistently done, has engaged what appears to be a large proportion of its resources. Though Hardwicke Rawnsley would have rejoiced in the National Trust's association with so romantic a concept, Octavia Hill and Robert Hunter would have surely been shocked at such a diversion of resources from more urgent needs.

The Neptune Appeal which had originally been conceived as a finite operation, lasting one, two or at the most three years, projected itself largely by its own success and after a while there was a tacit agreement that it should be allowed to go on until there arose some special reason why it should be stopped. In 1973 the Trust entered the Lord Mayor's Show with a Neptune float, to launch its new slogan – 'The Next Hundred Miles.' The description ran thus:

1. Neptune will be preceded by a spectacular sea-monster.
2. Behind will come girls dressed as sea nymphs ...
3. Then will come the Trust's Landrover, decked out in marine motifs which will in turn tow the chariot.
4. Urging this forward will be a dramatic figure of an Oceanic charioteer.
5. Next will be seated a splendid mermaid couched within a huge open scallop shell.
6. Behind her, raised on a high throne, Neptune himself will crown the chariot.
7. A sea attendant will work marvels at the back by launching balloons amid a wake of bubbles.
8. The rearguard will comprise a quartet of cavorting feminine sea horses.
9. Three baroque dolphins will sport round the chariot.

For contemporary fun and the information of posterity John Tetley recorded his impression in pen and ink. Lord Antrim on seeing the drawing was obliged to recognise a degree of likeness between Neptune and himself.

Progress continued on Enterprise Neptune although the pace dropped to about half of what it had been in the first five years. Ten years later, in September 1983, the campaign's slogan of the 'Next Hundred Miles' had been achieved. Moreover, the whole pattern of revenue for the appeal was changing. The Countryside Act of 1968 had brought into being the Countryside Commission with the power to make grants of Government money towards the acquisition of land for preservation. This proved much more flexible than the Treasury grant with which the appeal had been opened. This was to be augmented when the National Heritage Act 1980 was passed. Already in 1978 the percentage that Central Government contributed had risen to six per cent against the faithful local authorities' eight per cent, but, by 1982, the latter had fallen to three per cent and the former risen to fifty-nine per cent, an average over the five years of twenty-four per cent. But by far the most potent new source of revenue was that of legacies. Naturally, at the beginning, there was little time for a testator to make his will and then conveniently depart, but ten years later things were very different and legacies accumulated to become the second largest element of the appeal.

There were some notable additions to the coastal estate and, although it is not only difficult but probably invidious to attribute them to the personal efforts of individuals, it would be equally unfair not to recognise that this was often so. For example, in 1971 the Down Charitable Trust gave money with which the National Trust bought 700 acres of superb landscape running out to the sea at Foreland Point, Countisbury, from the Watersmeet property which it had with such difficulty acquired forty years earlier. This would not have come about but for the fact that the Area Agent in Devon, Dick Meyrick, had in the course of managing the Trust's neighbouring properties earned the respect and trust of the owner of the Glenthorne Estate who parted with his property on terms very favourable to the Trust.

In Pembrokeshire, the Trust's agent, Hugh Griffith, had been in private practice with his father, who was agent to that same Earl of Cawdor who had been very prickly at the time of the pre-war preservation scheme. On his death, his successor parted with the Stackpole Estate. Through long and intricate negotiations, in which his intimate knowledge of both property and personalities played a key part, Hugh Griffith succeeded, by using the 'in lieu' procedure of the Treasury, in securing 2,000 acres of the estate, including the fascinating freshwater lakes and eight miles of the most varied and dramatic coastline.

At Lands End in 1981, Michael Trinick had one of his rare reverses. The news that this furthest west point of England was coming on to the market aroused the country to a fever pitch even beyond that of Lundy. True, those who were most excited had never been there, and did not know that it had been horribly degraded, with a great barren area where cars and coaches parked, there were down-at-heel curio shops and cheap refreshment sheds, all dominated by a great square building near the cliff, a seedy hotel. On the cliffs themselves the vegetation and soil had been worn away and the only pleasure to be had was to turn one's back upon it and look out westward across the Longships lighthouse to the glory of the setting sun.

Trinick believed that this situation was reversible and that it lay in the path of the Trust's duty to restore and preserve the beauty that Lands End once had. He and his colleagues worked like slaves laying plans, which they concerted with Elizabeth Chesterton – an architect and landscapist with long associations with the Trust. The complications of what needed to be done were equalled by those of how to pay for it. To many it seemed as though no solid buyer would ever be found and that the Trust was being swept along on a tide of false values. But benefactors were found to back the scheme, with 'Union Jack' Hayward as generous as ever, and the vendors felt sure enough of themselves to set a closing date for tenders. The Trust offered over £1 million but – to the relief of some – was beaten by a good margin. In 1987 the property changed hands again following a private sale at a figure reported to be £6.7 million. It is to be hoped that the new owner will bring about the restoration so badly needed.

Christopher Gibbs' concept of the national appeal for the preservation of the coast has been a great and continuing success. There has most certainly been a national awakening of consciousness which was the first main object of his idea. Government, local authorities and private people have all accepted the principle and have worked to implement it. In May 1985, twenty years after its official launching, the appeal was given a re-launch. By that time £7 million had been raised (which does not include the value of land given), and the Trust had become the owner of coastland stretching over a distance of 454 miles, spread among thirty-one counties. In September 1988 the Trust celebrated the acquisition of its five hundredth mile of coastline under the Neptune scheme. Even so, as the 're-launch' implies, and as new surveys by the staff testify, much, much more remains to be done. And the measure of success is not to be found in the statistics, but by a direct personal assessment of the state of the land in the Trust's ownership. How well is it managed, and what happiness has all this effort brought to people? Not everything is right, not

214

everything well done, but it is likely that if the Quartet were to walk the coastal path – and perhaps they do – they would be well pleased.

CHAPTER XVI

Another Rawnsley
and
Reform

The increasingly intense activities of the early 1960s naturally produced some internal pressures in an organisation which was not geared to the pace. John Smith in particular was frustrated by the difference between the way things functioned in the world of business and the way the Trust operated. Rathbone, after twelve years as Secretary, during which he was most directly responsible to Lord Esher, whom he idolised, was upset and unnerved to find himself completely unable to meet the demands of his new General Purposes Committee Chairman.

In 1964 John Smith ceased to be the Chairman of the General Purposes Committee, but his valuable services continued to be enjoyed by the Trust in one form or another for a further twenty-one years. The new Chairman of the committee was Ran Antrim. He was almost certainly brought in by Lord Crawford because he intended to retire and wanted Antrim to replace him as Chairman of the Trust. David Crawford did retire in 1965. He had given twenty years to the Trust and had presided over the greatest period of growth in its history. Without diminishing in any way the contributions made by other people, it must be to him that credit is given for the standing which the Trust achieved in that time. Its membership had leaped from 7,850 in 1945 to 157,581 twenty years later. The Country Houses Scheme had successfully emerged from very shaky beginnings to become an established and integral part of its work. The preservation of gardens had been initiated and the great coastal appeal was under way. Government had acknowledged the value of the Trust and had paid it the compliment of following many of its pioneering ideas. In all this Lord Crawford had been a consistent leader, both within the organisation and without. His high qualities of intellect and humanity illuminated and inspired the work.

In Lord Crawford's last year as Chairman problems began to arise in the conduct of Enterprise Neptune. Antrim had been given the task of supervising the appeal towards the end of 1963, but the responsible committee was still the Executive, and anything outside routine business had to go to them. The whole process seemed to Conrad Rawnsley excessively cumbersome. The incident of the *Medway Queen* was symptomatic. With his undoubted flair for publicity Rawnsley had found a chance to link the appeal with the 'Miracle of Dunkirk'. A paddle steamer, which had been one of the 'little ships' which rescued the British Expeditionary Force in 1940, the

Medway Queen, was for sale. Rawnsley proposed to buy her, crew her, and use her as a floating publicity ship. This meant risking money which might or might not show a good return. The Executive Committee was extremely hesitant even when, in January 1964, John Smith offered to underwrite the cost – £2,050 – of moving her to Rotherhithe, and docking her there for survey. Rawnsley threw himself wholeheartedly into the preparation of a scheme for the ship which would be acceptable, to the extent that he wrote to Antrim that he had been unable to do certain other things because of '... detailed staff work on the *Medway Queen* which has occupied me almost entirely.' The scheme, amended and re-costed in different ways, came up to the Committee repeatedly but in the end it was rejected.

Similar frustration met Rawnsley's idea to finance, through the publishers David & Charles, a guidebook to the coast. Again the Executive Committee held back from expenditure which might not be recovered, while Rawnsley saw another cherished scheme abandoned. As early as 6 January 1964, he wrote Antrim a letter which sets out his feelings unambiguously:

> I seem to detect lately within the Executive Committee an under-current of criticism of my ideas and methods, which is unsettling and not conducive of one's best work, for it amounts to no less than a vote of no confidence. I am unused to voluntary organisations, or to working under a plethora of committees, and would be the first to admit that I have an awful lot to learn about the Trust – but this much is clear, that by any standards the Coastal Appeal has had more than its fair share of committee discussion and vacillation, and of decisions made at one meeting subsequently 'interpreted', altered or even reversed at later meetings. Can we (you and I) now have a clear mandate and be left to get on with the job in accordance with our own judgement? ... if we are expected to refer back before every step we take and be just the rubber stamps for the Executive Committee, then I begin to wonder whether I, at any rate, am the right man for the job.

The formation of a Neptune Campaign Committee in the summer of 1964 was long overdue and, if it had been in existence a year earlier, Conrad Rawnsley's sense of frustration might have been avoided. As it was, however, the committee was clearly intended to impose strict financial control, comprising as it did the Honorary Treasurer, Ruby Holland-Martin, and the two representatives of big business, Norman and Gibson. The only other member, apart from Antrim, Brigadier Lush, did indeed come from the Neptune organisation.

It was in that year that Rawnsley's 'Field Force' came into operation, and in considering the estimates for the following year the Committee applied the financial screw: they required that the payment of expenses to voluntary field workers be 'drastically curtailed', laid down that the cost of the campaign should not exceed five per cent of the amount raised, and authorised an expenditure not exceeding £75,000 for 1965. That was to be the launch year, and it seemed to go very well but the Executive Committee was still concerned about the cost and, in October, there was a move to apply a further brake. Earl De La Warr, Field Marshal Sir Gerald Templar and Peter Scott, Chairman of North-West region, all, in their different ways, formidable adversaries, are all recorded in the minutes as having expressed their concern about the expense of the appeal. It is not surprising that the 1966 limit on expenditure was to be the same as for 1965, even though the Director protested that it was less than half the amount required. A small sop to him was the promise of a review at the half year. By this time Antrim had become Chairman of the Trust and was consequently in a very dominant position. The Neptune Committee had been enlarged by the addition of Gabrielle Pike. She was Chairman of the National Federation of Womens' Institutes and it was to secure a link with that powerful nationwide organisation that she had been recruited to the Trust's committees.

Conrad Rawnsley persevered. In May 1966 he gave the Neptune Committee his reasons for proposing that the appeal should continue at least until the end of 1967 and possibly through 1968. The Committee heard his report and then took the peculiar course of going into private session – that is, excluding the staff – 'to consider the matter with a view to making a representation to the Executive Committee'. The Director must have read this as a signal that the Committee was in opposition to him because for their October meeting he circulated a paper entitled 'The Future of the Neptune Organisation'.

At the meeting he appears to have reported fully on the paper, the key paragraph of which read that the Director believed

> that the opportunity now open to the Trust through the Enterprise Neptune Organisation to improve its public image, ensure that its properties made the best contribution of which they were capable to the life of the community, and to broaden the base of representation in government was unique and one which would be unlikely ever to occur again in the foreseeable future. It would be difficult to envisage any other project on which the Trust might embark which would appeal so much to the public imagination, nor stimulate such universal response. It would not be profitable to discuss the possibility that the Neptune Field Force would find money-raising alone an acceptable activity. To keep the life and vigour of the organisation going it would be essential that the terms of reference should be wider and embrace all aspects of the work of the Trust and that its members should be vested with a suitable measure of authority, power of decision and representation in the government of the Trust.

It is hardly surprising that the Neptune Committee again went into private session to discuss the matter. Nothing more seemed to happen for the time being. Then Conrad Rawnsley went down to Devon where he presided at a Press Conference held at Saltram House near Plymouth, which had come to the Trust via the Treasury seven years earlier, and which had developed into the headquarters of the Devon and Cornwall Regional Committee.

What happened next was this: Conrad Rawnsley had indeed been told that his appointment as Appeals Director would be terminated at the end of March 1967, giving him five months' notice. He therefore decided that he would use the Press Conference to publicise his view of the way in which the Trust was run. He prepared a statement which he read to the meeting, copies of which were distributed to those present. He did not pull his punches.

> The National Trust is not bankrupt in that (financial) way. But there are other ways of being bankrupt. You can be bankrupt in ideas, bankrupt in the

common touch, bankrupt in your sense of what the people need and in your alacrity to provide it.

... [The Trust] was after all the child of my grandfather's imagination. I was not too young to remember the crusading spirit of this old man and his associates. Where was the fire and the enthusiasm of those early days ...? It seemed to me to have become part of the Establishment, an inert and amorphous organisation proceeding by the sheer momentum given to it by those who continued to bequeath their wealth to it, as often as not to escape death duties.

... Last Monday I was given the sack ... and the whole (Neptune) organisation looks as if it would collapse like a pack of cards.

Not surprisingly Conrad Rawnsley was suspended from duty pending the November meeting of the Executive Committee which would consider immediate dismissal. The following day he wrote to all his Neptune Regional Directors, enclosing copies of the papers he had prepared for the Committee and explaining his action. He wrote that the papers had not been discussed with him at all at the Neptune Committee meeting, that he was not permitted to know what recommendations would be made to the Executive nor whether the papers were submitted or read to them. There was no hope of getting the decisions reversed in committee and so he intended to try to do so through the Press and at the AGM which was to be held in November.

In fact the Executive had decided to 'integrate' the Neptune appeal within the general organisation of the Trust. This came as a surprise to those who had never considered that it was in any way separate. Indeed the word appears more like a euphemism to describe a pre-emptive strike against a *dis*-integration led by the Director. A submariner, Captain Tom (later Sir Thomas) Barlow who had been Rawnsley's Regional Director in the South East, took charge and called the Neptune Regional Directors to a meeting at which they recorded that they 'unanimously deplore the recent public pronouncements of their late Campaign Director and his calculated attack upon the National Trust ... they regret that he issued a statement ... without giving them any warning of his intentions ... they affirm their loyalty to the Trust.'

Barlow's County Commissioner for Somerset was Marshal of the Royal Air Force, Sir John Slessor. His response was perhaps representative of the average reaction of informed people to what had happened. '... my opinion of Rawnsley is unprintable, whatever right he had on his side (and there may be some.) 'I don't want to be unduly alarmist but unless the National Trust pulls its finger out and does something pretty drastic, and very soon, this fund raising campaign will go down the plug 'ole!'

Although the Press enjoyed the rumpus, it recognised the work done by the Trust in coastal preservation and emphasised the need for this to continue. Three provincial papers ran an identical leader with the heading 'Still needed'. All were prepared to quote Jack Rathbone's assurance that the campaign would go on, while the Director had himself announced at the meeting the acquisition of four separate coastal areas in Devon, and was duly reported.

Why did Conrad Rawnsley behave as he did? He had shown himself to be highly intelligent, yet he had proposed that the 'Field Force' should have a special, constitutionally privileged place within the Trust, an idea to which no-one, however open minded and unbiased, could possibly ascribe any merit. Then again, the proper course for anyone whose principles are in conflict with his office is to resign, and then take whatever action he feels he should. The explanation, if one there be, is certainly complex and may have its roots in the man's character. His grandfather was a man of strong passions. His father Noel must have inherited at least something of this. Conrad himself displays two quite distinct sides. In company he is lively, engaging and light-hearted, but when his mind turns to the exposition of a serious matter, or if he is speaking in public, his voice and demeanour take on the aspect of an Old Testament prophet. If, in his judgement, someone falls short of what Conrad believes is right, he may well be as unforgiving as Jehovah.

A curious accident of location may have prejudiced Conrad Rawnsley against the National Trust. He lived near Petworth, adjoining the Leconfield estate and close to the 700-acre park which, with the house, Lord Leconfield had given to the Trust in 1947. Now the house literally turns its back on the town of Petworth and in days gone by its owners seemed to do the same. The terms of the gift to the Trust did not permit of much alteration in terms of attitude or public access and it may have seemed to Conrad that the Trust's contribution was only to bolster privilege at the expense of the Exchequer. To cap everything, he suffered at the time from the most excruciating arthritic disability. He wrote to Antrim, 'One cannot work well without getting proper rest.'

He formed the opinion that the Executive Committee was composed of superannuated people without real interest in, or knowledge of, the National Trust, and he felt that the example of Petworth ran right through the organisation. He did not like what he saw of National Trust members either. These were mainly those who had joined Members' Centres and never comprised much more than ten per cent of the total. He thought they had the wrong attitude, that they fostered and encouraged snobbery and that Jack Rathbone compounded this by encouraging a feeling of privilege among members. In line with this, the Country House Schemes seemed to him to have been a great mistake and one which 'promoted a snob element and a tuft-hunting attitude'. Somehow this man, who has a great deal of friendliness and charm, never seemed to click in his personal relationship with the committees or the staff.

Characteristically Rawnsley set about the prosecution of his campaign with diligence and energy. He became a member of the National Trust and attended the Annual General Meeting held at Cheltenham in November. He tried to address the meeting but was prevented from doing so by the Chairman. Despite having no success there, he turned to the provision in the National Trust Act, 1907, whereby an Extraordinary General Meeting could be requisitioned by the signatures of thirty or more members. With membership of around 1,000 that was a fair percentage, but of 160,000 it had become a ludicrously small percentage. Advertisements were placed in newspapers throughout the country inviting those dissatisfied with the Trust to get in touch, and from the response he raised no less than 150 Requisitionists.

The Trust's response to the requisition was to fix the date of the Extraordinary General Meeting for 11 February 1967. In this they followed the rules of company law, to hold the meeting within three months' of requisition, although the Trust was not legally bound to do so. It may well have seemed not only best to get the disagreeable over but to give as little time as possible for a reform movement to gather strength. Conrad Rawnsley certainly found himself hampered by the shortage of time, though his preparations were characteristically thorough. He made his headquarters at the Naval and Military Club in Piccadilly – the In and Out – and set about trying to secure from the Trust information on which he could build his case on the lines he already believed to be correct.

He had only partial success: the Chairman instructed the staff that only the Legal Adviser, Bob Latham, should deal with Conrad Rawnsley who complained that, 'Letters to the Chairman and Secretary have been replied to by the solicitor and telephone calls automatically diverted to him.' Latham in fact worked very closely with the Chairman and in the exigencies of the time found him a great person for whom to work, and one whom he came to admire. Latham's responses to the enquiries made of the Trust were models of correct but distant politeness. Where the information was such as Counsel advised him was proper to be divulged, he did his best to collect it (not an easy matter in a diffuse organisation with no statistical department), and where it was not proper to do so he said so simply and without embroidery. Among the information withheld were the details of the terms of gift of country houses, rents paid by tenants, salaries and wages of staff, minutes of committees, and the details of finances beyond those contained in the published accounts.

Conrad Rawnsley had from the beginning envisaged a Reform Group but this does not seem to have taken shape until 7 January 1967 when a meeting of some twenty-six of the Requisitionists met at the In and Out. Conrad became Honorary Secretary and they elected Raymond Cochrane as their Chairman. By the very nature of the Reform Movement it was bound to attract those dissatisfied with the Trust. Mr Cochrane was one such. He had farmed with some success and had become an authority on dairying; before the Second War he published a definitive study *The Milch Cow in Britain*. In 1958 he moved to Guiting Power in the Cotswolds. This village was, and is, well-known as one of the most attractive in the country and Mr Cochrane offered it to the Trust. He was already in fairly close touch because his father had set up a Cathedrals Amenity Fund to be used to help Cathedral Chapters to maintain and improve the surroundings of their churches, and the Trust had agreed to administer the fund. His offer was refused and he was very hurt.

Whether the Trust's judgement was right is questionable. On the Executive Committee, Nicholas Ridley argued very strongly against acceptance on the ground that the village was not in danger. On the other hand it was, on merit, entirely eligible for preservation. To this grievance was added a strong disapproval of Captain Hill with whom Mr Cochrane equated National Trust management as he had observed it on the Coleshill Estate, regardless of the fact that, as has been seen, Captain Hill was not for long agent there after the Trust succeeded to the property. Mr Cochrane's position was not strengthened by a dispute at Guiting Power in 1965. He had tried – probably quite legitimately – to close to vehicles a path to the church, known as The Avenue, which went through the grounds of his house. That it was a public footpath he did not deny, nor did he try to stop people on foot, but the parish was up in arms and the local papers enjoyed the row and tended to cast Mr Cochrane in the role of villain.

221

'A Case for the Reform of the National Trust' was compiled by Conrad Rawnsley and was distributed to members by the Trust together with a statement by the Chairman of the Trust. The Case runs to eight densely printed pages, its style is often rhetorical, though its content is typically as exhaustive as all Conrad Rawnsley's work. The main sections were: a summary of the statutory position of the Trust; whether its purposes were being fulfilled; inadequacy of access to historic buildings; the ineffective, undemocratic, unrepresentative nature of the constitution; suggestions for constitutional reform; the fate of Enterprise Neptune; the appointment and dismissal of the Appeals Director. In heavy type at the end two main proposals were put forward: First, the setting up of an independent Committee of Enquiry of Members to investigate the Trust's affairs; second, the resolute prosecution of Enterprise Neptune (at least until May 1968) at full strength on former lines.

There followed some jockeying for positions over the form of the resolutions. In this the Trust held an advantage in that there were time limits laid down in the National Trust Act as to procedures. Conrad Rawnsley tried to recover the advantage lost to him by having antagonised the Trust; 'If the Council of the Trust is prepared to accept … Resolutions in the form in which they are written … I am to say that nothing would give the Reform Committee greater satisfaction and to suggest that, in such an event, the EGM might be made an occasion for a friendly discussion of ways and means rather than a contest of principle.' The prospect of that, if it ever existed, had long since gone and he obtained no change from the Trust. He did, however, succeed in obliging the Trust to accept the Reform resolutions save that they were reworded as recommendations rather than as mandatory.

The most important resolution called for a committee of enquiry with an independent chairman and eight members of the Trust, half to be appointed by the Executive Committee and half by the Requisitionists. The EGM was held in that strange and massive building facing Parliament Square, the Methodist Central Hall. In character, part place of worship, part concert or conference hall, it seats about 3,000 and in the event nearly 4,000 people attended with the result that a less than satisfactory overflow room with loudspeaker relay had to be provided.

The conduct of the meeting was not edifying. The *Sunday Times* reported it with some accuracy; 'Cdr. Rawnsley's onslaught was scathing. In October, when he had been dismissed, there was, he said, an incredible tale of blunder and mismanagement'. Also, 'there was a deliberate and sustained attempt by the Executive Committee by every means within its power to thwart and frustrate the purpose of this meeting and prevent a full and free discussion of these important matters.' Again, 'the entrenched few who wield power at Queen Anne's Gate watched a vigorous new Neptune springing up beside the old organisation. They saw it as a threat to bring democracy into the government of the Trust and whatever the cost to the national interest they were determined to prevent it.' The *Sunday Telegraph* called it, 'a rowdy special meeting' at which 'there were shouts of "rubbish", "shut up", "sit down" from both factions. The Earl of Antrim was shouted down when he refused to take a vote' on two resolutions which were held to be *ultra vires*. That was quite right: the first heckling came from a small group of Brownsea Island voluntary wardens who took exception to something on the opening proposition made by Robert Mowat. That, however, was nothing to the noise generated by the Reform clique which seemed to be concentrated in one of the balconies. In its turn this was as nothing to a thunderous growl of anger when Conrad Rawnsley attacked the staff, who were debarred from speaking in their own defence.

It went on all day, and it went on far too long. That was the fault of the chair and of two of the Trust's principal speakers, the Lords Chorley and Conesford. The former actually over-ran the thirty minute time limit by more than half as much again, but his forensic style was effective and his very deep roots in the past of the Trust an effective rebuttal of much of the criticism. He was speaking against the motion to set up a committee of enquiry, and he led off by treating the resolution as one of no confidence in the Council and Executive Committee, and the resolution was defeated. He had been supported by Mrs Gabrielle Pike whose style was perhaps not well attuned to the mood of the meeting. Referring to the criticism of the number of peers on the Committee she replied, 'yes, but let's face it, they are working earls'.

Upon the rejection of the first two resolutions, Conrad Rawnsley, white with fury, demanded a poll of the whole membership, which was provided for in the Act of 1907. The Chairman appealed to the meeting not to support this on the grounds of cost but Rawnsley replied, 'You should have thought of that before: it's too late now!' Indeed it was – under the rules the proposal needed the support of only twenty members and he got a lot more than that.

As the meeting progressed the Reform Group suffered defeat after defeat, though not without making a noisy fight of it. There was a break for lunch and the neighbouring public houses, especially the Two Chairmen in Queen Anne's Gate received a brief but boisterous boost to their trade. The resolution framed by Conrad Rawnsley to keep his Field Force in being was neatly turned by an amendment confirming the appeal 'within its authorised expenditure'. Maurice Lush and John Barrett spoke to this for the Council and made an excellent job of it. John Barrett was precisely one of those 'ordinary men' that the Reformers wished to run the Trust – except that in intelligence, commonsense, knowledgeability and the power to communicate he was quite outstanding. Mark Norman has written, 'He could move a committee of 20 or a meeting of 2,000 to a complete acceptance of his views.' The *Sunday Telegraph* picked him out as the speaker 'to state most clearly one of the main concerns of members. Because of the "irresponsible action" of those who had engineered the meeting a lot of money would not now be coming to the Trust or to Enterprise Neptune'. Some time about the middle of the afternoon, when the debate was beginning to be rather tedious, Len Clark, nominee of the YHA on the Trust's Council, happened to be standing near the microphone. Lord Antrim muttered, *sotto voce* 'Say *something* Mr Clark, say *something*.' He obliged, not accepting the strictures of the critics but proposing that it was time the Trust management looked carefully at its contacts with members and the public. A motion from John Betjeman supported the Council but wanted due consideration to be taken of what had been said at the meeting. These views reflected those of the large majority present.

The last resolution of the day was typical of the weakness of Conrad Rawnsley's allies. Vice-Admiral Sir Robert Elkins had some fifteen years earlier established himself in a house adjoining the Trust's property of Black Down just south of Haslemere. He had just retired from the Navy and had, he claimed, been the last Admiral to fly his flag in a battleship, the *Vanguard* having been the last such vessel in the Navy. He first came to the notice of the Trust when he sold a number of very

223

fine, large trees which did not belong to him, but to the Trust, which only discovered that he had done so when a number were cut down. A genuine mistake, no doubt, but a very careless and needless one since the boundary was clearly defined. He made some amends by serving on the Blackdown Local Committee but was unhappy about the circumstances endemic in the situation of his house. This was below the spring-line on the lower slopes of the 900-foot-hill, where the clay emerges from below the greensand. At first he was afraid of fire and wanted the Trust to maintain a firebreak round his property, and later became rather more justifiably alarmed to find that the area was inherently unstable and liable to slip in unpredictable places. He again sought to get the Trust to remedy a condition which was none of their making but his manner of negotiation did not promote much willing co-operation and so he chose to table a resolution for the EGM. His address in support was trivial and he refused to stop when his time was up, the Assistant Secretary, Jack Boles, being eventually obliged to remove the microphone. Everyone was tired and bored and the Chairman wisely accepted the resolution which simply 'invited the Trust to consider' doing something.

Next day the *Observer*'s headline was 'National Trust Rout for Rawnsley' and on paper it was. If he had ever really hoped to create for himself a power centre within the Trust he had completely failed, and he had failed because his strategy had been wrong from the start. But if he had wished to give the National Trust a thorough shake-up, to make it look at its origins and purposes, its methods and management, its successes and its mistakes, he had most certainly succeeded. To start with the very existence of the Neptune Appeal – and it must be remembered that its conception owed nothing to Conrad Rawnsley – had attracted more continuing attention from the Press than any other aspect of the Trust's work, and Rawnsley had seen to it that from the time of his first démarche at Saltram his case had full publicity. The EGM fuelled the blaze and hardly a day went by for months without some mention of the Trust.

The staff in the provinces, whose occupation had generally been a mystery to their acquaintances, now found that there was for the first time an awareness, indeed some understanding, of the nature of their work. The membership of the Trust, called upon to vote in poll on the first resolutions, were directly involved in a way which very few had been before. The result of the poll, announced in May 1967, gave a very large majority backing to the Council, and the Chairman announced that the Trust would set up its own committee of enquiry. In recognition of this Mr Cochrane undertook before the year's AGM to suspend organised opposition by the Reform Group.

It was Mark Norman who took Lord Antrim along to see his friend Henry Benson, who was a leading Chartered Accountant of his day, and a frequent choice for the job of chairing committees of enquiry. He accepted the task and was joined by Pat Gibson, Sir William Hayter (who was warden of New College, Oxford) and Len Clark. They began work in September 1967 and held their thirteenth and last meeting on 5 December of 1968. The terms of reference covered: The constitution: Council, Head Office Committees and Staffing; Regional Organisation; Economics and finances; Management – access – facilities at open spaces; Public relations and promotion; 'Other' including new fields of work. These terms were virtually all-embracing and it is largely due to Sir Henry (now Lord) Benson that they were fully covered in so short a time. Mark Norman describes him as 'a fiend for hard work'. Jack Boles, who, as, Assistant Secretary, was responsible for servicing the Committee, found that Benson worked with great concentration and that after a break he would return with a whole sheaf of notes in his hand. Much of the report he wrote himself.

The Committee decided to canvass opinions from individuals and organisations, including its critics. The Chairman wrote asking for views and received over 300 replies. They also interviewed thirty-three people. (The Reform Group later criticised with some justification the fact that all but four were either from committees or staff.) Not surprisingly they found that 'the difficulty of the task which was entrusted to us is emphasised by the fact that the views and opinions of many ... frequently contradicted the views and opinions of others.' This statement in the introduction to the report may perhaps have been entered as a ground for the Committee using its own judgement!

The written submissions and the record of interviews throws much more light on the character of the witnesses than it does on the welfare of the organisation, but there were some illuminating points. John Smith, for example, differentiated between entertainment, which was not the Trust's role, and enjoyment, which was. Jack Rathbone asserted that 'The Trust is not a business and what matters is not so much the financial results but how the properties in its care appear, and what is done by the Trust in the field.' Robert Mowat had really very little to say, and Conrad Rawnsley's oral evidence seemed to produce nothing more than his original complaints. He did, however, submit 'Notes on the Reconstitution and Reform of the National Trust' – 46 pages and three appendices. As in his earlier published statements, there is an almost inextricable mingling of high ideals and sound commonsense with prejudice, abuse and misrepresentation. There were five pages devoted to his appointment and dismissal, which includes an extract from a letter from John Smith dated 12 August 1964, warning him that he ran the risk of being sacked if he continued to 'stir things up'. This was no doubt intended as friendly advice but what occasioned it at that quite early date is not clear.

Among the committee and staff witnesses the two main preoccupations were regionalisation (which had already begun on a small scale) and the supposed rift between the Historic Buildings side and Estate Management. As to the first, there was a worry that it would lead to a loss of control at the centre. That was Latham's fear, and Wallace thought there should simply be advisory panels, not committees of management. One suggestion was that staff should remain responsible to Head Office, simply serving regional committees, thus retaining a direct link with Head Office authority. This also concerned outside witnesses. Lord Wakefield of Kendal, having had trouble getting his own way with Cubby Acland in the Lakes wrote, 'H.Q. are really powerless against the agent's knowledge of the locality and its problems. This can be disastrous if the local agent is an able man who considers he has a mission in life to interpret the N.T. policy as he thinks fit, irrespective of the views of anyone else.' Mr Cochrane on the other hand, in the course of a sensible and wide ranging submission, proposed that there should be autonomous regional trusts.

Rathbone wrote '... everything is going well on the ground. One exception is the relationship between Area Agents and Regional Representatives, and also the anomaly of Regional Secretaries. Agents do not have much taste.' Antrim was outspoken: 'In all matters efficiency and the hob-nailed boot should not take precedence over aesthetic considerations;' while John Smith saw the task of bridging the division as one of the main tasks before the Trust. He advised abolishing the post of Chief Agent and held that agents could never be trained as aesthetes but aesthetes could be trained as agents. Michael Trinick from his special position as agent, Representative and Regional Secretary advocated the combining of the Estates and Historic Buildings Committees, the appointment of regional secretaries who were solely administrators and the confining of land agents to professional work only. His Chairman, Julian Gascoigne, said that in default of a combined agent/aesthete (which he had) he would opt for a regional agent in charge to whom all regional staff should be responsible, including an aesthetic adviser.

Then there were an equal number who found no trouble in dealing with aesthetics, among them Cubby Acland and Ivor Blomfield, both land agents. Bobbie Gore, Adviser on Paintings and Representative in the South East, found that the 'association of area agent, representative and when necessary the Historic Buildings Secretary, in itself comprises a committee … no less satisfactory than a regional one', thus disposing of both issues with one delicate thrust.

Christopher Gibbs, just retiring as Chief Agent after thirty-two years with the Trust, reiterated the finding of the Nicholls Committee ten years earlier. The problem of combining management and aesthetics was, in his view, caused by the two parallel chains of command, one from the Estates Committee and the other from the Historic Buildings Committee.

The new Chief Agent, Ivan Hills, was entirely satisfied that it would be possible to recruit land agents who had an aesthetic sensibility and that, in any event, at Committee level there was insufficient weight given to natural history and to country matters in general. Conrad Rawnsley shared the view that the countryside did not receive the same attention in standards of management that houses did.

The historian and journalist John Grigg had one of the most radical suggestions, which was that the Trust should be placed under Parliamentary control in the manner of the National Gallery, with Trustees appointed by the Prime Minister, the Council an advisory body only, and members reduced to a supporters' club. When one considers how bitterly Conrad Rawnsley felt about what he deemed the 'Establishmentism' of the Trust one wonders what his reactions would have been to this. Equally he would certainly have taken issue with Lord Methuen who said, 'I see nothing particularly wrong with the set up of the National Trust, or its administration.'

Well before the Committee had finished its deliberations the Secretary, Jack Rathbone, became the first and only major casualty of the battle, other than Rawnsley himself. He had been against the appointment from the start, and Rawnsley in evidence to Benson said that he made no secret of the fact and repeatedly told him that he was not suitable for the job. Lord Antrim and his closest colleagues, among whom were Mark Norman and Pat Gibson, had two reasons for asking him to resign: first, there was genuine concern that his health was likely to break down again and that the damage might be more lasting; secondly was the generally accepted fact that by temperament he was not the right person to carry through the radical changes both in organisation and outlook which they knew had to come. It was Antrim who had to tell him and Rathbone says, 'The courage and sympathy with which Lord Antrim told me I ought to resign I shall never forget.' That sentence says a great deal in favour of both men.

It was Pat Gibson who found a successor. Someone with experience, authority and a strong character was wanted and it was thought that such a person might be found among the mandarins of the Civil Service. He consulted a brilliant, youngish ex-civil servant, Frederick Bishop. Bishop, in his words, 'had one of my few really brilliant ideas and suggested my old friend and colleague John Winnifrith who was shortly due to retire from the Permanent Secretaryship of the Ministry of Agriculture, Fisheries and Food (MAFF). I arranged a lunch meeting at the Ivy. It was a jolly good lunch and must have cost someone – I believe me – a lot!'

Winnifrith, who thought that the luncheon invitation had some connection with the Dowager Lady Antrim whose neighbour he had been at Edenbridge, was surprised to find himself invited to fill the newly created post of Director General of the National Trust, his primary role to be that of trouble shooter. He said out of politeness that he would think it over, intending to turn it down, but on telling his wife about what he regarded as a rather bad joke he discovered that she thought he ought to accept. 'Her main motive was to get me out of a job which involved long working hours, much attendance at public dinners and very little time with her or our family.' However, there was another factor and that was the prospect that the Labour Government then in office would drop its opposition to joining the Common Market. Winnifrith considered the prospect disastrous and thought that he might in any event have to resign rather than introduce a policy to which he was fundamentally opposed. He therefore agreed to come, accepting a drop in salary from £8,600 to £7,000 a year and a serious loss in pension. As a tease he had asked the Chairman if the Trust couldn't afford just £100 per annum pension, was taken seriously and is still in receipt of it! One stipulation he made was that he would only serve for three years.

He turned out to be precisely the right man, because not only was he a sound administrator, but he was warm and deeply interested in people and their welfare. He was a genuine agriculturalist and countryman, and could – and did when occasion offered – sing in the vernacular 'The Fly be on the Turmot'. Mark Norman says of him that 'he left behind him no enemies but only friends. There was a thick and skilful velvet glove on *his* iron fist.'

Rathbone's going was a personal tragedy. He had devoted himself to the Trust, saying on more than one occasion, 'You see I have no wife and no children and the Trust is my family.' To quote Mark Norman, '[Rathbone] was excellent for a small N.T. Intelligent, passionate, mercurial, disorganised and totally devoted to the Trust.' He had contributed in his twenty years much towards the success and development of the Trust and it was his misfortune rather than any fault that it now needed a very different man.

Because the office of Secretary is one with statutory duties under the 1907 Act, it was necessary to appoint a successor. Lady Dalton and Mark Norman were given the task of selection and they chose Jack Boles, who had been Assistant Secretary for three years. He had gone into the Rifle Brigade in 1943 and after the war joined the Colonial Service, his time abroad having been mainly in the Far East where his latest job was as Permanent Secretary to the Ministry of Land and Natural Resources. Both he and his wife had been National Trust members and she, before her marriage, had worked at Sotheby's. On the very day that they set foot in England when he retired from the Service, the job of Assistant Secretary to the Trust was advertised. He applied and got the job.

He was very well suited, with a country background in Devon where his father farmed. His early National Trust induction had included being sent to Cubby Acland in the Lakes (where the tiny housekeeper Miss Dugdale also had to approve), to Christopher Wall in Shropshire, and to the Devon Area Office near his old home.

Winnifrith was, to his dismay, faced with an overlap period which was made tolerable by Rathbone's friendly reception and the task of working as an assessor to the Benson Committee. The Committee's report was eventually published in December 1968. It ran to 158 pages including appendices and, considering its scope and complexity, was lucid and compressed, and its recommendations were summarised in fifty-eight short paragraphs. It is not easily further summarised but the main points concerned amendments to the constitution which tightened up the committee system, penalised non-attendance and introduced a system of proxy voting; the organisational structure was somewhat decentralised – although the Council was still to decide policy; published accounts were to be simplified, membership was to be stepped up; and Enterprise Neptune was to be phased out and an appeal for £5 million for the General Fund launched. Public relations were to be improved!

This was not very well received by the Reformers. E.W. Hodge, writing to Mr Cochrane from Elterwater Hall, near Ambleside, commented 'Its obvious lack of impartiality, though not unexpected, is very disappointing …' and complained of 'a total ban on democratic criticism, or responsibility to grass roots membership.' John Grigg, writing to Conrad Rawnsley said, 'My view of Benson is slightly less gloomy than yours, though I certainly don't think it goes anything like far enough on the remedial side. Its chief merit is that it endorses, by implication, most of the criticisms which you and the rest of us put forward.' John Winnifrith had no illusions about the question of impartiality: 'No one could describe this as an independent committee. It was a cosy family party. All three members were on the Trust's Council and even Sir Henry was one of the Trust's shooting tenants! However in practice the Committee took an independent line. Far from all their recommendations were welcome to the Trust's die-hards – Committee members and staff.'

It fell to the new Director General to steer the recommendations of the Report through the Executive Committee and Council, and it was a somewhat wearisome business, with the minutiae of the Report discussed backwards and forwards, and it was quite a tricky one too. He found 'the Council … contained a number of loose horses, liable to bolt when the red rag of their pet like or dislike struck their eyes.' (One supposes that his country background led him into that interesting mixture of animal metaphors). Jack Boles says that 'this was Winnifrith's triumph completely. After complete discussion he ensured complete acceptance.'

In the course of discussion there was a lot of informed comment which affected the recommendations by way of emphasis, but little in the way of outright rejection. The main points of amendment were:

– the Council to retain a right to call an EGM;

– voting rights to apply (in general terms) to all classes of members and not to exclude those below the age of majority;

– that the target of money to be raised to fund improvements and administration should be reviewed, and probably reduced;

– that an eventual optimum for access to houses of five days a week for eleven months each year might be modified by circumstance;

– that Regional Agents and Custodians should not have equal status and that the former should be in charge;

– that Neptune should be continued.

In retrospect the last two items have been the Council's most significant, and probably most rewarding, interventions.

All this had to run the gauntlet of the 1969 AGM and then Parliament. Winnifrith prepared for both meticulously. The Annual Report, in addition to reporting as fully as usual on the year's events, contained an appendix of thirty-nine pages with the Council's comments and decisions on every single recommendation in the summary of the Report. Then prior to the meeting, for which the Trust again hired the Central Hall, the most careful attention was given to the physical arrangements for the conduct of the meeting, especially communications. Lord Antrim was subjected to a series of dummy runs with John Winnifrith 'taking on the role of Mr Mowat, Mr Cochrane (leader of the rebels) and other well known teases. He said the mock examinations were far worse than the real thing.' In the event all went well with enough speakers who were sufficiently convincing against the opposition to make it clear that the arguments as well as the votes supported Benson.

Then it was Parliament. Bob Latham had to instruct Parliamentary Agents to draft the Bill. The provisions of the Bill were limited, with one exception, to matters arising from the Benson recommendations. This was John Winnifrith's decision, and had the object of limiting objections to things which had already been fully documented and discussed. The exception was Latham's own initiative and concerned the inter-application of the statutes governing the operation of the Wey and Godalming Navigations so that the two could be effectively managed as one. When the Bill came before a Select Committee, John Winnifrith was the Trust's witness and Robert Mowat for the opposition. The Chairman, Michael English MP, is remembered for his 'professional delight in taking points for criticism'. Mowat pushed very hard for the continuance of provisions for an EGM and English was concerned that the Trust in conceding that was trying to negate it by requiring, in one per cent of membership, too high a number of requisitionists to be in practice obtainable. The compromise of one twentieth of one per cent seemed to Winnifrith too low (i.e. 100 out of a 200,000 membership), but the growth in membership which was wholly unforeseen within ten years raised the figure to 500. In any event John Winnifrith was realistic enough to recognise that 'babies had to be thrown to the wolves'.

The preamble to the Act, which received the Royal Assent on 17 February 1971 asserted, 'Since the incorporation of the National Trust as aforesaid the membership of the National Trust, the property in its ownership and its responsibilities have all greatly increased and it is expedient that the constitution of the National Trust should be amended as in this Act provided.' And so it was. Latham, looking back over seventeen years, reckons that it has done satisfactorily what it was intended to and that it has genuinely brought the constitution up to date.

All those named in this chapter are entitled in their different ways to be credited with a share in the responsibility for what is a satisfactory outcome, but Lord Benson has given one special credit to the National Trust as such. In 1983 he gestured towards the shelves in his room at the Bank of England: 'These are copies of all the Reports that I have done and out of all that number the National Trust is the only one to have carried out my recommendations in full.'

Mr Mowat was to become an institution in himself regularly attending AGMs and keeping a sharp eye on the Trust's finances and accounts, and regularly urging upon it that the acquisition of country houses as opposed to countryside was an unwise and potentially damaging policy. His criticisms were level-headed and his attitude one of reason, and he achieved with the platform, and in particular with Mark Norman, a relationship of mutual respect.

What of Conrad Rawnsley? The course of events had been a personal tragedy for him and his family, regardless of the rights and wrongs of his conduct. The common opinion of him among the Committee men and senior Head Office staff who dealt with him continues to be in recollection severe and unforgiving. Jack Rathbone, however, has written, 'In retrospect I think I was wrong and that in the long run Rawnsley was of true benefit to the Trust ... the expensive shake up [the EGM] which he initiated has been of benefit to the Trust. The way he initiated the shake up was deplorable ... and he was rightly given the sack, but we in the Trust were too complacent and inward-looking.' Bob Latham, whose adverse comments are repeated earlier, takes a similar view. Conrad Rawnsley has come up smiling in the end. He is still hurt by what he considers the injustice of his treatment, his business flourishes under the very walls of Petworth Park, and he has this satisfaction: 'At least I have kicked the National Trust into the twentieth century!'

CHAPTER XVII

Inalienable Lands

As the new Director General, Winnifrith was faced in his first year not only with the consequences of the Benson Report but with the first of a series of challenges to the principle of inalienability. This is the status – unique in Great Britain and probably in the world – given under the powers of the 1907 Act, whereby if the Executive Committee so resolve, property held for preservation may not be disposed of by the National Trust. Since that time, under general legislation, it has been possible to apply compulsory acquisition to such land but only after the consent of both Houses of Parliament has been obtained through what is called Special Parliamentary Procedure. This the Trust can invoke if it thinks it right to do so. The special status works for preservation in two different ways: first, it means that donors of land know that only in the most exceptional circumstances could land be taken away from the Trust, and, second, it prevents the Trust from divesting itself of responsibilities which it has found to be onerous or perhaps politically tiresome.

A system evolved in the late 1940s whereby, before declaring land inalienable, the Trust consulted the Ministry of Town and Country Planning (the work of which, after several changes, is now done by the Department of the Environment). The Ministry circularised Planning Authorities, other departments and nationalised industries to see whether this would conflict with proposed requirements for the land. It was open to the Trust to adopt a resolution of inalienability regardless of the response, but if it did so in the face of a known requirement it could not then expect the Ministry to support it. This procedure operated in 1957 when the Treasury gave Saltram House and 291 acres of parkland just east of Plymouth to the Trust. The enquiry showed that in order to relieve the village of Plympton St Mary, through which on the A 38 trunk road all the traffic to and from Plymouth and much of that for Cornwall passed, it was intended to build a four-lane dual carriageway through the park. For reasons which are wholly obscure the Trust decided nevertheless to declare the whole of the gift inalienable.

By 1963 it looked as though the road project would really go ahead. Anthony Martineau asked the Charity Commission to advise on what action the Trust should take, and was told that it should be opposed. When he pointed out that the road proposal had been known before the land became inalienable, the Charity

231

Commission, with absolute justification, replied that the Trust had 'courted this consequence'.

Michael Trinick, in whose management area Saltram was, and who was shortly to become Regional Secretary, was reported to have been opposed to the road but by 1964 had changed his mind. He now felt that, subject to negotiation on details of the route, any new road must go through the park. The Executive Committee followed this opinion and sought to avoid putting it to the test of Special Parliamentary Procedure. The Charity Commission however, were quite firm and insisted on the principle that where land was to be taken for something which would do positive harm to the Trust's land, Parliament must be allowed to decide.

From then on the Trust sought to find some way out of what seemed certain defeat. R.T. James, a retired civil engineer of great experience who had helped the Trust voluntarily on other matters, tried to find an alternative route but the best he could contrive was one which involved an embankment 100 feet high, towering above the village, so that some of the houses, it was reckoned, would not see the sun for a third of each year. Michael Rosse as Chairman of the Historic Buildings Council superintended these efforts, attended meetings with the Ministry and Planners at Saltram and tried his charm on the Minister, Barbara Castle, but even that bore no result. The Trust's valuer, Tony Archer-Lock of Plymouth who had been negotiating improved conditions should the work go ahead, summed things up when he wrote to Latham in January 1968. The Trust was on very bad ground: there had been no objection to the County Plan which first featured the road; modifications had been made to the proposals at the Trust's request which diminished the adverse effect on the property; finally there was no practical alternative. For these reasons the Trust's position was untenable and it should not object.

Nevertheless the Trust had to and did so at the public enquiry, Latham setting out the very dubious grounds: 1) The by-pass is unnecessary and a waste of public funds; 2) If it is necessary (which is denied) there are alternative less damaging routes; 3) The amount of land required is excessive; 4) The land is inalienable and the proposal is therefore objectionable.

The Inspector's report was against the Trust and so was the Minister's decision, and the Trust duly invoked Special Parliamentary Procedure. The hearing began on 9 November 1968. Michael Trinick was the Trust's principal witness and found the business of examination, cross-examination and re-examination completely exhausting. On 26 November, the Joint Select Committee found against the Trust. Now the A38 dual carriageway of six lanes runs through the park at Saltram. Although the park is diminished in space and beauty, the damage to the house and grounds is less than might have been expected since the road is in a deep cutting as it passes by.

The worst damage done was to the sanctity of the principle of inalienability and for this the Trust was wholly to blame. It was bad enough to be obliged to explain this to the membership and to the public, just one year after the Rawnsley row, but it was to have very serious consequences a few years later.

Even while the Saltram affair was coming to a head, John Winnifrith had to prepare for another battle to protect inalienable land. This time the enemy was Bath City Council, with which relationships had not been easy ever since the war, when the City had tried to get out of its responsibility for the Assembly Rooms. South-east of the city by just one mile on the flat top of Claverton Down, which rises to over 600 feet before dropping steeply to the Avon, is a property of 362 acres. The greater part of this is Rainbow Wood Farm, and there are restrictive covenants protecting a further sixteen acres of woodland adjoining. Nearly all this land came to the Trust through the Mallett family, the first tentative enquiry being made in 1931.

In 1946 Mrs Mallett enquired of the Trust whether the property would be accepted for preservation in its present unspoiled state were she to devise it by will at her death. So close was it to the city that it was obvious that the land might be required by some authority and the Trust decided to make sure. The Ministry of Town and Country Planning replied that there were no planning objections to the land being declared inalienable and so Mrs Mallett's offer was accepted. Before it became effective, indeed just two years later, Bath had changed its mind and wished to zone the area for house building in its development plan. After enquiry, at which the Trust gave evidence, the proposal was dropped, and no further attempt was made on the land until ten years later when the Mayor, personally, made strenuous efforts to obtain it as a permanent site for the Bath and West showground.

A year later Mrs Mallett died and her devise became effective, and the Trust again enquired of the Ministry (by now styled 'Housing and Local Government') and again received clearance for a resolution of inalienability. At the same time an informal approach was made by the Town Clerk to see whether the farm could be used as playing fields to free other playing fields for use as the showground, an approach which the Trust rejected. However, the City did dispose of that land for use as the site of the new University and in 1968 issued a compulsory purchase order against the Trust for Rainbow Wood Farm.

The enquiry was held at the same time as the Joint Select Committee was dealing with Saltram. The Director General gave evidence for the Trust, and emphasised two main points – the role of the Trust in preservation and its need to inspire confidence that it could do its job, and the consistency with which it had first ensured that it was not cutting across any planning intentions and then maintain that position against attempted incursions. He pointed out, moreover, that there were perfectly satisfactory alternatives. Anthony Greenwood, the Minister, did not give his decision until the end of March 1969 when he refused to confirm the compulsory purchase order and at the same time planning permission for the change of use. The terms of his decision letter are very important. He wrote: 'Because of the terms under which it was donated and because it has been declared to be inalienable, the Minister regards it as a pre-requisite of approval to take such land that no reasonable alternatives exist, and that the development proposed to be carried out causes the minimum amount of harm to the National Trust property affected.'

Not only had John Winnifrith's authoritative evidence been very effective but there were a total of 118 objections and during the hearing the Inspector received nearly 1,300 letters, mostly objecting too. This was a splendid victory, and fortunately timed because it came just long enough after the Saltram debacle not to lose any of its significance by comparison. It gave reassurance to members, committees and staff alike, and was also noted by those authorities which might otherwise have decided that the status of inalienability was not after all impregnable.

It did not, however, deter the Calderdale Water Board from introducing a Bill in the House of Lords to take part of the Trust's property of Hardcastle Crags in

Hebden Dale for making a reservoir. There were some similarities here with the Saltram case in that before resolving the land to be inalienable when it was given by Lord Savile in 1950, the usual enquiries had disclosed the existence of a scheme for a reservoir which had fallen into abeyance but might be revived. The Trust had felt that the valley with its famous crags should be protected and had decided to run the risk of confrontation and make the land inalienable. A petition to the Select Committee in the Lords, in which the Trust was joined by Lord Savile, the Hepton District Council, the CPRE and local preservationists, failed, but the Trust decided to mobilise support in the Commons. John Winnifrith co-ordinated the operation: he delighted in putting his experience of Parliament to use on behalf of the Trust, and he was very good at it. The constituency member, Douglas Houghton, was engaged to rally Labour, Marcus Worsley (who had become Chairman of the Trust's Regional Committee for Yorkshire), the Conservatives and Peter Bessell, the Liberals. Winnifrith backed this with circular letters emphasising, not only the need for preservation, but also the wholly unconvincing argument by the Water Board that there was no alternative. The Bill was rejected on Second Reading by 73 votes to 35 and the National Trust had won again.

Besides giving credit to the MPs mentioned, the Annual Report 1969 also mentions Mr Tarton and Mr Waddington, two Conservatives, but Winnifrith gives credit to John Smith, who had entered Parliament for the City of Westminster in 1975, and Peter Jackson, the member for the High Peak. Jackson was a Socialist academic with a fellowship at the University of Hull, and his appearance on the Executive Committee was an improving experience for both parties. He and John Smith were natural allies in their enthusiasm and their disregard of established precedents. They became more closely involved with each other when John Smith's Landmark Trust bought the fine, early nineteenth-century Edale Mill in the High Peak. Not only was Peter Jackson keen to promote preservation in his constituency but he took a direct share in it, buying one of the flats into which the mill was converted. It seems very possible that these two, from each of the two main parties, with their energy and enthusiasm, may have made a significant behind-the-scenes contribution to this second success.

John Winnifrith felt that Government and Local Authorities may have been wrongly encouraged by the defeat of the Trust at Saltram, a case which he considered lost from the start. Certainly the Ministry of Transport was prepared to take on the Trust again. The 6,000 acre Killerton Estate lies across the approach to Exeter from the north east and through it passed the A 38 carrying traffic from the Midlands down to central and southern Devon and to Cornwall. The County Development Plan had provided for a new road which would pass through the estate but the land had been made inalienable ten years before that and the Trust duly entered an objection. It did so again when the plan was reviewed in 1975. On that occasion the Trust put forward two possible alternative routes, one passing to the west and the other to the east, each taking some land from the estate but neither as disastrously destructive of the landscape and the unity of the estate.

Despite these objections, the Ministry built a section of the road to by-pass the little town of Cullompton a few miles to the north on a line the natural extension of which was aimed at the heart of the Trust's property. In 1971, the Ministry took its next step and issued a compulsory purchase order for some three miles of a route which passed through the narrow col linking the valleys of the Culm and Clyst. Sir Richard Acland, who had given the property to the Trust nearly thirty years earlier, was living in the dower house and in accordance with the terms of his memorandum of wishes was kept in touch with events. He was opposed to the chosen route and received from the Executive Committee a promise that the Trust would object very strongly. It could hardly do less, one would suppose, but the Regional Committee was far from resolute. By this time John Winnifrith's three promised years had passed and there was a new Director General, Frederick Bishop, who reported to Lord Antrim that the Regional Chairman, Sir Julian Gascoigne, was worried about opposing the order and that his committee considered the route the best one from the general point of view.

In fact the reasons for the Regional Committee's cold feet were several. To start with, they had only three years before worked themselves into a state of righteous indignation over the Saltram case, only to find themselves wholly in the wrong. Then the projected new road had been the subject of intense political activity in the counties of Devon and Cornwall for many years. A dozen local interests were all crying out for a 'spine road' which would transform communications with the heart of England and with it the prosperity of local trade and industry. The Regional Committee both individually and collectively were reluctant to appear obstructive. There was also a sense in which Trust property would benefit, in that the congestion and danger on the road which served the hamlets and village was appalling and almost any relief from that seemed worthwhile.

However, the Trust did enter an objection and at the public enquiry Bishop gave evidence. He was by nature a manipulator and negotiator, and he felt that the Trust had not been very clever in the earlier stages, and that there was little prospect of success. Acland, who also gave evidence, expressed the feelings which had moved him to donate his land: 'A man does not give his land away because he hates it. If he hates it he sells it. He gives it away to the National Trust because he loves it.' Neither reason nor emotion prevailed and the Minister confirmed the order, his decision letter boiling down to the belief that there was no alternative. The Trust decided not to invoke Special Parliamentary Procedure on the ground that it would lose, and this time Latham was careful not to consult the Charity Commission until the period in which the procedure could be called for had expired. Curiously enough the Commission, which had been so insistent about the Trust's duty to go to Parliament a few years early, made no comment whatsoever.

Was it a correct decision? Sir Richard Acland thought at the time that it was wrong: he is now not so sure, and recognises that it was a very difficult decision to make. Bishop is quite sure that it was right. The issue which neither the Inspector nor the Minister would accept was that under the protection of the Trust that landscape which was, as Sylvia Crowe said in evidence on the Trust's behalf, exceptionally beautifully in scale, content and variety, would have been preserved in that form. It was a point which Parliament might have accepted, and in any event it may be thought that the principle was one for which the Trust should have fought all the way.

It was at about the same time that West Sussex County Council decided that it must relieve the intolerable congestion on the narrow road which winds between the blank back quarters of Petworth House and the streets of the little town. The solution was fairly simple – to drive a new road through the park. Now opinions differ about the architectural merits of Petworth House: some have said it is 'as good as anything in France', which is intended as high praise, and others that there used to be better barracks in Aldershot. But about the park, still in form much as designed by Capability Brown and with records of its development in several paintings by Turner hanging in the house, there is universal agreement as to its beauty and importance.

The Trust at once took measures to defend the property, retaining the eminent road expert, Professor Colin Buchanan, to advise on alternatives. These were not easy to find. The obvious one, east of the town, which was recommended, ran through a pleasant valley which provided the nearest country walk for townspeople. They, having very much the same feelings about the restrictive conditions for the use of the park as did Conrad Rawnsley, were united and vociferous in their opposition. There was a great deal of press comment and public meetings were held. Out of all this a proposal came from Jack Speed, a local resident, that two single carriage-way roads should be developed, one to the east and one right beyond the park to the west. This was adopted by the consultants and became confusingly known as 'the Speed Route'.

The County Council had other ideas and adopted a new proposal which was literally a short cut – a route through the pleasure grounds and less than fifty yards in front of the house, where it was to be thinly disguised as a tunnel made on the 'cut and cover' principle. By that time it was 1975 and the Trust mounted a splendidly-orchestrated publicity campaign against the proposal. The route was marked out on the ground so that visitors could see its impact, a most effective poster was commissioned from David Gentleman, and the Press stirred up. A form of Petition, addressed to the Secretary of State for the Environment was prepared and distributed to the Trust's properties throughout the country, collecting by the season's end over 350,000 signatures.

Then, just one year later, the public enquiry which was to have been held in the summer of 1976 was postponed for a year, and has not in fact yet taken place, while the traffic still grinds its slow way through the streets of the town. This is due at least in some measure to three factors: the ineptitude of the County Council; the legacy of resentment in the town against the Leconfield Estate; and the vigorous counter-offensive of the National Trust. Should the issue ever come to trial it does now seem improbable that Parliament will fail to uphold the safety of that inalienable land.

As a postscript it should be recorded that the Trust, with the co-operation of Lord Egremont, who is the second generation to succeed the donor, has liberalised and made greatly more welcoming access for visitors to both the house and the park and perhaps with the passage of time the resentment factor will diminish.

There was a further trial of strength in the early 1970s when the National Trust for Scotland was threatened with compulsory purchase of its coastal property at Drumbuie for development in connection with the North Sea oil and gas fields on a scale which would have meant the virtual destruction of the landscape. Since the NTS shared similar status, and had to some extent developed on similar lines, an attack on one Trust was an attack on the other, and every support was given in terms of publicity and influence from England. Freddie Bishop went to Scotland and gave evidence at the long public enquiry. The proposal was eventually rejected by the

Secretary of State for Scotland. In some ways this was the most important case because, in terms of the money involved, and the urgency and importance of establishing the new industry, it must have been politically very tempting to disregard the inalienable status of the land.

Where it has seemed to the Trust that no reasonable alternative to some necessary public use of inalienable land existed and where the damage to the Trust's interests was not too serious (or alternatively that the damage would be worse if the development were to be shifted onto neighbouring land) the device of making the land available on leasehold has been adopted. In its annual report for 1981 a section was devoted to explaining this, prompted by criticism of the Trust's agreement to lease twelve acres of the 1,100 acre Bradenham Estate to the Ministry of Defence. It was needed for an extension of the underground RAF communications centre which had been built nearly fifty years earlier on adjacent land. The site was an inconspicuous corner of a large property and an unobjectionable farm field which contributed nothing to the landscape and had become inalienable simply as a result of the terms of Ernest Cook's will. Such alternative sites as existed were less desirable from every point of view and it was clear that unless terms were agreed compulsory purchase would be inevitable.

What had not occurred to the Trust – and the whole business had been raked over in great detail by both Regional Committee, Executive and Council – was that a pressure group from outside would try to use the Trust as a weapon against the Government of whose defence policy they disapproved. When the Trust went ahead and granted the lease, the group requisitioned an EGM which was held in November 1982, on the same day as the AGM in the Wembley Conference Centre. The critical amendments were defeated heavily.

Aside from the underlying purpose of the group there was an important matter of principle which Conrad Rawnsley, who appeared as a self-styled 'superannuated rebel', intended to raise. Unfortunately his oratory outran the prescribed time for speakers and the points were not then put, but he did subsequently present them in a letter to the Director General, the essence of them being that it was certainly unwise and possible *ultra vires* for the Trust to grant leases which involved the development of inalienable land. This issue was taken to the High Court by Lord Beaumont of Whitley who sought a declaration, 'that the Trust has no power to grant a lease for purposes which are inconsistent with the purposes of the Trust ...' and that the lease to the Ministry of Defence was inconsistent. The Ministry, the Charity Commission and the Attorney General were all joined with the Trust as defendants!

Mr Justice Nichols found against Lord Beaumont, but the reasoning in his judgement is of great importance and brings right up to date an examination of the Trust's duty towards the care of its inalienable land. He started by pointing out that the Trust's power to grant leases was given to it by statute in order to assist it to carry out its own purposes. If a lease were to be granted which was aimed at the maintenance of a historic house or beautiful land that would be an obvious example of a lease which would further the Trust's purposes. By way of contrast, a lease of beautiful land which would result in it being altered for ever by building would, *prima facie*, not be so. However, there might well be circumstances in which, despite development arising out of the grant of a lease, where the Trust might justifiably grant such a lease, having regard to the importance or otherwise of the particular area for preservation, the impact of the development on the rest of the property, and the likely consequences if the lease were not granted. The Judge summarised the general position in such a case: '... in deciding to grant the lease the Trust would be doing no more than recognising that the grant of such a lease in all the circumstances was likely to be less damaging to the Trust's preservation purposes than the adoption of any alternative course open to it. The lease would be granted as representing the best means available to the Trust of minimising the damage to the preservation of its estate.'

It is interesting to speculate what the founding Quartet would have thought of this. Grosvenor, Hunter and Octavia Hill were all in their different ways pragmatic even in their crusades and would probably have recognised that the management of such a huge estate as that now owned by the Trust could not be maintained against other legitimate national interests without at least a little flexibility. Hardwicke Rawnsley would perhaps have taken a different line and advocated the course of no concession. They would all have welcomed Mr Justice Nichols's final comment: '... nothing drawn to my attention in this case has given me cause to doubt that, when making their decisions the Council and committees of the Trust are (to use Mr Macdonald's [counsel for Lord Beaumont] expression) "unequivocally on the side of preservation," and that if anybody has any fears on this score they are unfounded.'

The events covered in this chapter have been followed in detail because, in the final analysis, it is the status of inalienability which has been and remains the one feature of the constitution of the Trust which sets it aside from all the authorities, organisations and individuals whose interests are in any way similar. It is a status given by Parliament and one which Parliament can take away, and it must be conscientiously and wisely applied if it is to endure.

CHAPTER XVIII

A New Professionalism

T he appointment of a new Director General, Frederick Bishop, in January 1971, was the result of Winnifrith's decision to stick to the limit of his three-year term. He had enjoyed the work and his relations with his Chairman, Lord Antrim, had been happy. 'He trusted me and didn't try to do my job. I asked him once where he kept his papers and he replied, "In the waste paper basket", a good answer because it was my job to see that he had the papers he needed when he needed them. There were very few of the staff I didn't like or trust and above all I had the great comfort of having Miss Kearney as my personal assistant.' Mary Kearney had succeeded Florence Paterson and had acted as secretary to Jack Rathbone. Winnifrith, only too well aware that the circumstances of Rathbone's departure might breed resentment against the new man, was deeply appreciative of the way in which Mary Kearney gave him loyal support without in any way relinquishing her loyalty to and affection for Jack Rathbone.

Winnifrith's successor was the very man who had suggested his name in the first place. Bishop was not particularly well suited to business life and consequently not very happy with J. Pearson and Son, and it fitted well with all interests concerned that he should take on the job of running the National Trust. He had had a brilliant career. After the war, in which he served as a ferry pilot, he transferred to the administrative grade of the Civil Service, where he had a very distinguished record, being promoted finally at the young age of forty-nine after a spell in the Cabinet Office, to be Permanent Secretary of the newly formed Ministry of Land and Natural Resources. Unfortunately that department did not long endure and when offered a job in Pearson's by Oliver Poole (then their Chief Executive) he accepted. For the National Trust a man who had been at the very centre of Government for nine years, and who knew and was known to so many people in positions of power and influence, was a great catch.

He and his new colleagues in the Trust found themselves well suited to one another.

The relatively small size of the Trust's organisation at that time reminded me very much of the sort of 'team' that I had enjoyed greatly in the Cabinet Office and No. 10. It was the sort of unit that could perform efficiently while still remaining human and friendly and even (in the case of the National

Trust) amateur. Lord Antrim was right for the Trust then: really an inspired amateur, unsystematic, slightly eccentric, often diffident. But he had a very wide knowledge of people, splendidly balanced aesthetic judgement and a great personal knowledge of both houses and countryside. He was extremely funny and immensely humane.

Bishop particularly enjoyed the aesthetic side of the Trust's work which was to him largely – but not entirely – a new field.

> The detailed and devoted application to aesthetic problems of such people as Robin Fedden, Bobbie Gore and others was a revelation and a joy. In particular I shall always be grateful to Robin, that remarkable and many faceted character, for the patience and trouble and tolerance he showed to me as a newcomer. This characteristic of 'amateurism', in the real and best sense of the word, seems to me to be the essence of the National Trust.

What Freddie Bishop has written about the Trust as he found it has been quoted because, like John Winnifrith, he is as independent a witness as can be found, and one whose experiences of working in Government and commerce gave him ample comparisons. Neither of the first two Directors General stayed long enough in office to be committed by their length of service to anything other than an objective opinion. Regrettably Bishop went through a bad time in terms of fitness and after something less than five years he felt obliged to give up. The job of running the Trust had never been a sinecure – Matheson, Bevir, Rathbone and Winnifrith all attest to that – and it was if anything getting harder.

During his time in office, however, Bishop was very valuable. To start with, he was very well liked by both committees and staff and so continued the process begun by his predecessor of restoring mutual confidence within the organisation. Beyond that he had the task of enlarging the professional staff in the ways not only proposed in the Benson Report but seen as necessary by the Head Office committees and staff.

The first necessity was to make sure that there was a sound and reasonably remunerative framework of employment. Although conditions of service had improved in the 1960s, things were somewhat haphazard and uneven, with such elements as the pension scheme leaving much to be desired. At Head Office the main areas to be reinforced were the finance and public relations departments, and a wholly new arrangement was needed for the membership department. A new Chief Finance Officer had been appointed in 1969. Jimmy Wheeler had come from Unilever's Indian organisation and continued to talk of money in terms of *Lakhs* and a warehouse always remained for him a godown. An indication of the awareness of the Trust of the inadequacy of salaries then paid is Mark Norman's question, 'Can you afford to work for us?' to which Wheeler truthfully replied, 'Not really!' Norman had just assumed the position of Chairman of the Finance Committee, the office of Honorary Treasurer having been dropped. He found Wheeler a tremendous asset, and Bishop and Boles did too.

Wheeler found the Trust's properties being run on an accounting system which had been evolved in 1954 to decentralise accounts to areas, and which had at that time worked very well indeed. The enormous increase in work since that time had produced an overload under which the system functioned only with difficulty. Areas had been pressing for years for an improved system which could employ more mechanical aids. Wheeler, however, had a simple remedy: he dismembered the system and re-centralised the accounts, leaving the regions (as they had become) with virtually no coherent system through which to manage their affairs, a state which was to endure until, in the 1980s, the accounting responsibility was returned to them. Not that it seemed at the time to matter much and it did enable the Chief Finance Officer to supply his Finance Committee and Director General with the information they wanted for strategic purposes.

Wheeler it was, with his fresh outlook and cheerful insouciance, to whom Bishop and Boles turned for guidance and action in matters such as bringing salary scales and conditions of service into line with comparable jobs elsewhere. To him also was entrusted the removal of the bulk of his department from London in accordance with the Benson recommendations. By 1974 it was re-established on an industrial estate at Melksham in Wiltshire and furnished with a computer. Although it functioned, it did so only with great efforts on the part of the staff there, and great forebearance from their colleagues up and down the country until decentralisation again to regions went far towards putting matters right.

Conrad Rawnsley had quite rightly criticised the Trust for its lack of a public relations organisation on a countrywide basis. Considering that a Publicity Committee had been formed over thirty years earlier it is remarkable that there had been so little development. The reason may have been the post-war belief in the extreme poverty of the Trust and a distaste for publicity as such, an attitude exemplified by the reluctance to appeal for funds, which has been mentioned earlier. In 1969 a Director of Public Relations was appointed. He was not to work to a committee but a member of the Executive was given the special responsibility of working with him. The Benson Committee devised this idea in order to eliminate a sub-committee. They suggested that the person for this should have experience in the field and the lot fell upon Simon Hornby (knighted in the 1988 New Years Honours List). He was a director of the newsagent and stationery retailers, W.H. Smith who had been on the Executive for several years and was young, energetic, full of ideas and very keen on the Trust.

The man chosen as Director of Public Relations was Edward Fawcett. He came of the same family as Dames Millicent and Mildred who had founded the Fawcett Society for Female Emancipation, and the Professor Henry Fawcett who, as an MP was a leading Commons Society member and who, when Postmaster General, appointed Robert Hunter to be Solicitor to the Post Office. He was at school at Uppingham as Hardwicke Rawnsley had been and then entered the wartime Navy. In the war he served in the navy and afterwards he read history of art and French at London with Nikolaus Pevsner and John Summerson as teachers, and then went on to the LSE for a course in personnel management.

It may be imagined that this was only partly a suitable preparation for commercial life but, by the age of fifty, he had become Overseas Sales Director for the car component firm Lucas. He clearly felt the need for a change and lying ill at home he read in the newspaper about the Benson Report. He got a copy of the report and studied it very thoroughly. He had been a National Trust member for ten years, joining when he visited Stourhead which moved him very much, as it had done Jack

Rathbone, and he plotted to secure a position on the staff. His first move was to entertain Robin Fedden, whom he knew, at the Golden Sole, starting off with two large Martinis and fish soup. The rest of the meal must have been good for the result was a formal interview with Robin, who wanted him to take over the Historic Buildings work in the South East. He then saw Sir John Winnifrith, and after that Lord Antrim at his house in Moor Street, where the interview panel included Mark Norman and Pat Gibson. There he was accepted for the post of Director of Public Relations and looking back admiringly on the process he says, 'The National Trust is the last remaining organisation which is prepared to frame jobs round people.'

Ted Fawcett found a public relations department of seven, headed by Lawrence Rich, one of the handsomest and most charming of men to grace the staff of the Trust. He acted as Press Secretary, and he was assisted by three others and three typists. In the regions there were two full time Information Officers – Christopher Hanson-Smith in the North-west, and Warren Davis in Devon and Cornwall. In Wales Claude Page divided his time between looking after the Tudor Merchant House at Tenby and public relations, towards which his skill with pen, pencil and colour made a great contribution.

It was with this meagre force that Ted Fawcett began his primary task, to achieve the Benson target of half a million individual members in fifteen years. The previous attitude of the Trust to this was crystallised for him when Robin Fedden admonished him with the words, 'Mr Fawcett, you must realise that the National Trust has nothing to do with people.' Indeed, the idea of direct recruitment, although it had been initiated in the mid-1960s had hardly taken root in the regions, and was only prosecuted vigorously in two. Acland's 'Cubby-holes' in the Lake District adopted the device of offering something for sale – maps and guidebooks mainly – to attract the casual visitor who was then told about the Trust and persuaded, if possible, to join. In Devon and Cornwall Michael Trinick was pursuing his own ideas of what should be done in the presentation of houses open to the public and in Fawcett's words:

> Houses were not thought of simply as architecture, or as containers for collections of furniture and works of art, but places where families had lived, where kitchens, laundries and stables were realised to be as interesting as a Louis XIV commode, or a Devis portrait. It was also realised that visitors need loos, enjoy eating, and like being treated as human beings. Under these circumstances the response to the question, 'Would you like to join the National Trust?' was frequently 'Yes', and almost invariably with the comment, 'I never knew we could'.

Trinick was very well supported by his Regional Information Officer, Warren Davis, an extremely good communicator who instantly produced in the South-West the very best sort of relationship with the press, radio and television. He is now the national Press and Public Relations Manager in charge of publicity at Queen Anne's Gate.

Fawcett held up this shining example to other regions and gradually the attitude of the Trust – committees and staff alike, began to change. It would be wrong to attribute this change entirely to Ted Fawcett: there were many other factors both within and without the Trust which had been developing for a long time, but it was he who seized upon it as the first weapon in the battle for membership. In 1970 membership was up by 49,000 on the previous year's 177,000, and went up rapidly each year so that, by 1975, it topped the half million which Benson had set as a target over fifteen years. In May 1981 it went over a million, in celebration of which members were given notices to stick in the windows of their motor cars proclaiming, 'I'm one in a million!' By autumn 1987 the figure was over 1.5 million.

Jim Wheeler made a major contribution to this success. It is no good recruiting a member who does not maintain his subscription and the annual collection is not only expensive but also provides an excuse for dropping out. The banks had evolved a system known as Variable Direct Debit which if adopted by a subscriber meant that not only was the subscription paid automatically by the bank but also at any different figure. This results in membership continuing regardless of increasing costs unless the subscriber takes positive action to stop it. Wheeler, supported by Fawcett, had to overcome stern resistance from his Finance Committee before the system could be promoted. The Finance Committee Chairman said, 'I would never allow my wife to sign such a thing: it is equivalent to a blank cheque!' So it is, but from the Trust's point of view it was a great advantage.

Fawcett saw the Lake District Cubby-holes, five per cent shop and ninety-five per cent publicity and recruitment as being right in concept and he determined to apply the principle more widely and also to try to make more money that way. The Brownsea Island shop had been operated profitably for six years. At Saltram in Devon the first proper shop to be made in a country house was opened. Until that time the 'hall table' was used to sell guide books and postcards and the average spending by visitors was, in addition to an entrance fee, only about two (old) pence a head. Even at that level he proved that the Trust could do a lot better. When with the help of his assistant Tom Burr he designed a guide book and postcard dispenser and, with difficulty, got them installed in some one hundred houses, sales quadrupled.

Trading as such really began after Fawcett engaged Ray Hallett as Sales and Marketing Organiser in 1970. He was chosen from among other applicants 'because he was different in that he could draw (he had been to Art School), and he could add up'. A cheerful, phlegmatic, beer-drinking character, an ardent bicyclist (despite having made his living in the motor industry) only Hallett or someone like him could have risen above the innumerable hindrances which confronted him. He worked from Queen Anne's Gate assisted by half a girl who was permanently in tears of vexation and despair. His warehouse was the narrow entrance passage of No. 42 and it is a moot point whether he more inconvenienced those going in and out or vice versa. In the regions he had to guide wholly inexperienced colleagues – representatives, agents, custodians and volunteers – not all of them by any means co-operative and enthusiastic – on the elements of retailing from the location and equipping the shop, to stocking it and running it. Not only did he succeed in that, but he converted obstruction into enthusiasm. In twelve months under his leadership the Trust opened thirty new retail outlets and, because everything was done on a shoe string, they all by and large made a lot of money and won high praise from visitors.

One of Hallett's great gifts was to be able to choose designers who understood the sort of thing the Trust wanted and were prepared to design for them. In this way

243

successful partnerships developed, the outstanding one probably being that with Pat Albeck.

The third area to be put right was membership. The department was housed in that elegant eighteenth-century building the Blewcoat School, not a quarter of a mile from Queen Anne's Gate and acquired by Carew Wallace for the Trust in 1954. It consists of one very large and lofty room over basements and at one time had a small room added at one corner for the ushers. It was no doubt bedlam when filled with charity school boys and bedlam it was again when some forty devoted ladies sought to maintain the growing membership records on an antiquated manual system. Jack Boles was put in charge when he was Assistant Secretary in 1965. He realised then that 'it was quivering on the edge of collapse through sheer pressure of work'. With expansion of membership likely to continue, he saw that the system must be mechanised, but knew that it was essential to combine that with a personal service.

When he was promoted to be Secretary under the new Director General he retained the responsibility for membership and put his intentions into effect. He says himself that he took immense pains over developing a new system, building in a series of sieves which would extract as wide a range of information as possible. Advised by the Finance Committee, he selected a firm at Beckenham in Kent called Ravensbourne (a subsidiary of Barings and Cooper Bros), resisting the pressure of his new colleague Wheeler to make use of the computer being acquired for accounting. He discovered that membership records had much in common with the maintenance of a share registry for which there were already reliable computer programmes and he was able to build the Trust's special requirements into an existing system.

That, however, was only one side of the job. The other was to keep the personal touch. To achieve that Ravensbourne gave the Trust the exclusive use of a small department. The men in charge, at first Alan Smith and later Roy Budd, were deliberately asked to give, and create in their team, loyalty to, and enthusiasm for the National Trust. The result was successful beyond belief and the efficiency of the system and its operators combined with a helpful courtesy produced results in which the change was made with very little complaint. Designed originally to cope with a roll of half a million it has proved capable of handling one and a half million, and it has one virtue which is beyond price – it is absolutely secure and National Trust subscribers need not fear that because they are on that list they will be on the receiving end of an avalanche of unwanted approaches.

All these developments were taking place when Freddie Bishop became Director General. His style of direction was unobtrusive. That things went smoothly and with increasing rapidity was due in large part to the conditions he created. Provided that his colleagues were going in the right direction he did not interfere with detail, ensured that they were not unduly hampered by committees and gave them the backing they needed to get things done.

There was one major stroke for which he alone must take the credit and one which, if only it had been secured long before, would have made an immense difference to the evolution of the Trust. We have seen how from time to time Governments had made concessions of privilege in terms of tax relief on gifts to the

Trust. However, the situation was still complicated and tax was liable to be paid in certain cases on gifts and bequests whether in money or property. Freddie Bishop knew both the Prime Minister, Edward Heath, and the Chancellor of the Exchequer, Anthony Barber, and made what he describes as 'repeated representations' to them for better taxation treatment for the Trust. Ministers are generally well screened by their officials from importunate requests, and not only was Bishop's direct access to them very useful but the Chancellor in particular held him in high regard. The upshot was that in the Finance Act 1972 the Trust (and some other national institutions) were relieved from any taxes whatsoever on gifts or legacies of any kind and under any circumstances. This not only has the obvious benefit of making the whole of any gift available to the Trust but simplifies the donor's decision of how to make a tax free gift. If there were nothing else for which to thank him – and there is much – that alone would stand as a sufficient contribution from the Trust's second Director General.

Both Winnifrith and Bishop were served by a new Chief Agent, Ivan Hills, who succeeded Christopher Gibbs in January 1969, having been Area Agent for the counties of Kent, Surrey and Sussex since 1948. Christopher Gibbs had been remarkably relaxed during his period of office, which had been a happy and successful time for him. His mark was indelibly made with his creation of the coastal preservation campaign, and for the rest he tidied up and built on the structure laid out by Hubert Smith and encouraged the staff in their various enterprises. He liked to be consulted, and might complain mildly, even if there had been nothing about which to consult, if the flow of communications dried up from one Area or another.

Hills's area was not an easy one to manage in some ways. It was very close to Head Office and both his predecessors as Chief Agent had their homes not far away. Surrey was also one of the strongholds of the early Trust, with large numbers of entrenched local committees. There was also the greatest concentration of members in London and Surrey. All in all it was an exposed position and one in which he had learned the value of diplomacy. The properties in it had, however, enabled him to exploit his knowledge and love of natural history, the North Downs and the Surrey Heaths having been one of the most researched and prized areas ever since Gilbert White wrote his *Natural History of Selborne*. In the 1960s the Trust began to come under some criticism for not developing the opportunities which its wide range of possessions gave it. The National Trust for Scotland had led the way with the appointment of graduates as Naturalist Wardens and on the magnificent mountain of Ben Lawers, managed as a National Nature Reserve, built a 'Visitor Centre' which first explained the place to those who came to see it and then sent them off on 'nature trails', often with the Warden Naturalist, to see for themselves.

At that time too County Naturalists' Trusts were forming rapidly, generally modelled on the lines of the veteran Norfolk Trust. Their objects were to accumulate knowledge, physically preserve natural history where needed, and then disseminate that knowledge both for the benefit of others and to influence conservation. Struggling as they had to for funds, and able at first only to practise preservation on a very few small sites, they naturally looked towards the Trust whose massive land holdings seemed ready-made for nature conservation. They were not always well received, although many of the Trust's agents did take an active part and worked on the County Trusts' Committees.

This was the beginning of a conscious revival of the Trust's positive interest in nature conservation. John Workman, proud of being a Forestry Adviser, suddenly found himself styled Adviser on Conservation and Woodlands. He was admirably suited for this and eventually became accustomed, though not resigned, to the new title. About fifteen years later he read one day that the Trust had appointed a 'Surveyor of Conservation'.

Ivan Hills's expertise on the subject and his anxiety to ensure the better standing of the Trust, led him to embark on an enterprise at Witley on the Surrey heaths which was designed, like Workman's new title, to show the world that the Trust did care. On the heath, sheltered among the pinewoods, the Trust's first Visitor Centre was built. The money was conjured by Hills from Government agencies, benefactors and special funds held by the Trust. The property was selected for a variety of reasons: good communications, by road and rail; a robust ecosystem which would stand up to intensive public access; a good and interesting variety of habitats; a recent history of military use in two wars which prevented possible charges of improper development. Perhaps the most potent reason was that in the warden, Ted Chambers, the Trust had one of those very self-taught but expert naturalists who not only know and love their subject, but can impart information to others, especially the young, in a way which is both intelligible and interesting.

Ivan Hills took up his duties at Queen Anne's Gate as Chief Agent in January 1969, co-incidentally designated European Conservation Year, and his first special task was to continue the process of mending fences with nature conservation interests. The Nature Conservancy Council was even more critical of the Trust than were the County Trusts, probably because the organisation was largely staffed by specialist scientists whose interests tended to be concentrated on their own field. They too saw the Trust as having the disposal of a great many of the choicest of natural history sites and, apparently, neither doing anything with them nor even caring about them.

Lord Antrim was made sharply aware of the Nature Conservancy Council's hostility by its Chairman and, not wishing to have more attacks upon the Trust, gave Hills the job of putting matters right. At first things were put on a formal basis with quarterly meetings between him and the Conservancy's Director, Duncan Poore, but as relationships improved that became unnecessary. The rapprochement was cemented by a conference attended by many of the Trust's agents and NCC staff at their Monks Wood Research Station. It is to the credit of the Trust that it was prepared to learn and profit from the ideas of others. In the two post-war decades it had not quite been like that. By and large the Trust had been ahead of other organisations and Government and became somewhat authoritarian and intolerant of criticism. Perhaps it was due in part to Conrad Rawnsley that it shook off that attitude. When a member of the Council, Dr Eric Duffey, an ecologist, suggested to Ivan Hills that the Trust really ought to know the conservation qualities of its properties and have plans to manage them he did, after a certain amount of prodding, get the Trust's agreement to the setting up of three pilot surveys in Yorkshire, Norfolk and Kent, carried out by university staff.

These proved to be of practical use and illustrated quite clearly the risks involved in not knowing even in general terms what might need looking after. As a result the Trust instituted its own survey. By 1985 this had covered about three-quarters of the properties and, besides producing advice on management regimes, had discovered all sorts of hitherto unsuspected matters of natural history importance. By the end of 1987 the survey was complete, and there was a permanent survey team of four people. Workman's role had been reinforced in 1967 by the appointment of Dr T.W. Wright as his assistant. Bill Wright had left Oundle for the Army in 1942, survived the Normandy landings and the war in Europe, and took a degree in Forestry from Aberdeen University in 1950, going then to research on forest soils at the Macauley Institute for nine years, gaining his doctorate with a study on the afforestation of the Culbin Sands. At the age of thirty-five he forsook research and went south to work for the English Forestry Association as their nurseries and contracts manager, and then went in 1965 to be Head Forester for the Trust in Devon. When his motives were questioned, he simply replied, 'I just want to grow trees.'

Alas, the Trust found him far too valuable to be left to do only that. Two quite different qualities made him particularly useful: he had a scientific training and an analytical mind, and academic experience which earned him the automatic respect of people in that walk of life. He was also very practical and ready to turn his hand to all the physical problems involved in land management including the use of machinery and the ever growing use of chemicals. He was good with people and prepared to devote his skills to the training and encouragement of woodmen and wardens. Early on he became known as 'the Under Workman', and later, when he became involved with studying legislation as it went through Parliament he became first 'Countryside Bill' and then 'Deer Bill'.

Although Hills tended to be dismissive of academic qualification – he would say of those who wished to be National Trust wardens 'They think all they need to have is a Ph.D and a beard!' – he recognised where it was needed and strengthened the staff still further when in 1974 he appointed Jim Hemsley as a second assistant. Hemsley was a botanist who had become Regional Officer for the Nature Conservancy Council in the South West before going out to Tasmania for ten years where he set up the Government conservation service. His addition to the Trust's team made clear beyond any shadow of doubt its commitment to serious nature conservation. In time this advisory staff, together with the Gardens Advisers, were set up in an office in Cirencester. If any further confirmation were needed of the importance of the Trust's role in nature conservation it emerged in 1977 when the N.C.C. published its Conservation Review which for the first time listed and graded all designated Sites of Special Scientific Interest. It showed that the Trust owned 117 Grade 1 sites, 42 Grade 2 and 183 others with a total area of 203,000 acres, making it the largest by far of any private owner of such land.

It is to Ivan Hills that the Trust owes the revival and firm re-establishment of this element in the Trust's work. Other things, however, were to absorb his attention and most particularly the new role of the Chief Agent. In his two predecessors' times the Chief Agent and the Historic Buildings Secretary were, *de jure* and *de facto* in direct charge of the staff in the country as well as their own miniscule staff at Head Office. Benson's regionalisation plans removed this from them entirely and placed the *vis-à-vis* staff in the country, on a purely advisory basis. Ivan Hills, having initially had some twenty-nine land agents responsible to him, found himself required to carry out the same job with no real authority whatsoever. When asked

247

why he didn't do this or that he would say, 'How can I? I have no power; I'm an adviser; I am a eunuch!' Mercifully things didn't work like that in practice.

The past regime had been based on mutual respect and tolerance. Since discipline had been by consent, its theoretical removal had remarkably little effect and the management staff in the country continued to treat the Chief Agent, who was after all a friend and colleague, very much as though there had been no change. If there were difficulties they were generally caused by new and powerful Regional Chairmen flexing their muscles to show that power really had been delegated to them.

A greater problem in the event was caused by the expansion of activities and staff. Hills's land agents in charge of Regions had to cope with the disruption of the accounting system, the steady addition of Historic Buildings Representatives, Regional Information Officers and later Trading and Catering Managers, and to reorganise the properties open to the public to deal with longer opening hours and the other activities which were being introduced. Trading and catering in particular made increasing demands upon custodians (now more usually styled 'administrators') and both the public in general and members in particular began to swell the number of visitors, sometimes to a point at which a house could hardly cope with them. At the same time Head Office and Regional Committees began to demand a better service in terms of information and the volume of office work increased accordingly.

The main channel between region (or area) and Head Office had for a very long time been the Chief Agent. Although the Director General and other Heads of Department began to take a larger part, it was to Hills that the regional agents turned first for help. The role of adjuster was all the harder for him because he was not by nature an expansionist, and he had for a long time felt that the Trust was trying to go too far too fast.

There was another change at the centre when Robin Fedden retired in 1973. It is impossible to speak too highly of his influence on the Trust and in discussion with anyone who knew him there will inevitably be the sort of admiring remarks which have been quoted in this story. Perhaps the most telling in respect of his influence is Fawcett's aphorism 'what Robin Fedden said was what the Trust thought.' Not that everything was right or beneficial – his elitism, for one thing, and the disregard for opinions which were not in tune with his for another. But for the Trust in the quarter century after the war there could have been no-one better able to lift and sustain its aims and efforts.

For his successor, Bobby Gore, he was a difficult man to follow, and wisely he did not try. He said himself of Fedden, 'How difficult for anyone, let alone me, stepping into his shoes – perfectly fitting, always in fashion and with flair, moulded by experience but still as good as new, able to dance in a ballroom or kick a thug, and worn with authority.'

Gore was really the first representative who had a training for the work. He had been born into a Suffolk family in 1921 and went to his father's old school, Wellington. His upbringing was wholly country, and his favourite pastimes shooting and hunting. The war took him into a machine gun regiment and then to

TOP Brownsea Island in Poole Harbour, off the Dorset coast. In 1961 Mrs Bonham-Christie, the island's reclusive owner, died and this mysterious place, with its wealth of wild life, was taken over by the Trust.

ABOVE Cape Cornwall, an important breeding site for many birds, was purchased for the Trust in 1987 by H. J. Heinz Limited. Signs of Bronze Age habitation have been found there.

ABOVE The Blewcoat School in Victoria is one of the Trust's few London properties. The School, built in 1709, is now used by the Trust as its London shop and information centre.

RIGHT The Trust's London headquarters at Queen Anne's Gate. On the left is one of the 18th-century houses in which the Trust lived from 1945 to 1983, when the staff moved across the road to 36 Queen Anne's Gate, an Edwardian building originally occupied by the Anglo-American Oil Company.

North Africa and Italy, during the course of which he was twice wounded, and the second – a shoulder wound – was of some importance in his career. This mild-mannered, diffident and quietly spoken individual perceives himself as always having been something of a rebel. He expressed this while in Italy by going off on his own to look at paintings in the neighbourhood while his fellow soldiers were generally relaxing in a very different way.

His shoulder never did mend properly and that meant that he could no longer with comfort shoot or ride, and this was a factor in deciding him to take a three year course at the Courtauld Institute of fine arts after being demobilised. He did not much care for the style of teaching, which was directed mainly towards passing examinations, and found that, since he was only directed to looking at good pictures, he found merit difficult to judge. He spent as much time as possible in self-education, looking at pictures on the Continent, but in any event he passed the three year course in two years and went to work for Sotheby's for three years. There he learned what he had missed at the Courtauld – a necessary knowledge of bad pictures and the ability to form judgements.

After that initiation he was occupied for several years cataloguing various collections until one day he was invited by Professor (later Sir) Anthony Blunt to join him for a drink and to meet Lord Crawford. Blunt was Gore's *beau ideal*. He had known him since his days at the Courtauld and found him thoughtful and friendly, cultivated and a superb and knowledgeable judge of paintings. Besides his appointments at the National Gallery and to the Queen he was Honorary Adviser to the National Trust. When they met Lord Crawford told Gore that the Trust intended to appoint a paid, although not full-time, adviser on paintings. They discussed the proposal and Gore gave Lord Crawford a lift home, on the way saying that if they eventually decided to offer him the job he would like to take it. 'Oh, but we have decided; we would like to have you.' And that was that.

Blunt must almost certainly have instigated the move, and have proposed Bobby Gore for the job. It is clear that he thought highly of his abilities, for he would never have entrusted what was already a very important collection to a second rater. Blunt had been very active on behalf of the Trust but, although he remained Honorary Adviser, he did not do a great deal after Gore began work. Looking back at his influence on the Trust's attitude towards, and care of, its paintings Bobby Gore sees it as consistently highly principled and wholly beneficial. When Blunt's treachery to the country was eventually exposed, it must have caused shock and distress to many people, including Gore, but his professional standards and integrity appear always to have been maintained wholly separate from other activities.

As Adviser on Paintings Gore found he had two main tasks, the first being restoration and the second cataloguing. Neither had been tackled seriously before, and both involved not only technical problems but also the application of tact and persuasiveness in dealing with the various people who were concerned – donors, representatives, custodians – and judgement not only as to what was needed but also what was appropriate. Gore gives himself the credit of seeing paintings as part of the decoration of a room and not simply as objects in isolation. To clean and restore just one picture out of many simply on the grounds of its individual importance does, he feels, disregard and upset the balance of the furnishings.

In 1964 Gore went as Representative to the South East and he regards it as the happiest time of his working life, both because of the interest of the work and the excellent working relationship he had with Ivan Hills as Area Agent, and with his assistant and successor Ivor Blomfield. In that post he formed the views which, when he succeeded Fedden as Historic Buildings Secretary, dictated his objectives.

Before promotion Bobby Gore had become concerned about the care of the multitude of objects in the Trust's houses. Until about 1960 these had been looked after by people who had been brought up in the housekeeping disciplines of the nineteenth century, which had at least been adequate to ensure their survival without excessive deterioration. As the last of that generation went their less well-instructed successors coincided with the increase in numbers of visitors and the consequent wear and tear which that brought. At the same time, museums were becoming much more scientific and positive in the way in which they looked after things. Just as the nature conservationists had, the academics and administrators of the museum world cast disapproving and somewhat jealous eyes on the fabulous but in their opinion sadly neglected collections of the National Trust.

Gore's close connection with that world – he continued to be adviser on Pictures – made him aware of what he describes as 'an attitude of potential or actual hostility'. He tried to persuade Robin Fedden to take some measures to combat it, but without success. The museums and picture galleries were concerned only with the preservation and display of objects in isolation while the Trust also wished to preserve but to retain objects in their settings and as parts of a coherent story. Robin Fedden was reluctant to believe that objects which had apparently survived for one or two hundred years without special attention must now be regarded as fragile. On succeeding Fedden as Historic Buildings Secretary, Gore set up four aims for himself: to fend off and neutralise museum hostility; to institute preventative conservation and revive the old housekeeping disciplines; to employ specialist advice on interior decoration; to achieve a full and proper cataloguing of all the possessions in the Trust's care.

He summed up his ambitions when asked by Ted Fawcett what he hoped to achieve: 'I hope to bring curatorship up to museum standards, while maintaining the atmosphere of a private house, and to give visitors whatever the Trust can offer them, but not necessarily what they expect.'

The museums were by nature not enemies but friends, and had been consistently helpful with advice and the provision of specialist facilities for the repair of particularly precious objects. Gore's recipe for rapprochement was to bring influential individuals into the National Trust fold.

The Benson streamlining of committees was both sensible and practical but it left the Trust without the direct involvement of all but one or two influential people, who sat on the Properties Committee, in its several main fields of work. This deficiency was gradually remedied by the creation of informal panels – Estates, Nature Conservation, Gardens and the Arts. This last was Gore's creation and he brought on to it some who had been displaced from membership of the Historic Buildings Committee and others directly from the sphere which he wished to identify with the interests of the Trust. One such was a man whom he first met back in his days at the Courtauld, Michael Jaffé, Director of the Fitzwilliam Museum in Cambridge. In this he succeeded so well that Jaffé quite soon joined the Trust's Wessex Regional Committee on which he is still serving.

Gore eventually succeeded in his own words in getting people from such institutions as the British Museum, the National Gallery and National Portrait Galleries and the V & A, to form a team to bat for the National Trust.'

The business of preventative conservation, once seriously contemplated, revealed itself as an immense undertaking. The Trust had in its care the accumulated chattels of some four hundred years, and they included fabrics, furniture, paintings, china, glass, silver, ironwork, pewter, copper, brass, lead, marble, stone. The oldest and rarest were often least at risk because their conservation needs were known and catered for. In other cases the Trust was aware that work must be done but there was a scarcity of skilled workshops and of money too. There remained a mass of things which just needed a bit of old-fashioned care.

It was the last category which gave rise to the engagement of Sheila Stainton and Hermione Sandwith. Sheila had worked on textile repairs for the Trust since 1961 but her interests and common sense enabled her to take on formally in 1977 the title of Housekeeper. Hermione had a more specialist training and in 1974 was engaged to undertake the care of pictures, generally at the property to which they belonged, which avoided the risks and problems of bringing them to London. In 1980 a Surveyor of Conservation, David Winfield, was appointed, and Miss Sandwith became his Deputy. She with Miss Stainton worked for several years on a *Manual of Housekeeping*. This was originally intended as an internal guide for the Trust's custodians, but was so practical and excellent that it was published for sale in 1984.

Seventeenth-century textiles – often in the form of tapestry or embroidery – are among the most fragile and easily damaged articles in country houses and the problem of those at Knole resulted in the setting up of a repair workshop there. That was followed by one at Blickling and another at Hughenden, much of the work done by relays of devoted volunteers under the instruction and supervision of a professional. It was obviously desirable to extend the system to other crafts and furniture seemed to be the obvious choice. The pros and cons were discussed but eventually, mainly because of the availability of suitable people, sculpture and metalwork were preferred. All this has taken more than a decade to evolve, but the pattern and standard has been set and the disappearance of skilled conservation which so alarmed Gore twenty years ago has been reversed.

Interior decoration has proved more difficult. While representative in the South East, Gore was responsible for the restoration of the interior of Clandon, for which, he employed John Fowler, of the Mayfair firm of Colefax & Fowler (an episode dealt with later in more detail). This was highly successful and set new standards for the Trust, although there were a good many critics at the time. Gore had suddenly realised how deficient in taste and knowledge the Trust was when, after visiting one of its houses he stopped at a roadhouse for dinner on the way home and found that the newly papered room he had seen had the same wallpaper as the bar he was in!

The fourth objective should have been the simplest, but proved quite the most difficult to attain. Cataloguing the contents of a house involved identifying every object, no matter how small or large, giving it a number, a written description with as much accurate information about it as possible, a note of its position in the house, marking it with its number and finally photographing it. This tedious, time-consuming but absolutely essential work was the task of Representatives, and it was one which was almost universally disliked and avoided as long as possible. Historic

Buildings Representatives were thin on the ground. When Gore took over there were seven – Michael Trinick who was also Regional Secretary and four Honoraries. Five years later there were eight (with Trinick again doing another job as well), one assistant and three Honoraries. It was not easy to find new recruits. There were very few people available who were knowledgeable, mature and with some experience of the conduct of business, and there was not then a sufficiency of experienced staff in the Trust to take in and train those who had a suitable academic training, with the result that young graduates in, say, history of art, were taken on and pitched straight into executive jobs of complexity and responsibility before they had even learned to look after themselves. This caused strain for them and stress for their colleagues. Most survived to become competent at their job, but in the meantime many things went to the wall, cataloguing being one.

The changes that Frederick Bishop presided over until he retired in 1975 meant that the Trust had become a much more modern and professional organisation. There were major developments which affected virtually everyone concerned in the Trust, committees and staff throughout the country, members and the general public. When he felt that he had to give up he left the Trust extending its expertise and the range of its responsibilities.

Chapter XIX

Interpreting History

I n the end what really matters in the life of the National Trust is the preservation of its properties and their enjoyment by the public. For the first sixty years of its existence most, if not all, the initiatives in this direction started at the top and were passed downwards. With the gradual growth of a professional staff in the provinces, the tide began to turn the other way and most good ideas in terms of property management were produced there and were adopted by, and disseminated from, Head Office staff and committees.

In the history of preservation it is right to start with Cubby Acland in the Lake District. The ingredients for the National Trust's success were all there – beautiful scenery, intense public interest, a tradition of preservation, and extensive ownership by the Trust. Acland brought to his work here an acute mind, an unconventional imagination, energy in execution and a somewhat autocratic attitude towards obstructions and hindrances. In short, he got things done.

Central to his management policy was the belief that the hill sheep farm formed the landscape and that the landscape's continued survival depended upon this system. He thought of sheep as lawn mowers and landscape gardeners. In the two decades after the war, and later on too, there was a general trend towards larger and fewer farms, and pressure for higher rents. While that may have been appropriate in the lowlands, it would not serve for the genuine hill farm and Acland said so. He was determined to maintain a viable community which would accept the hard work and moderate returns of the hill farm, but he saw too that the system needed help. He pushed for and got as much money as possible to invest in better housing conditions for the farming families, and for buildings to make farming more profitable. Where possible, he tried to provide facilities which would enable farmers to share in the money to be made from tourists, either through taking in guests, or by providing self-catering accommodation.

He also did his best to preserve the landlord and tenant system by keeping on the Trust's estate the so called 'farming ladder', with small places where a man could start part-time, then larger ones which were full-time for a single-handed farmer and finally ones which would give work to a whole family. In this context the landlord's herd of 'hefted' sheep was very important. Hefted means born and bred and accustomed to live on a particular area of fell. If there are no such sheep on a farm it is a difficult and expensive process to instal a new flock. For that reason it is customary in many places for the landlord to own the sheep and then the flock can never – legitimately – be removed, and, moreover, a new tenant with small capital does not have to find the cash to buy them: he pays for them in the rent.

This attitude of Acland's was not original, and indeed as we have seen, it follows directly upon Beatrix Heelis's ideas as expressed in her lifetime and in her will. His contribution was to insist upon the observance of that policy and to support it with practical measures when the accepted ideas of the time would have eroded it beyond recall. The general lines of his work were followed by other agents of the Trust in the hills of Wales and Northern England.

The other side of the coin for Acland was the enjoyment which this countryside could give. To the Trust before his time 'open space' was just that – commons, moorland and so on – but public access to farmland was only possible if there existed a *public* footpath. Hence the bitter struggles to prevent those rights being stopped up. It is, of course, always open to a landowner to give the public permission to enter his property and this the Trust had done in limited circumstances. Farms, however, were occupied by farm tenants and unless special rights were reserved in the tenancy agreement the owner could not unilaterally invite the public to cross a field. Cubby Acland decided that if it were desirable for the public to walk on farmland then a right to give them permission must be negotiated with the farm tenant.

This is what he did, and uphill work it was too for many years. Public access is often a genuine disadvantage to a farmer and particularly so in stone wall country where field divisions are so easily damaged, but Acland, whose sense of fairness was almost an obsession, was perfectly prepared to offer some *quid pro quo* – 'mod cons' for the house or better stockhousing. Today the so called 'permissive path' is a common-place device of management, and generally provision is made for it in the tenancy agreement and any real agricultural disadvantage is reflected in a lower rent. But it was Acland who showed how it could and should be done.

Cubby loved growing trees, a trait inherited from his father, but he also believed in using them for as many purposes as possible. The screening of car parks, caravans and camp sites are all of great importance in the Lake District and Cubby used trees boldly for this purpose. The National Park Authority did not always agree with his ideas, nor did some members of the Trust's Head Office committees. Cubby's first site for touring caravans was achieved with the help of the Caravan Club. It was in woodland at Manesty on the shores of Derwentwater, entirely charming within and wholly unobtrusive from without, and it provided a pattern for other sites.

Camping in the Lakes had been popular for a very long time but before the Second War the number of campers was not overwhelming and their khaki tents inoffensive in the landscape. Everything changed in the twenty years which followed that war. Numbers increased enormously in step with paid holidays and personal transport, and the khaki tent was replaced by brilliant blue or orange. The dale heads began to acquire a scatter of these brilliant points of colour which disrupted the composition of the landscape. Cubby Acland's solution was to withdraw the tents from the farms into camp sites where they could be somewhat screened by trees and where lavatories and wash places could be provided.

Acland also attacked from another angle. He had already produced a chart of colours acceptable for static caravans (those placed on a permanent site on which they stayed throughout the year), and the idea was taken up by Planning Authorities.

254

He now began to campaign for the elimination of brightly coloured tents, and produced another chart of acceptable colours. He toured the annual Camping Exhibition at Olympia actually sticking National Trust approval labels on such tents as he deemed satisfactory, and persuaded firms to advertise their products as having been given a National Trust seal. To any who turned up on a camp site with such a tent he gave one night's free camping.

The Trust's holiday cottage business began with Acland in the Lakes. Quite a number of small dwellings of one kind or another came into the Trust's ownership almost by accident and some of these were quite unsuited to permanent habitation. There were any number of reasons – difficulty of access, no possibility of electricity, poor water supply or simply unfitness as a building. On the other hand they could often provide accommodation for holidaymakers who wanted little more than a base from which to go walking, or a retreat a bit more comfortable than a tent. Acland accordingly furnished such places on minimum standards and made holiday lettings at lowish rents. This lead was followed first by Michael Trinick in Cornwall, although he swung the product to the other extremity, providing luxury accommodation at very considerable capital cost and let at the very highest prices possible. There are now over 160 National Trust holiday cottages in many parts of the country.

Acland also pioneered the provision of basic accommodation for groups of young people who needed a base for walking, climbing, canoeing and other activities which were being promoted by organisations like the Outward Bound scheme. This he did by using small barns or old quarry buildings, making them wind and water tight, providing water and some sort of sanitation, and simple cooking arrangements. These he called 'bothies', the old term for workers' lodgings. Later he organised at Wray on Windermere a purpose-built complex which provided for the same purpose but with much more accommodation and better equipment. It was styled 'Base Camp NT' a mountaineering flavour deliberately implied because the intention was that it should be used to enable youth groups to explore the Trust's Lake District properties. It was opened on 13 September 1969 by Jack Longland, a notable climber, and by that date the Director of Education for Derbyshire and a Countryside Commissioner. A condition of occupation was that each group should undertake at least one day's work in a week on conservation tasks. This lead was also followed by Cubby's colleagues and 'basecamps' may now be found in Devon, Derbyshire, Wiltshire, Norfolk, Northumberland, Shropshire, Sussex and several other counties.

All Acland's concern to combine the preservation of the Lakes with the fullest possible enjoyment of the area by the public is expressed in his development of Fell Foot at the southern extremity of Windermere. These eighteen acres had been accepted as a gift from Mrs E.L. Hedley, as a memorial to her husband. It was undistinguished as landscape and already much used by the boating fraternity, and it boasted a splendid, large boathouse. There had been no intention to hold it for preservation but simply to give access to the lake, but 'by accident' it was included in the items listed for the Executive Committee to resolve to be inalienable, and inalienable it became. Acland saw Fell Foot as a place at which the Trust could properly provide for the sort of popular use inappropriate to most of its properties.

The Charity Commission, having considered the circumstances, said that just this once it would be acceptable, and so Acland went ahead. The relatively new Countryside Commission was at that time promoting the idea of 'country parks': places in the country which could bear a very considerable intensity of public use, in that way relieving pressure on other places, and were prepared to give substantial grants to establish them. So Fell Foot became the first 'country park' on Trust property. It now provides car parking, sites for twenty-six touring caravans, a slipway for launching boats (but no motor boats), bathing and picnic places, rowing boats for hire, a tea room and a shop (and, inevitably, visitors' lavatories) and self-catering chalets to sleep six.

With that one leap forward Acland went beyond anything that his colleagues could imitate, but the example opened their eyes to other and different opportunities. Anthony Lord, who was Cubby's assistant from 1958, and who succeeded him on his retirement in 1972, said, 'He put the Trust on the map, was a marvellous speaker, with tremendous enthusiasm, a great raconteur and host. He gave himself unstintingly in support of the Trust, more than anyone else I have ever known, perhaps because the Trust was his life.'

Tony Lord had to learn to admire Cubby Acland the hard way, and one day he was a passenger in Cubby's car following an articulated lorry down Dunmail Raise before the old road was widened. 'The driver threw a cigarette packet out of the window; Cubby roared with fury, opened his door at 20 m.p.h. picking up the packet, overtook the lorry on a blind bend, slammed on his brakes having swerved across the road so that no one could pass. The lorry just stopped after an eight wheel skid. Cubby leaped out and berated the poor driver who by that time was a gibbering wreck anyhow, returned, jumped into the car and said, 'How bloody some people are!'

Working in a very different environment, Michael Trinick was cast in something of the same mould, always ready to look for ways to improve the presentation of the Trust's properties and to increase the enjoyment which could be gained from them. He was the first person in the National Trust to try to show a visitor to a house something more than the state rooms and the fine furnishings. As often happens, it was necessity that first sent him along that road. At Compton Castle, just outside Torbay, there was really not very much for a tourist to see. The donor, Commander Gilbert, a descendant of the family which produced Humphrey Gilbert and Walter Raleigh, had bought back the property in 1930 after a gap of 130 years, and rebuilt the great hall, which lies across the centre of the castle courtyard. That and the chapel were the only parts of the interior which could be shown. With Commander Gilbert's enthusiastic support, Trinick decided to try to re-equip the old kitchen, which was little more than a derelict stone-floored space in the base of one of the Towers. A spit, pot hooks, an iron door for the old bread oven, a plain deal table and some ancient kitchenware brought it to life and greatly increased a visitor's sense of reality.

From there it was only a small step to do the same at Saltram, with the difference that the scope there was tremendous. It merited a pamphlet of its own which lists the elaborate cooking range of about 1810 and the spits turned by a fan driven by the hot air in the chimney, and the much later hot plates and ovens of the free standing stove with its under-floor flue. There is a *batterie de cuisine* of 600 pieces, and who should have provided most of them but John Smith. So the list goes on, right down to cockroach traps which were filled with stale beer.

Even the Great Kitchen at Saltram was later surpassed in interest by the late nineteenth-century domestic offices at Lanhydrock, where the full range of pantries and larders survived with their equipment.

Michael Trinick's contribution to the ever-widening efforts of the Trust was to look beyond the qualities of architectural and artistic interest and to try to restore houses to a human scale. The usual attitude of the promoters of the Country Houses Scheme had been that only the public face of the house was of interest. It was Trinick who demonstrated that the whole household was both of historic importance and of popular interest. He re-opened bedrooms at Arlington Court and a nursery too. Although the kitchens there had lost their equipment and were used as a restaurant, he hung the walls with evocative enlargements of photographs from Rosalie Chichester's albums which display in great detail the place as it was at the beginning of the century, and the cook and kitchen maids too.

One leading member of the Trust's Head Office Committees who had a considerable influence on the efforts made by the staff to enlarge the attractions available to visitors to the Trust's properties was Lord De La Warr. Underlying much of what he did, was a strong desire that the world should become a better place in which to live. He very much wanted what was preserved to be enjoyed. How had the country house been enjoyed in private ownership? By the owner inviting guests and offering them whatever entertainment he could. What better then than to treat visitors as guests? Certainly they could not be asked for a whole weekend, nor compelled to play charades, but they could be offered enough to enable them to spend an entire day enjoying themselves. As Chairman of the Estates Committee he was a constant traveller around the Trust's properties and in regular and close touch with the agents, who came to know that enterprises on those lines would be welcomed and supported.

John Tetley had a special problem on his hands in the shape of the incredible Norman Gothick Penrhyn Castle, near Bangor. Of that immense building only some eight rooms were open to visitors and public taste in the 1950s scarcely encompassed appreciation of the peculiar qualities of the place. Tetley's struggle with a combination of disastrous disrepair and a complete absence of income are touched on later, but one result was to make revenue from visitors a necessity. A circular from Head Office reported the offer from the Industrial Locomotive Preservation Society of a small steam tank engine. That gave Tetley the idea that the stables – 'a gaunt, unfriendly area with neither horse nor carriage to give it interest or meaning' – might be used to house a collection of such locomotives. He saw that as steam engines went out of use, those that were preserved would gain in rarity and interest, while there was an especial justification in associating industrial locomotives with Penrhyn, whose owners had amassed their fortune from the great slate quarries in which such engines had become the main form of transport.

The decision was perhaps the easiest part: the practical problems were daunting. That they were successfully overcome was due to John Tetley's quiet tenacity and to the resource and enthusiasm of Richard Parry, the Trust's first administrator at the Castle. There was also the very fortunate arrival on the scene of young Iowerth Jones. He was working as an engine driver in the Penrhyn Quarry. He could see that his job was likely to go and he not only needed another but he wanted it to be with steam engines, and so he came to the Trust. Vernon Davies was already on the staff. He was a skilled joiner by trade, and like many others in that line, could turn his hand to many other building trades. These two between them did all the work of receiving, restoring and installing the nine locomotives in the collection. They stripped them down, cleaned them up, discovering under layers of dirt what lay beneath, then rebuilt them, repainted them in their original livery, including the fine line work which that involved, each operation taking weeks of painstaking work.

Among the locomotives lent to the collection was one named 'Charles' which drew the slate trucks from the Bethesda Quarry to Port Penrhyn; it could not have had a more appropriate retirement home. There was also the 'Fire Queen', a real veteran which had worked in the Dinorwic Quarries from the 1840s for some fifty years. It will by this time come as no surprise to learn that the man who saved it and then loaned it to the Trust was none other than John Smith.

Getting these bulky and very heavy machines into the stable yard was a task in itself. They were brought by road on low loader trailers but first had to be got through the entrance archway of the Grand Lodge, half a mile from their destination. Two had to have smoke stacks removed and in one case a length of track laid for it through the archway. It was then unloaded on to the track, pushed through and then picked up again by the low loader which had been sent round by another route. The manoeuvres in the stable yard had to be precise. Having got the engine off its trailer and on to a specially laid section of track, the whole lot, track with engine on it weighing several tons, had to be moved sideways with crow bars until it lay under the covered arcade which would be its home. John Tetley emphasises the extraordinarily hard work and care that Jones and Davies had to put into the business of getting the locomotives in. 'It is to their undying credit,' he says, 'that we never had one toppled or over-running the track.'

The locomotive collection most certainly did its job of increasing the interest of visitors to the Castle, and so did the collection of dolls which John Tetley accepted as a gift from Miss Philippa Judge for display in the house. These antique toys are of great charm.

It was a few years later, in 1964, that a similar offer was circulated to areas. This time it was the Museum of Wales which had been given a collection of nineteenth-century carriages by the Marquis of Bute. They had his state coach on display at St Fagan's but had no room for the other eight. There were two bids, one from Clumber Park in Nottinghamshire and the other from Arlington Court in Devon, each having a stable block in which the vehicles could be housed. Arlington was chosen, and the carriages which were lying in open-ended Nissen huts at St Fagan's were put on low loaders, fortuitously attracting their first publicity each time the drivers stopped for tea on the long haul round the head of the Bristol Channel.

There was no one on the staff of the Trust in Devon who knew much about horse-drawn vehicles beyond farm carts, waggons and pony traps. Dick Meyrick had just arrived as Assistant Land Agent and had the responsibility of managing the North Devon properties and so he naturally got the job of dealing with the carriages. However, the mere mention by the press of the advent of the Bute carriages was enough to attract an enquiry from young Eric Homewood of London who had worked for coachbuilders and in the film industry but who wanted to set up on his own as a restorer of carriages. He had little money, and needed premises and work to start him off.

Dick Meyrick took the plunge. The little small-holding of Arlington Mill had just fallen vacant and the house was let to Homewood, and an estate building close to the stables made into a workshop. The first requirement for that was that it should be rendered dust free lest the high gloss of the varnish should be marred. The carriages were put on display in the coach house and arcade of the stableyard and withdrawn one by one for restoration, forming an additional attraction for visitors. Among those who came to see them was Hugh McCausland who subsequently wrote to the Trust to say that one of the vehicles was wrongly named. Meyrick's nose for expert guidance led him to think that McCausland was likely to be very knowledgeable. He was indeed knowledgeable and was prepared to put that knowledge freely at the disposal of the Trust, not only for Arlington but for any other purpose and eventually he was formally appointed as Honorary Adviser to the Trust.

It was Meyrick's inspiration in enlisting Hugh McCausland's help that changed the enterprise from the limited one of exhibiting the Bute carriages to forming a representative collection. At one time McCausland thought that Arlington might house a national collection but there were practical objections to that, including the feeling that the stables were not nearly big enough, and the location, remote in the hills of North Devon, was not right. Nevertheless the thing took off and in 1966 the Trust launched an appeal for £2,000 to help pay for further restoration. Meyrick heard that the Crown Equerry, the member of the royal household responsible for the Royal Mews, had paid a visit, and on McCausland's advice wrote to ask if he might consult with him. This resulted in a visit to the Mews and a great deal of helpful advice from Colonel Sir John Miller. It was McCausland, too, who persuaded the notable whip, Sir Dymoke White to leave some of his vehicles to the Trust.

Carriages without horses are in some ways rather sad and there was an early attempt to remedy that. Bob, a strong black bob-tailed superannuated cob, came from a home for retired horses, because everything in this sort of exercise had to be contrived with little or no money. There was a tub (or 'governess') cart in good running order and the idea was that Bob should give rides to visitors, and a girl keen on horses was engaged to look after him. Keen she may have been but experienced not. Immediately Bob was unboxed he was dressed and put into the shafts, and expressed his displeasure by trying to kick harness and tub cart to pieces. That was not his true character and having been allowed to settle down and given a refresher course, he turned out to be tractable, willing and steady.

Again at McCausland's suggestion, Dick Meyrick approached the Science Museum to see whether they would lend some of their surplus vehicles, which they did, Philip Sumner of the museum giving further help and advice. The collection so prospered that by 1972 there were twenty-six vehicles drawn by horses, motor cars of 1899, 1926 and 1946 (the last being a Daimler built for Queen Mary), a score of farm and estate vehicles, half a dozen perambulators and the harness room revived and full of tack. By great good luck the stables were built into a steepish slope and it was possible to get access to the forage loft by building a bridge from the higher ground behind. That held the greater part of the collection, the farm carts being put into a simple open fronted shed along one side of the yard.

The great day came when Sir John Miller found a pair of bays which the now more prosperous collection could afford to buy. After the death of the old cob they gave visitors rides down the long drive to the lake in a waggonette. The first coachman was a local farmer, Alec Pugh. He was later succeeded by Russell Forehead who in aspect and character would have been indistinguishable from one of the great mail-coach whips of the pre-railway era. Among his qualifications when he applied for the job was that he had been responsible for camels and horses used in making the film *Lawrence of Arabia*. Meyrick understandably had his reservations but made another inspired decision and engaged him. Forehead subsequently proved him right by making a tremendous success of a job calling for skill and care combined with showmanship.

These two land agents and Meyrick, with no special knowledge but with flair and judgement each made notable contributions to De La Warr's idea of extending the pleasure of visiting a house. Both properties are in the hinterland of holiday coasts and both are a boon to holiday makers on a wet day. Everything benefits: the visitor; the revenue; the cause of preservation in the widest sense.

The work of Bobby Gore at Clandon, near Guildford, has already been referred to, but needs to be looked at in more detail because, by its example, it lifted the care and presentation of country houses to a new level. The house was rather sad when it came to the National Trust in 1956. It had been the home of the Onslow family since it was built in the 1730s and they had owned the property for seventy years before that. The interior decoration had naturally undergone a number of vicissitudes, the latest of which involved a lot of that whiting-over with which the twentieth century sought to cure the indigestion of late Victorian flamboyance. Then from 1941 until the end of that war it was used as a repository for the Public Records Office, which was no doubt less damaging than other wartime uses but represented a period of neglect and accumulating dirt. The 6th Earl, having gone through the Western Desert and Italy with 7th Armoured Division, was captured in Normandy and spent the rest of the war in a prison camp. On his release and return to England his father died and he determined to live at Clandon. He did so under increasing difficulties for five years, but was eventually driven by rising costs and high taxation to move to a small house on the edge of the park. Clandon stood empty until his aunt, the Countess of Iveagh, came to the rescue, acquired the house from her nephew and gave it to the National Trust.

The structural condition was taken care of to a large extent by grants from the Historic Buildings Council, but Gore, taking up his job as Representative in 1964, found a cold looking, bare house, underfurnished and desperately in need of care.

In 1968 Mrs David Gubbay died. She had been a woman of considerable wealth and one of the great connoisseur collectors of her generation. She bequeathed her collection – furniture, porcelain, jade, metal work, textiles and carpets – to the National Trust. Along with the collection itself came a handsome residual legacy of £114,000.

It was Gore who saw that this was Clandon's chance. He knew that if only money could be found, much of the original interior decoration, which was mostly there under the later work and the grime, could be restored. He felt that the Gubbay objects would be beautifully suited to the rooms. There was opposition, of course, and among the objections it was said that the furniture was too small to furnish rooms on the Clandon scale, but as Bobby Gore pointed out there was enough big stuff there already to provide a frame.

So it was agreed that the collection should go to Clandon and that the money could quite properly be used to fit the house for its reception. This was Gore's opportunity to demonstrate what could be done by a skilled interior decorator with a knowledge of and respect for the techniques and practices of the past; Gore turned to John Fowler, of Colefax & Fowler. This was by no means the first work Fowler had done for the Trust. He had been involved over the previous ten years with the redecoration of individual rooms at Claydon, Petworth, West Wycombe and Shugborough. Clandon, however, was to be the apogee of his National Trust work for reasons which are difficult to explain, but the effects of which were dramatic.

John Cornforth, who contributed a penetrating and sympathetic essay to the 1979 edition of *National Trust Studies*, after John Fowler's death, says 'it was there that John Fowler's gifts as a teacher became apparent'. Fowler completely immersed himself in every aspect of the interior: not just in the painting or papering but in the curtains, drapes and upholsteries. He studied in immense detail how the Gubbay collection should be married to the very grand Onslow pieces.

So self-effacing is Bobby Gore that it is difficult to look beyond the effervescent, extrovert Fowler, but it is quite certain that without Gore to encourage and to ease the innumerable problems, the work would not have had the stupendous success that it did. Gore worked with the then Assistant Agent, John Garrett who was responsible for the ordering of the work and accounting for it. Fired by the opportunities at Clandon he devoted himself to making Mrs Gubbay's legacy stretch as far – indeed further – than it could reasonably have been expected to.

Gore was with the Director General one day when Philip Henman called to say that he had heard someone giving a lecture announce that money was needed for Clandon and to ask how much was wanted. The unrecognised lecturer had been Gore, but the money needed had already been subscribed by another benefactor, Kenneth Levy.

A shop and a restaurant in the basement completed the preparations for visitors. This was one of the first times a shop had been provided in a country house. The restaurant was put in the hands of a licensee whose menu was required to match Bobby's most exacting standards. Clandon was re-opened in 1971 to crowds of visitors and universal acclaim. Bobby Gore summed the achievement up under three heads – decoration; preservation; presentation.

In Graham Stuart Thomas the Trust harboured not only an outstanding adviser for its gardens but an authority on roses. He had gradually been collecting examples of the older shrub roses and had been looking for somewhere in which to establish a permanent collection. In gardens owned by the Trust it is seldom possible to be drastically innovative because that is likely to damage or destroy what ought to be preserved, and so it was not easy to accommodate a wholly new element. However, in 1971 Mrs Gilbert Russell, who had given Mottisfont Abbey in the Hampshire basin to the Trust, reserving some things to her own use, decided to give up the kitchen garden which she had retained, and the Trust agreed to establish Graham Thomas's collection there. The site was easy of access both in its general position and in itself, with space for cars to park and, within its own walls, separate from the pleasure grounds. Curiously enough the soil was far from ideal, but that was capable of improvement.

Would the carriages at Arlington have endured on their own longer than the old roses? The roses at least could renew themselves but once lost they would be lost for ever and are not capable of being reproduced in imitation. Thomas's own description sounds like a battle cry and a roll of honour. His living roses are – 'Gallicas, Damasks, Centifolias, Mosses, early hybrids of the China Rose, like the Bourbon and Noisette'. The National Trust can be proud that this most unusual and fragile of collections has been entrusted to its care, and Graham Stuart Thomas can be satisfied that he has set an example of an essay in permanency which inspires the professional and the lay horticultural world.

Some new ideas that have emerged in the last twenty years are not new at all, but simply revivals or altered applications of well-established traditions; one such is the ornamental stocking of park lands. The deer park and the coney warren were mediaeval methods of ensuring a food supply with, in the case of deer, the chance of a bit of a chase thrown in. Later the deer became appreciated for their decorative character. Nine parks with herds of deer are owned by the Trust, of which all but one are of genuine antiquity (Attingham Park, Shropshire; Charlecote Park, Warwickshire; Dunham Massey, Greater Manchester; Dyrham Park, Avon; Knole, Kent; Lyme Park, Cheshire; Nostell Priory, West Yorkshire; Petworth, West Sussex; Waddesdon Manor, Buckinghamshire). Many more parks did once have deer herds, but they were put down for a variety of reasons, generally economic ones. However, parks did require grazing and, as well as taking in domestic farm stock, there was often some attempt to keep either animals which were decorative or were the owner's particular interest. As a result the Trust somewhat incidentally acquired flocks of the horned black and white Jacob sheep and Shetland ponies at Arlington and more Jacobs at Charlecote, where they shared the park with the descendants of those fallow deer among which the young Shakespeare is said to have gone poaching. At Stourhead, Sir Henry Hoare left a herd of Dairy Shorthorn cattle which subsequently the Trust allowed to go on the doubtful grounds of economy. More recently Ralph Bankes's splendid herd of Red Devon cattle have come with the park at Kingston Lacy.

More generally, however, and especially after the exigencies of the Second War turned most parks into farmland, the Trust became satisfied with any ordinary farm stock which would pay for its keep. Not only did this result in the almost universal sight of the inappropriate black and white Friesian, but the drive for profit resulted in pressure for the 'improvement' (agriculturally), of parks by draining, liming, spraying and fencing into paddocks which bade fair to ruin the park as such. By 1970 the Trust had begun to see the error of its ways and to try to reverse the process. This coincided with a national awakening to the fact that historic breeds were diminishing to the point of extinction. At Hardwick Hall in Derbyshire the park which had been badly damaged by dairy farming, came to hand and it seemed sensible to stock it with animals which were appropriate to the area, interesting to look at and which would contribute to the preservation of breeds which were in danger of disappearing.

The choice was not difficult. The Longhorn cattle which once dominated the rural scene had not originated in the Midlands but had been developed there 200 years before by the great breeder Bakewell, not thirty miles away in Leicestershire. With varied colours from an orange brindle through to reds and whites, and with their immense spread of horn, they are exciting to look at, while at the same time extremely docile. Then there was a breed of sheep, the horned White Faced Woodland from the Peak District estates of the Dukes of Devonshire. Since the Trust had inherited both Hardwick and the Hope Woodlands it seemed appropriate to give a home to a breed, to the improvement of which the 6th Duke a hundred or so years before had given both time and money. Finally that most agreeable of all pigs, the ginger-haired Tamworth, had not only originated in the next county but was ideally suited to an outdoor life.

The establishment of these animals at Hardwick Hall, provided a solution both practical and appropriate to the use of the park. It also prepared the ground for a different approach by the Trust to its management potential. Farm and stable yards with no animals are unreal places, no matter how venerable or grand their architecture, and the re-introduction of animals – sound and smell as well as sight – was subsequently practised in several places. So at the Argory in County Armagh the almost extinct moiled red cattle of Ulster ('moiled' because they have bumps on their foreheads but not horns) have been introduced. At Ardress, also in County Armagh, there are barnyard fowls and squealing pigs to lend verisimilitude to the assembly of farm implements. At Shugborough, Staffordshire, Longhorns and other breeds are now kept in the Home Farm buildings, and at Parke in Devon, where the Dartmoor National Park is tenant of the house, the farm buildings again house stock.

But the biggest enterprise is at Wimpole in Cambridgeshire where the near-derelict Home Farm buildings turned out to be the remains of a model farmstead by the architect John Soane. It was a necessity to repair them and to find a use for them so the Regional Director, Michael Rogers, persuaded the committees of the Trust to establish a 'Rare Breeds Farm'. The objectives were to provide a use for the buildings; to decorate the park; to perpetuate the breeds; to make money, both from stock and visitors; to provide an additional attraction to support the house. There were assembled three ancient breeds of cattle, half a dozen each of sheep, goats, pigs and poultry. In this, rather as in its rose collection, the Trust has stepped outside its usual role. There are risks in these diversions, but an organisation which has become possessed of such immense resources in terms of property must surely be prepared to accommodate enterprises which are appropriate even if they are not wholly in the mainstream of the Trust's work.

John Cripwell joined the Trust as an Assistant Agent to Ivan Hills in the South East in 1958 but quite soon went to form the new Area covering Shropshire, Staffordshire and South Lancashire (up to then it had been in the care of Colin Jones, operating from Ross-on-Wye!). Cripwell was a product of that practical, down-to-earth institution, the Royal Agricultural College, where he had known Anthony Lord and Ivor Blomfield, and he was to become the most far-sighted and innovative of all the Trust's land agents.

His first major individual contribution was to persuade his masters to let him launch an appeal for the purchase of the Long Mynd, greatest and most beautiful of the Shropshire Hills. In the early 1960s the Secretary was still not enthusiastic about appeals in general, and there was some validity in the argument that since the hill was largely common land 'nothing could happen to it'. It was a surprise to his colleagues that the diffident Cripwell did get his way, very successfully raised the money and bought the property in 1965.

A year or so later he went to take over the Wessex Area where he pressed forward with the putting together of the Golden Cap Estate, begun five years before to protect the West Dorset coast. He brought it to a point where, in 1985, there were only a few more additions needed to bring the conception to a perfect fulfilment. In Wessex too he initiated another appeal on a very important subject – the preservation of downland. The chalk hills dominate much of Wiltshire and reach out down into Dorset where they meet the sea in the Isle of Purbeck. Well within living memory they were in many places un-enclosed and characterised by a short springy turf, evolved through centuries of sheep and rabbit grazing. Stonehenge Down had been like that before the Second War but, as we have seen, was then ploughed and fenced and so was an immense area of similar land elsewhere, and there was very little indeed left of what had been. The landscape as such suffered less than might have been expected, the great sweeps of cornland providing a different sort of beauty and often emphasising the contours in a new way. Ugliness came more from the fencing. What had disappeared, seemingly irrevocably, was the downland flora with its population of butterflies and other creatures which had been one of the chief joys of that country.

John Cripwell set himself the task, on behalf of the Trust, of trying to gather up the fragments that remained. In this he was encouraged and strongly supported by members of his Regional Committee, especially Helen Brotherton, who had become Chairman, and Bill Copland who had been a Regional Officer of the Nature Conservancy Council and was blessed with an unusual breadth of vision. Between 1976 and 1985 Cripwell had secured five separate properties with a combined area of over 800 acres beautiful in themselves, and all but one important for their plants and insects and with prehistoric remains of considerable significance.

The odd one out is perhaps the most interesting of the lot. Ballard Down is a ridge of the Purbecks north of Swanage which drops into the sea near the mouth of Poole Harbour, forming the Old Harry Rocks. The relatively gentle, whaleback slopes of the ridge permitted the use of machinery, and when bought it had been farmed in arable for several years. Had the downland flora 'irrevocably' gone? With help from Bill Copland and with advice from the Nature Conservancy Council the arable was sown with a seed mixture of the principal downland grasses and herbs and, after establishment, a sheep grazing regime imposed. Within a remarkably short time the main pattern of vegetation became similar to what had once been there, and although a good many more years must elapse before recovery is complete, the practicability of the idea is proven.

In all this, the vision to see the need and the perseverance to see it through, were Cripwell's own contribution. And he has been ready to launch or further campaigns of preservation wherever possible, for example, along the southern edge of the Mendip Hills, and for the skyline of Bath. Another, perhaps more unusual project of his has been his interest in William Henry Fox Talbot, who was born in 1800 and died in 1877. He was one of the earliest pioneers of photography and did much of his work at Lacock which his granddaughter, Matilda, had given to the Trust. In 1949 some of the attics of the Abbey were still littered with bits of his apparatus and copper plates on which views of the house and neighbouring buildings could be discerned. Cripwell felt that Fox Talbot's connection with Lacock should be acknowledged, and he proposed that a museum of early photography should be made in the tithe barn not far from the house, then no longer needed for farm use.

Lord Head, Chairman of the Wessex Regional Committee, took up the idea with enthusiasm. An appeal was launched, supported by a committee with a number of experts on the subject. These included Sir Cecil Beaton, Dr Harrison, who was President of the Royal Photographic Society, and Roy Strong, Director of the National Portrait Gallery. An important member was George Jones who represented Ilford Ltd, the manufacturers of film and photographic materials. They were supported by a Technical Sub-Committee on which Ilford again, Kodak, the National Portrait Gallery, the Smithsonian Institution and the Science Museum were all represented.

The appeal target was £50,000 and there was a particular effort to underline the scientific and scholarly side of the enterprise by aiming to produce an archive and index of all Fox Talbot's materials and contemporary sources.

The Australian designer Robin Wade, who had been concerned with the Witley Visitor Centre, was engaged. His two level design was devised to provide for a permanent exhibition related directly to Fox Talbot on the ground floor and changing exhibitions, three or four different ones a year, up in the gallery which also has an audio-visual display. It worked well from the start and still does so.

The Fox Talbot Museum was contrived in a period when that sort of thing – often called an 'interpretative centre' – was very fashionable. John Cripwell's special merit was to choose a subject which was entirely relevant to the place, of genuine historic interest and one which was likely to endure. He believes that his own best contribution was to appoint as Curator Bob Lassam, who for twenty years had been Exhibition Manager for Kodak and who has, he says, '... given the Museum a national – perhaps an international – reputation.'

Among the new recruits of the early 1970s, brought in to strengthen the Historic Buildings side, was Merlin Waterson. He was born in 1947, the son of a minor Canon of Ripon Cathedral, and in due course went up to King's, Cambridge, to read history and fine arts, and became a university prizeman. The usual post-graduate spell of doing something different and seeing a bit of the world took him to Persia to study carpet making and on his return he looked at possible careers. Christopher Gibbs was a family friend and advised him. In 1970 he was working as Robin Fedden's Assistant before going to the Regional Office at Attingham as Historic Buildings Representative for the North West Midlands and North West. He was very young and might have suffered from the problems of inexperience in administration that so hampered some of his colleagues had it not been for the fact that he was extremely methodical and conscientious in his approach to work and was prepared to learn and conform with procedures and practices.

His place in this chapter is due to the fact that Philip Yorke, the last Squire of Erddig near Wrexham, whose family had owned the place for 240 years, eventually decided in 1973 to give it to the National Trust. Mr Yorke had been trying to make up his mind for a long time. He lived all alone in the big house which he had inherited from his elder brother in 1966, sleeping with the silver under his bed and a shotgun by his side. Much of his time was spent manoeuvering pots, pans and baths to catch the rain as it came through the roof. The whole building was affected by subsidence from the workings of the Bersham Colliery immediately below. Outside the gardens were kept tidy by sheep.

The Trust thus became possessed of Erddig, a house that had always been plain and was now nearly derelict as well, but full of the most lovely things and undespoiled by modernisation or by sales. It was a frightening prospect, having to cope physically with a place in that condition, let alone having to find the money for it. When it came before the Properties Committee for final acceptance Sir Terence Morrison-Scott was taking the chair. After a medical and scientific training Morrison-Scott had become a career administrator and ended up as Director of the Natural History Museum and of the Science Museum as well, being given the second job as something of a trouble shooter. He worked very hard for the Trust as a committee-man, taking on any and every job for which others had either not got the standing or the stomach. He was, however, the reverse of a crusader. Small wonder then that he said to the Properties Committee, 'We've just got to get out of this one, haven't we?'

Well they didn't: and in the event they didn't need to because by a sheer stroke of luck an outlying part of the estate was wanted for development. The sale was handled, very competently and at the very peak of a boom, by the firm of Savilles and it brought in £1 million.

The circumstances were then precisely right for Merlin Waterson to make his mark on a wholly new approach to the management and presentation of a country house. The Trust had also acquired a young Research Assistant for the Historic Buildings Secretary. Gervase Jackson-Stops had combined history and architectural history at Oxford and thus had very much the same intellectual background as Merlin Waterson. Together they began to go through the documents, which had been exceptionally well cared for by Mr Yorke's father. They were very thorough, dividing the work roughly between them with the social history going to Waterson and the architecture and decorative arts to Jackson-Stops. Later, as they went on from documents to objects, everything was card-indexed and cross referenced. Waterson writes, 'This was very academic – we were both fresh from reading history – but it was important. It represented a departure from the "good eye" and "good taste" approach of Robin Fedden, Lord Rosse and others. John Cornforth urged that we should do the work on the documents and papers before restoration and not afterwards (as at Clandon).' Cornforth also encouraged him to approach the social history in a serious and scholarly way. John Fowler agreed, suggesting that it was perhaps the property's most interesting attribute.

Two factors combined to produce in Merlin Waterson another departure from the norm. In 1975 he went at the expense of the Countryside Commission to the United States of America to study the new cult of interpretation. In the course of his visit he was greatly impressed by houses such as Mount Vernon, where the presentation of domestic offices and outbuildings were features which he thought very well handled. He had also, early in his time with the Trust, been sent down to Cornwall and had seen Michael Trinick's development of the social and working life of the houses there. He determined on two things, first that Erddig was best approached through the labyrinth of yards and through the basement passages and domestic offices rather than in mock grandeur through the front door, and secondly that these areas should be as alive as possible. He did not easily get his own way: Gervase Jackson-Stops and Elizabeth Beasley, who had been appointed as consultant, both thought it wrong. The decision at the time it had to be made was by no means straightforward, no matter how right it may now seem to be. It had to be argued out long and hard and Waterson must have been absolutely sure of himself on the point to get his own way.

While acknowledging the way in which Cornwall and the States opened his eyes to the possibilities, he says now, 'the crucial influence was Erddig itself. The social history and its importance hit you between the eyes: all those paintings and photographs [of the servants] were crying out for attention, for explanation, for elucidation.' So it is that the visitor finds joiners at work in their shop and the blacksmith in his, horses in the stables, sawmill and mortar mill and the carts, carriages and cars accumulated by the Yorkes in their appropriate places, while the kitchen is fully equipped.

What Waterson did for Erddig set a pattern for the Trust's approach to the new responsibilities which were to come thick and fast in the next few years. It finally extended the Trust's concept of preservation and presentation to the limits of the historical significance of the country house.

This chapter has told the story of the contribution made by a handful of the Trust's staff, with a marginal mention of some others who influenced and helped them. It must be emphasised that it would be difficult to find many – indeed any – of their colleagues at any level of seniority who have not made an individual contribution in some way or other. That this is so is rooted in the nature of the National Trust and the scope and opportunity which working for it brings.

CHAPTER XX

Principality and Province:
Wales and Ireland

It is not easy to know how far the founders of the Trust intended their organisation to operate. The British Empire was approaching its greatest extent at that time and it might well have seemed natural that an English organisation could properly undertake work almost anywhere. Robin Fedden in his book *The Continuing Purpose* records that, on an approach from the Colonial Office, the Trust was prepared to take on the Knights Templars' Castle at Kolossi in Cyprus, and that there was talk of taking property in the West Indies.

These came to nothing, but Wales had from the beginning been in the Trust's orbit with the acquisition right at the start of Dinas Oleu. Scotland was also to be in the Trust's sphere: in the first twenty years there were several interventions but no property was acquired. In 1899 a motion was passed by the Council advocating the creation of a branch in Scotland; Canon Rawnsley was to be sent to Edinburgh to promote the idea. This came to nothing, but in 1931 the gap was filled by the institution of the National Trust for Scotland as a wholly separate, if similar, body. It was incorporated by statute in 1935.

As to Ireland, despite the political troubles of the time there is every indication that the Trust intended to work there. Indeed in 1899 at the time when the Killarney sale was alarming everyone the Executive passed a resolution 'that it is desirable that branches of the National Trust be established in Ireland and Scotland.' Octavia Hill seconded that motion.

The Trust did indeed acquire Kanturk Castle in County Cork in 1900 but nothing more before the partition of the country in 1922 and thereafter its work was confined to the Province of Northern Ireland. The Trust's organisation is now established in both Wales and Northern Ireland on exactly similar lines to England but there are significant differences in the way its work is conducted and its policies framed.

Clough Williams-Ellis, writing *In Trust for the Nation* in 1947 said that Wales was '... miserably under-represented by Trust possessions ...' and went on to list several reasons: 'the mistaken notion that just because a place may be remote and wild, so it will always be safe ...; a still surviving mistrustfulness of English institutions run from London and generally of anything not arranged for Welshmen by Welshmen for themselves after long discussion – in Welsh! ... few notable buildings of the middling manor house sort and still fewer comparable to the great country houses ...'

There were other reasons. The population and the wealth of the Principality are disposed very unevenly. The native Welsh, if one may use that expression for those whose first language it is and whose heredity is rooted in the country, are divided as between north and south, using the language with differences. They tend to continue to be based on agriculture and rural industry, and to be left with the less productive and more difficult land. That is most easily seen in Pembrokeshire, where the Normans contented themselves with the conquest of the fertile south, leaving the Welsh the mountain land north of their castles which still mark the Landsker line. Fedden, writing of how things were in the 1940s, said, 'there existed in Wales neither the public interest nor financial backing to support an effective independent Trust.' That there is some truth in that statement is given some force by the fact that in 1948 there were only 500 members of the Trust resident in Wales, by 1968 the number had grown only to 2,500 and in 1987, despite great success in preservation and presentation and a determined effort to promote the Trust, especially in South Wales, the members number only 31,857.

On the wider stage of Welsh nationalism, the Trust has only appeared once, in 1943, when the Montgomeryshire County Council tried to move the foundation of a separate organisation for the Principality. The Trust was entirely prepared to abdicate if a competent body could be set up in its place, but that proved impossible and so the Trust has continued its work in Wales.

Despite Clough Williams-Ellis's strictures, the Trust had accomplished something by the time it had passed its half-century. The abortive Pembrokeshire Coast Appeal had gone far enough to set a pattern for coastal preservation, especially around St Brides Bay and St Davids. The romantic, ruined castles of Cilgerran and Skenfrith had both been entrusted to its care, despite being under the guardianship of the Ancient Monuments Department. The Pass of Aberglaslyn and Dolmelynllyn with its Black Waterfall were representative of the sort of landscape which the English valued most highly in Wales. At Tenby the remarkable survival known as the Tudor Merchant's House had been given in 1937, and at Llanrwst in 1945 Tu Hwnt i'r Bont the tiny fifteenth-century courthouse came from the local authorities. The fourteenth-century Aberconwy House was given in 1934. The very early acquisition of the Kymin, which was given in 1902, represented the taste for viewpoints and follies; with its Round House built for a dining club of local gentlemen; it perches on the 800 foot summit, with the naval memorial, built in 1800 by the same club, nearby. Thirty years later the two great hills near Abergavenny, the Sugar Loaf, close on 2500 feet and Skirrid Fawr just 400 feet less, were given.

Those and a number of other properties, including the 322-acre Hafod Lwytog given by Williams-Ellis himself, might seem to represent a fair degree of success, but perhaps he had compared it with the extent of the country and its immense wealth of scenic beauty both inland and on its long coast. There was progress in the four years after his book was published, but nothing sensational other than Lord Aberconway's gift of his garden at Bodnant in 1949. Even this seems to have little connection with Wales save the fact that it is located there, its existence being more an act of colonisation than a native growth, although there is no question of its beauty and importance in the horticultural world.

The whole scene changed when, in 1951, the Douglas-Pennant family offered to the Treasury in lieu of estate duty the extraordinary Penrhyn Castle, built between 1827 and 1840 to the designs of Thomas Hopper. It is a vast building and although much of the decorative work is in the Norman manner, the military aspect is freely extended into the sophistication of late mediaeval architecture. Nevertheless, without and within, the place demands big adjectives – 'stately, massive and stupendous'. The roots of the family went back to Welsh families of the Middle Ages but their wealth was derived first from Jamaica and second from slate quarrying.

In terms of the use of the 'in lieu' procedure the transfer of the castle via the Treasury was nothing more nor less than the unloading of a massive white elephant to the advantage of the estate. There was no cash endowment and no protective land, income producing or otherwise, was offered apart from the grounds around the building. Why then, un-endowed and certain to require large sums in upkeep, was it accepted by the Trust? On offer with the castle was the estate of Ysbyty Ifan, lying inland and covering nearly 42,000 acres. Of this huge expanse 16,000 acres comprised the Carneddau, a glorious hump of mountain at the head of the Nant Ffrancon pass, rising above 3,000 feet to the crests of the Glyders and Tryfan, and enclosing the romantic Cwm Idwal and its Devil's Chimney. The Ysbyty Estate proper dropped from the high, rolling moorland of the Migneint through hilly farms and woodlands into the valley of the Conwy at Betws-y-Coed and the south side of Telford's great road, now the A5. This was presented as an income-producing property which would yield a sufficient surplus to cope with anything needed for the castle.

The whole transaction from the Trust's point of view was an exercise in wishful thinking and self-deception compounded by a degree of urgency and shortage of staff which prevented any proper assessment of the problems involved. The Trust's agent in Wales, appointed after the war, was Frank Armitage. He was based in Tenby, which is almost as far away from the north-west corner of Wales as it is possible to get. Petrol was rationed and the number of visits he could contrive were limited by that and other calls on his time. One suspects that much of the substance of his report was derived from enquiries of the Penrhyn Estate which were very likely to be answered from a different standpoint than the Trust's. At the same time the Head Office committees and staff were dazzled by the prospect of this immense and important gift, and probably did not wish to prejudice the operation of the Land Fund which was still a relatively new affair.

It was all settled before the Trust's new Land Agent appeared on the scene. Wales was to be divided between the south and the north and John Tetley gave up his job looking after Geoffrey Wolryche-Whitmore's Dudmaston Estate in Shropshire to take on the north and its new giant property. Very tall and lean, with a slight limp from polio contracted during the war in Italy, John Tetley contrived not to look or act excessively English. Indeed his second name, Howell, was given him by his Welsh mother, and Frank Armitage, experienced in the difficulties of working in Wales, seriously advised him to use it instead of the English 'John'.

The subsequent history of the Trust in Wales is so strongly influenced by Tetley and Ysbyty that their story must be told in some detail. The castle of Penrhyn, though important in itself and to the Trust, was little different in its problems from many other of the Trust's houses except in size. It absorbed time and huge amounts of money – indeed it still does – but Tetley did not regard it as central to his task. What he saw as central and indispensable was the laying of the foundations of long term good-will and confidence.

He knew that he was confronted with a tenantry which was resentful of the transfer of their farms to a new owner which was an alien, London-based, Government dominated, English organisation without any interest in them or any affinity with Welsh ways. They were disappointed too that there had been no death duty sale which would have given them the chance to buy the farms they occupied. Tetley writes, 'I very soon realised that in addition to the superbly beautiful area that had come under our protection we had also acquired an area where the pattern of Welsh life in the hills still retained its hold on the three valley communities embraced in the estate. Each valley had its group of farms nearly all with an acclimatised flock summered on a sheep walk, or cynhefin, on the open mountain. Each community had its chapel at the lower end of the valley which held an annual eisteddfod. The whole represented a way of life long established in the hills of Wales which combined the provision of mutual aid in hard or difficult times with the ability to create communal entertainment to help pass the long winter.'

Tetley's initial problem was that Welsh is the first language of that part of the world, always spoken at home. Even today many have difficulty in finding enough English to express fully what they mean. Tetley wanted to learn but regrets that approaching forty and with the demands of work on his time and energy he never properly succeeded, although once at a meeting in the village hall when the seven preceding speakers had used nothing but Welsh, he did so too, receiving a generous round of applause for his effort.

The first coup for Tetley and the Trust was to retain the services of John Williams, the Estate foreman. He had been brought up on the estate at Penrhyn, trained in forestry, and was in general the sort of man who could turn his hand to anything. He had met Tetley before the estate had actually been conveyed to the Trust, making a reconnaissance in the company of Hubert Smith, Frank Armitage and Humphrey Evans (newly engaged as an Assistant Secretary at Queen Anne's Gate). Williams was presumably pleased with the sort of people who worked for the Trust and he may have thought that at least the new arrangements would keep intact an estate which he loved. At any rate he turned down tempting offers to go elsewhere and went to work for the new owners. Not only was his knowledge of the neighbourhood as a whole and the estate in particular intimate and thorough but as – or more – important he was well liked and respected. That such a man had thrown in his lot with the Trust was a great bonus.

Williams was later joined by John Morris, also a respected personality, a member and later Chairman of the Nantconwy District Council. He too chose the Trust, rather than vice-versa. Hearing that the new agent and tiny office needed a secretary he volunteered to teach himself to type and learn office methods. He had been lecturing on behalf of the RSPCA to schools all over the Principality for the useful salary of £10 a week. All John Tetley could offer was £4.10s. for a job within walking distance of home and it was accepted: 'Oh, I think that's very fair. I'll be here on Monday.'

With Williams and Morris to consult on tricky local issues and to act as two-way interpreters (they were both fluent bi-linguals) there was a team with which Tetley could pursue the course which he believed to be necessary, but it was he who determined that course. His masters in London would have modified it greatly had they had their way. The state of agriculture in the 1950s has been described in an earlier chapter, and at Ysbyty all the problems existed but generally in an intensified form.

Small wonder that the Estates Committee should press upon Tetley the urgency of reducing the burden by amalgamating farms and allowing the redundant houses and buildings to decay. As with Acland in the Lakeland fells, Tetley saw in this not only the certain destruction of the social fabric but the practical disadvantages which would, on this marginal land, flow from having farms which were too large for one family to handle. The expense of hiring labour would lead to neglect of fences and drains, money would be needed for new larger, labour saving buildings and the land under ranching would decline in productivity. Fortunately, in the early days shortage of staff and pressure of work kept Head Office staff from breathing down his neck, and nearly three years were to pass before the Chief Agent paid him a visit. That gave him the time to establish his own policies.

The first element in his self-imposed regime was one which all land agents would do well to emulate. He would never refuse to see a tenant who came to the office, or to the house, at any time. Amongst other things he recognised that they could not easily leave their farms during the working day. Secondly, 'if any awkwardness had arisen between a tenant and myself I would go to his farm and have it out face to face across the table, rather than writing a pompous request for him to call at the office. If there was likely to be any difficulty with the language John Williams would be ready to come along and if need be take an active part in the argument or negotiation.'

The process of rehabilitation of the estate slowly went ahead, Tetley concentrating on bringing to the little grey stone farmhouses the amenities of water, bathrooms, lavatories and drainage, while for the farms themselves there were roads, water, electricity and better buildings. For improvements there was an increased rent to pay, but he got special dispensation to fix it at six per cent on the cost instead of the ten per cent quite reasonably required by the Trust in other places. Tenants then began to wish to do improvement work on their own, encouraged by Tetley who undertook to pay compensation should their tenancy come to an end. There was Government help for the hill farms in those days and special schemes had to be prepared; then, as the work was carried out over a period, grants of half the cost were made. This was a great help, but it was also a great labour, yet no less than forty-four farms were the subject of such schemes.

The principal pre-war interest of the Douglas-Pennants in Ysbyty had been the shooting, and the requirements of the Head Keeper took priority over everything else. Until the war eight keepers had been employed with beats on the moor and several thousand pheasants reared on the lower ground near Glanconwy. This probably accounts in large part for the run down of the farms and that in its turn to a degree of stagnation which discouraged young tenants and left the Trust on its succession with an elderly tenantry. At least the advanced age of the farm tenants meant that vacancies occurred with frequency, and John Tetley's policy of improving the houses and the farms began to attract younger couples. In the early 1960s a film about the National Trust featured John Tetley and Ysbyty. There was a shot of the school playground swarming with children and the commentator said, 'When the agent came here ten years ago there were only eight children in the school: now there are over forty.' Tetley modestly disclaims direct responsibility for the increase, but he does like to think that it is evidence of a renewal of vitality to which his policies have contributed.

To visit the Ysbyty Estate today and to meet its people with their friendliness and superb courtesy, their vigour and independence, is to feel deeply thankful that Tetley not only saw what had to be done but had the ability and temperament to do it.

> I feel pretty sure that once it was realised that our aim was not only to be conscientious landlords but to respect, protect and enjoy the truly Welsh ways of the estate, *as part of the Trust's responsibility in holding it*, the initial suspicion of us as an enemy to be defeated might be changed to a realisation that we were an ally, who would do all it could to work with them in improving their conditions and protecting the centuries old character of the district in a way which would have been far more difficult for any other landlord in these changing times.

The importance for the work of the Trust in Wales lies in the words in italics. From Tetley's arrival in the north onwards through his colleagues and successors there had been a recognition, reflected in a revision of attitudes at the centre of the Trust, that there is a special and additional duty not just to the land and buildings of Wales but to the Welsh.

The 1943 proposal for a separate Trust for Wales, even though it came to nothing, prompted Lords Zetland and Matheson to give at least a token participation to Wales and, in 1945, an Advisory Committee was formed. When John Tetley came to work in Wales six years later he was not much impressed as to its usefulness. 'It was composed of eminent personages in the Principality, few of whom could speak Welsh. It met twice a year; once in the south and once in the north, and received a report from the Agent, who tended to report only what he wanted them to hear and show them only what he wanted them to see.'

In the circumstances of the time the Committee's lack of involvement did not greatly matter. The problems of the Trust were largely practical ones and matters which the agents could cope with on their own. In South Wales, when Armitage left, the Trust put its work into the hands of Hugh Griffith who was in partnership with his father in Carmarthen. The Trust's holdings in the south were still not extensive and only engaged a part of his time. The gift of Powis Castle in 1952, coming so soon after Penrhyn, was a notable event. Not only is the castle, perched on its crag near Welshpool, a romantic building in itself but its terraced gardens, developed from the late seventeenth century onwards, are among the most fascinating in the country. It was also important to the Trust that this came as a gift from the 4th Earl of Powis, with an endowment, and was not one of the then increasing flow of Treasury transfers, although, in 1965, the Land Fund did take, and pass on loan to the Trust, the principal contents.

Growth was slow to come, and perhaps that was just as well, because when it did the organisation was more nearly ready to cope with it. In 1964 the Government, somewhat belatedly, recognised the separate identity of the Principality by establishing a Secretary of State for Wales, although in doing so they underlined the extraordinary deficiency of a real centre for the country. To locate its new department in Cardiff may have been administratively sensible, close to the bulk of the population and with good and improving communications with London, but to the Welsh of the north it was almost as distant and foreign as Whitehall. The Trust had already converted its Advisory Committee into a Regional Committee, with the executive responsibility which that entails, and under the chairmanship of Captain Wynne Finch it began to become an effective source of authority.

It was to start with a large committee with twenty or more members, due to a wish to ensure a good geographical spread and to include at least five Welsh speakers. Captain Wynne Finch secured for his committee the services of two particularly useful people. The Marquess of Anglesey lived at Plas Newydd on the Menai Strait and knew the north well. Robin Herbert lived at the other end of the country, near Abergavenny. Both had wide interests inside and outside Wales.

As Chairman, Wynne Finch gave evidence to the Benson Committee and could foresee that there would be a retirement rule which would oblige him to give up, and he determined to go of his own volition. His first choice as successor was Colonel Crawshay (later Sir William, and a Chairman of the Arts Council) but he could not do it and suggested Robin Herbert, who was a friend of his. It may have been Herbert's relative youth – he was then 35 – that made him second choice, but he accepted and took the chair from 1969 until he was retired in 1984 under the then current fifteen-year retirement rule (since reduced to ten years). Lord Anglesey became Deputy and together they were able to cover the country. Herbert was not only a landowner, but he had been to that forcing house of the commercial world, the Harvard Business School, subsequently joining the merchant bankers Leopold Joseph, of which in due course he became Chairman. His experience of rural conservation work was widened when, in 1971, he became a member of the Countryside Commission, of which he was later Deputy Chairman.

The system of the two agents dealing separately with the Committee was continued. Robin Herbert is satisfied that it is important that there is only one committee with two offices responsible to it. 'It enables the Trust to speak with greater authority when dealing with the outside world and it endorses a committed approach to the Welsh conservation scene. The weakness (if any) of the structure has been that there is no Chief Executive N.T. Wales, but I doubt if the cost of this would be justified by the results.' He too finds the Committee well balanced, 'always some lady members and some (usually one third) Welsh speaking. The lack has been of people with enough financial and managerial ability to assist the Committee as members. The availability of good conservation advice has always been easier to find.'

The expansion of the Trust's work in South Wales is first noticeable on the Gower Peninsula, which thrusts deep and wide into the Bristol Channel west of Swansea. Almost entirely unspoiled and yet very close to the densely populated industrial towns, its preservation was probably more urgent than that of the Pembrokeshire coast. It began in a small way in 1933 when Mr and Mrs Stephen Lee gave the fifty three acres of Thurba Head and there were two more gifts before the war amounting to 128 acres. Then in 1954 Miss E. R. Lee bought up five acres on Notthill. It had been divided into building lots and she bought them in one by one until she could give the whole to the Trust. In the same year the secluded Bishopston Valley was given, and 158 acres of Pennard Cliff.

The establishment of footholds is often an important, sometimes essential, preliminary to a major campaign of acquisition and those gifts were to prove of immense importance when Enterprise Neptune was launched. Indeed the first success of the campaign was the purchase of Whitford Burrows at the north-west tip of the peninsula, and it was followed by a further nine properties over the following years, of which the most spectacular is the 1,000-acre stretch of the Rhossili beaches and the Worms Head. The campaign was initiated and carried out by Hugh Griffith whose labyrinthine channels of contact with local interests were invaluable.

Neptune also prompted further acquisitions in Pembrokeshire and Cardigan, although progress was not nearly so dramatic there as in the south west of England. Griffith's contacts did, however, operate again to produce in 1976 an addition of the utmost importance. The Cawdor Estate decided to dispose of its Stackpole property and although the greater part was sold on the open market, the trustees were persuaded by their former agent to offer to the Treasury 2,000 acres, stretching along eight miles of splendid cliffs and broad bays. This included the site of Stackpole Court (which Griffith had himself, on behalf of the Estate, demolished) and a series of freshwater lakes extending almost to the sea. There was a hiccup when the Pembrokeshire Coast National Park thought it more appropriate that the property should be in their care, but in the end it did come to the Trust and it offers a great and continuing opportunity for preservation combined with intensive and increasing enjoyment for the public.

Those who deal in the sort of work that the Trust does are accustomed to have to live for a long time to see the fruits of their labours, but seldom can it be as long as the twenty-one years which passed between acceptance by the Trust of Clytha Park far to the east near Raglan, and its eventual transfer. The owner, Richard Hanbury-Tenison, had transferred it to the Government subject to a retention of the right to occupation, and with the intent that the ownership should be vested in the Trust. That was in 1957, and it was 1978 before the Welsh Office conveyed it to the Trust.

While the coastal preservation work was going on, South Wales received a tremendous gift from Sir Brian Mountain, who gave over 8,000 acres of the Brecon Beacons, including the 3,000-foot Penyfan, in 1965. It was, and remains, by far the most extensive property owned by the Trust in the south, and it was augmented four years later when, with the help of the then newly established Countryside Commission, the Trust bought Blaenglyn Farm, over 900 acres on the western edge of the Beacons. As in most hill country the use of the moorland depends upon the farms around the moor-edge and it is generally right that the two should be in one ownership, so the purchase of Blaenglyn was a major embellishment to Sir Brian's gift.

The advance in the south was matched and later exceeded in the north. There had been early gifts along the coast of Anglesey and with the launch of Neptune these were substantially extended. Inland tracts of hill farm and mountain, widely scattered over the Cambrian Mountains, came in first by gift and were then often extended by purchase. Where there is so much beautiful scenery it is hard to praise one place above another, but Clough Williams-Ellis must have been gratified with

275

what had been achieved when in his eighty-eighth year he resigned from the Committee for Wales. That was in 1970, and more than thirty years had passed since he had lamented the lack of progress.

Five years earlier he had seen the Trust take one of its exceptionally bold steps off its beaten path. The suspension bridge, build by Thomas Telford over the river at Conwy had finally gone out of use and the borough council was reluctant to remain responsible for it. The permanent preservation of a complicated iron structure already 139 years old is not a task lightly to be undertaken, but it was a monument to British skill and inventiveness and the Trust did take it on.

Lord Anglesey added a new dimension to the Trust's standing in the north by giving his own house in 1974. The house with its Gothick exterior by James Wyatt and its partly Repton grounds would be out standing anywhere, but in North Wales, looking across the waters of the Strait to the mountains of Snowdonia it is exceptional. The 1st Marquess had shown a considerable degree of dash in command of the cavalry at Waterloo, where in the closing moments shot smashed his right leg as he rode beside Wellington. His boot, his ruined trousers and his wooden leg remain in the house to this day.

The dining room was decorated in the 1930s by Rex Whistler with *trompe l'oeil* murals which are sheer masterpieces of wit, imagination and beauty. The whole adds up to a place of such charm that the Trust was bold enough to accept the house unendowed, relying on income from visitors to meet the cost of maintenance. It was undoubtedly risky, but if the gamble succeeds, that will be splendid. If it does not, the Trust will not regret having to find the means to preserve so lovely a place.

When memories of those who worked for the preservation of beautiful things in Wales has dimmed there will still be a bright recollection of the three Misses Keating of Plas-yn-Rhiw, Pwllheli. South of the Menai Strait, the Peninsula of the Lleyn thrusts south westward into the Irish Sea and, toward its furthest tip, is the hill of Rhiw below which snuggles the manor house. Mediaeval in origin, it has Tudor and Georgian additions and around it a garden, luxuriant in that kind climate, drops down the streamside to the sea. The coastline has exceptional charm, being soft and intimate and small in scale, while at the same time giving a feeling of space not always found in more dramatic scenery. That something approaching 400 acres is protected by the National Trust is due entirely to the sisters. John Tetley knew them very well indeed and they are best described in his own words:

> The Misses Eileen, Lorna and Honora [Honor], in order of age, worked as a very effective team in fighting for the beauty of Lleyn whenever, and by whomsoever it was threatened.
>
> Miss Eileen was gentle, quiet spoken and charming, with the hidden iron in her soul that was to be found in her two sisters when it came to a fight.... Miss Lorna was a bustling character, broadly the mistress of the house ... Very determined, but tending to withdraw when her sisters were in the chair, she nevertheless backed them wholeheartedly in battle. Miss Honor was the spokesman and general campaign manager for the party. She represented herself and her sisters, with the active support on occasion of her elder sister, at countless enquiries, and took an active part in the work of the Council for the Preservation of Wales. She had received the O.B.E. for

her work in child care between the wars, and had been a land girl in the First War.

They spoke for their countryside in a way which most men find some diffidence in matching, brushing aside 'practical' counter-evidence as of insufficient weight.... As might be expected I was brought into every case where it seemed to them that for some reason or other the Trust might be affected. Much of their battle planning was carried out in their upstairs sitting-room, in loud whispers in case it should be heard from the road, fifty yards away.

Robin Herbert, looking back over his years with the Committee for Wales, sees the growth of an established and accepted place for the work of the Trust in Wales and for Wales in the policies of the Trust. The major obstacles in the 1950s and 1960s were lack of resources in terms of money and staff. In the early 1960s he had been to look at the Trust's Cornish properties and 'found that the standards of presentation were very much higher and the moneys available were riches beyond my dreams. When I suggested that we ought to emulate this I got a frightful wigging from John Tetley!'

Tetley was probably right in those days. Care through good husbandry was a better policy to win respect in Wales than an outpouring of easy money. It was not until 1974 that he was given management help in the person of Gordon Hall, a highly intelligent and energetic land agent, and the difference was immediately noticeable. John Tetley retired in 1975 having brought the Trust in North Wales to a point at which its base was secure and it could advance with confidence. This suited his successor, Ian Kennaway, who had been working in the South East, first with Ivan Hills and then with Ivor Blomfield. Freed from the hard, uphill slog that had for so long been the lot of his predecessor he was able to pursue the extension of the Trust's preservation work in Wales, as in England.

The final proof of arrival was that Hugh Griffith and Kennaway were able in 1980 to launch 'Wales in Trust' an appeal both within the Principality and in England for money for preservation. By 1987 it had succeeded in raising nearly £700,000 for a cause and from an area which would have been thought, probably rightly, quite hopeless twenty years ago.

If there were problems in Wales for an English organisation, what of its prospects in the Province of Northern Ireland? In 1922 the Irish Free State had come into being and the six counties of Ulster immediately exercised their right to contract out, thus dividing the country, a process completed when the Republic of Eire was formally constituted in 1937. Small wonder that under these circumstances the operations of the Trust in Ireland were much curtailed; the surprise is that they were pursued at all.

Until 1945, there were only five properties owned in the Province and Kanturk Castle in the Republic, but they were of more significance than might have been supposed. The woods at Ballymayer and Killynether were just pleasant places, but Lisnabreeny, 160 acres right on the edge of Belfast was of strategic importance: it provided a check to the spread of the city, and has preserved a rural lung of significance far greater than its extent. The gem, however, is White Park Bay on the coast of County Antrim, with its mile of fine sand, shoulders of white cliffs and backing of dunelands. Moreover, it was the only property of the five to come by purchase as opposed to gift, and represents the first positive initiative shown by the National Trust in the Province.

These first properties had been acquired after the setting up of a Regional Committee in 1936, an arrangement which was in line with the Executive Committee resolution of 1899 referred to at the beginning of this chapter. The Trust benefited at once by the Stormont Parliament bringing its legislation into line with that of Whitehall, including an exemption from estate duty of property given or left to the Trust. For reasons which are not clear the Committee, in 1943, expressed a wish to be autonomous. In the event, nothing more happened, perhaps because the Committee could not see its way, or get enough local backing, to stand alone. Two years later Lord Antrim became Chairman of the Northern Ireland Committee and began to prepare the way for a more enterprising and progressive policy.

The work of the Trust in Ulster suffered handicaps similar in some respects to those in Wales. The Province was far from rich, and the greater part of its population concentrated in and around Belfast. Industry was much dependent on ship building, and away from the capital the economy was almost wholly agrarian. The Irish Land Acts of 1881 and later had applied to the whole of Ireland although the rural poverty and resentment against absentee Anglo-Irish landlords had been far less intense than in the south. The effect had been to break up all the great estates, placing the land in the ownership of the occupiers and leaving the landowner with his house and the demesne lands – roughly the grounds and parkland. This meant that almost any programme of land acquisition required negotiation with several owners and, moreover, there remained a suspicion of and prejudice against any large land-holding in one ownership.

On the other hand there were peculiar advantages. The Province is ornamented with a number of very beautiful country houses, the lack of which Clough Williams-Ellis had bemoaned in Wales; there was no language problem and above all there was a Government for the Province, as distinct from an office of the Whitehall Government. It also operated to the advantage of the Trust that, while there were highly efficient Government agencies for agriculture and forestry, there was none for the conservation of buildings, countryside or wild life and consequently when need arose there was a tendency to look to the Trust for help.

Not that there was instant progress when Antrim became Chairman for Northern Ireland. New properties were acquired indeed but they were not of any special importance. Coney Island, a mile or so off the southern shore of the great expanse of water that is Lough Neagh, was in little danger of having its tranquillity disturbed. Collin Glen, fifty acres of rough woodland valley only a mile from the edge of Belfast was indeed at risk, but its extent and position were not such as to affect the spread of the city. Perhaps the third of the places to be given to the Trust in the five years to 1950 was after all rather special. Mussenden Temple is a remarkable object in itself, a domed rotunda perched on the very edge of the cliffs, high above the Atlantic looking west across the Foyle to Donegal and east along the rugged Antrim coast. It was built in 1785 by Frederick Hervey, Earl of Bristol and Bishop of Derry, as a library on the demesne of Downhill. He was a builder and collector (he built Ickworth in Suffolk, again with a rotunda) but in the context of Irish history it is most notable that he was not only a conscientious prelate, but one of generous tolerance towards Protestant and Roman Catholic alike. In the undercroft of Mussenden Temple mass was celebrated on Sundays for local Roman Catholics, which was in those times a remarkable demonstration of Christian forebearance.

In 1948 the Committee appointed a full time Secretary. Harry White, Commander, RNVR, was a genial man, well liked by both Committee and staff. He was not in any way a professional, being little interested in the countryside, but he provided a permanent focus for the tiny office which was first in Castle Street, Belfast and subsequently moved to Dublin Road.

It was a good job that Lord Antrim had provided the rudiments of an administrative system because things really did begin to move in 1951. In the next seven years no less than five country houses and two gardens of the greatest quality came to the Trust. The inspiration of this remarkable flood of preservation success was Lord Antrim: the means were provided by the Ulster Land Fund. The fund had been set up by the Ulster Land Fund Act of 1949, which was a direct derivative of Dr Dalton's 1946 initiative. The difference from England was that the Treasury was not involved in its administration and the Finance Department of the Northern Ireland Government was prepared to use the provisions of the Act to their fullest extent, and was imaginative and flexible in applying them.

In 1951 Castle Coole, not far from Enniskillen in County Fermanagh, was accepted from the Earl of Belmore by the Fund and given to the Trust. His successor continues to live there and the furniture in the house is his. The perfection of the lines of the house, the cool crispness of its Portland stone, and the way it stands on, as it were, a däis in a bowl of parkland, give a pleasure not often equalled. No other building could more fittingly have opened the National Trust's new role in Ulster.*

This was followed in the next year by a house of a wholly different character although almost coeval with Castle Coole. Derrymore House, near Newry, was built by Isaac Corry, MP for that town for forty years. It is small, single storied and built on three sides of a courtyard, and roofed with thatch. Two opposing sides are in the form of the traditional long-house of the country, while linking them is a larger pavilion entered by a wide glazed bay, which gives some slight resemblance to an orangery. That may be an unfortunate comparison in the circumstances for it is said that inside it the Treaty of Union of 1800 was drafted. It might just have worked if Pitt and Castlereagh's intention to enfranchise Roman Catholics had not been blocked by George III's refusal to regard emancipation as compatible with his coronation oath. As it was the Act was hated then, and Corry's coach was stoned as it passed through Newry, nor did it ever achieve what was hoped for it. Derrymore came into the care of the Trust by gift from John Richardson, but acceptance was only made possible by the Ulster Land Fund providing money for its restoration.

In 1953 the Trust was given a property which became, and remains, the most popular of all with visitors: Castle Ward. Its popularity rests on its variety, but is firmly based on its setting in the curving bay on the shore of Strangford Lough, near to its southernmost end. Behind it the land rises in an irregular amphitheatre of park

---

*Castle Coole has been closed for five years while an extensive programme of repair on its fabric has been undertaken. In addition, the splendid neo-Classical and Regency interior has been carefully redecorated. The house re-opened in June 1988.

and fields and wood towards the wall of the demesne. The house itself stands dignified between lawns and gardens, and since the two fronts, wholly different in style, cannot be seen together this capricious use of strict classicism on one face, and Gothick on the other amuses and does not jar. The land drops from the house to the stable yard and from there past a tower house (the later Irish version of the pele tower) to estate workshops and the shore with its jetties and little quay. Unexpectedly, on the north side, in line with that arm of Strangford Bay is a formal, ornamental canal with beyond it an embanked walk and a classic temple, while above the quay on the shoulder of the bay itself is another tower house. On the death of the 6th Viscount Bangor in 1950, his son felt that he could no longer undertake the maintenance of the property and it was acquired by the Northern Ireland Government and later it was given with an endowment to the Trust.

Florence Court in 1954, the gardens at Mount Stewart and the gardens and house of Rowallane in 1955, and Springhill in 1957: all this was due in the first place to Lord Antrim. But the position of the former owners in all this must not be overlooked. Quite apart from the outright gifts – four out of seven – the transfers to the Ulster Land Fund required the positive intention and co-operation of the owner. Antrim's standing and warmly agreeable personality were a prime factor in presenting ownership by the Trust as an acceptable, even desirable, outcome. Equally the Government had to see the Trust in the light of a competent agency to ensure the preservation of these properties.

The partnership has continued up to the present day with a string of acquisitions made possible in whole or part by the Northern Ireland Government. John Lewis-Crosby, describing the workings of this in his time, attributes the excellent relationship to the question of scale. It was possible, he says, for one person on behalf of the Trust to have a direct link with one person in the Department of Finance: the Secretary of the National Trust's Committee had regular access to the Assistant Secretary of the Department, and he in turn to his Minister. Politics were irrelevant, nor was there any need to orchestrate pressure through the news media.

As in Wales so in Ulster, Enterprise Neptune provided a new initiative, and a very valuable one since in the 1950s there were few acquisitions other than houses. Virtually all the Ulster coast is of merit, much is of great beauty – sometimes of surpassing beauty – but the question of purchase on the scale achieved in England was never contemplated, largely because of the problems of land tenure. On the other hand the deficiencies of statutory protection as opposed to that in England and Wales, and the complete absence of any provision for access (as had been provided in the National Parks and Access to the Countryside Act 1949 which did not apply to the Province) constituted a different challenge. Harry White had died after being ill for some time and John Lewis-Crosby started work as the new Secretary in 1960. A Dubliner with a county background but who had been working in Northern Ireland, he was appointed by Lord Antrim and the Northern Ireland Committee.

Lewis-Crosby was an admirable choice for the time. Tall, active and energetic, he is capable of great charm and a fluent and convincing speaker. In his work the end was everything.

It is often difficult to discern whether the credit for an enterprise should go to one or more of the people concerned in it. Often it should be shared, and that is the case with the first major démarche made after Lewis-Crosby's appointment – the Antrim Coast Appeal. As recorded earlier the idea of a coastal preservation appeal had been put to the Executive – of which Antrim was a member – by Christopher Gibbs in 1962. In the following year the Northern Ireland Committee launched their appeal – two full years before Neptune's official launch. It was almost certainly prompted by Lord Antrim, and his impatience to get on with a good idea. It was, however, Lewis-Crosby who gave form to it.

The Trust already owned the mile long stretch of White Park Bay, and in 1961 had added the remarkable Giant's Causeway to its list. This gift was another in which the Ulster Land Fund was concerned as part-donor with Sir Antony Macnaghten. It had been a 'Beauty Spot' from time immemorial, the terminal of the basalt ridge forming a causeway beneath the sea to Scotland along which the Giants of long forgotten times made their way from one land to another. The hexagonal pipes of basalt had fascinated generations. At one time a tramway brought day trippers in their thousands. This had bred a little huddle of buildings where the road runs down to the sea and along the shore a line of little shanties selling refreshments and souvenirs.

The tramway fell into disuse, the Second War came to hinder that sort of recreation and after it the great flow of visitors began to revive but slowly. Still the little shops traded as well as they could, and when the Trust became the owner the site was as much of a moribund specimen of Edwardian seaside recreation as a place of myth and natural beauty. Nevertheless, it was that still, and a household name throughout the British Isles. To reinforce its attractions the Trust was given one year later the scant but romantic remains of Dunseverick Castle. This, like the castle of Dunluce some miles to the west, is perched on a sheer faced rock high above the sea linked to the land by the narrowest isthmus. It had been fortified for at least two thousand years and one of the five roads from the palace of the High King of Tara ended there. In 1641 Giliaduf O'Cahan, its then lord, joined the rebellion against the Commonwealth and his lands and life were forfeit and his castle slighted. It remains a singularly beautiful and exciting place.

The Trust working in England would have aimed at protecting the coast by linking these three properties by more or less continuous ownership. In Ulster this would have been quite impracticable; instead it was planned to create a coastal path. In England paths along the coast had been in existence for centuries, started by fishermen, gulls-egg collectors, smugglers and excisemen, lighthouse keepers and coastguards. Such paths had had statutory protection for a hundred years and since 1949 there had been powers to create new ones. This was not so in Ulster and the Trust broke completely new ground with its scheme. It was not easy. Negotiations either for purchase of a strip or just of a right of passage had to be carried out with dozens of owners, mainly farmers, who could not see much advantage to themselves, or indeed to anyone else. Their privacy or security against trespass seemed at stake and the need to fence was often imposed. However, by 1967 Lewis-Crosby had succeeded in creating an eleven-mile path from Ballintoy in the east to Runkerry in the west.

The work of construction was only made possible by the use of the Development Services Scheme, an unemployment relief scheme wholly financed by the Government, and which in different guises has continued ever since. The walk, which runs variously below, along the face or on top of the cliffs, offers an experience unrivalled in the British Isles, from the extraordinary construction of the cliff faces to the distant views of the Hebridean Islands. Equal in importance was the splendid publicity derived from the enterprise, and the acknowledged public leadership shown by the Trust.

1965 saw two coastal preservation projects without comparison in England or Wales save on the Northumbrian coast at Low Newton some years later. These were the acquisition of two seaside villages, Cushendun in Antrim and Kearney on the seaward side of the eastern arm of Strangford Lough in County Down. Each has its special merits, but what they both share is a unity of composition with little intrusion of discordant objects.

Cushendun, lying within a gentle sweep of fields and woods at the foot of Glendun, one of the nine great glens of Antrim, is mainly a village of whitewashed cottages strung out along the road behind the long beach, but they are curiously mingled with a number of agreeable but totally dissimilar houses. These were built before the Second War in what is supposed to be the Cornish manner, and are a memorial to a Cornishwoman, the wife of the first Lord Cushendun. The architect was Clough Williams-Ellis.

Kearney is by contrast simple, compact and restrained to the point of severity. The land is level and almost treeless, the beach is scarcely separate from the little village of thirteen houses, all low, slate-roofed and rough cast. Its complete serenity and separation from the pulse of the life of the province and its identity with the shore and the sea bring it nearly into Neptune's Kingdom.

What Neptune in Ulster lacked in acreage it made up in quality and novelty. At Carrick-a-Rede a steeply sloping grass path leads down to the cliffs and to the rope bridge which connects it with an islet off-shore. Two salmon fisheries, owned by the Trust, operate from there. Far to the south just short of the Mourne mountains at Murlough, Dundrum, the Ulster Land Fund gave a great range of duneland on the south side of the harbour mouth, behind a splendid beach. Never was land more in need of protective management for inland were caravan sites and cars parked along the roadway from which streams of holidaymakers poured across the dunes to the sea. Feet are very destructive of dunes and where the form and crust are broken the wind follows to complete the damage. Had there been a Government agency for nature conservation the property would certainly have gone to its care, but only the National Trust was available to do the job. The place was of such importance that Queen's University, Belfast, joined with the Trust to manage it, contributing to the cost. In 1977 it was given the status of a National Nature Reserve.

It seems that it is difficult to write of Northern Ireland without hyperbole, but despite the interest and grandeur of so much of its coasts there is something special about another Murlough, a bay on the north east of Antrim. The bay is backed by a high amphitheatre of pasture, woodland and thicket with little streams tumbling to the shore. The 760 acres were paid for by Enterprise Neptune in 1968 and never was money better spent. To this was added a further 180 acres ten years later as a memorial to Lord Antrim, who had died the year before.

Lord Antrim had given up the Chairmanship of the Northern Ireland Committee in 1963 when he was becoming more involved with Head Office work. His style had been one of direction rather than participation at executive level, and his influence had been exerted on Government and benefactors, potential and actual. He was succeeded by Gillie Clanwilliam. The 6th Earl of Clanwilliam, Lord Lieutenant of County Down, was then just on fifty. Very tall, very reserved, he had a very different method of exercising his responsibilities. In common with the rest of the Trust's administrative arrangements those in Northern Ireland were well below the margin of minimal need, and indeed they were to remain so for a long time. At the same time the work in the Province had grown enormously and the houses and gardens demanded a great deal of specialist care and generated a turnover of money running into tens of thousands of pounds.

Clanwilliam's course was to constitute himself an Executive Chairman. He attended the office regularly one day a week and dealt in conjunction with the Secretary in all current detail. In particular he took upon himself the duties carried out elsewhere by the Representative. Lewis-Crosby found him deeply involved in the work of the Trust, but thought that in management matters he needed to be persuaded to take a detailed interest. However that may be – and Clanwilliam certainly took an active part in trying to find a substitute for the mutually unsatisfactory annual land tenure known as 'conacre' – he was probably closer to the work in the Province than any Chairman of a Region in England and Wales. He also devoted a great deal of attention to the ticklish business of integrating the Northern Ireland Committee more closely with its parent organisation. In this he succeeded, drawing from the centre money, expertise and a high degree of moral support which became of great importance in the 1970s.

It was Lewis-Crosby who proposed a scheme of preservation unique in the National Trust involving Strangford Lough. The lough is a long narrow inlet which runs south from the town of Newtownards, which is itself very close to Belfast. To the east the twenty-mile arm of land is but two or three miles wide for much of its length, but the west is backed by the prosperous rolling countryside of Down. It has every quality to make it the seaside playground of the city. The Trust owned two very special properties on the lough – Castle Ward and the gardens of Mount Stewart – but the prospect of large scale acquisition was non-existent and Lewis-Crosby's solution was the Strangford Lough Scheme, the Trust's only campaign of preservation to rest upon the co-operation of other owners, local authorities and independent organisations. The Strangford Lough Information Centre opened in July 1988.

Immense numbers of water birds winter or breed on the Lough. At the northern end at ebb tide there are thousands of acres uncovered which provide a fertile feeding ground, and the slitch-grass or zostera is a vital food for geese. The initial idea was to gain overall control by leases of the foreshore from the main owners and then to set up refuges for wildfowl and to regulate shooting elsewhere by granting licences. The owners co-operated willingly – the Crown, the Lady Mairi Bury and four others granting leases – and seven refuges were set up. This simply would not have worked had not Lewis-Crosby found another first rate warden. Arthur Irvine had retired from the Royal Ulster Constabulary with the rank of Head Constable. He was an ardent sportsman and convinced conservationist, and it is due to him that the wildfowlers, who were potential antagonists, were converted to be conservationists too.

It was not until 1979 that more land was acquired, but between then and 1984 seven islands up and down the lough were bought, with a total area of nearly 250 acres, and about 70 acres on the mainland. One of the latter, the Glastry Ponds, which are old clay pits, was used by Arthur Irvine as a working area in ecology for school parties, and like everything he touched it was a great success. In 1982 Lady Mairi agreed to the purchase by the Trust of over, 5,000 acres at the head of the lough which was already under lease, and that fairly set the seal on the scheme.

It was Lewis-Crosby too who urged the Trust to try to preserve at least some remnants of the great linen industry on which the rural wealth of the Province had been based. Part of the process of manufacture was scutching, the beating of the retted flax to dress it, and the final process was beetling, when the cloth was hammered to produce a sheen on the surface. Both processes can be done by hand but were mechanised in the eighteenth century. Lewis-Crosby found a beetling mill at Wellbrook, County Tyrone, dating from that time, modified in the nineteenth century. He secured it as a gift and after an appeal for funds, restored it, again using the Development Services Scheme to help. It had been working until a few years before and now with its leat rebuilt to power the presses it works again.

So devoted was Lewis-Crosby to the cause that for his retirement he bought at Marybrook a complex of house, smallholding, corn and scutch mills, then completely derelict and now privately restored and preserved.

Clanwilliam's objectives included the continuation of the leadership in conservation which the Trust had already given. For example, he commissioned the listing of buildings in Armagh which were of historic or architectural importance. The lead was followed by the Ulster Architectural Heritage Society which pressed for and secured legislation for listing throughout the Province. The National Trust for Scotland had launched in Fife their successful and popular 'Little Houses' Scheme through which run-down houses of good quality were bought, restored and re-sold subject to restrictive covenants on the basis of a revolving fund. Northern Ireland set out to do the same, sponsoring an organisation with the acronym of HEARTH, as a Friendly Society to take advantage of grants available. It was funded with a £20,000 interest free loan jointly from the National Trust and the Pilgrim Trust. Very slow to start, it has probably not made anything like the impact of the NTS scheme but it most certainly was the first measure of its kind in the Province.

There is a refreshing eclecticism about the readiness of the Northern Ireland Committee at least to consider taking on almost everything, and a somewhat alarming uncertainty as to whether there has been a sufficiently thorough appreciation of the long-term results. It was an inspired confidence which prompted them to take on, in co-operation with the owners, a High Victorian gin-palace, the Crown Liquor Saloon in Belfast. At the time of the offer it was a sad and dreary place, its windows shuttered after repeated repercussions from the bombing of the Europa Hotel across and down the street. Now restored in all the glory of its mahogany cubicles, ornamentation and coloured glass it is a warm and lively relic of what had been a great feature of the city a hundred years ago.

The Committee also undertook management on behalf of others, only done in England, with reluctance, in respect of Heveningham. No less than ten Presidents of the United States were of Scotch-Irish descent, their families originating in Ulster, and the Government was ready to try to preserve their homes. The Trust managed the Wilson House, owned by the Scotch-Irish Trust, and was prepared to do the same for the Mellon House, home of the progenitors of that multi-millionaire, and the home of Judge Arthur Mellon.

The American connection is also celebrated by the preservation in Strabane of Gray's printing press where according to tradition the printer of the Declaration of Independence, John Dunlap learned his trade, and where the grandfather of President Wilson was also an apprentice. The press at the back of the house behind a little shop on the street which leads to the bridge over the River Bane into the Republic, is intact, and one day could well be at work again.

Lord Clanwilliam retired from the Chairmanship in 1978 and he summarises those fifteen years as having achieved growth both in terms of preservation and of popular support, and of true integration with the National Trust as a whole. The outstanding element has, in his view, been the imaginative generosity of the way in which Government has used the Ulster Land Fund. Looking back through this chapter there can be no doubt that he is right.

Integration became an evident fact when a year after Lord Clanwilliam retired the Committee gladly accepted the appointment of Anthony Lord to replace the retiring Lewis-Crosby, and exchanged the title of Secretary with that of Regional Director, then recently introduced elsewhere. Tony Lord had been Cubby Acland's assistant and successor in the Lake District. Thoughtful, patient and determined, but with an adventurous spirit, he proved to be an excellent next-step for the Trust in the Province, very gradually working to put a sound administrative base on which to sustain what had been done and from which to do more.

It would be idle to pretend there were never any difficulties. Florence Court had been given to the Trust, with a very small patch of land, by Viscount Cole, son of the 5th Earl Enniskillen. He died while still a young man and his cousin who succeeded him could not get on with the Trust at all. The arrangement was that he should live in the house and that his furniture should remain there on 'permanent loan'. The disagreement went very deep, so that for a long period he would give no access to the Trust (during which time there was a serious outbreak of dry rot) nor respect the loan agreement. Lewis-Crosby once went there with Lord Antrim, the Trust's national Chairman, and Lord Clanwilliam as Northern Ireland Chairman, to try to mend matters. At lunchtime Lord Enniskillen was served with sherry and withdrew to enjoy luncheon while the National Trust Lords and their Secretary picnicked in the hall. Eventually Lord Enniskillen was obliged to leave, but with his land actually abutting on the house he was in a position, if he wished, to put it almost into a state of siege. Eventually this was resolved by the acquisition of land from Lord Enniskillen.

The business of insufficient land to protect a house was common to perhaps a majority of all those acquired by the Trust in early days. It was true also of Castle Coole where less than a fifth of the 420-acre park had been acquired, which, since the glory of the setting was at least an equal part of the beauty of the house, could have been a disaster, as the Local Authority coveted it for use as a golf course. As at Florence Court this problem was solved by purchase from Lord Belmore.

Castle Coole also produced another crisis. The superbly precise ashlar work of Portland stone – brought by sea to Ballyshannon, thence by ox-cart ten miles to Lough Erne, and by water again to Enniskillen – had been, as was the eighteenth-century custom, secured by iron cramps. By the 1970s the rusting and expansion of the cramps had begun to cause an extensive spalling, or splitting off, of the surfaces of the stone. The Ulster Land Fund had given money for repair when the house was bought for the Trust but it had included nothing like this which required the dismantling of the outer surface, section by section, and rebuilding with cramps of stainless steel and the replacement of many blocks. It is to the National Heritage Memorial Fund that the Trust owes the funding of this immense operation of repair. Castle Coole has been closed for several years while the repair work was undertaken and at the same time the heavy neo-classical and Regency exterior have been painstakingly restored. It re-opened to the public in June 1988.

No one will wish to dwell upon the Troubles which flared up again in 1969 and have been in intermittent eruption ever since. It has been to the credit of the conduct of the work of the Northern Ireland Committee that the Trust, an easy target for terrorism, has apparently not been seen as an enemy.

There was just one occasion on which the Trust was a target, and even that may have been mainly an action against the Belfast City Council. They were the owners of Malone House, a fine building in the parkland of Barnet Demesne. The National Trust took a lease and transferred its office there. It was part of the arrangement that some of the rooms should be open to the public and that refreshments should be available. National Trust members were encouraged to use this as a social centre, and the Committee had an information room with a display of craft goods. Soon after the office opened on 11 November 1976 three boys and a girl, all armed, burst in, planted two bombs, making the staff lie on the floor and warning them not to move before three minutes had passed. No sooner had the raiders gone than the staff left too, and none too soon for the bombs exploded almost at once. A fire started and the fire brigade arrived, checking to see that no lives were in danger. Then, being on strike they sat outside and watched the house burn while the staff rescued what they could. So outraged by this was public opinion that the strike ended but the loss of its records, which was almost complete, was a most damaging injury to the Trust.

The response of the staff was an instant hardening of resolve to recover and continue. They set up a new office in the house at Rowallane where the Lewis-Crosbys moved over to give them as much room as possible.

The story of the National Trust in Northern Ireland is one of enterprise in difficult circumstances. The success, which has merited all the support given to it by the central organisation, would have been impossible without the help of the dedicated staff and committee members. Three who deserve a particular mention are Charles Brett who has been a valuable member of the Committee throughout its existence, Dr Alan Burgess, Chairman of the Committee from 1978 to 1981 and Lord O'Neill, the current Chairman.

CHAPTER XXI

Marks for Good Conduct

In the commercial world a business has principally to satisfy its shareholders, and the measure of their satisfaction is profit. In the process of achieving profits the business generally has to satisfy its customers. For the National Trust there is no simple yardstick of satisfaction. It does have to answer to several groups – its members, its benefactors and 'the nation' for whose benefit it works – but perhaps the only way of telling whether they are satisfied is by discovering whether they continue their support.

It seems that 'the nation', in so far as it is represented by Parliament and successive Governments, is satisfied with the Trust: it has promoted such legislation as has been put before it, and has gradually – very gradually – rewarded it with relief from certain taxes, which has been an enormous help.

It is true that at one point a Minister did consider 'nationalising' the National Trust. Richard Crossman proposed to the Prime Minister, Harold Wilson, a complete Government takeover of the whole of the functions and property of the National Trust. It is not clear what prompted this, because the idea hardly matches even the most dogmatic interpretation of centralised state socialism. It may be that with the legislation which was to lead to the Countryside Act 1968 already being worked up in the Ministry of Housing and Local Government someone may have thought it a good idea to endow the proposed Countryside Commission with a nice slice of property, or perhaps the museum world, dissatisfied with and jealous of the Trust at that time as we know, may have made the suggestion. Kenneth Robinson, then Minister of Health, is inclined to dismiss it as just another somewhat irresponsible quirk of Crossman's. At all events, Mr Wilson consulted Robinson who advised him against it, and nothing more was heard of the idea, nor has it since been revived.

Membership is best judged by numbers and continuing support – especially the proportion of those who renew their membership regularly over a fair number of years. The character of the membership has certainly changed over the years, and will probably continue to change. From the first one hundred in 1895, and for over fifty years, members were a very small band of like-minded people, conscious of the need for preservation and determined to support and work for the cause. This membership grew, drawing more recruits from that class of responsible and reasonably well-off people who are prepared to support charities as much out of a sense of duty as special interest. The change may really have dated from 1950, when the membership topped 20,000 for the first time, after which the increase to 100,000 took only ten years. The Extraordinary General Meeting of 1967 may have had much to do with this: it certainly stirred up a large body of loyal support.

Neptune and the EGM also produced a new and different membership, inspired by Benson's campaign to increase numbers. Never before had the public been so well-informed about the Trust and, not since the early days, had so many people been keen to do something in addition to paying their subscriptions. As the total swelled year by year – ¼ million by 1971; ½ million in 1975; ¾ million in 1978; over the million in 1981; 1½ million in 1987 – this same characteristic seems to have remained dominant. It can, perhaps, be measured by the activity of the so-called member centres. These groups of members are, at least in theory, self-generating, and are not constitutionally a part of the Trust. They exist primarily to support the work of the Trust. They engage the interest of members who join them with a variety of National Trust orientated social events. The first to be founded was in Manchester, by Mrs Dorothy Barton, who later served for very many years on the Council of the Trust. By 1967 there were thirteen such centres, and ten years later 78. They have averaged something like 10 per cent of the total membership. The 167 centres in 1987 possibly represent some 150,000 people actively interesting themselves in the Trust's work and raising money for it – to the tune of the best part of 450,000. Besides that the centre members give all sorts of voluntary help, such as staffing exhibitions and acting as room stewards in houses open to the public, stewarding at AGMs, and promoting local appeals and recruiting new members. This continuing surge of voluntary effort can only mean that these members at least believe in the Trust.

Another register of confidence was provided in 1982 when an Extraordinary General Meeting was requisitioned by a group representing wholly outside interests. The resolutions were in terms of out-and-out no confidence in the Chairman and Director General, and by inference the Committees and staff. The vote went overwhelmingly against the requisitionists. What the membership did say, however, was that they wished to be even better informed and given the chance to be even more closely involved. While that in itself is an indication of strong support for the Trust, it shows that the organisation must remain sensitive to the feelings of ordinary members.

This leaves us to consider the Trust's benefactors and especially those who have given property. Without their gifts the Trust would never have become what it is today. Why did they give property to the Trust, and what did they expect would be the result? How has it all turned out for them and are they too, satisfied customers? It may be better to start the other way round and to look first for dissatisfaction, fortunately rare.

One gift that did go wrong was that of the 4th Lord St Oswald's of his Yorkshire house Nostell Priory. The method of conveyance was most unusual, Lord St Oswald introducing a private Bill in the Lords which was designed to provide for the resolution of family trusts. In the course of its passage it was in some measure amended, and became less easily workable as a result. The fault of the Trust lay in its acceptance of the gift on terms which were almost certain to be unsatisfactory. The house contained an outstanding collection of Chippendale furniture, which was made specially for it. This was retained by Lord St Oswald, but the Act provided that a loan agreement should be made and the furniture kept in the house, insured at the expense of the Trust.

His son, the 5th Lord St Oswald who succeeded to Nostell in 1957, soon found himself in disagreement with the Trust. This may have prompted him to defer the completion of the loan agreement for the furniture. It was fortunate indeed that the Trust decided that it would fulfil its share of that particular arrangement unilaterally and insure the contents for, in 1980, a fire destroyed two rooms and damaged four others.

Not that there was a direct benefit to the Trust, for the money passed to the Trustees of Lord St Oswald's estate. The Trust eventually felt that it was not deriving or giving any benefit by continuing to press upon Lord St Oswald its ideas about how the house should be managed and presented to the public, but though there was some rapprochement before Lord St Oswald died in 1984, the situation remained fundamentally unchanged. That is a sad thing to have happened, and a warning to the Trust to do all that it can to avoid acceptance of property on terms which do not seem certain to be workable. Unfortunately there have been too many other examples of that mistake.

The question of the ownership of the contents of houses has been the cause of several of the Trust's problems. It was realised from the inception of the Country Houses Scheme that the house depended upon its contents for an illustration of the true appearance of a home. Beyond that the collections which so many country houses contained were of themselves an integral part of the social and cultural phenomenon which they represent. However, in the earlier days of the scheme it was assumed that if a donor agreed to keep the contents in the house, they would safely stay there, and generally they did. There was less urgency then to persuade the donor to make an outright gift of them as well as the house and land, or to try to raise the money to buy them.

What nobody could foresee was the immense increase in the value of objects of all sorts which began in the 1960s and in the 1980s soared to astronomical heights. In these changed circumstances those who succeeded to the ownership of pictures and furniture left in National Trust houses on so called 'permanent loan', found themselves possessed of objects which would bring them very large sums of money if sold. Quite often they were not themselves in particularly affluent circumstances and there was a great temptation, often a real need, to realise their assets.

Lord Clanwilliam's experience at Florence Court led him to declare that never again should the Trust again countenance a 'permanent loan'. Elsewhere there were problems. At Uppark the urgency was such that the Trust has since been obliged to find quite considerable sums in order to retain in the house objects which were almost as much a part of it as the bricks and mortar. There was a similar emergency when the Trustees for the Earl of Powys decided that they must raise a substantial sum and at short notice removed from Powis Castle a picture by Bellotto, a 'View of Verona'. The major part of the contents of the house had been transferred to the Trust in 1952 but not this picture. It is of high artistic merit but the special thing about it is that it is one of the few remaining of the collection formed by Clive of India, whose son became Earl of Powis, and for most of its existence had hung in that house. Sotheby's, on behalf of the Trustees, offered it to the National Gallery which, quite properly, decided to buy it. What then became the issue was not the preservation of the picture but whether or not it really ought to stay in its own home. The Trust thought that it should and set about raising the money. With magnificent help from the National Heritage Memorial Fund, the National Art Collections Fund, Victoria and Albert Museum grant-in-aid and private benefactions it succeeded, and the picture is now at Powis for ever.

There can be no objection to the Trustees disposing of an asset for the benefit of their Trust, nor to the National Gallery taking up the offer of a fine picture, but the incident does highlight an aspect of the relationship between some donors or their successors and the National Trust which is liable to be under some strain in circumstances of that kind.

In very many cases some idea of what a donor might feel about the fate of property he has given may after his – or her – death be quite reliably expressed by someone who was closely acquainted with his – or, again, her – ideas. It has seemed useful to consider the case of Sir Charles Trevelyan and Wallington, because as we have seen relationships with him were not entirely satisfactory – although always friendly – during the closing decade of his life. His elder daughter, Pauline Dower, is in no doubt about how her father would feel about the Trust's stewardship. On behalf of her sister as well as for herself she writes, 'I can certainly say that we certainly consider that Sir Charles's wishes and hopes are being fulfilled as regards Wallington, its surroundings and the fine gardens.' She acknowledges the Trust's expertise on questions of art, and is particularly warm in her appreciation of Sheila Pettit who, first in an honorary capacity and later on the paid staff, was the Trust's Representative. Mrs Dower notes the problems of wear and tear and the control of large numbers of visitors, and the difficulty of keeping the appearance under those conditions compatible with a home and not a museum. 'But the most usual comment we hear is that Wallington is "homely" – which we consider a compliment both to the house itself as our family used it, and to its tenure by the Trust who have kept its character most carefully.'

Mrs Dower might well have been critical of the Trust's estate management policy since it has been from the beginning very different from her father's. Certainly she has misgivings about the recent policy of letting houses on long lease for a premium. This course has been forced on the Trust by legislation highly unfavourable to landlords letting for shorter terms on annual rents. It has been made acceptable by the social and economic changes which have drastically reduced the number of country people who actually have their livelihood from the farms and the estates. 'Our local people fear that there will be newcomers who have no real connection with this estate and who will be leased houses and cottages which local people need. My own view is that the place belongs to the Trust and that a landlord must run his estate as he sees fit.'

It is indeed the policies forced upon it by changing circumstances that are most likely to incur the regret if not the displeasure of a donor, and no change has been greater in the last forty years than that of the rural economy. A landlord's new policy can, and the Trust's should, be tempered to avoid undue hardship, but it is improbable that change can be completely resisted except in such very special circumstances as in the Lakes and North Wales. It is not everyone who would accept, as Mrs Dower does, that the Trust cannot be asked to do more than its best.

There is a curious conflict to be resolved if one tries to decide whether Sir Harold Nicolson and his wife (Vita Sackville-West) would be pleased with the Trust for trying to preserve their home, Sissinghurst Castle in Kent. In the first place they were not the donors. They had found the place derelict in 1930, made of it a very special kind of home and formed around it a garden of great beauty. They did not do this with the expenditure of a lot of money. Neither was rich and they did it with their heads, hands and hearts. To them Sissinghurst was a precious and personal thing, not an inheritance from forbears nor a creation for posterity.

Vita died in 1962 and her two sons, Nigel and Ben, were faced with finding the money to meet Estate Duty which could only be done by selling up the property. The decision to offer it instead to the Treasury for transfer to the National Trust cannot have been easy. The Trust would not be able to take the house and garden unendowed and there was not enough money for that, so that the only way to manage was to include the 285 acre farm with its revenue. That was a sacrifice because, if the farm had been sold, there would have been something left over after duty had been paid. More importantly Vita Sackville-West had most certainly been against the idea. She had hated her childhood home, Knole, going out of the family and her son Nigel found that she had written in her diary about the same fate for Sissinghurst, 'Never, never, never that hard little plate at my door'.

However, the Nicolsons were resolved to do their best to preserve their parents' home and the garden they had created and so in 1967 the conveyance to the Trust from the Treasury finally took place, and Nigel Nicolson gave as much as he could, £15,000, to add to the endowment. He was to all intents and purposes at least part donor with the Treasury, for without him the transaction could not have been begun, and he continues to live in the house as resident donor.

From that position he gives his opinion on the result:

> I am absolutely delighted. It is the wisest thing my family has done. You see, there are very strong emotional ties. Father and Mother made this place and died here, and my brother and I were brought up here. I have not had one moment's regret. Firstly I have no great financial worry. If I were to have tried to manage it myself there would have been the problem of fluctuation in revenue from visitors: I am relieved of that. Then the income to run the garden is tax free. Without that it could not be maintained. These are overwhelming reasons. I hope my son Adam, who is married, may want to live here, and that would give me great pleasure.

That Nigel Nicolson can be so emphatic when the major element in the property is that most difficult thing to preserve, a garden, is particularly remarkable. Moreover it is a garden made by two people for their own pleasure, intimate and personal. There have been and are critics of the way in which the garden has changed over the last fifteen years. Generally the criticism is that it has become too tidy, too well-disciplined.

Nigel Nicolson rejects that criticism. 'The garden was always different in my Mother's time: she was always experimenting. It is right to preserve the spirit and the functional nature of the garden; it is wrong slavishly to repeat a plant or plants. 90 per cent of the garden is the same as it was, 10 per cent of it is new but in the same spirit.'

On his death in 1942, Sir Francis D'Arcy Cooper left to the Trust his 1,000 acre estate of Drovers, which lies among folds of the South Downs between Midhurst and Chichester. There was a condition that his nephew, Henry Benson, should be entitled, if he wished, to take the shooting. Here, where the Downs begin to broaden as they spread westward towards Hampshire they shelter scenes which represent the rustic orderliness which eighteenth-century enclosure imposed. Also, with their long and narrow copses of hazel underwood growing beneath standards of oak, they offer the best of pheasant shooting. It was Henry Benson, of course, who took the chair of the Trust's Advisory Committee in 1969. His connection with the donor, his long subsequent association with the Drovers Estate and his penetrating inquiry into the conduct of the Trust qualify him to give an opinion on how his uncle would regard the way in which the Trust had fulfilled his intentions as donor. 'The impelling spirit of every donor,' he says, 'is to preserve the heritage of buildings and their contents, and the landscape for their continued enjoyment by those in whose family possession they have been, while sharing them with the public.'

If that is applied to Drovers, what is the Trust's record? There have been mistakes Lord Benson says, for example the over-enthusiastic forestry of thirty years ago which led to overplanting, especially with conifers. Then again later there was a period when the estate cottages were left too long in some disrepair. His view is, however, that the Trust has overall made a good job of the management and that one of the most serious risks – damage to the landscape and to the sport by agricultural improvements – has been avoided. From his personal point of view he has found the Trust considerate in consultation with him over matters which directly affect his interests such as forestry work and public access.

To the question, 'Do you think that your uncle would have been satisfied that the National Trust has done its job properly?' he gives an unqualified answer: 'Yes, he would.'

It is noticeable time and time again in the Trust's story how there are personal links between all sorts of different people connected in one way or another with its work. Harold Nicolson's sister married the 3rd Baron St Levan, who with his son John gave St Michael's Mount in Marazion Bay, Cornwall, to the Trust in 1954.

There was no automatic decision to give the island to the Trust: a viable alternative would have been the formation of a company on the pattern established at Woburn by the Duke of Bedford, and by Lord Montagu at Beaulieu. They did in fact turn to the Trust for the wholly altruistic reason that it represented a Trustee on whom they could depend in perpetuity. They were not entirely confident that the scheme would work satisfactorily and to start with thought of giving just a part of the island, but in the end they took the course of making a gift of the freehold and taking a lease back. Even then they insured their independence in case of conflict by retaining ownership of the two terrace gardens below the south cliff under the house, and of part of the village and part of the harbour.

Their agent Claude Pendlebury, was expert with the various devices which could be adopted to make the arrangements as favourable as he could for the donors. For example, in those days income tax was payable on the annual value of property, although the valuation for 'Schedule A' was always very far below the real value. He set the rent payable at the Schedule A level so that no one could challenge his valuation – and at £200 a year that was no great hardship on the tenants.

Furthermore for the dual purpose of giving the St Levans control over the entertainment of visitors and an earned income for tax purposes, he introduced into the lease a provision that they should have the right to operate the tourist trade. Finally, the lease was very restrictive of public access: on Wednesdays and Fridays the church and blue drawing room were shown to guided parties only at fixed times between four and six times each day in October and May, although tourists were admitted more frequently during June to September. It is small wonder that St Michael's Mount was one of the places singled out by Conrad Rawnsley as an example of how the rich used the Trust for a tax refuge.

It was, of course, entirely up to the Trust whether or not they accepted such terms, and if it was wrong to do so the fault first lay with the senior staff in London. They left young Michael Trinick, inexperienced and very new in Cornwall, to deal with the negotiations entirely on his own. Trinick, to whom food was an essential part of life, was nearly deprived of his pudding at his very first visit because the butler would not hold a rather hard treacle tart sufficiently steady for him to cut into it. Probably his greatest success in those early days was to find the courage to say rather sharply, 'If you would please put it on the table perhaps I shall be able to have some.' He did not manage well and in the face of Lord St Levan's grandeur and Claude Pendlebury's devious skill he was outgunned.

The present Lord St Levan, looking back at that time and with the benefit of long experience on the Estates Committee, believes that the Trust was wrong to have taken the Mount on the terms it did, but on the other hand the gift would not have been made on other terms.

From this really rather unpromising start which might well have settled down to permanent private and public dissatisfaction, there has been a remarkably happy outcome. To this the Trust's only contribution – but perhaps a vital one – 'has been', in John St Levan's words, 'to have abided by its promises, and to have been a faithful trustee'. The rest lies to his credit, because he has greatly liberalised and improved public access, he has promoted the tourist trade to its utmost, giving all his profits to the Trust, and he has substantially added to the endowment from his own pocket; all this in consultation and with the agreement of the Trust but entirely on his own initiative. Public access is now given twice a week through the winter, four days a week in spring and five through the summer, and the number of visitors is about or over 170,000 a year.

Lord St Levan says that his expectations as joint donor have been fulfilled. He and his wife have their home there, and the Mount as a whole has been well maintained and improved in a variety of ways. The 'tourist trade licence' has worked as intended: he runs it as a business for the benefit of the property. He is confident of the future, and expects that his nephew and heir will be able to live there, although to do so he will need that revenue and the benefit of his uncle's other commercial interests.

A curious effect of the growth of National Trust membership has been the way in which the members' privilege of free access to places where a charge is made has affected properties which rely for solvency on admission fees. Even a property accepted as recently as Plas Newydd in 1976 – has had its estimates falsified by the ever increasing proportion of members to paying visitors. That is not so serious for properties to which the money comes back again in terms of Head Office subvention, but for places which have to finance themselves the problem has been serious, and the Trust's slowness to help to resolve it has been Lord St Levan's only serious criticism. In recent years things have been in some measure adjusted by internal book-keeping.

The clearest indication that a large number of benefactors are satisfied with the Trust is that many who give money for its various needs keep on doing the same thing again and again. Such men as Philip Henman, and Kenneth Levy would certainly not have come regularly to the aid of the Trust if they had thought their money was ill spent, and a very large number of similar examples can be culled from a study of the benefactors' lists in the annual reports. Even so, they probably do not provide as important an illustration of the motivation and subsequent reaction as do those who have given property with which they and their families are involved, and of such none offers subject for such a rewarding study as does Sir Richard Acland, to whom and to whose family there have already been a number of references.

In Devon there are still a number of families that bear the name of the place from which they sprang and where they still live – Cruwys of Cruwys Morchard, Fursdon of Fursdon, Fulford of Great Fulford. The Aclands of Acland Barton are of the same stock but, mainly by marrying well, they became possessed of great estates in Somerset and Cornwall as well as Devon, reaching a peak of both land and money in the late-eighteenth century. Richard Dyke Acland was born in 1906. His great-grandfather, the 11th Baronet, had two sons, Charlie, the elder, who died childless and Arthur who had a family of three. Francis was the elder son and married Eleanor Cropper of Kendal and he, Richard, was their eldest son.

His grandfather Arthur is important in the story because of his character. He was brilliant, intense, somewhat erratic, but in the end highly successful in politics. Although not averse to a degree of wealth he had absolutely no interest whatsoever in landed property and had he come into any would have sold it and spent the proceeds on his political career. In 1892, after some years in Parliament during which time he had made a reputation for himself as a champion of the artisans of the northern and midland counties, he was hoping for a junior ministerial appointment when he suddenly found himself in charge of the Education Office with a seat in the Cabinet. This was Gladstone's appointment, but made on the recommendation of Haldane. He is described at that point as being 'a first-rate administrator, an experienced educationalist, and a red-hot social reformer'.

Provision was made that on Charlie's death the lands should by-pass Arthur and go to his son Francis, and that is what happened in 1919.

Just two years earlier Uncle Charlie had taken a quite remarkable step in leasing to the National Trust some 7,000 acres of his Holnicote Estate in West Somerset. Lord Plymouth in his letter to *The Times* announcing this said: 'The substance of it is that Sir Thomas [as Uncle Charlie was formally known] and his successors will continue to enjoy the rents and profits and all the ordinary rights and powers of an owner, except that the owner will have no power to develop the estate as a building estate and the Trust obtains such control over the exercise of his other powers as may be necessary to preserve the property, so far as possible, in its present beauty and natural condition.'

Hardwicke Rawnsley, making his tour of the West Country in the high summer of the following year, was taken round the Trust's leasehold by the agent. Mounted on Exmoor ponies they climbed North Hill, which lies between the sea and the

Porlock Vale, admiring the *cottages ornées* of Selworthy as they went. 'We saw many houses that day upon the Holnicote Estate and not one of them ... but made us feel that an artist had planned it and would wish to have the chance of drawing it.' They dropped down from the crest, having looked upon the Bristol Channel, through the woods above Bossington, '... filled with silver fir, spruce, Douglas pine (sic), and Scotch fir, chestnuts and Wellingtonias, planted by the grandfather of the present owner ... Carefully made grassy rides passed off left and right of the main track. What a delightful wander round on a hot summer day would this cool woodland give to future generations.'

Over the old packhorse bridge at Allerford they went and across the vale to Horner, with its walnut groves, exclaiming as they rode up Horner Water to Cloutsham of the beauty of its oakwoods, and musing on the more than ten centuries of stag hunting for which the place had been a famous centre. Next day they went further afield to Winsford Hill where among the Celtic field banks Rawnsley was much taken by the Caratacus Stone. They went down the old clapper bridge of Tarr Steps. But the highlight of his day was at Old Ashway farm where the Aclands' herd of Exmoor ponies was kept. 'The master of the house was away, but his only daughter, a pure Celt, with her raven-black hair and dark eyes, gave us courteous welcome ...' It is hard to tell after that whether it was the ponies, 'delicate limbed creatures with mealy muzzles' or this hard riding 'Diana of the Moor' as she went to round up the herd, captivated the Canon the more.

Hardwicke Rawnsley's unqualified raptures not only were surely justified at that time but would be equally justifiable today. Out of all the beautiful places in England, Wales and Northern Ireland – and it would be right in respect of some of them to use the word 'incomparable' – there is none that can produce a variety of aspect, history and feeling as is encompassed by the Holnicote Estate, and its excellence is perhaps the key to Uncle Charlie's decision to seek the Trust's protection for it and is certainly relevant to his great nephew's gift twenty-five years later.

Richard Acland, cast somewhat in the same way as his grandfather Arthur, followed his father and grandfather in a political career. Francis gave Holnicote to him in 1927 in order to avoid Estate Duty by a gift made seven years before his death – which he did indeed achieve. However, he retained the rents and profits from the estate and paid his son an allowance, and in any event, on his own and his wife Anne's evidence, Richard had little real interest in the estates as such at any time. He enjoyed the excellent shooting which Holnicote afforded and dabbled in projects for housing development designed to be unobtrusive. Unhappily it did not go as he wanted it and the ribbon development along the lane from Porlock to Bossington is the result.

He stood for Parliament, unsuccessfully, when he was only nineteen, but did get elected as Liberal M.P. for North Devon ten years later. Reading Maynard Keynes' General Theory almost as soon as it was published converted him to socialism, but the Liberal party policy of collective security against war, which he embraced himself most strongly, kept him tied to the Liberal party. In 1936 he married Anne Alford whom he met when he, briefly, and she, staying on to receive an Honours Diploma, were students at the School of Architecture. It is an Acland characteristic, especially well developed in Richard, that to think a thing is to put it into practice, and so when the Second War began he started to work on the creation of a new political party based on the idea that common ownership of wealth was not only sound economics but morally right. His Commonwealth party won several wartime by-elections but was overwhelmed by the Labour landslide of 1945. He faced reality, joined Labour and was elected for Gravesend in 1947 and held it until he resigned in protest against the Labour party's decision to approve the manufacture of the hydrogen bomb. He failed to get re-elected and spent the rest of his working life teaching, first at a very big comprehensive school in Wandsworth and then lecturing at St Luke's College, Exeter, of which his great-grandfather had been a co-founder.

When he succeeded to the baronetcy, the 15th in line, his estates were reduced by sales to meet Estate Duty to those of Holnicote and Killerton, in acreage about half of what there had been one hundred and fifty years before, and in money value probably a lot less than half. Holni- (pronounced 'Honey')- cote has had a brief description through the Canon's eyes. Killerton is entirely different. Half of it consists of farms on some of the best of the Devon red-soils. The other half is on the nastiest possible sort of clay. There are out of its 6,000 acres a full thousand of woodland, including the great block of Ashclyst Forest which was planted on farmland which fell derelict after the Napoleonic Wars. The house sits on the edge of the red-soil, facing south and backed by a hump of volcanic trap-rock, producing an oasis of acid soil in a plain of fertile alkilinity. Here the Aclands had indulged their passion for plants in creating and improving a garden where the rarity of the stock was only out-done by its quality. The house looked towards the village of Broadclyst which, with several other hamlets, gave the estate a very considerable population. In beauty of composition Killerton could not hold a candle to Holnicote, but in terms of its garden, its woods, its farms, its buildings and its people it was the essence of rural England.

In 1944 Richard Acland gave the two estates, in their entirety, to the National Trust. Both he and his wife Anne had a romantic appreciation of the beauty of the land and an emotional admiration for the qualities and action of great-uncle Charlie. They were certain that the next lot of death duties would break up the properties – Holnicote would go on Richard's death; what would be left at their son's death? Above all, in common with many at that time they believed that the old order had passed away for ever. 'If the Archangel Gabriel had come to me in 1943 and said that in forty years time there would be a Government in power with the policies of this one [Mrs Thatcher's] I should have replied, "You're lying! You're not a real Archangel: you must be the Devil!" '

Anne Acland jumped at the idea of a gift to the National Trust. 'It really did seem the most responsible thing to do with all this that had come to us and for which we felt tremendously answerable.' Her work on the Killerton Estate had grafted on to her socialism the paternalistic attitude of trusteeship which had been the sterling characteristic of Uncle Charlie.

So an offer was made to the Trust. Though Richard Acland does not recall any doubts expressed by the Trust it was not a straightforward decision. The doubts which Benny Horne had expressed about acceptance of farmland at Wallington applied with equal force to the Killerton farms. On the face of things, while Holnicote was clearly worthy of preservation for its landscape, farms, villages and all, Killerton by the standards of the time was not.

For Richard Acland it was all or nothing. He and his wife looked askance at the way in which Sir Charles Trevelyan had retained a life interest from his gift of Wallington and they were ashamed that several farms on each estate were tied by the terms of a marriage settlement and could be sold but not given away. Hubert Smith thought that it was George Trevelyan's advocacy alone that overcame the Trust's doubts. Providentially the Trust had received Mrs Greville's legacy and was able to buy in the marriage settlement farms with that.

Sir Richard and Lady Acland broke the news to the estate staff in that traditional place of assembly, the sawmill in the estate yard, and later that evening in the Victory Hall in Broadclyst to the farm tenants. It never occurred to them that their sons and those whom Anne describes as 'the extended family' of the estate, would not see it the same way as they did. Alas, it was not so. From their varying standpoints there was initial disbelief, puzzlement and then a feeling of rejection and betrayal, and this was also the feeling of others far removed from personal involvement. There were bitter letters to *The Times* about abdication of responsibility and those feelings were shared, and retained for a very long time, by other county families. George Trevelyan took their part in *The Times* correspondence and Anthony Martineau got a letter of support published too.

Is Sir Richard satisfied that his expectations and aspirations have been realised? 'Well, yes, but let's face it; the National Trust has a mental block about living donors. Donors are supposed to be dead! To be fair, in essence my intentions have been realised but because organisations are subject to the human frailties of those engaged in them there have been problems.'

Those problems had all sorts of causes, but a thread which runs through the relationship between the donor and the Trust is that the latter had accepted a detailed memorandum of wishes, a key feature of which was that the Trust undertook to consult him and his wife on all aspects of estate management. Of course, they were not so consulted, and indeed in practice they could not be, since for some years they were seldom in Devon and never in Somerset, and even when they were at Killerton they were fifty-five difficult miles from Holnicote.

So the first ten years were not happy ones, but really all this sprang from the emotional upset which accompanied the gift. The passage of time alone would have soothed these feelings, but that process was helped by the way in which everyone concerned became swept along with the better times that began in the late 1950s. On the estate agriculture began to get positively prosperous, buildings were improved, houses and cottages modernised, there was over-full employment and wages rose rapidly. One by one the older tenants gave way to their sons whose attachment to the old days and to the Acland family was second-hand, and in that family itself the three boys grew up, took degrees or professional qualifications and went their separate ways. Richard Acland and his wife had been living at Killerton since the early 1960s, first in a flat in the house and later in the dower house they had occupied when he first succeeded his father. They were easier of access and consultation on important aspects of management policy was a more practicable affair.

In retrospect Sir Richard and Lady Acland think that not only did they do what they then believed to be right, but that the outcome has been as satisfactory as could be expected. The estates are preserved almost intact – only the M5 motorway having taken away anything given to the Trust for preservation.

The change from paternalism is a matter for regret but it would certainly have happened anyhow. Acland tells the story of Mrs Rawle at West Lynch, a fine barley-growing farm on the Holnicote Estate. Since the Trust became the owners 'everything had gone wrong'. That boiled down to 'boys in the orchards, screaming'.

'But Mrs Rawle, didn't that happen before?'

'Oh yes, but we should have sent word up to Sir Charles and he would have sent down word to their parents to stop it – and stop it they would!'

There are some traditions which the National Trust simply cannot hope to preserve.

CHAPTER XXII

Retrospect

In 1975 Jack Boles succeeded Sir Frederick Bishop as the Trust's third Director General, retiring to a farm in Devon with a knighthood in the autumn of 1983 at the age of fifty-eight. Looking back after his retirement on his experience of the Trust he is in a good position to see things in perspective.

That perspective view contains remarkably little that is critical of the Trust, yet there have been aspects of its conduct which have attracted criticism.

The one outstanding new initiative has been its Country Houses Scheme. Jack Boles feels that 'If it had failed to try to rescue great country houses it would have failed in its duty to members, its founders and its constitution. Without its country houses the Trust would have grown much more slowly, be less well known and respected, and would have shown culpable inadequacy in the face of the threat to the greatest English contribution to the arts.' He acknowledges that the pendulum may have swung too far at times towards that side of its work, and that at one time the Trust's involvement with it tended to be impersonal and superior but, '... in any case I believe the arguments about the distinction between country house preservation and landscape preservation to be quite bogus, as the English tradition is to combine house, garden, park, woods, lakes and countryside as a whole, and that is what people wish the Trust to preserve as part of its work for the nation.'

The growth in membership Sir Jack rightly regards as both the reward for, and evidence of, success, but he is concerned about specialist interest which, for example, may wish to put archaeology above nature conservation, or nature conservation above landscape or any of those above public enjoyment, and equally the same in reverse. With a small membership which was wholly behind the leaders of the Trust and scarcely consulted about policy it was generally easy for the Trust to achieve its own necessary compromise. With a very large membership that is not so easy. When the Benson Committee chose the enlargement of membership as the way forward for the Trust they were thinking very much in terms of financial support and Lord Benson, Lord Gibson, Len Clark or Sir Jack Boles cannot remember anticipating at all the other consequences, good or bad, that might flow from it.

Sectional interests, however, are not new. As long ago as 1934 Mr W.A. Sibley gave notice of his intention to raise the question of hunting at the AGM and although he in the event did not take part, Commander Cather, seconded by Mr Lloyd, did propose, 'that in view of the cruelties involved in killing for sport the

Trust rescind any existing authorisations and prohibit all future hunting and shooting ...' and adduced three reasons for doing so. Ronnie Norman spoke against the motion, having been primed by Chorley who told him about the practical necessities of killing foxes in the Lake District fells and the practical impossibility of preventing it. The motion 'was put, and lost by a very large majority'.

The divergent views on the subject were well known and certain donors took pains to ensure that the Trust should be bound to act in one way or another. We have seen that Miss Chichester had already taken her own measures to protect her sanctuary and wished the Trust to continue her policy. Sir Richard Acland on the contrary made it an absolute condition of his gift of Holnicote that stag hunting, which had actually served to preserve red deer on Exmoor, should be allowed to continue. Ernest Cook obtained written confirmation from Matheson that the Trust 'would abide by Mr Cook's wishes in relation to ... permission for blood sports [meaning that they should be permitted].'

It is an especially interesting philosophical issue, not confined to this particular question, as to whether the Trust's membership is morally entitled to use its powers as trustee to secure an object which is outside the terms of its trust. It must be very tempting to do so but it is almost certainly wrong.

Boles was acutely conscious that another and similar problem might well divide the Trust for the wrong reason. The Atlantic grey seal had always used the Farne Islands as a breeding ground. This species comes ashore from about mid-October to mid-November, the pups are born and suckled and the adults mate. It is only at that time that the seals can be identified as being connected with any particular territory and a time at which they are exceptionally vulnerable, especially the pups which do not take to the water until deserted by their mothers. Seals eat fish of all sorts and as early as 1938 the salmon fishermen were complaining that their catches were reduced, and the river netsmen in particular that their nets were being damaged. The complaints were revived after the war and at the same time the colony on the Farnes began to increase dramatically in numbers. By counting the almost immobile pups it is possible to get an accurate figure of the number of breeding females and this count rose from about 800 after the war to 3,500 in 1960.

In a sense this was a triumph of conservation, but the fishermen and the Government thought otherwise and the Ministry of Agriculture and Fisheries asked permission to reduce the colony by culling the pups. This the Trust agreed under protest to allow, but members, dismayed by sensational press reporting, were up in arms and after a three year trial the Executive Committee decided to withhold consent unless it were sanctioned by a vote at an AGM. They were swayed not only by members' views but also by the emergence of responsible opinion which cast doubt on the validity of the reasons for a cull, and of the effectiveness of what was being done even if the reasons were sound.

Numbers continued to rise until by the early 1970s they had about doubled and new problems arose. Some of the islands are just rocks but the Brownsman, Staple, the Inner Farne and some smaller ones have a covering of soil which is important for the breeding of many of the sea birds and absolutely essential for puffins, which nest in burrows. The huge numbers of seals – and full grown they are very large animals – began to erode these soils with alarming rapidity, and it was clear that the fragile soil caps would go in a very short time. The seals themselves were desperately overcrowded, the breeding grounds and the pups were clearly suffering. For these quite different reasons the Trust itself decided to reduce the colony, but the numbers were so large that it was necessary to employ a Norwegian sealing company. This involved shooting the cows, getting the carcasses on board their ship and processing them there. The need for this had been accepted unanimously by members at the AGM in 1971 but when it happened in the autumn of 1972 it attracted a number of unfavourable and somewhat lurid press reports, and the operation was harassed by protesters. It is after all not reasonable to expect to be able to shoot and then butcher over 700 large animals without creating a very unpleasant scene. There was a repeat in 1975 because the first cull had made little impression on the size of the colony, but it failed to take out anything like the number needed and again attracted unfavourable attention. Since this commercial culling was both bad publicity and ineffective it was abandoned after 1975 and instead it was decided only to kill seals which attempted to use the soil-capped islands. Within three years that had remarkable results. Very few seals had to be killed and the simple presence of men on those islands was enough to deny the seals the use of them. They continued to make full use of all the other islands, but the number of cows breeding dropped dramatically. At first this was a mystery but they were later discovered in a newly formed colony on the Isle of May in the Firth of Forth.

In all this the management of the Trust had been obliged to feel its way to a solution in circumstances where there was no experience to act as a guide. The commercial culls were a great mistake but not one which could have been shown to be in advance. Throughout the whole difficult time members gave the management of the Trust their full backing. Had they not done so the solution would never have emerged and the Farne Islands as a nature reserve would have been badly damaged and the Trust would have failed in its duty.

Sir Jack Boles, looking back on the results of setting up Regional Committees, seems still to be feeling some relief that the Trust did not disintegrate into a number of more or less autonomous baronies. 'There were problems caused to Head Office by the great talents and zeal of Lord Head as Regional Chairman for Wessex. We wanted to appoint distinguished people to these posts and a cabinet minister of his calibre was quite a catch. Nevertheless he wanted quite a degree of autonomy and I think there was some danger in the post-Benson days of some regions going their own way too extensively. We always feared some UDI movement and several regional chairmen thought we were dragging our feet.'

This is where a peculiar problem surfaces. The Trust is now an organisation with immense responsibilities and has needed, and succeeded in attracting to its committees, people whose experience is commensurate with the task. That has produced a swing towards those in the stratosphere of the business world – Pat Gibson, Mark Norman, John Smith have already been much mentioned. Simon Hornby, Nicholas Baring are others who have played leading roles. In simple terms – no doubt excessively simple – the subsidiaries of groups in industry are controlled from the centre by the supply or withholding of money, and their performance is measured by profit. Lord Benson, himself a product of the same world, believed that regionalisation could be controlled in the same way, and drew a diagram to illustrate that. At the time his Committee was at work, Boles thought that its conclusions were too much influenced by company law and business practice, and in this he is supported by Sir Kenneth Robinson whose position on the Finance Committee for the last ten years gave him plenty of opportunity to watch the Trust at work. The difficulty is that regional performance cannot be measured in the same way as a business enterprise; it is not a 'profit centre'. Pat Gibson – who after a stint as Chairman of the Arts Council and with a life peerage succeeded to the Chairmanship of the Trust on the death of Lord Antrim in 1977 – recognises this. 'I have always been interested in organisation and devolution of responsibility', he has said, 'but in the National Trust it is much more difficult than in business. It is much more like the problem which the Government and the Treasury have to face. Some departments will have achieved a level of funding and consequently standards of performance, which it is very difficult to reduce.'

The fissiparous tendencies of regionalisation were to have been countered by the regional chairmen being *ex officio* members of the Executive Committee, a measure very strongly urged by Mark Norman, and it does seem that this has been effective up to a point, but financial control and regulation has proved much more difficult. The many problems of committee structure and staff functions led the Executive to set up a working party under the chairmanship of Simon Hornby, and they reported in 1984. Not unexpectedly their conclusion was to bring the Trust closer to the pattern of the business world. 'In effect the Head Office committees should acknowledge that they are in the position of a Board of Directors rather than a management committee.'

Their recipe for better control is to restore to the staff the authority that had, in theory at least, been taken away from it by the Benson Committee. 'The Director General's position should be clearly established as the Chief Executive of the Trust and the terms of reference for his job and that of other senior staff should be re-written to give them authority to manage; they should likewise be accountable for the good management of the Trust.' An even more significant reversal is that the Regional Director, and in consequence his staff, are to be responsible to the Director General and not to the Regional Chairman.

The new status of senior staff at Head Office is symbolised by becoming members of committees, as they might under other circumstances join a Board of Directors, 'rather than, as now,' runs the Report, 'an adviser and servant of it.' Sir Jack Boles would not have thought that a good thing, but since the occasions when Head Office committees have voted on anything have been rare indeed for the last forty years, it probably will not matter much one way or another.

At the time he became Director General in 1975 Boles had been instrumental in making a very important decision as to who should follow him as Secretary. This post has always been the second most responsible after the Director General and, by virtue of the fact that it was formerly the principal one in the Trust, carries an equivalent prestige. The person chosen was Ivor Blomfield, who had been Regional Agent in the South East since 1967. The appointment was made partly because Boles knew that Blomfield was a careful and meticulous administrator, with experience both of property management and of those other aspects of National Trust interests – members; donors; local committees – which are particularly thick on the ground in the South East. He wished to bring the experience of work in the provinces into Head Office, and to demonstrate that the staff could re-form like a self-regenerating family, and that its professionals of any discipline could move to the wider tasks of administration. The move was certainly welcomed by his fellow land agents for those reasons, but equally because, although quiet and unobtrusive in manner, without the talent for showmanship which had brought some of his colleagues into prominence, Blomfield was known to be efficient, fair minded and friendly, with a sympathetic warmth not too often displayed, and was very well liked indeed. In 1985 after ten years in office as Secretary he was needed for something quite different. If the Regional Directors were to become once more directly responsible to the centre, the Director General needed someone who would be the channel, and who better to make Director for Regions than someone who had done their job and a central one as well? It was a wise move to give Ivor Blomfield that job and it may well be that in ten years time it may stand out as the most effective result of the Hornby reforms.

The United States has always seemed to the Trust to have a great potential in support of the Trust's work. Canon Rawnsley crossed the Atlantic in 1899 for a five-week visit, at the suggesstion of the Duke of Westminster, to advertise the aims of the Trust, although he did it mainly by lecturing on his favourite theme, the Literary Associations of the Lake District. He got a warm commendation from Professor Van Dyke of Princeton but a dusty reception from a fellow passenger on a steamer up the Hudson: 'You talk about the beauty of natural scenery. I tell you, sir, there ain't a red cent in it!' He did succeed in procuring the help of Professor Rolfe, of Concord, Massachusetts, as Honorary Organising Secretary, and there were six 'corresponding members', all in the Eastern States, by 1900. This number rose to fifteen two years later, which was a very creditable result, and it was maintained until the 1920s, by which time there were outposts in Ohio and Missouri.

This sort of contact was maintained, with people going over at intervals on lecture tours, Jack Rathbone, for example, in the fall of 1956 addressing among others the AGM of the American National Trust and the Trustees of the Reservations of Massachusetts. There seems, however, to have been no major response in terms of financial support, which was certainly at the back of everyone's mind. Nor had the Trust been particularly forward in promoting the preservation of properties with American connections. Sulgrave Manor, the home of the Washington family, was on offer in 1903, but refused on the grounds that £5000 would be needed. Since it is a fine house in its own right and the value of the American connection was already recognised it seems strange that the Trust did not strain every effort to raise that sum. It is true that in 1956 the medieval home of the Washington family, the Old Hall in Washington, just south of the Tyne near Newcastle was accepted. But the connection is somewhat remote and the surroundings far from romantic.

It was not until 1975 that the Trust set up an American public charity with American trustees, the Royal Oak Foundation, the purpose of which was described, somewhat disingenuously, in the Annual Report as being, 'to help the Trust's friends in the United States to support conservation projects that may take their fancy.' In fact the object was primarily to set up a system whereby, under the very complicated tax laws of the USA donations to the work of the National Trust could be tax-exempt, and since that is a comparatively rare privilege the existence of the Foundation must be regarded as a success in itself.

The Trust set out to nurture it in various ways: – a titular twenty-one year lease of Washington Old Hall was presented to the Chairman of the American Revolution Bicentennial Administration; Lawrence Rich went over as a member of the eight man British Bicentennial Heritage Mission; in England a number of sponsorships for American students were arranged, and at Cliveden, appropriately, there was a garden party for prominent Americans living in Britain, graced by Mrs Armstrong the United States Ambassador. 1977 saw the President of the USA, Jimmy Carter, at the Old Hall, where Peter Orde as Chairman of the Northumbria Region, presented him with a Life Member's silver medal. The British Prime Minister, James Callaghan, who accompanied the President, was also offered one but rather sharply refused to accept it. Subsequently it was sent to him by post at Downing Street.

Five years from its creation the Foundation numbered some 3,000 members and had produced grants for quite a wide range of the Trust's undertakings. One of the reasons for the slow start lay in the need to give the cultural side of the Foundation at least an equal part with its fund raising. Its first Executive Director, Arete Swartz, was very good at the promotion of those cultural activities, but less so perhaps at money raising. Nevertheless progress there is, and work to improve it goes on. Sir Jack himself went over in 1983 to lecture, and in 1985 the Trust surpassed itself by not only being the major contributor to very successful 'The Treasure Houses of Britain' exhibition in Washington but also by seconding Gervase Jackson-Stops as Director of the Exhibition. Lord Gibson went to the opening, both the Prince and Princess of Wales paid the exhibition a visit, and the Director General followed to exploit the success.

Boles is sharply self-critical. 'Of the things with which I reproach myself, the partial success of the Trust's American effort is one that I particularly regret. We had and we still have a real opportunity there and it saddens me that we have made only modest progress towards realising our ambitions.' The extent to which it matters probably depends on the reality of the 'special relationship' which is believed to exist between the two countries. Upon that as much as on the efficiency of the organisation the usefulness to the Trust of Royal Oak depends.

Whatever the vicissitudes of its various endeavours the National Trust has been consistently fortunate in the support it has received from the Royal Family. Born in 1848, just ten years younger than Octavia Hill, Princess Louise, fourth daughter of Queen Victoria, was one of Octavia's earliest and most faithful supporters in her housing work. She was a talented artist, a watercolourist and sculptor. The statue of Queen Victoria in Kensington Gardens is her work. She married at the age of twenty-three the heir to the dukedom of Argyll. She was known as the Marchioness of Lorne for much of her long life. It was for Octavia that she accepted the Presidency of the Trust in 1902, and for her that she attended the opening of Brandelhow in the same year. But her interest was directly engaged and throughout her long life she was actively concerned to follow the Trust's progress and to exert her influence on its behalf and also on its policies. For many years she presided at the AGM and right up to her death in 1939 her secretary kept her informed about significant changes and issues.

The position of President remained vacant until it was honoured in 1944 by

304

Queen Mary, whose husband George V had been a benefactor early in his reign. She in her turn was succeeded in 1953 by Queen Elizabeth, the Queen Mother. Other members of the family have given generous support. At the 40th Anniversary dinner in 1935 the then Prince of Wales was typically forthright: 'The National Trust is really everyone's concern, and everyone can do his part to help it in its great work. We all know, most of us here tonight, the heavy demands that are made on our purses by the many charitable institutions and organisations in this country, but I feel that we have a duty to our countryside as well.' That by itself is interesting in its implicit acceptance that no other charity catered for the countryside. He went on to say: 'And if it were better known throughout Great Britain the Trust would be able to do even more than it is doing today to preserve those features of British life which have meant so much to those who live in our great cities and indeed to all who love our countryside.'

Prince Philip's consent to become Patron of the coastal appeal, Enterprise Neptune, in 1966 was of great importance. He had acquired the reputation of being a no-nonsense man who was not ready to suffer fools gladly, and for an organisation which had scarcely emerged from the stigma of 'shabby gentility' to have his support was a tremendous advantage. Not that it was a protection from what he might on occasion say, as while pausing at the Trust's stand when the Royal Show was at Norwich, he contemplated a tableau designed to illustrate the various pests which troubled its woodlands. At the sight of stuffed rabbit and grey squirrel he exclaimed 'My God! Are they preserving vermin now?'

As the Trust in the 1970s became more adventurous and event-minded the current generation of Royals rallied round. The Queen's Silver Jubilee in 1977 was a high point when, among the festivities organised by the Trust, Princess Alexandra attended a garden party at Attingham. A fortnight earlier the Prince of Wales, ever ready to help in his Principality, opened Erddig. He was met at the drive gate by Mr Yorke with a penny-farthing bicycle and very sportingly agreed to try to ride up to the house, but failed after a valiant attempt.

The Prince had just the year before done his most signal service to the Trust in the Principality by agreeing to become Patron of its appeal 'Wales in Trust', giving the project a unity and prestige which it could not have gained in any other way.

The Duke of Gloucester, an architect by training, went in 1979 to open Cragside, the extraordinary mansion of the armament manufacturer Lord Armstrong, in Northumberland. In Norman Shaw's 'Old English' style, the house, just one hundred years old, rivals Penrhyn for its complete disregard of the practicalities of resistance to weather, ease of routine maintenance, and in the quirks and quiddities of its architectural conceits. The Duke was fascinated, and after a most thorough inspection went home to Northamptonshire to write a long and helpful appreciation, with advice for future management. The same summer his cousins were also at work for the Trust, Princess Margaret re-opening the Assembly Rooms at Bath (the third such occasion since 1931), and Prince Michael of Kent doing the same for Basildon Park in Berkshire.

The member of the Royal Family who has contributed most is the Trust's President, the Queen Mother. She seemed thoroughly to have enjoyed opening the Stratford Canal in 1964. Her active participation continued in 1970 when she attended a garden party at Cliveden, where two thousand members and some of the staff were gathered in celebration of the Trust's seventy-fifth birthday. The Annual Report speaks of 'Her Majesty's evident pleasure' and it is in her open and apparently inexhaustible pleasure at meeting people on these occasions which has made them so memorable for so many.

In 1974 there was another occasion with which the Queen Mother had a special connection. The chapel on the family property at Gibside in Tyne and Wear was given to the Trust by the Executors of the 16th Earl of Strathmore, her brother. The beautiful little building, which had originally been intended to be a family mausoleum, had been restored by the Trust, and she performed the opening ceremony.

For the Trust's eightieth birthday in 1975 the Queen Mother brought royal sunshine to 2,000 members gathered at Montacute. Two years later a very special event was arranged to celebrate her daughter's Silver Jubilee. At Polesden Lacey, where she had spent part of her honeymoon, she lunched with Lord Antrim and a few selected guests including that recurrent benefactor of the Trust, Kenneth Levy. In the afternoon she presented to more than forty members of the staff who had served the Trust for more than twenty-five years silver medals and commemorative certificates. The small scale of the event – for there were no other guests apart from the families of the recipients – and the Queen Mother's wholehearted participation and informality made it a very happy day, and one on which it was possible to see a cross-section of those on whom the work of the Trust depended. There was Margaret Sach, typing at Queen Anne's Gate since 1946, Mrs Lanchbery-Brown who had been at the switchboard for about the same time; there were carpenters, gardeners, woodmen, wardens, land agents, administrators. It was also right that on the lawns at Polesden which are stiff with trees planted by royalty, the Queen Mother should add one more. (Polesden Lacey, like many other gardens in the south-east suffered from the Great Storm of 1987. The royal trees were particular casualties: the only one to survive was the blue spruce planted by the Queen Mother on her honeymoon.)

The Queen Mother celebrated her own eightieth birthday in 1980 and attended a garden party in her honour at Knole. Lord Sackville kept her so long at lunch talking to his old retainers that the programme went haywire, and to complicate the issue the usual luck with the weather also broke, with torrential rain and a lightning strike which brought out the fire brigade, fortunately for a false alarm. Neither the weather nor her eighty years seemed to weigh upon her in the very least, nor as a consequence on the 1,400 or more who were gathered to meet her.

These royal events are not the aim and object of the Trust, but they are a mark of its worth and of its success, and a celebration of the happiness of its history which so very far outweighs the things that may have gone wrong.

It is a far cry from Dinas Oleu and the Clergy House at Alfriston, and in the ninety years or so that have passed there have been so many great events and undreamed of changes in the wide world around that it seems almost impertinent of the Trust to have survived and prospered.

Not that it is itself by any means unchanged. Should it have been? When she was making her speech of thanks upon the presentation to her of her portrait by Sargent, Octavia Hill said:

'When I am gone I hope my friends will not try to carry on any special system, or to follow blindly in the track which I have trodden. New circumstances require various efforts; and it is the spirit, not the dead form, that should be perpetuated.'

CHAPTER XXIII

The
Wider Accountability

It has sometimes been hard, in recent decades, to avoid an Elgarian sense of Pomp and Circumstance about the story of the National Trust. For although a non-acquisitive policy has been reaffirmed on several occasions, the Trust's success in adding new properties to its estate – sometimes at a remarkable rate – creates the impression of 'Wider still and wider, Shall thy bounds be set.' At the same time it can create the image of a tight-rope walker, the spectators' awe not unmixed with speculation that the performer might be heading for a fall. Occasionally there may even be a perverse hope that this would happen. The episode known in shorthand as 'Bradenham' provided such an opportunity for critics.

The Bradenham Estate, comprising 1,111 acres near High Wycombe, had been accepted in 1956 under the will of Mr Ernest Cook, a notable benefactor to the Trust. A condition of the gift was that the land would be declared inalienable. The landscape importance of Bradenham lies in the views down the valley, flanked by mature beech woodland towards the Manor House and village. A small section on the plateau, comprising 40 acres to the east of the village and known as Hollybush Farm, is not of intrinsic landscape importance. It was let on a grazing licence. The neighbouring land houses the Headquarters of RAF Strike Command which maintained an underground command centre dating back to the Second World War. From time to time, the Trust had been in negotiations with its neighbour about boundary issues of mutual interest, such as the establishment of a caravan site by the Trust in the 1970s. It emerged, though not immediately, that the Ministry of Defence was unenthusiastic about caravans because of its wish to 'safeguard' the site. But not until April 1979 did it transpire that it wished to modernise its communications centre by building an underground structure at Hollybush. For this it would need from the Trust a ninety-nine-year lease of twelve acres of inalienable land. The MOD had rejected what it regarded as the only other feasible site on its own land because of its destructive effect on Grim's Ditch.

From the start there were fears among the Trust's staff that the Government's demands, because of their security aspect, were liable to increase as discussions proceeded; and although such an intention was denied, it was admitted that the operational aspects of the new construction were constantly changing, with consequent effects on the precise nature of the request.

The staff became increasingly wary of the proposition. It was clear, however, that the MOD was determined to proceed with the scheme, and it was considered that outright objection, with ultimate appeal to the special parliamentary procedure, was bound to end in failure.

As a number of important environmental issues were involved, the Trust sought to achieve the best outcome in safeguarding the village of Bradenham, especially during the construction period, in protecting the woodlands, and landscaping the hump which would be the visible consequence of the underground bunker. It was believed that it was better to negotiate these points in advance rather than to rely on their being satisfied through the political process of the parliamentary committee. The Executive Committee accepted this view.

Consultations at an early stage with amenity bodies, such as the Chilterns Society and the Council for the Protection of Rural England, did not elicit any major objections. Almost certainly it was the defence issue and the intervention of the Wycombe Peace Council which raised Bradenham to a *cause célèbre*. The issue clearly had mileage for the media, and the Trust was put on the defensive. Objectors fell into several quite different categories. There were some who hated the scheme because of its purpose; others, fearing that the land would be raped, objected on the grounds of natural beauty (though the case was weak); a third category felt that, irrespective of landscape merit, the inalienability factor should be regarded as inviolate; and a great many others expressed an unease that, whatever the rights or wrongs of the decision, they should have been told more about it before it became a *fait accompli*. During the autumn of 1981, a furore developed on a scale not seen before, and more and more staff time was spent on trying to defend the Trust's decision.

A leading figure in the objection lobby was a local Trust member and peace activist named Audrey Urry. She and her family had become members in the 1970s, chiefly in order to visit properties in the area where they lived. She recalls that it was her spontaneous indignation at a peace group meeting in her Wycombe home that propelled her into the role of Honorary Secretary for the constituency of indignation. There was no need to court publicity. Mrs Urry quickly had a heavy postbag, most of it from objectors. Her encounters with the Trust's officials did not serve to narrow the gap. The row, now firmly in the public domain, was no longer a domestic controversy confined to the membership.

As with most democratic crises, the great majority of the Trust's million members were however not much moved by it. Misunderstanding was increased by the unjustified public statement from Mr Jerry Wiggins, a junior Defence Minister. In effect Mr Wiggins said that, in agreeing to lease the land, the Trust had taken regard of the needs of national defence. The Trust had agreed, he claimed, 'because of the vital nature of the project'. This presumed a Trust stance on the defence issue, which at no time had governed its decision. The Executive Committee was indignant at the innuendo, which was later – none too convincingly – withdrawn.

Anxieties among Trust members were widespread enough to lead to a demand for an Extraordinary General Meeting. This was held at the Wembley Conference Centre on 1 November 1982, on the same day as the Annual General Meeting. With memories of the overflow meeting at the Westminster Central Hall in 1967, as a result of the Rawnsley-Neptune affair, care was taken not to underprovide for the potential attendance. In the event there were many empty seats and the meetings were something of an anti-climax. But it has to be said that the debates were of a high standard and civilised in character. The tenor of the meetings owed much to the fair-handed and tolerant way in which Lord Gibson handled the proceedings. He was a master of moderation and much respected for his genuine concern to see that the critics had a fair hearing. There remained resentment, however, in some quarters of his view that the occasion represented a challenge to a Board of Directors and his insistence on reserving the right to the final speech.

Including proxy votes, the critical motions at the Extraordinary General Meeting were defeated by 169,984 to 26,619, and by 144,264 to 18,794 at the less well attended AGM in the afternoon. This was not altogether the end of the argument. Lord Beaumont of Whitley, a prominent objector, issued a writ against the Trust in the High Court. After proceeding for a year in a desultory fashion, this finally failed; but the scars took longer to heal.

Bradenham was not the only issue on which a Trust decision provoked some organised opposition. In 1978 a scheme had been developed for opening an interpretative centre in the three-storeyed water-mill and maltings at Burnham Overy on the North Norfolk coast. They had been held since 1939 but had remained empty since 1960 after a fire. Objections were raised by local residents (many of them of some influence) because of the fear that it would bring yet more people to a coastal road already congested in the summer months. It was decided that members of the Council should go to a public meeting called by the Trust at Wells-next-the-Sea, primarily to hear local views. It was crowded out, and again Lord Gibson won appreciation for showing himself a good listener. After further discussion, the Trust decided to bow to local feeling.

At Friday Street, the picturesque hamlet on the side of Leith Hill, a minor Bradenham erupted in 1982. This was over a plan to lease a woodland known as Severall's Copse to a neighbouring landowner whose forestry policies were reputed to be somewhat over-zealous. The copse had been bought fifty years earlier by local subscription, and the local community wanted it left undisturbed. Once again village halls resounded to the voice of grassroots democrats. In the outcome, an alternative plan for management was agreed, with the Friends of Severall's Copse once again becoming Friends of the National Trust. Although management plans are essential for the Trust to discharge its responsibilities to future generations, they are bound from time to time to offend local traditionalists. Except when the public is kept fully in the picture on management issues, it is not unexpected for locals to get up in arms, for example, about well-loved yet over-mature trees being felled in the interests of younger growth, or to forestall damage, or to open up new views.

Two main strands emerged from the Bradenham affair. The first was a reinforced concern to entertain with extreme reserve any proposals, especially from the Government, which would make an incursion into inalienable land. In point of fact, despite the critics, the Trust had never been a soft option for would-be developers – as had been shown in campaigns ranging from its spirited defence of Rainbow Wood Farm in 1969 to that a decade later against a bypass being driven through 'Capability' Brown's landscape at Petworth Park. However, as a result of Bradenham, the Trust became increasingly tough, and several current demands on its land are being strongly resisted, at least one of which is likely to end in the Parliamentary lap.

The second outcome of Bradenham was the realisation that the Trust needed to be much more positive in informing members and the public of its thinking and actions. Just as the Neptune controversy had begotten the Benson Report, so Bradenham begat the Arkell (and in some measure the Hornby) reviews.

Since 1970 John Arkell had been a nominee on the Trust's Council of the Council for the Protection of Rural England but had never had a very prominent role. In his last two years before retirement, however, he gave invaluable service helping to guide a sensible group of Council members to sensible conclusions. Arkell's administrative background with the BBC, and Boots the Chemist, served him in good stead. The members of the Arkell Committee were John Anfield, Michael Cadbury, Ron Rowland and Elizabeth Sargeant, all active members of the Council. They brought together a wealth of knowledge and understanding in dealing with Trust members and Centres, with local authorities and the general public.

Although in fact the way the Bradenham issue unfolded had not lent itself to dialogue among a million members, there remained a feeling that the Trust had been somewhat naive: in retrospect, it should have been expected that many members would be perturbed at a lease being granted to the Ministry of Defence. The 1981 Annual Report spoke of 'a recent example which attracted some attention in the newspapers and caused concern to some members'. This was something of an understatement, and the following year the Director General had to concede in the Annual Report; 'To many at Head Office and to some in the Regions that autumn was dominated by the Extraordinary General Meeting. Normally, the Trust is free of internal dissension and it is not often involved in battles other than defending its properties ....'

The terms of reference for Arkell were to consider the relationship between the members and the Council and the management of the Trust, and to consider procedures for dealing with inalienability. On the latter question, the Committee saw a need to explain the nature of inalienability more clearly to the members, and for a declared presumption against leasing such land, however useful the intention. Because of the complexity and wide-ranging character of modern development plans, it also recommended that the Trust should be highly discriminating when declaring a property inalienable.

Most of the Committee's time was spent on finding ways of achieving wider management accountability to those both within and outside the membership. In a sense the Trust had become public property, and it derived much support from those who do not hold an admission card. Since Benson, devolution to Regional Committees had been seen to be inescapable as well as desirable. There was now a clear need to widen the basis of the Regional Committees' membership. Arkell considered carefully but rejected the idea of directly elected committee membership, largely because it felt that the aim would not be achieved and that Centre members would predominate. Instead it recommended more open invitation for offers to join Regional Committees so as to attract a wider spectrum of geography, interests and experience.

Along with Arkell's other recommendations, this conclusion needs to be reviewed to see how far the spectrum has in fact been widened. By means of a more frequent magazine, through information boards at properties and through open meetings Arkell hoped to get more membership participation and also greater interest in standing for election to the Council. It was not until 1987, when there were thirty-one nominations for eight Council seats, that this option was noticeably taken up.

The Hornby Working Party addressed itself to internal management and the committee structure. Sir Simon Hornby, Chairman of W. H. Smith and the Design Council, who deprecatingly calls himself 'a newsagent', had for years injected an extra touch of imagination and thrust into the business aspects of the Trust. His Working Party concluded that the sheer volume of management decisions taken to committee brought into focus what was already tacitly accepted – that the Council and Committees should be for deciding policy and the staff for executing it. It is the endemic disease of committees to have an addiction for detail, to which they all too readily give the halo of policy. Because of the monthly cycle of committees, the staff were on a treadmill of preparation for, attending and executing the consequences of those committees. Hornby proposed a two-monthly cycle, and that the Director General should have wide delegated powers to act within overall policies.

A key member of the deliberations of both Arkell and Hornby was Angus Stirling, who had joined the staff as Deputy Director General in 1979 and was widely seen as the Crown Prince. He duly succeeded Sir Jack Boles in 1983 and since then his influence on the Trust has been unmistakeable. His background, by Trust traditions was impeccable: Eton, City Banking and the Arts Council. But undoubtedly the choice was a good one. From the outset Angus Stirling was committed to the principle of the wider accountability, without rejecting the traditions on which the Trust had achieved such notable successes. He has shown a quiet confidence in the increasingly complex handling of the Trust's management, a readiness to listen to new approaches, and a clear but cautious determination about the way forward.

A more outward looking stance has also been reflected in other recent appointments. David Beeton came from having been Chief Executive of Bath City Council to succeed Ivor Blomfield as Secretary of the Trust when the latter became Director for the Regions. Alastair Muir from ICI was appointed Director of Public Relations, and on his retirement in 1987 was succeeded by Brian Lang. Besides having been Secretary, since its formation, of the National Heritage Memorial Fund, Brian Lang brought with him a doctorate in social anthropology and experience as a driver of a fork-lift truck! The in-house loyalty which was the seed bed of past Trust successes has not been perceptibly impaired.

In the field of education, too, the Trust has begun to look outwardly with less nervousness. Its Education Adviser, John Hodgson, has brought great imagination to his task, building on his experience of running the Geffrye Museum in East London and the Museum of Childhood at Sudbury Hall. In something of the tradition of William Morris, he has thrown a new light on ways in which many properties, previously thought to be of interest only to the mature and aesthetically minded, can equally be presented to fascinate the young. A number of them have been brought vividly to life by the productions of the Young National Trust Theatre. Education had once been considered a word of doubtful taste at Queen Anne's Gate. It is now fully embraced as a means of realising what the Trust has to offer the nation rather than as a didactic exercise.

Meanwhile a steadily increasing professionalism was being brought to the management of the Trust's finances. The foundations of this were laid by Jimmy Wheeler. They enabled the Trust to embark on and pursue its ever more complex role, and Jimmy's sense of consistency in direction continued under Gordon Lawrence as Director of Finance. It is greatly to the credit of both Jimmy and Gordon that the Trust remained buoyant while being permanently – as always – short of funds. This has been particularly so at a time when public subsidy has been politically out of fashion, and when the Trust has had to rely even more heavily on the private sector and the support of its members.

There has been a long tradition of providing gift shops and catering points at heavily visited properties. The first shop was opened at Saltram in 1965, while legend has it that the Trust's catering began with a cup of tea served through the window of a gardener's cottage at Hidcote. In recent years, however, the cutting edge has been much sharpened. The trading arm, known as National Trust Enterprises, has enjoyed the benefit of chairmen from the world of business – currently Ladislas Rice, formerly of the Burton Group – and of full-time Directors of Trading, such as Roy Preece, formerly General Manager of Selfridges, and currently Martin Moss who had been Managing Director of Simpsons of Piccadilly. In addition to selling points at houses, redolent of National Trust soap and pot-pourri, trading thrives through thirty 'town shops' in key tourist towns and cities. Restaurants and tea rooms have enjoyed a similar expansion in numbers and viability. Trading and catering have grown from a base in 1981 of £7.7 million turnover and a profit of £860,000 to just under £20 million in 1987 with a contribution of £3.2 million.

This rapid expansion has been matched by the Trust's book publishing activities. These began with the publication in association with Jonathan Cape of *The National Trust Guide*, a survey of all the Trust's different kinds of properties, back in 1973. The success of this, allied with Graham Stuart Thomas's *Gardens of the National Trust* and Nigel Nicolson's companion volume on houses, laid the foundation of a thriving book list which today contains nearly eighty titles, ranging from cookery books to the more esoteric delights of the catalogue of Robert Clive's exquisite collection of Indian treasures at Powis Castle. Children's books now form an important and growing part of the list, including the beautifully illustrated edition of the *Just So Stories*. This continues to pay the Trust a royalty, even though copyright ran out in 1987 to the detriment of Wimpole Hall in Cambridgeshire, which had depended on the Kipling estate for part of its income.

The traditional guidebooks that the National Trust has produced over the past decade are now thought by some to be too erudite and indigestible for visitors making their way around a house. The Trust's Publisher, Margaret Willes, has been given the challenge of producing a new style of guidebook, and the prototype of this programme was launched at Blickling Hall in the summer of 1987.

With the far from adequate title of Historic Buildings Secretary (no better has emerged) Martin Drury has overall responsibility for the aesthetic aspects of the Trust's endeavour. In tune with the times, he does not see his role simply as the last bastion against the marketeers and popularisers, although he and his staff fight tenaciously for standards. Having been the Trust's Adviser on Furniture, and also Historic Buildings Representative for two Regions in the South-East with the heaviest concentration of members and visitors, Martin Drury is well aware that the public interest is not to be gainsaid.

It has become increasingly appreciated that some properties are ripe for good and profitable entertainment. Landscape parks come high on this list. They lend themselves readily to *fêtes champêtres* and garden parties, usually ending in lakeside fireworks, which are essentially folk *fiesta*. Those at Stourhead and Claremont have become an annual feature with many regular adherents; and the large numbers at a recent Family Day at Polesden Lacey provided headaches for the local traffic police until its organisation was brought under tighter control. Music, too, is more often heard at properties – both indoors and out – than at one time; and the catholic taste of this most traditional body embraces Humphrey Lyttleton and Acker Bilk as well as Hummel and Alfred Brendel.

Without any lapse of taste, all these enterprises can be seen as consistent with the Trust's commitment to preserve places of beauty 'for the benefit of the nation'. Benefit does not exclude enjoyment. Insofar as the enterprises are profitable, moreover, Octavia Hill's note to Robert Hunter is apposite. She advised him to call their brainchild a Trust rather than a limited company. 'You will do better, I believe, to bring forward its benevolent rather than its commercial character. People don't like unsuccessful business, but do like Charity, where a little money does go a long way because of good commercial management.' And the Trust has come a long way since then.

Most charities whose objects stir the emotions of their supporters are subject to internal controversy. All too easily this can give rise to demonstrations less charitable than the common aim: the heretic is always treated more harshly than the heathen. Yet despite the Neptune and Bradenham controversies, the Trust has been relatively fortunate. This does not mean that there are grounds for complacency, for there will always be unresolved debates in the minds of at least some parts of the membership.

The Trust's estate is now remarkably diverse. Nowhere is this more eloquently demonstrated than in the seemingly dry pages of its List of Properties. Twenty categories are itemised in the preamble, including churches and pubs, landscape parks and water mills, nature reserves and Roman antiquities, barns and castles, historic houses and industrial monuments. Yet the public perception still puts emphasis on the historic houses with their overtones of architectural distinction, fine art collections and social privilege.

From time to time, the dichotomy between houses and untamed open spaces is presented as a conflict of the Trust's basic interests. This may be unfair, but the image in the public mind cannot be brushed aside. There are of course differing preoccupations and concerns. Long ago, Sir John Smith distinguished the Trust's Historic Building Representatives and its Land Agents as 'the lily and the hobnailed boot'.

By historical chance, in the past few years a whole series of historic houses in the Midlands have called for adoption by the Trust. Canons Ashby in Northamptonshire was the first, followed by Belton House, Calke Abbey and Kedleston Hall. Each was very different, each of national importance, and each in turn required very large sums of money before being brought under the Trust's management and opened to the public. In the cases of Belton and Kedleston, the major expense was to buy the contents from their owners, for without these the gift of the house and park was not enough to justify opening. It was enough to lend colour to the argument that the Trust's over-riding sympathy lay with the aesthetes and the privileged. Left to itself, said one slightly acerbic commentator, the Trust would revert to scrub – a very aristocratic scrub, of course!

But this does less than justice to the facts. Although the processes of acquiring, repairing, fitting out and showing a great historic house are dramatic and inevitably steal the headlines, surveys have consistently shown the high regard for the Trust's open space properties in the minds of its members. Nor has there ever been a period when these have taken second place. In 1983, there was the purchase of Kinder Scout, flagship of the organised Ramblers' Movement. Hardly a committee meeting passes without decisions to extend the holdings in the Lake District (now well over a quarter of the whole National Park) and other National Parks, or stretches of important coastline under Enterprise Neptune. And in the very heart of mid-Wales the Trust recently bought 16,000 acres of wilderness known as the Abergwesyn Commons. There is nothing wrong with healthy competition for the available resources of the Trust. The claims of archaeology, nature conservation, industrial archaeology and wilderness landscapes are regularly pressed as strongly as those for architecture, paintings and furniture.

The continuing debate was fuelled in an *Observer* article in 1986 by Dr David Clark, MP for South Shields. Like his predecessor at South Shields, Arthur Blenkinsop, he is a member of the Executive Committee and was sharply critical of the preoccupation with Kedleston to the possible detriment of the open spaces. Even if his criticisms seemed to some to be not entirely fair, they served to stimulate awareness of what is still a widely held public impression.

The major issue now facing the Trust is how best to respond to its high and justified public expectations. Some high expectations it should not try to meet. In regard to future acquisitions, and its widening of interest, such as helping to preserve small houses, Sir Jack Boles would take a conservative stance. Indeed, he would also have rejected Kedleston at the time that it was offered, suggesting a deferred approach to allow the Trust to digest the heavy load already on hand. His successor is probably more pragmatic, although well aware of the dangers of being tempted forward too often. And while there is much to be said for self-denial, the immediate item on the agenda always attracts its special advocates and is not easily shelved.

Angus Stirling views with marked confidence the Trust's ability to meet the challenges ahead. He would not reject new types of property within the remit of the National Trust Act, but he welcomes the initiatives of private owners, English Heritage and other voluntary organisations to share the care of the heritage. Except for its continuing concern with the coastline the Trust should not be seen to be the prime instrument, though it was the first in the field and still has a major and unique contribution to make.

Today the environmental debate is high on the country's agenda, and the Trust is often urged to take a more prominent role in that debate. Traditionally, this has been left to other bodies more specifically designed to help mould public opinion. However it is now accepted that it is right on occasions for the Trust to make its views public where they affect not only its existing properties but the seamless garment of the wider countryside. One such occasion was in 1987, when in response to a government paper the Trust made a public submission on the future of agricultural land. Its firm views had considerable impact. There are some who fear that such statements may prejudice the effectiveness of the quiet, behind-the-scenes diplomacy which has sometimes worked well in the past. But if the concept of wider accountability is to prevail this is outweighed by being seen and sometimes counted. No amenity organisation, however eminent, is an environmental island. This is very much the view of the Director General.

During his time with the Arts Council Angus Stirling had been acutely aware of the vital importance of a good rapport between staff and the governing body. The National Trust's Council, comprising 26 elected members and the same number nominated by an approved list of bodies, has become notably more lively in recent years. Too often in the past it had seemed politely muted while effective decisions remained the preserve of the Executive Committee. The Council is now a more effective debating forum to which the Director General provides papers on broad questions of principle. Among those making a significant impact are younger members – Jacob Simon from the National Portrait Gallery, who was first elected to the Council while still a student at Cambridge; Carrie Cocke, a lively Family Member who chaired the Panel for Youth; Malcolm Petyt, head of a University Extra Mural Department and nominee of the Ramblers' Association, who brings to debates a robust Yorkshire common-sense. Each of these has been a member for a number of years so has absorbed the not inconsiderable background of Trust tradition and practice. And it is encouraging that others of similar mould are joining the Council.

In this profile of the Trust's history Angus Stirling must be seen not only as a figure in the landscape but as something of a signpost, while equally significant as a signpost has been the appointment to the chair of Dame Jennifer Jenkins. Lord Gibson retired under the age rule in 1986, having steered the organisation with an extremely deft touch through eight years of unprecedented expansion and some controversy.

For more than sixty years the Trust had been led by landowners and figures of State. Pat Gibson's successor broke new ground. Not only is she the first woman to take the chair, but her Fabian background and diverse experience open a special sensitivity to public feeling. Besides holding several successful business directorships she has been Chairman of the Consumers' Association and the Historic Buildings Council as well as a member of the Design Council, the Wallace Collection and President of the Ancient Monuments Society.

Chairman and Director General are very much at one on future objectives and the means of achieving them. Dame Jennifer regards inalienability as the corner-stone of all the Trust's work, and she is open to new types of acquisition if they pass the test of merit. She is especially keen that there should be a greater presence in Wales: the scheme for safeguarding small houses in the valleys is one of her enthusiasms. But financial pressures may well apply a brake on expansion. Factors outside the Trust's control can greatly affect income. Thus changes in the standard rate of income tax have a major effect on the value of covenanted subscriptions; and the value of the MSC scheme, which has been measured in millions every year, may decline.

Dame Jennifer would like to see a further broadening of the range of those serving on Committees, and an extension of membership to social groups which are at present proportionally under-represented. Many of her ideas seem to echo down the decades as if uttered by one of the founders. It is tempting to think of a reincarnation. For many years a portrait of Octavia Hill has surveyed the board room at Queen Anne's Gate, as if keeping a watching eye on the proceedings. Perhaps the same influence can now be detected in the chair itself.

This book has been a story of the National Trust written around some of the large number of people who have supplied colour and notable dedication to its progress. Inevitably there are many others whose contributions have been no less valuable who go unmentioned or only in passing reference; not least John Gaze who, sadly, died before the book was completed and whose part in some of the triumphs and achievements recorded is discreetly hidden. Beyond the figures in the landscape lies the landscape itself, comprising countless people who have helped, criticised and enjoyed the Trust and its work. A very recent event brings them into focus.

The violent storm of 15–16 October 1987 destroyed a quarter of a million trees on Trust properties across the south-east of England and in East Anglia. Within a couple of months members and supporters had donated £1 million towards the restoration of landscapes. Their devotion is eloquent of what Robin Fedden called the 'continuing purpose' of a truly remarkable body.

STRUCTURE OF MAIN COMMITTEES 1895–1988

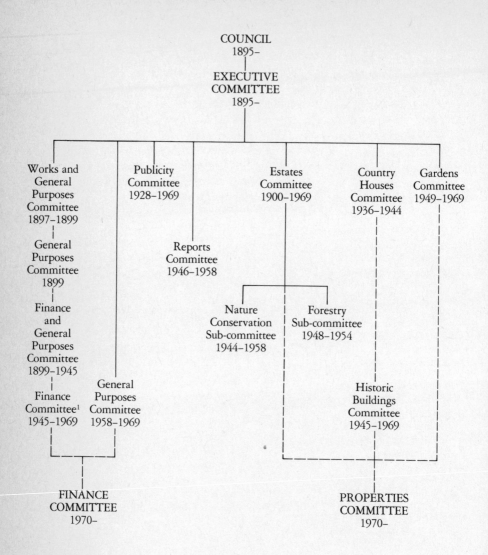

COUNCIL
1895–

EXECUTIVE
COMMITTEE
1895–

Works and
General
Purposes
Committee
1897–1899

General
Purposes
Committee
1899

Finance
and
General
Purposes
Committee
1899–1945

Finance
Committee[1]
1945–1969

Publicity
Committee
1928–1969

Reports
Committee
1946–1958

General
Purposes
Committee
1958–1969

Estates
Committee
1900–1969

Nature
Conservation
Sub-committee
1944–1958

Forestry
Sub-committee
1948–1954

Country
Houses
Committee
1936–1944

Gardens
Committee
1949–1969

Historic
Buildings
Committee
1945–1969

FINANCE
COMMITTEE
1970–

PROPERTIES
COMMITTEE
1970–

———— Sub-committees
–––– Replaced by

[1] Reconstituted in 1958, when many
functions were taken over by GP Committee

Present day committees in CAPITALS

Index

Florence Court, Co. Fermanagh 280, 285, 289
Flyd, Arthur 191
Forde Abbey, Dorset 124
Forehead, Russell 260
Foreland Point, Devon 214
Forestry and the National Trust 102, 177–81
Forestry Act, 1948 178
Forestry Association 247
Forestry Commission 117, 1200, 179, 180
Forfarshire, The 75
Forster, E. M. 100
Fortescue, 4th Earl 89
Fowler, John 251, 261, 266
Fox, Sir Cyril 87
Fox House Inn, South Yorkshire 67
Fox Talbot Museum 265
Fox Talbot, William Henry 264–5
Fox, Dr Wilfred 168
Freeman, Mr and Mrs 38
Freshwater Place, Marylebone, London 16, 17, 27, 28
Friar's Crag, Cumbria 43
Friday Street, Surrey 310
Friends of the Lake District *see* Lake District Defence Society
Frithsden Copse, Ashridge, Hertfordshire 71
Frogmore Farm, Cornwall 211
Furzey Island, Dorset 205

Gainsborough, Thomas 10
Gaitskell, Rt. Hon. Hugh 151
Galava Fort, Cumbria 40, 78
Galbraith, Professor John Kenneth 198
Gallimore, Ethel 64, 66–8
Gardens Advisory staff of the National Trust 247
Gardens of the National Trust 313
Gardens of the National Trust 165–173
Garrett, John 261
Gas Light and Coke Company 98
Gascoigne, Major-General Sir Julian 212, 226, 235
Gaskell family 103
Gatliff, Herbert 102, 176
Gatton Park, Surrey 52
Gavin, Sir William 176
Gaze, John 317
Geffrye Museum 312
Gentleman, David 236
George III, King 279
George V, King 20
George VI, King 128
Georgian Group 193
Giant's Causeway, Co. Antrim 81, 281
Gibbs, Christopher 50, 97, 98–9, 100, 102, 103,

114, 134, 137, 139, 147, 159, 176, 180, 186, 190, 197, 202, 203, 205–6, 207, 215, 226, 245, 265, 281
Gibside Chapel, Tyne and Wear 306
Gibson, Lord 171, 196, 204–5, 208, 216, 224, 226, 227, 242, 299, 301, 302, 304, 310
Gibson, Lord 316
Gilbert, Commander W. R. 256
Gilbert, Sir Humphrey 256
Gilbert, Revd 53
Gillerthwaite Estate, Cumbria 69
Girouard, Dr Mark 189
Gladstone, William Ewart 13
Glastonbury Tor, Somerset 41
Glastry Ponds, Strangford Lough, Co. Down 284
Glenarm Castle, Co. Antrim 194
Glencoyne Farm, Cumbria 197
Glendun, Co. Antrim 282
Glendurgan Garden, Cornwall 170
Glenthorne Estate, Devon 214
Gloucester, Duke of, HRH Richard 305
Glyders, the, Gwynedd 270
Goddards, Abinger, Surrey 100
Godfrey, Arthur 172
Golden Cap Estate, Dorset 210, 264
Golden Treasury 13
Goldsmid, Sir Julian 24
Goodhart-Rendel, H. S. (Harry) 132
Goodwin, Miss A. M. 120
Gore, St. John (Bobby) 226, 240, 248–50, 260–61
Goss, Herbert 72
Government: concessions 123
Government: financial help 145–157, 175, 209
Gowbarrow Park, Cumbria 39, 45
Gower Peninsular, W. Glamorgan 274
Gowers, Committee and Report 150, 151
Gowers, Sir Ernest 149
Grafton, 11th Duke of 154, 186, 188, 196
Grand Union Canal 199
Grange Fell, Borrowdale, Cumbria 39
Grant, Duncan 164
Grasmere, Cumbria 9
Gray, Thomas 10, 87
Gray's Printing Press, Strabane, Co. Tyrone 285
Great Gable, Cumbria 68, 197
Greater Manchester County Council 154
Greenlands Estate, Hambledon, Surrey 189
Greenwood, Anthony 233
Greville, Mrs Ronald 128, 132, 297
Grey of Falloden, Viscount 70, 76, 82
Griffin, Herbert 61
Griffith, Hugh 214, 273, 275, 277
Grigg, John 226, 228
Grim's Ditch 308
Grindleford, Derbyshire 67

Royal Photographic Society 265
Royal Society for the Protection of Birds 77
Royal Ulster Constabulary 282
Royal Zoological Society 70
Rugby School 12, 13
Rumps, The, Cornwall 206
Runkerry, Co. Down 281
Runnymede, Surrey 127, 139
Ruskin, John 15, 16, 18, 21, 22, 28, 30, 31, 32, 35,
    125; memorial stone 43
Ruskin Reserve, Cothill, Oxfordshire 74, 187
Russell, 1st Earl 13
Russell, Mrs Gilbert 261
Ryan, Peter 114
Rydal Mount, Cumbria 9
Rye, East Sussex 164
Ryle, George 179–80

Sach, Margaret 139, 306
Sackville, 4th Baron 131–2
Sackville, 6th Baron 306
Sackville-West, Edward 138
Sackville-West, Vita 101, 166, 290–291
St Aubyn, John *see* St Levan, 4th Baron
St Barbe, Mrs F. E. N. 211
St Bertram's Well, Ilam, Derbyshire 66
St Boniface Down, Isle of Wight 53, 54
St Bride's Bay, Dyfed 269
St Catherine's Hill or Point, Isle of Wight 54–5
St Davids, Dyfed 269
St Gabriels, Dorset 210
St Helen's Common, Isle of Wight 54, 74
St John's College, Cambridge 9
St John's Jerusalem, Kent 168
St Levan, 3rd and 4th Baron 292–3
St Mary le Bow, Cheapside 37
St Mary's, Marylebone, London 18
St Michael's Mount, Cornwall 292–3
St Oswald, 4th and 5th Baron 288–9
Sales, John 171
Salisbury, Edward 61, 73, 76
Salisbury, Joiner's Hall, Wiltshire 87
Salisbury, 5th Marquess of 26, 61, 123, 124–5
Salomons, Leopold 41, 52
Salter, Harold 182
Saltram, Devon 152, 153, 190, 218, 231–3, 124,
    235, 236–7
Sandbanks, Dorset 202
Sandringham Gardens, Norfolk 106
Sandwich tern 75, 76
Sandwith, Hermione 251
Sangar, Owen 120
Sargeant, Elizabeth 311
Savile, 3rd Baron 234
Sawrey, Cumbria 107

Sayes Court, Deptford 32
Scafell Pike, Cumbria 68
SCAPA 61
Scarsdale, 3rd Viscount 88, 92
Science Museum 259, 265, 266
Scots Gap (Northumbria Regional Office) 192
Scott, Peter 217
Scott, Sir Samuel Haslam 105
Scout and Guide Movements, the 204
Seahouses, Northumberland 75
Seal culling 300–301
Seeley, John 19
Seeley, Leonard 19
Seeley, Major General Jack 53
Selworthy, Somerset 294
Senior, George 140, 190, 192
Sennen, Cornwall 110
Seven Lamps of Architecture 16, 31
Seven Pillars of Wisdom 161
Seven Sisters Cliffs, East Sussex 115, 116
Severell's Copse, Leith Hill, Surrey 310
Shaftesbury, 7th Earl of 18
Shakespeare, William 262
Shalford Mill, Surrey 110
Shaw, George Bernard 126, 160–161
Shaw, Norman 305
Shawe-Taylor, Desmond 138
Shaw's Corner, Ayot St Lawrence, Hertfordshire
    160–61
Shaw-Lefevre, Charles 23, 24, 28, 29, 33, 81, 90
Sheffield Association for Protection of Local
    Scenery 67
Sheffield Park, East Sussex 168–9, 170
Sherriff, R. C. 210
Shetland ponies 262
Shining Cliff Wood, Derbyshire 65
Shops *see* Trading
Shugborough, Staffordshire 153, 261, 263
Sibley, W. A. 299
Simon, Jacob 316
Simpson, Eleanor 22, 42
Sissinghurst Castle, Kent 290–291
Skenfrith Castle, Gwent 269
Skiddaw, Cumbria 138
Skinner, Archie 169
Skirrid Fawr, Gwent 269
Slessor, Sir John 219
Slindon Estate, West Sussex 174, 178
Smallhythe Place, Kent 174, 178
Smith, Alan 244
Smith, Arthur 135
Smith, Augustus 24, 30, 69
Smith, Clifford 126
Smith, Hubert 135, 137, 140, 141, 142, 147, 161,
    165, 168, 170, 178, 180, 185, 186, 190, 197,
    199, 245, 271